THE
FIRST U-BOAT
FLOTILLA

THE
FIRST U-BOAT
FLOTILLA

by

LAWRENCE PATERSON

LEO COOPER

First Published in Great Britain 2002 by
LEO COOPER
an imprint of Pen & Sword Books Ltd
47 Church Street
Barnsley, S. Yorkshire, S70 2AS

ISBN 0 85052 816 X

A CIP record for this book is available from The British Library

Typeset in 10/12.5 Plantin by
Phoenix Typesetting, Ilkley, West Yorkshire.

Printed by CPI UK.

To Robert Strauss and Jon Gawne
For starting it all

CONTENTS

ACKNOWLEDGEMENTS

Many people have helped with the writing of this book. I would particularly like to thank Sarah Burbridge; Audrey and Shane Paterson; Jon Gawne; Urbain Ureel; Hans Milkert (President of Cuxhaven Kameradschaft); Yannick Creach, Hannelore and Gesa Suhren; Frank James and Angus MacLean Thuermer for their help with information and research. Ralf Bublitz – one of life's good guys – helped enormously with German translations, as did Robert Strauss – mentor, agent and squirrel hunter. Neville Burbridge and Jan Dekeijser assisted me a great deal by proof reading the first draft and kicking me when I needed it, while Elizabeth Burbidge kindly let me invade her front room while writing the first draft. From the Royal Navy Submarine Museum at Gosport, Maggie Bidmead (Head of Archives) and Debbie Corner (Head of Photographic Department) were extremely helpful with both reference material and photographs. The Brest Naval Library and Altenbruch's U-Boot Archiv also provided many excellent reference sources. I would also like to thank Jak Mallmann Showell, Eberhard Hoffman, Jürgen Weber (München U-Boot Kameradschaft) and Günther Hartmann (Verband Deutscher U-Bootfahrer). Egbert Kaibert, Peter Wimmer, Paul Darcy and Nicolo Thierry all provided valuable photographs for inclusion within this book, and Ranieri Meloni created the wonderful illustrations of the three U-boat types used by 1st U-Flotilla. I would also like to thank my editor, Tom Hartman, and everybody at Pen & Sword. Of course very special thanks go to the U-boat veterans who took the time to answer queries of mine, in particular: Georg Seitz (*U604* & *U873*); Erich Topp (*U57, U552* & *U2513*); Günther Poser (*U59* & *U202*); Claus-Peter Carlsen (*U251* & *U732*); Peter Wimmer (*U556*) and Paul Helmchen (*U441* & *U1407*).

Photographic Acknowledgements:
Ranieri Meloni, Plate 1; National Archives and Records Administration, Plates 2, 23, 32, 38; Royal Navy Submarine Museum, 12, 15, 19, 20, 21, 26, 30, 36; Author's Collection 3, 5, 6, 7, 9, 11, 16, 24, 25, 27, 29, 33, 34, 35; Egbert Kaibert (Peter Wimmer), 13; Siftung Traditionsarchiv Unterseeboote, 4, 17; Nicolo Thierry, 10, 14, 18, 28, 37; Paul Darcy, 22.

FOREWORD

Military units are renowned for their strictly regimented administration. Each decision, movement or event receives its official documentation filed within the paper archives for that particular formation. In times of conflict another administrative volume is added to the list – the War Diary. Drawn largely from the War Diary (*Kriegstagebuch*) of the Second World War's 1st U-boat Flotilla, this book seeks to chart the momentous events between 1935 and 1944, the years of formation and dissolution. The course of the book closely follows the entries recorded by various flotilla commanders over this period, beginning in August 1939 as war threatened Europe. The flotilla War Diary was a formal record of administrative matters and combat results, compiled by the flotilla commander. While his was not necessarily the only hand to record notations within its pages, the words belonged to him and he was entirely responsible for the diary's contents.

A Flotilla by definition is a grouping of vessels of an undetermined size. Germany's U-boats were constantly shuffling between flotillas, the unit providing an administrative, not tactical, control over U-boats and their operation. Tactics and operational jurisdiction was held firmly in the hands of BdU. This is not, however, a history of the Battle of the Atlantic or U-boats in general; those stories are told in numerous excellent and authoritative published works. The events of the war at sea provide a backdrop against which the drama of Germany's premier submarine unit was played out. The U-boats from this unit began their war laying mines along Britain's eastern seaboard and ended it fighting desperate and hopeless running battles against Allied naval forces intent on their destruction. The roller-coaster fortunes of Karl Dönitz's 'Grey Wolves' as a whole are mirrored in the events that occupy the following pages. By necessity there is a brief history of the rebuilding of Germany's U-boat arm following the humiliation of defeat in 1918. This has relevance to Karl Dönitz's entry into the story and the birth of the 'Weddigen' Flotilla – embryo of 1st U-boat Flotilla.

By its very essence a War Diary records the operational events affecting the unit concerned. Within the pages of 1st U-Flotilla's Diary are multiple references to U-boats occupying the same port. Apart from early stages of the war or where particularly relevant I have omitted these U-boats – their flotillas have their own stories to tell. Long periods of time were spent with no recorded duties; therefore this is not a literal day-by-day translation of the Diary in its entirety. Several patrols undertaken produced no result and achieved nothing. They have sometimes also been omitted. Again, there are available excellent reference sources for sailing dates and patrol areas and I have not replicated them here. Sinking reports are included wherever they are mentioned in the War Diary. The dates of the presumed or known loss of a U-boat will be mentioned and, as far as possible, the story of its demise told retrospectively. Sadly there are many of them.

Many words remain in their original German accompanied by translations, the non-English word italicized for clarity. Ranks I have also sometimes retained in full. I hope that the length and apparent complexity of many of these German words and titles will not deter non-German-speaking readers. Of all the words encountered within the following pages there is one in particular that repeats all too often – *Vermisst*, which in English means 'missing'.

GLOSSARY

Rank table

German	(medical)	British/American
Grossadmiral		Admiral of the Fleet/ Fleet Admiral
Admiral		Admiral
Vizeadmiral	(Admiralstabsarzt)	Vice-Admiral
Konteradmiral (KA)	(Admiralarzt)	Rear Admiral
Kommodore		Commodore
Kapitän zur See (KaptzS)	(Flottenarzt)	Captain
Fregattenkapitän (FK)	(Geschwarderarzt)	Commander
Korvettenkapitän (KK)	(Marineoberstabsarzt)	Commander
Kapitänleutnant (Kptl)	(Marinestabsarzt)	Lt Commander
Oberleutnant zur See (ObltzS)	(Marineoberassistenzarzt)	Lieutenant
Leutnant zur See (LtzS)	(Marineassistenzarzt)	Sub Lieutenant/ Lieutenant (jg)
Fähnrich		Midshipman
Oberbootman		Chief Petty Officer
Obermaat		Petty Officer
Obermatrose		Leading Seaman
Vollmatrose		Able Seaman
Leichtmatrose		Ordinary Seaman

ASDIC – term applied to the sonar equipment used for locating submarines. A powerful and effective weapon, it emitted a distinct 'ping' when locating the target. The word ASDIC is apparently an acronym for 'Anti-Submarine Detection Committee', the organization that began research into this device in 1917, although some historians dispute this.

BdU – (German) *Befehlshaber der Unterseeboote*; Commander of all U-boats.

BdU.Ops – (German) *Befehlshaber der Unterseeboote Operationen*; Commander (Operations) of all U-Boats.

BETASOM – (Italian) Italian submarine command for operations in the Atlantic. Established in Bordeaux during 1940, becoming operational in September that year and totalling 32 submarines before Italy's surrender in September 1943.

Bold – (German) Short for *Kobold* (goblin), an acoustic decoy, known also as the 'submarine bubble target' that comprised a small cylindrical mesh container filled with calcium hydride. When ejected from a submerged U-boat the compound reacted with sea-water and gave off hydrogen bubbles, and thus a false echo to ASDIC operators. Simple but effective.

BRT – (German) *Brutto Register Tonne* – Gross Registered Tons.

Dampfer – (German) steamer.

Degaussing – A method of reducing the magnetic polarity inherently present around iron-hulled ships, thereby eliminating the threat of magnetic mines. This involved electrical cables carrying a strong electrical charge stretched around a ship's hull that reduced or even reversed the hull's magnetic field (known to the Allies as 'degaussing', and still in use today). Merchant vessels were given temporary degaussing treatment at naval degaussing stations rather than the permanent equipment installed aboard military ships.

Displacement – The actual weight (in tons) of a ship, measured by the weight of the volume of water it displaces when afloat.

Eel – (German) *Aal* – Slang expression for torpedo.

Enigma – (German) Coding machine used by German Armed Forces throughout World War Two.

Fallschirmjäger – (German) Paratroops.

FAT – (German) *Feder-Apparat-Torpedo;* Zig-zagging torpedo head that followed a preset course. The warhead could be attached to both G7a and G7e torpedoes.

FdU – (German) *Führer der Unterseeboote;* Flag Officer for submarines responsible for a particular geographical region.

Fido – Air-launched Allied acoustically homing torpedo – correct designation the 'Mark 24 mine' – first used by VLR Liberators May 1943.

Flibo – (German) *Fliegerbombe* – Air launched bombs.

Gnat – Allied designation used for the *Zaunkönig* torpedo.

Goulet de Brest – (French) Narrows of Brest.

GRT – Gross Registered Tonnage (one ton equals 100 cubic feet cargo capacity), a standard way of judging merchant shipping size.

Heer – (German) Army.

(jg) – (American) Junior Grade, i.e.Lieutenant (Junior Grade)

Kriegsmarine – (German) Navy of the Third Reich.

La Royale – (French) Colloquial term for the French Navy.

Lords – (German) Slang term for Naval Ratings.

LL sweep – Thick steel cable loops suspended by floats and towed behind a minesweeping ship. An electrical current was passed through the cable, which generated a strong magnetic field capable of detonating nearby magnetic mines.

Luftwaffe – (German) Air Force.

MAD – Magnetic Anomoly Detector. Device of American design by which large ferrous metal object (such as a submerged U-boat) can be detected by its inherent magnetism.

Minensuchboot – (German) Minesweeper.

OKH – (German) *Oberkommando der Heer* ; Supreme Army Command.

OKL – (German) *Oberkommando der Luftwaffe*; Supreme Airforce Command.

OKM – (German) *Oberkommando der Kriegsmarine*; Supreme Navy Command.

OKW – (German) *Oberkommando der Wehrmacht*; Supreme Armed Forces Command.

Rade de Brest – (French) Brest harbour.

Reichsmarine – German Republican Navy, pre-Third Reich.

Ritterkreuz – (German) Knight's Cross of the Iron Cross.

Sperrbrecher – (German) Barrage breaker, a specialized mine destructor vessel.

Torpedoboot – (German) Designation given to light destroyers.

Turm – (German) Abbreviation of *Turmumbau* – conning tower.

U-Ausbildungsflottille – U-boat training flotilla.

U-Bootwaffe – (German) U-boat service.

U-Boot Jäger – (German) Submarine hunter, usually a converted trawler.

VLR – (British) Very Long Range, used in conjunction with aircraft, often Liberators.

Vorpostenboot – (German) Coastal Defence Ship.

Wabo – (German) *Wasserbombe* – depth charges.

Wacheoffizier – (German) Watch Officer. There were three separate U-boat watch crews, each consisting of an officer, Petty Officer and two ratings. The ship's First Watch Officer (IWO) would be the Executive Officer (second in command), the Second Watch Officer (IIWO) the ship's designated Second Officer, and the Third Watch Officer (IIIWO) often the *Obersteuermann* (Navigation Officer). Their duties were typically divided into the following time frames: 0800–1200 (1st Watch), 1200–1500 (2nd Watch), 1500–1700 (3rd Watch); then 1700–2000 (1st Watch), 2000–2400 (2nd Watch), 2400–0400 (3rd Watch); ending with 0400–0800 (1st Watch); thus the times were staggered and gradually revolved with each day.

The duties of the IWO included torpedo and firing system care and maintenance as well as control of surface attacks; the IIWO handled administration regarding food and supplies as well as the operation of deck and flak weapons.

Wehrmacht – (German) Armed Forces.

Wintergarten – (German) Nickname given to the open railed extension astern of the conning tower, built to accommodate increased flak weaponry. Known to the Allies as a 'bandstand'.

Zaunkönig – (German) Title given to German T5 torpedo (literally meaning 'Wren'), acoustically guided and used particularly against escort ships, tuned to the pitch of their propellers. Known to Allies as the 'Gnat'.

Zerstörer – (German) Destroyer.

INTRODUCTION

During the closing months of World War Two Allied armies were converging on the heart of the Third Reich, driving before them the shattered remains of Germany's military forces. Defiant to the end they may have been, but there was no possibility of reversing the catastrophic chain of defeats suffered by Hitler's exhausted fighting men. From the east the Russian steamroller ground through Germany aimed squarely at the capital city, Berlin, one eye already on establishing post-war dominance in Europe. From the west, American, British and French troops battled doggedly through crumbling defences, their goal Germany's capital and the possible capture of Adolf Hitler. Unbeknown to the men in the field, however, these potent symbols of all they had fought against had already been denied them by political manoeuverings. Among the American units racing through Germany, General George S. Patton's Third Army was already covered in fame and glory, a reputation for thrusting bravery established since the battle of Normandy the previous June. While endless columns of Sherman tanks and half-tracked infantry roared through subdued German villages, a small British unit hardly merited any attention from the surrounding troops. The men of 30 Assault Unit, Royal Marines, had been in the company of the Allied front-line fighting formations since the bloody Normandy landings. The small commando unit had specialist tasks, a primary role being to operate behind enemy lines in advance of the leading Allied units and to sieze enemy personnel, documents, codes and ciphers. While America's most famous General ordered his Army deeper into Germany, the men of 30 Assault Unit were fixed on a somewhat more exact objective. Sixty miles north of Nuremberg on the edge of the *Thüringer Wald* (Thüringer Forest) lay *Schloss Tambach* (Tambach Castle) a beautiful medieval fortress nestled among thick forest near the town of Coburg. Within the stone citadel lay nearly 100 years of German history – the records of the German Navy, moved from Berlin in 1943 by Grand Admiral Dönitz in order to escape the escalating Allied bombing.

By 1945 Hitler's forces throughout what territory they still held were frantically destroying or hiding documents related to their years of war on the orders of their Supreme Commander, possessed of a mania to leave nothing but ashes for the conquering Allies. However, Dönitz's concept of honour forbade the destruction of so much German history and, stating that his Navy had nothing to hide, he ordered the storage and preservation of the records within Tambach Castle, designated 'Admiralty/War Science Department' (*Seekriegsleitung/Kriegswissenschaft Abteilung*), guarded by a unit of German Marines. At sunset on 9 April Lieutenant Commander Jim Glanville, DSC, RNVR, and his small group of men found and took control of the castle without a shot fired. *Konteradmirals* Walter Gladisch, Kurt Assmann and Arno Spindler surrendered the citadel and its garrison to Glanville, German and British Marines both standing side-by-side to guard the precious cache from possible attack by nearby Waffen SS units still stubbornly and fanatically resisting Germany's final collapse.

So it transpired that the records and diaries of six years of bitter naval war were taken by the small unit of Royal Marines and spirited away for analysis and storage. In the years following the end of the Second World War British authorities handed over the priceless documents to the Americans as previously arranged in 1944 as a form of 'payment' for American cooperation and assistance. Copied onto microfilm and stored within the National Archives and Records Adminstration, Washington DC, the originals were finally returned to federal Germany some fifty years later. Within the massive collection of German documents lie thousands of pages of battle reports, ship movements, administrative records and war diaries from BdU, flotillas and individual ships. From sixteen operational U-boat flotillas very few complete war diaries remain. One of the few that does tells the story of Germany's premier submarine unit of the Third Reich. The recorded history of the 1st U-Boat Flotilla remains intact and provides a fascinating insight into one of the most important naval campaigns of history.

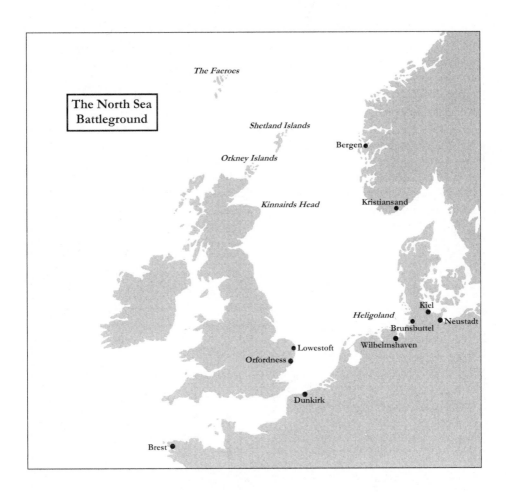

The North Sea
Battleground

The Faeroes

Shetland Islands

Orkney Islands

Bergen●

Kinnairds Head

Kristiansand●

Kiel
Heligoland ● ●
●Neustadt
Brunsbuttel
Wilhelmshaven●

●Lowestoft
Orfordness●

Dunkirk●

Brest●

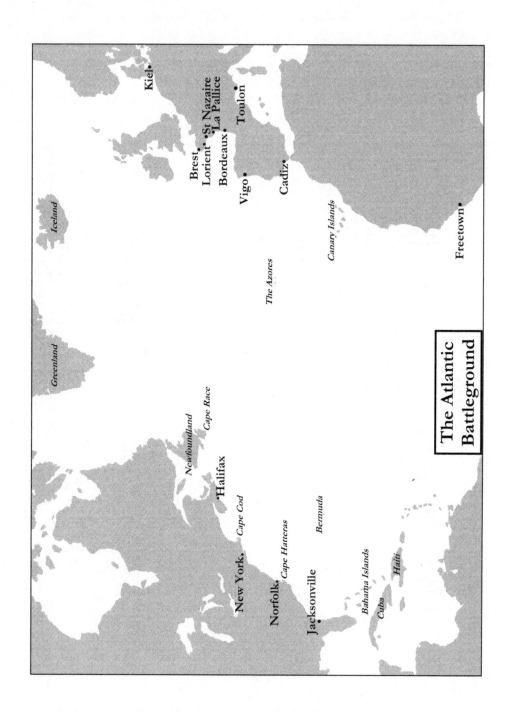

The Atlantic Battleground

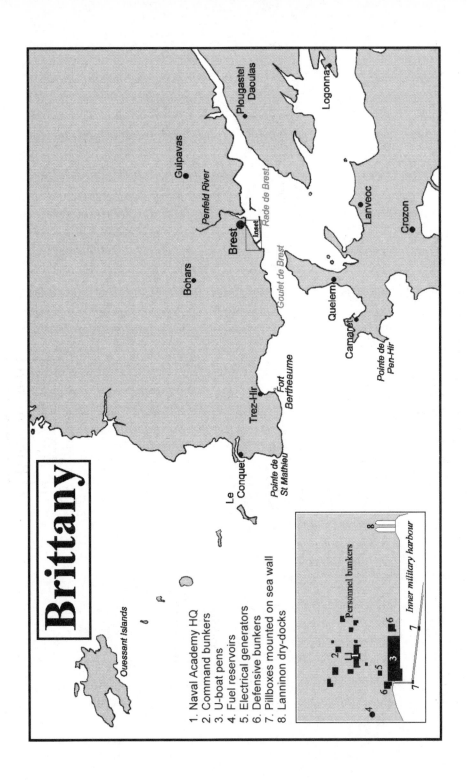

Brittany

Ouessant Islands

Guipavas

Penfeld River

Plougastel
Daoulas

Logonna

Rade de Brest

Brest

Inset

Goulet de Brest

Bohars

Lanveoc

Crozon

Quelern

Camaret

Pointe de
Pen-Hir

Trez-Hir

Fort
Bertheaume

Le
Conquet

Pointe de
St Mathieu

1. Naval Academy HQ
2. Command bunkers
3. U-boat pens
4. Fuel reservoirs
5. Electrical generators
6. Defensive bunkers
7. Pillboxes mounted on sea wall
8. Lanninon dry-docks

Personnel bunkers

8

2

5

6

3

6

7

7

4

Inner military harbour

1.

PRE-WAR FORMATION 1935 to 1939

'We are the U-Boat men, the Grey Wolves on grey seas.
Before us runs pale death, and ships are our quarry.
Here today, tomorrow at sea, our Admiral gives us orders:
"Comrades, always think – attack, pursue, sink!"'[1]

During the course of six years of war between 1939 and 1945 German U-boats branded an indelible image of cunning brutality and destruction in the minds of their enemies, an image equally applicable to submariners of all countries, and of all wars. Their 'silent service' necessitated stealth and intelligence, followed by swift, destructive assault. In essence the Third Reich's U-boat service existed for only ten years and yet their legacy outlives them, still alive at the beginning of the following century. In order to begin to examine the operational life of the 1st U-Flotilla there must first of all be a summary of Nazi Germany's rearmament of her Armed Forces in the years between the end of the First World War – the 'War to end all Wars' – and the beginning of the Second, twenty-one years later.

Following the end of the First World War Germany lay emasculated and in ruins. A population devastated by five years of brutal land, sea and air combat was further tormented by harsh peace treaty terms, war reparations and squalid political violence fermented in an air of revolution. After the turbulent rise of Adolf Hitler to the pinnacle of power within Germany – the post of Führer of the Greater German Reich – the severely restricted Reichsmarine (State Navy) received a new title. From 1935 onward it was to be known as the Kriegsmarine (Combat Navy) and it began a new existence, casting off the stain on its honour caused by the Bolshevik revolution aboard the idle High Seas Fleet in Kiel in 1918. An essential component of this newly unveiled naval power was the tiny *Unterseebootwaffe* (U-boat Arm). Despite ruthless terms of the Versailles Treaty forbidding a German submarine force, memories of a merciless campaign at sea between 1914 and 1918 still fresh in the minds of the victorious Allied nations, Germany had managed to keep

---

[1] U-Bootlied.

1

abreast of developments in underwater warfare systems even before Hitler's assumption of power.[2]

As early as 1922 the German government had financed design work by thirty of their engineers based in friendly Finland, Turkey and Spain under cover of a Dutch-registered firm named IVS. Prototype designs for three different submarine models were completed on paper: one small 250-ton vessel, one medium 500-ton vessel and a 750-ton large model. Three of the small types (*Vessikos*) and three mediums (*Vetehinens*) were constructed in Finland, while a single large submarine (*E1*) and all initial torpedoes and torpedo tubes were built in Spain. Meanwhile, back in the Fatherland a covert training programme was established for prospective submariners at the newly created 'Torpedo and Radio School' in Flensburg-Mürwik.

By November 1934 foreign-based German submarine development had advanced to such a state that component frames of twelve U-boats had been constructed in the Ruhr. Copied directly from tried and tested IVS designs, they were transferred to Kiel in the utmost secrecy and stored under armed guard in shipbuilding warehouses of Germaniawerft and Deutschewerke during January 1935. Diesel and electric engines followed, and then finally delivery was taken of the U-boats' teeth – torpedo tube armament. On Saturday 16 March 1935 Hitler decreed Germany's rearmament, formally abandoning the Versailles Treaty, announcing Army conscription, the establishment of the Luftwaffe and construction of new battleships. During mid-morning on 15 June 1935 a massive floating crane at Kiel's Deutschewerke shipyards launched the small Type IIA coastal submarine *U1*, commanded by Kptlt. Klaus Ewerth and commissioned into the U-boat school flotilla (*Unterseebootesschulflottille*) in Kiel.[3]

Ignoring the fact that Hitler's government had obviously constructed U-boats while forbidden to do so by the Versailles Treaty, German submarine strength became subject to an Anglo-German agreement signed in London on 18 June 1935. Under this naval accord the German Navy's underwater fleet could be '60 per cent of Britain's and, if exceptional circumstances arose, might be 100 per cent'. The other major European naval powers, France and Italy, were not consulted. The brakes were now effectively off German U-boat production. By 27 September the 'Weddigen' Flotilla, first unit of the Kriegsmarine U-boat arm (*Unterseebootwaffe*) and equipped entirely with Type IIB boats, was established at the port of Kiel, ensconced in the city's northern suburb of Wik, under the command of FK Karl Dönitz.

Dönitz himself fully understood the potential power of a revived U-boat arm. He had begun his naval career in the Imperial German Navy (*Kaiserliche*

---

[2] See Appendix Two for a fuller description of German submarine development during the inter-war period.

[3] This training school moved to Neustadt in May 1937.

Marine) during April 1910. Initially his duty as an officer was aboard the cruiser SMS *Breslau* operating in the Mediterranean, based largely in Istanbul[4]. In October 1916 Dönitz transferred to U-boats. He served initially as First Watch Officer (*I-Wacheoffizier*) aboard *U39* (for five patrols), before rising to command *UC25* (two patrols) and then *UB68* (one patrol) with the rank of Oberleutnant zur See. His latter command was sunk in 1918 following a catastrophic loss of longitudinal stability during an attack on British shipping in the Mediterranean. The stricken U-boat plunged out of control to 300ft before rocketing to the surface where it lay at the mercy of Allied guns.[5] Six men were killed and the remainder, including their commander, captured. After nine months in an English prison camp, Dönitz was released after feigning mental illness and returned to a ruined Germany. Following a brief stint as a Torpedo Boat captain, he was promoted to command the cruiser *Emden*, aboard which prospective naval officers received basic training during a year-long world cruise. In 1935 Kriegsmarine C-in-C Erich Raeder offered Dönitz command of the 'Weddigen' Flotilla. Despite brief initial reservations, he accepted the posting and arrived in June 1935 primarily as commander of the tiny U-boat School at Neustadt which boasted a strength of six U-boats – *U1* to *U6*. On 27 September 1935 Dönitz became commander of the three U-boats comprising 'Weddigen' Flotilla officially formed that day – the kernel of the 1st U-boat Flotilla. This is where our story begins.

---

[4] SMS *Breslau* and SMS *Goeben* were a constant presence in the Dardanelles area during the First World War, handed over to the Turks by Germany and crewed by men of both nations. They emerged from the Straits and headed for the Aegean on 20 January 1918, opposed by British destroyers and monitors. Both ships evaded the British but struck mines off Imbros, *Breslau* sinking immediately, *Goeben*, badly holed, beached herself in the Dardanelles Narrows.

[5] The sinking was attributed primarily to HMS *Snapdragon*.

2.

THE 'WEDDIGEN' FLOTILLA

Early U-boat flotillas were named rather than numbered, these names belonging to previous German U-boat heroes, men of the Great War who became the first of the U-boat 'Aces'. The premier flotilla was named 'Weddigen' in honour of Kptlt. Otto Weddigen, wartime commander of *U9*. He, perhaps more than any other, had been responsible for an uneasy and somewhat belated British awareness of the submarine's destructive power when he torpedoed and sank three 12 000-ton British cruisers – HMS *Aboukir*, *Cressy* and *Hogue* – in little more than one hour on 22 September 1914.[6]

In the autumn of 1935, however, Germany was still four years from war. When FK Dönitz arrived to take charge of the flotilla it numbered only three boats – *U7* (Kptlt. Kurt Freiwald), *U8* (Kptlt. Harald Grosse) and *U9* (Kptlt. Hans-Günther Looff). Shortly afterwards the strength of this unit was raised by the addition of further Type IIB boats commissioned directly into the flotilla after weeks of 'working up' in the Baltic. The first three reinforcements – *U10* (Oblt.z.S. Heinz Scheringer), *U11* (Kptlt. Hans Rösing), *U12* (Oblt.z.S. Werner von Schmidt) – arrived before the year was out. There is still a common misconception that Karl Dönitz exercised complete power over early development of the U-boat Arm. In fact this was not so. At that stage of his career he was responsible for little more than operational control over his small command. The real power regarding submarine development, construction programmes, training schedules and naval policy was held firmly by OKM's U-boat Division in Berlin, commanded by KA Leopold Siemens, ex-Naval Attaché to London.

On 1 October 1935, after less than a month of command Dönitz was promoted to Kapitän. Within the first year of his guidance, Dönitz, with close assistance from 49-year-old flotilla Engineer Kapitän Otto 'Papa' Thedsen another First World War U-boat veteran, had honed the men of the 'Weddigen' Flotilla into a small tightly knit unit enjoying elite status and was able to pick and choose those admitted to its ranks. At this stage of U-boat development, the men of the flotilla were truly volunteers for the U-boat arm (*Freiwillig zur Unterseebootwaffe*).

---

[6] Weddigen was killed on 18 March 1915 when his second U-boat *U29* was rammed by the British battleship HMS *Dreadnought* in the North Sea.

Initial training for prospective submariners was hard in the extreme. Seamanship skills were honed aboard one of three square-rigged sailing ships – *Gorch Foch*, *Albert Schlageter* and *Horst Wessel*. Eventually the eager prospective U-boat men slipped from dock aboard one of Germany's precious new submarines, blood-red swastika flags streaming from the boats' conning towers. In the Baltic's frigid waters emergency dives, deep dives, underwater navigation and simulated submerged and surfaced torpedo attacks were undertaken for numbingly long hours, day after day. Captain and crews had to undertake sixty-six surface and sixty-six submerged practice attacks using compressed air 'water slugs' before they graduated onto real torpedoes with dummy warheads. The crews alternated between manning U-boats and KK Rudolf Wiegner's submarine tender *Saar*, playing the role of enemy convoys. Launched on 5 April 1934, this 2,710-ton ship provided an excellent training platform and accommodation for U-boat officers, all under the critical eye of Dönitz, recently nicknamed 'The Lion' by his men. Written examinations added to the exhausting workload, the physical and psychological demands placed upon cadets designed to push them to the limits of endurance and gauge their effectiveness under high levels of stress. Those who survived to receive the coveted status of submariner felt truly justified in claiming membership to an elite force. Within the 'Weddigen' Flotilla morale soared. Perhaps serving to illustrate the self-assured confidence of Germany's new submariners, flotilla Senior Officer Hans-Günther Looff (captain of flotilla command ship *U9*) persuaded the 'Weddigen' U-boat skippers to autograph a telegram to the British publishers of Lowell Thomas's book Raiders of the Deep. Their brief message, written in English, was simple and direct – 'We're back.'

On 1 January 1936 Dönitz relinquished direct command of the 'Weddigen' Flotilla to Kapt. Otto Loycke, while beginning his new post of FdU (*Führer der Unterseeboote* – commander of all U-boats). He took with him Otto Thedsen and a small talented staff including Eberhard Godt as Operations Chief. However, the tempo of 'Weddigen' training and exercises never slackened. During May the proud new 'Weddigen' flotilla passed in review before Hitler aboard his state yacht *Grille*. By September 1936 a second flotilla was formed at Kiel, named 'Saltzwedel', under the command of FK Werner Scheer and comprising 9 Type VII submarines (*U27* having been the first of the new Type VII models to be launched on 24 June 1936) and with the two unstable and heavy Type I designs constructed along the lines of the Spanish *E1* prototype, *U25* and *U26*, attached. Within weeks this new flotilla had transferred to Wilhelmshaven.

By November 1936 the 'Weddigen' Flotilla numbered ten Type IIB boats – *U12*, *U13*, *U14*, *U15*, *U16*, *U17*, *U18*, *U19*, *U21* and *U23*, supported by the two submarine tenders *Saar* and *T23*. That same month the unit suffered its first casualties. On 20 November 1936 *U18* was manoeuvring on exercise in Lübeck Bay, submerged, but only to periscope depth. Without warning a jarring crash suddenly threw the small submarine onto her side. It was the lethal impact of German escort ship *T156*, unaware of the submarine's presence beneath her knife-edge bows. Flooding rapidly, the crew struggled to escape their sinking vessel. Of the twenty men aboard eight went to the bottom, their bodies recovered later by Kriegsmarine divers.[7]

The high pace of training and induction into Kriegsmarine U-boat Flotillas continued into 1937. International attention was now acutely aware of Germany's burgeoning submarine fleet, but turned what amounted to a blind eye to this and Hitler's other activities that disregarded previous arms treaties. Appeasement from the Allied nations continued along its ultimately futile path. In October 1937 a third new flotilla – 'Lohs' – was formed from Type IIB boats to share Kiel harbour with 'Weddigen'. The following year three more U-boat Flotillas were created from newly commissioned U-boats – 'Wegener' (Type VIIBs) in June, 'Hundius' (Type IXs – improved design of the two already constructed Type I submarines) during October and 'Emsmann' (Type IICs) in December of 1938.

German military progress benefited from another international development during the mid-thirties. On 17 July 1936 General Francisco Franco triggered a military revolt in Spanish Morocco, which soon developed into full civil war on the Spanish mainland. Franco's Nationalist forces possessed no submarines whereas their opponents, the Soviet-backed Republicans, had twelve available for combat. In Paris, Spanish Naval Attaché Lieutenant Commander (*Capitán de Corbeta*) Arturo Génova resigned his post and joined Franco's staff. His thoughts were that the Nationalist cause required at least two submarines in order to take the war to sea against the Republicans. Through his old personal friend Admiral Wilhelm Canaris he asked for German assistance but was rebuffed by Canaris' superior, KA Günther Guse (Chief of Naval Command Office, OKM).[8] Italy on the other hand showed no such hesitation and immediately offered two submarines with their crews to Franco's naval commander. By 8 November 1936 the Italians were operational in Spanish Mediterranean waters.

Hitler, not wishing to miss an opportunity to test his new weapons, ordered a similar German undertaking. OKM relented and agreed to send two brand new Type VII submarines to Spain under the operational title 'Training Exercise (*Ausbildungsüben*) Ursula' (the name of Dönitz's only daughter). With all identification marks painted out and under complete secrecy *U33* and *U34* departed from the Elbe on 20 November 1936, penetrating the Straits of Gibraltar seven nights later and commencing operations on 29 November. In

---

[7] *U18* was raised eight days later, repaired and recommissioned into the 'Lohs' Flotilla on 30 September 1937.

[8] Wilhelm Canaris – then at the rank of Korvettenkapitän – had been sent by the Reichsmarine as an intermediary in Spanish armament deals during the late 1920s, establishing a friendly rapport with Génova.

the meantime the Italian submarine *Torricelli* had claimed the first casualty of this covert submarine war. On 22 November the Italian torpedoed Republican cruiser *Miguel de Cervantes* causing severe damage to her machinery and putting the ship out of commission for months. Republican and foreign Press reports pinned the attack on to 'foreign submarines', causing great apprehension in Berlin, OKM fearing possible exposure of their secret U-boat missions.

Despite the remainder of Europe declaring their non-interventionist intentions towards the Spanish war, Germany began to use the conflict more openly as a convenient testing ground for its new military equipment. Small units of men, aiding the Nationalist forces under Franco, went into action to begin honing their military skills and perfecting modern techniques. Although fair to say that the Luftwaffe's 'Condor Legion' and Heer's *Panzertruppen* derived the most useful experience, the two U-boats operating within the Mediterranean derived valuable skills from their exposure to combat conditions.

However, German naval operations around Spain were beginning to drain the resolve of Hitler and his Chiefs of Staff. Mussolini's submarines had started to wage a more aggressive 'covert' war. Kriegsmarine commanders, however, became hesitant to commit further vessels to the struggle, sensing the possibility of extreme international complications if U-boat operations were discovered. On 10 December Field Marshal Blomberg finally ordered U-boat operations halted. It was on the point of returning to the Fatherland that *U34* scored the sole German victory of this silent war, torpedoing and sinking Republican submarine *C3* off Málaga. Only three men of the Spaniard's forty-man crew survived but, fortunately for Germany no evidence was recovered to suggest anything but an internal explosion.

Following the curtailment of 'Ursula' U-boats were again present around Spain, but this time as part of the multi-national 'peace-keeping' force. There they 'enforced' the supposed blockade of Spain by non-interventionist countries while monitoring British and French ships operating within Spanish waters as anti-submarine vessels under the Nyon Agreement.[9] In these warlike conditions captains and crews alike developed their techniques of stealth and concealment. From the 'Weddigen' Flotilla, *U14* commanded by Victor Oehrn served in the Spanish region between 16 July and 30 August 1937, *U19* commanded by Viktor Schütze during the same period and *U23* commanded by Eberhard Godt between late July and 10 August. 1938. Other flotillas also provided U-boats, aboard which were men such as Günther Prien and Otto Kretschmer, both serving as Watch Officers on 'Salzwedel' boats *U26* and *U35* respectively, and

---

[9] Several Italian ships had torpedoed cargo ships bound for Republican harbours in direct violation of international law. The Nyon Agreement (so named because it was signed in Nyon Switzerland 10 September 1937) allowed for ASW patrols to operate in support of all coastal shipping and for the safe escorting of ships carrying foreign nationals from war-torn Spain.

both soon to become part of U-boat history. Between July 1936 and April 1939, when the Spanish Civil War officially ended, fifteen separate U-boats had operated during forty-seven patrols around the Spanish coast.[10]

In October 1937 the 'Weddigen' U-boat Flotilla received its second change of command. Kapt. Loycke departed to be replaced by 21-year-old Kptlt. Hans Günther Looff, formerly the commander on *U9*. For the next two years the world watched as Hitler made repeated gambles in his desire for territory in which to spread the boundaries of the Third Reich. Neighbouring countries were annexed and occupied amid vague grumbling and placatory gestures from Britain and France. The Kriegsmarine as a whole also continued to expand, although production of U-boats could never be fast enough. For the 'Weddigen' men they remained equipped with Type II coastal submarines – nicknamed 'dugout canoes' (*Einbaum*) – while other units continued to receive larger, more modern Type VII and ocean-going Type IX boats. In the spring of 1939 Dönitz – after promotion to the rank of Kommodore on 28 January – launched the U-boat arm into large-scale Atlantic exercises to test his theory regarding submarine attacks. In a simulated assault on British supply arteries he and his men rehearsed the *Rudeltaktik* approach to convoy attacks, made famous in English as the 'Wolf Pack'. This technique had been developed during the Great War but never properly instituted in combat. Despite the exercises being heavily weighted in favour of the U-boats, Dönitz read the encouraging results as a complete vindication of his principles for waging a future mercantile war.

Aboard the Type II submarines, however, there was neither the available range nor torpedo-carrying capability to conduct full-scale convoy warfare. While Type VII submarines could rove over 6,500 miles in search of a target for any of their fourteen torpedoes, and Type IX boats further still, the small Type IIs could only range 3,100 miles and carry an absolute maximum of six torpedoes. Their role remained clear. While the larger U-boats would roam outward in search of merchant shipping, Type II units would conduct primarily mine-laying missions around England's south and west coasts as well as harassment of British naval forces in the North Sea.

Further complicating Kriegsmarine strategy, Germany did not possess a sufficiently large stockpile of magnetic mines for thick, extensive barrages to be immediately laid around England's sea-lanes. At the early stages of rearmament the Kriegsmarine had worked closely with armaments company Rheinmetall-Borsig, who also were engaged in developing a series of electro-mechanical bomb fuses for the Luftwaffe. The resulting magnetic mine design was finally ready for production by late 1936. Unfortunately Germany could do nothing to compensate for a heavily diversified armaments manufacturing plan using limited resources, and mines remained a low priority. Neither were there sufficient means of deploying these weapons. *Reichsmarschall* Göring in

[10] *U14, U19, U23, U25, U26, U27, U28, U29, U30, U31, U32, U33, U34, U35* and *U36*.

a fit of pique, had virtually denied major use of the Luftwaffe for mine-laying, leaving the burden squarely on the Kriegsmarine. While surface vessels were capable of laying up to sixty mines at a time they were often unable closely to approach Britain's guarded ports. The answer therefore was for the Kriegsmarine's small submarines strategically to place twelve or so mines each mission immediately in front of important British harbours.

Even with this planned method of blockade taken into account, the Kriegsmarine remained too weak to wage full-scale warfare against the Allies. Britain's Royal Navy rated as the largest professional navy in the world, while Germany was still in the early stages of an ambitious naval building programme. Grossadmiral Erich Raeder, Commander-in-Chief, was well aware of his forces' limitations, but still hoped for more time before any demands were placed upon his fleet. He had sought and received Hitler's 'guarantees' that war should not be expected before 1944 at the earliest.

During September 1938, the eve of Chamberlain's visit to Munich, Germany's U-boats had been placed on full alert pending political results. This was the second time that hasty deployments for 'exercises' had been ordered by Dönitz, the first accompanying German occupation of the Sudetenland earlier that year. As 'Weddigen' boats lay out in the North Sea at their exercise stations not all officers were happy about the possible prospect of war. *U23*, under command of her new skipper Otto Kretschmer, was one such boat cruising silently off England's east coast. Aboard, Kretschmer and his Watch Officer Adalbert Schnee discussed the future possible crisis. Schnee expressed concern at probing the seemingly formidable British anti-submarine defences. He noted that, years previously, British submarine *M2* had been lost in a training accident, her wreck later located by surface ships using 'some form of listening device'. To the majority of German crewmen ASDIC was a thing of the future and a truly ominous development. Dönitz, on the other hand, viewed British ASDIC and other anti-submarine measures as 'overrated' and with serious technical weaknesses. British sonar had a range of little more than 1,000-metres, while U-boat torpedoes were capable of firing several times that far. The U-boat could stand off and shoot without any fear of likely detection. Besides, war was not likely before 1944 according to Germany's apparently invincible leader.

However, by the beginning of August 1939 the writing was on the wall for all to see. If Raeder was concerned with the Fleet in Being, Dönitz was under no illusion about his U-boat strength. He had hoped for a submarine arm some 300-strong before any conflict, allowing 100 to be at sea at any given time, rotating with those under repair or being replenished. Under the grandiose naval building scheme of January 1939, known as '*Ziel* (Target) Plan', Hitler had promised 130 new U-boats in 1942, 194 in 1944 and 229 in 1945. Instead, by the end of August 1939, Dönitz had just fifty-seven operational U-boats, of which thirty were small coastal Type IIs.

Raising the international political stakes even higher on 28 April 1939,

Hitler had formally shaken off any pretence of abiding by naval strength restrictions of the Anglo-German Naval Agreement of 1935. He had already announced on 12 December 1937 that Germany was preparing to go to 100% submarine strength as allowed under the Anglo-German Agreement; now he removed the treaty stumbling block altogether. In an address to the Reichstag Hitler alluded to his excuse for his actions that England had removed the 'basis of friendship' that the treaty had been founded upon by their pledge of support to Poland in case of attack, he said:

> 'Since England today, both through the Press and officially, upholds the view that Germany should be opposed in all circumstances, and confirms this by the policy of encirclement known to us, the basis of the Naval Treaty has been removed.'

Irrespective of these grave political manoeuvrings U-boat commanders and crews maintained their extremely high state of readiness and morale. Through their exhaustive training and the deep camaraderie fostered from Dönitz downwards they possessed an extreme confidence in themselves and their abilities. During August 1939 Kiel enjoyed its last summer of peace and played host to its annual sailing regatta. While gaily-coloured yachts gathered to enjoy the festival atmosphere war clouds darkened the near horizon and Germany's submarines were deployed accordingly. On 21 August 1939 Dönitz recorded in the BdU War Diary:

> 'The North Sea patrols planned can start as soon as the 1st U-Flotilla has fitted out. I consider Group West's complaint that the Northern Sector of the North Sea is insufficiently defended is justified. I therefore intend to hasten the training of four of the seven school boats so that they can be at the disposal of Group West from 30th August.'

To meet possible developments concerning Poland the majority of U-boats were stationed in the Baltic. Dönitz and his staff embarked upon their command ship *Erich Wassner* (this ship having taken over the role from *Saar*) at Kiel and sailed to Swinemünde.

The decision was taken that if the situation with England and France began to deteriorate Dönitz would then proceed to Wilhelmshaven in order to control all submarine deployment against the west personally. Already there was the temporary FdU West Hans Ibbeken (commanding officer 'Saltzwedel' Flotilla) and his also temporary deputy Hans-Günther Looff. Those U-boats then remaining facing the Poles in the Baltic were to be controlled by KK Schomburg at Swinemünde. As it transpired this was exactly what happened, Dönitz arriving in Wilhelmshaven on 31 August. By then Hans-Günther Looff had returned from a holiday abroad and proceeded to begin fitting out his boats for combat.

Beneath the clear skies of late summer yachts from dozens of nations gathered in the Kiel estuary to celebrate the regatta. Amidst teeming sails and brightly coloured flags and bunting nobody paid much heed to the sight of sleek grey U-boats slipping from their moorings and taking to the North Sea for yet more exercises. These were not boats of the 'Weddigen' Flotilla but rather the larger Type VII 'Wegener' boats, the only unit still operating from this crowded estuary. Kiel's other normal occupants had temporarily relocated to Wilhelmshaven, a port allowing easier access to the North Sea and eastern English Channel. But casual observers of the discreet sailings may well have taken more notice if they had known that other German harbours were witnessing similar movements and that on 23 August 1939 new 'Weddigen' Flotilla commander 34-year-old KK Hans Eckermann, former skipper of *U20* and replacement for Hans-Günther Looff, made the first entry into the unblemished pages of 'Weddigen' Flotilla's *Kriegstagebuch* – the War Diary.[11] Curiously perhaps all of the initial entries concern boats from the 'Lohs' U-Flotilla. In fact it had been decided by Dönitz and FdU West that several 'Lohs' boats took the places of 'Weddigen' units in the task of minelaying, the freed machines under Eckermann's command destined to be sent instead to prowl in search of torpedo targets.

Wednesday 23 August: *U14*, *U18* and *U22* (all of the 'Lohs' U-Flotilla) departed for the forward staging harbour of Memel. From this East Prussian port these U-boats would be able to operate in support of any military action taken against Poland, although as far as the crews were concerned they merely continued to exercise in the Baltic Sea. Their cover designation was *Transportübung Lübeck* (Transport exercise Lübeck). This tenure within the Baltic was to be limited, however, that same day Russia and Germany signing a non-agression pact that removed the threat of hostile Russian forces.

24 August: In the early morning stillness *U12* ('Lohs' Flotilla) departed Wilhelmshaven to patrol England's east coast, slipping her mooring at 0600hrs. She quietly nosed through the harbour before heading north for her station on the Great Fisher Bank in the North Sea. *U16* and *U24* (both of the 'Lohs' Flotilla) departed Wilhelmshaven alongside their flotilla mate for brief patrols of the North Sea as much to keep the crews at their peak mettle as to observe foreign naval activity. Miles to the east, over the flat lands of Schleswig Holstein, a final 'Lohs' Flotilla submarine was putting to sea. *U20* began its transfer journey from Kiel to Wilhelmshaven, a voyage that would take seven days to complete, arriving at its destination on 31 August.

25 August: At 0130hrs the codewords *'Sonderkommando Ulla'* were received at Dönitz's headquarters – signalling that the sailing of boats to their war

[11] Outgoing Flotilla commander Kapitänleutnant Looff spent the next week as deputy to FdU West Hans Ibbeken. Later he went back to operational U-boats in 2nd UF's *U122*. He was killed in action on 22 June 1940 in the Eastern Atlantic.

stations should be increased. *U19* (Kptlt. Hans Meckel), *U21* (Kptlt. Fritz Frauenheim) and *U23* departed from Wilhelmshaven, the former two for reconnaissance patrols. Aboard *U23* her young commander, Kptlt. Otto Kretschmer, in his ninth year of naval duty and already a veteran of Spanish operations aboard *U35*, had orders to proceed to his designated quadrant within the North Sea and await further instructions. His U-boat carried an ominous and deadly cargo – a payload of 12 TMA (*Torpedo mine A*) magnetic mines; the standard pre-war designed floating mine. Stored aboard the U-boat in the same manner as torpedoes, TMA mines were shorter than 'eels', measuring only 3.64 metres long, including the anchor by which it was moored to the seabed plus its connecting cable. Detonated by magnetic influence, the warhead was relatively small, weighing only 215kg, which soon proved inadequate.

The following six days are omitted form the Flotilla's War Diary. During this period U-boats were positioning themselves either throughout the North Sea or in forward ports from which to launch the first wave of war patrols. There was considerable uncertainty within the ranks of these men, none doubting that conflict was ahead, but unsure with whom or indeed when. Devoid of the overall strategic picture privy to the men of Dönitz's staff, those sailors aboard the gently rolling U-boats were unaware of their carefully orchestrated fleet movement. There was only their own small part of the sea, brought to the boat by men wrapped in the warmth of grey Kriegsmarine leathers clutching binoculars and constantly sweeping the horizons. Politics replaced the more customary topics of sailors' conversation from the torpedo room to the officers' mess.

On 31 August 1939 Germany unwittingly enjoyed its last day of peace for the next five and a half years. The great gambler in Berlin's Chancellery was about to plunge his country into a war the likes of which had never been seen before. During this calm Thursday both *U20* and *U16* put into port at Wilhelmshaven. Another 'Lohs' boat, *U14*, left Memel to patrol Poland's brief stretch of coastline. The following day the storm in his assigned sector finally broke.

3.

COMBAT 1 SEPTEMBER 1939
to 31 DECEMBER 1939

Friday 1 September 1939: This slightly overcast day dawned in Germany with martial fanfares on national radio announcing the invasion of Poland. Hitler issued a proclamation to his military forces at 0540hrs to declare the opening of hostilities, five minutes before the first shells rained down on Polish soil. As Germany unleashed its Blitzkrieg there was little for the U-boat arm to do – Poland possessed very little coastline and an even smaller Navy. Nevertheless nine U-boats of various units operated in support of the invasion. The majority were deployed in order to prevent any Polish naval vessels from escaping to England while their country was rapidly overrun. Three 'Saltzwedel' Flotilla Type VII boats were immediately withdrawn when it was discovered that Polish destroyers *Grom*, *Blyskawica* and *Burza* had already slipped through the German net. There were two attacks against sighted Polish submarines reported to FdU as successful, although in both cases they were not, the torpedoes having prematurely detonated. Poland's two submarines *Wilk* and *Orzel* escaped to England.

The 'Weddigen' Flotilla comprised just six boats at the declaration of war: *U13* (Kptlt. Daublebsky von Eichhain); *U15* (Kptlt. Heinz Buchholz); *U17* (Kptlt. Harald Jeppener-Haltenhoff); *U19* (Kptlt. Hans Mackel); *U21* (Kptlt. Fritz Frauenheim) and *U23* (Kptlt. Otto Kretschmer).

While the War Diary makes no entries relating to any of these submarines until 10 September they were in no way idle. *U23* and *U21* had been at sea since 25 August. *U13*, *U15* and *U17* were all engaged upon mine-laying missions off England's coast. As they sailed during the first two days of September Germany was not yet at war with England or France but the boats proceeded to their stations in the event of such hostilities opening. Britain and France had pledged support to Poland in the event of any aggression against her, and they delivered an ultimatum to Hitler – withdraw his troops from Polish soil or face war with the Allies. The expiry time given was 1100hrs on 3 September. By that time the crews of these four 'Weddigen' U-boats were already poised over their wireless receivers ready for the orders launching their part of the Kriegsmarine mine offensive.

3 September: The entries for this day take up two small lines that shook the world:

> '1100hrs War with England.
> 1700hrs War with France.'

At Wilhelmshaven FdU Dönitz sat before the huge wall maps inside his head-quarters. Small blue flags marked the positions of his active U-boats, tiny markings lost within the expanses of the North Sea and north-eastern Atlantic. Within minutes of the official declaration of war from Great Britain he and his staff received an intercepted British Admiralty message. The two code words 'Total Germany' were ordering the Royal Navy to commence hostilities. Holding the flimsy paper intercept in his hand Dönitz sat immobile for several seconds before exclaiming: '*Verdammt!* That this has to happen to me again.' He stalked from the room, as his Staff Officers remained motionless and silent. Within thirty minutes 'The Lion' had returned, reconciled to his task. Orders came quickly and within minutes the direction of the U-boat war had begun.

Aboard 'Weddigen' boats the following message was received:

> '1105/3/9
> From Naval Command stop.
> To Commander-in-Chief and Commanders afloat stop.
> Great Britain and France have declared war on Germany stop Battle stations immediate in accordance with battle instructions for the navy already promulgated stop.'

Minutes later Dönitz added his own message for the men already at sea and preparing to break the seal on their orders' brown envelopes:

> '1116/3/9
> From Commander-in-Chief U-boats stop
> To Commanding Officers afloat stop
> Battle instructions for the U-boat arm of the Navy are now in force stop Troop ships and merchant ships carrying military equipment to be attacked in accordance with prize regulations of the Hague Convention stop Enemy convoys to be attacked without warning only on condition that all passenger liners carrying passengers are allowed to proceed in safety stop These vessels are immune from attack even in convoy stop Dönitz.'

The declarations of war found *U19* still on patrol, prowling the east coast of Scotland following a sweep of the North Sea to the east of 0° meridian. She did not return to Kiel until 15 September, the second week of war with England. *U17* laid an unsuccessful Minefield off Dover while *U15* achieved greater success, SS *Goodwood* and SS *Orsa* being sunk on 10 September and 21 October respectively.

U13 was ordered to proceed to the area of Orfordness. There, on 4 September, she laid her mines astride the heavily travelled shipping lane. Once her deadly cargo had been released the U-boat returned to her base, arriving two days later. The small field that she had deposited lay lethal and untouched until 10 September. During the course of that day the steel hull of British steamer 8,641-ton SS *Magdapur* activated one of the mines and she sank within minutes. Six days later British cargo ship SS *City of Paris* was damaged by a mine explosion, while on 24 September French ship SS *Phyrné*, a 2,660-ton steamer of the *Société Navale Caennaise* was sunk while steaming one and a half miles north-west of the marker buoys for Harwich's Adleburgh bank. She had also activated a mine laid twenty days previously by Kptlt. Karl Daublebsky von Eichhain's *U13*. Listing heavily to port she wallowed in the swell as her crew abandoned ship. Rescued by an Adleburgh lifeboat, they watched while *Phyrné*'s number three hold slowly flooded, dragging their ship below. This latter sinking was the first French merchant loss of the war. Her U-boat opponent had not got away scot-free, however. Returning to Kiel *U13* developed serious engine trouble. The boat's Chief Engineering Officer (*Leitender Ingenieur* known as the boat's 'LI') Oblt. (Ing) Rolf Brinker had managed on-board repairs enabling the U-boat to continue her home run, although bizarrely the diesels could only be run at full speed or not at all. Approaching the eastern entrance to the Kaiser Wilhelm Canal at Brunsbüttel Kptlt. von Eichhain requested permission to come through the waterway at top speed as opposed to the normal enforced speed limit. His request was greeted with derision at Kiel, taken as over-eager crewmen attempting to gain liberty ashore as soon as possible, and flatly refused. Von Eichhain promptly asked for a ship to tow his boat through the 99-kilometre canal and, following further radio discussion, *U13* was finally allowed to proceed unaided at full speed. The remarkable sight of a small U-boat hurtling to her mooring against Tirpitz Pier in a flurry of spray was long remembered by onlookers on shore. Kptlt. Daublebsky von Eichhain and Oblt.z.S. Brinker were held aboard their boat until Flotilla engineers verified the mechanical problem. Despite this extraordinary entrance to port Dönitz awarded several Iron Crosses Second Class to commander and crew members.

Aboard *U23* Kretschmer opened his orders on the morning of 3 September. His instructions were to head west to the Humber estuary where he was to deposit mines in the most advantageous area. Ordering full ahead to his engine room the twin 350-horsepower diesels thundered below decks, thrashing screws to maximum revolutions. The game was now on and look-outs, poised on a knife-edge of tension, searched for the tell-tale black smoke or mastheads of a British warship, all signs of lethargy shed. If forced to dive, the small U-boat had seconds in which to vanish from sight beneath the dull green sea. Seagulls soon appeared in the dusk sky above the U-boat heralding the closing coastline and Kretschmer adopted a stealthier submerged approach. Slipping carefully into position after nightfall he reached a point five miles from the channel buoys marking the Humber entrance. While trying to assess with his First Watch Officer the best way to approach the sticky problem of mine-laying he was understandably chagrined to be recalled to Kiel as he was about to give orders releasing *U23*'s deadly cargo. The operation had been cancelled and twelve mines would make the return journey to Wilhelmshaven. Kretschmer's was not the only boat recalled as twelve U-boats trekked home, ordered to do so by Dönitz.

The following day Kretschmer followed Dönitz's former command, the cruiser *Emden*, into Wilhelmshaven harbour. As the aged cruiser tied up at dockside air-raid sirens screamed their shrill warning. Ten RAF Blenheim bombers were attempting their first attack on the German Naval yards. Kretschmer hurriedly took his boat away from shore to the centre of the bay, but as quickly as it had begun the raid was over. Casualties aboard the *Emden* had been caused by flaming wreckage of a single British aircraft crashing on to its decks, providing a poignant memorial to the RAF crew and their failed raid.[12] It was, however, an augury of things to come for Germany's dockyards during the next five years.

The weeks that followed in the War Diary are remarkably clear of entries related to 'Weddigen' boats. The Flotilla's first war patrols were over. A somewhat inauspicious start, although eventually enemy losses totalled 15,575 tons of Allied shipping sent to the bottom by 'patiently waiting' lethal ground mines laid by 'Weddigen' U-boats. Most of the returned submarines required at least a week for shipyard maintenance and repair while the crews were given leave. These consignments of U-boats to the maintenance yards caused great frustration to BdU – there simply were not enough boats to keep the Flotillas in constant action.

Dönitz was unhappy about the emphasis placed by Kriegsmarine command on mine-laying operations. If Raeder's plan to sow fields in all of Britain's major ports, choking the waterways with lethal traps, was undertaken, the entire U-boat arm would have to be committed to the task. At FdU headquarters, Dönitz and his staff were convinced of the need to continue torpedo attacks, both to allow his commanders and crews to gain experience in real combat and also for the devastating psychological impact upon Allied sailors of a surprise U-boat assault. Dönitz pressed for U-boats to operate in the North Sea and Atlantic where they could threaten Britain's trade, but had to be content with a compromise solution. During new moon periods where the nights were pitch dark he would allocate roughly one third of his U-boats for mine laying, the 'Weddigen' boats targeted at England's east coast.

Elsewhere U-boats were crashing headlong into their enemy, writing their place in history's pages with bold strokes. The first day of war with England had resulted in the disastrous sinking of SS *Athenia* by Fritz-Julius Lemp's *U30* of Wilhelmshaven's 'Saltzwedel' Flotilla. An attack against the 'rules of

---

[12] Three direct hits had been acheived on the pocket battleship *Admiral Scheer* – all three bombs duds.

war', German authorities denied the sinking. Flotilla mates of Lemp aboard *U31*, another Type VII submarine, caused havoc with the first convoy attack of the Second World War on 16 September. Penetrating the small convoy OB 4 south-west of Ireland, *U31* torpedoed and sank SS *Aviemore* (4,060t). Other names were already emerging with glory from the U-boat arm: Günther Prien, captain of Type VIIB *U47* of Kiel's 'Wegener' Flotilla sank three British ships with torpedoes and gunfire on his first patrol, returning home triumphantly.

Meanwhile the 'Weddigen' Flotilla command returned to their home port of Kiel on Tuesday 5 September, the 160-kilometre journey completed by most of its staff within the day. The Flotilla's boats undertook their second group of missions immediately after maintenance had been completed. Quickly restocking their vessels with supplies and ammunition, captains were anxious to get back to the expanding battle with the Royal Navy.

In Berlin, however, there was some hesitation about how much free rein to allow the Kriegsmarine. Hitler was ecstatic over his Army's invincible march into Poland, but remained cautious regarding the western Allies. He felt that France in particular was acting with 'political and military restraint', making no move against Germany's thinly held frontier, and until the situation in Europe became clearer he had no wish to provoke them further. U-boat commanders had been authorized to take only defensive action against French warships and shipping. Raeder initially agreed with this approach, stating in conference with Hitler on 7 September that, in his opinion, there were two important factors to consider with regard to the French:

'a. Great Britain is unable to draw France into the war unconditionally;
b. France fails to see any war aim and is therefore trying to stay out of the war.'

For two weeks the general policy of war at sea was to 'exercise restraint', as Raeder put it in his Diary. Hitler forbade attacks on passenger liners and any French shipping at all. However, Raeder soon revised his opinion, strongly backed by Dönitz who had previously sardonically remarked in his own War Diary: 'So the French merchant ships are to be treated better than the neutrals!'. Waging limited submarine warfare was not a viable option for such a small navy in the face of the combined power of France and Britain. In further conferences at OKW, Raeder virtually pleaded with Hitler to remove the brakes from the Kriegsmarine. The Führer gradually complied as it became apparent that his peace overtures to England and attempts to sow discord between the Allies were bearing no fruit. The dictator submitted to his admirals' wishes and on 24 September cancelled the order to spare French shipping:

'Naval operations against France are to be carried out as against Britain. French ships are to be treated in the same way as British ships.'[13]

13 Hessler, Vol. 1, p. 41.

9 September: Kptlt. Fritz Frauenheim's *U21* put to sea from Wilhelmshaven. It was an unsuccessful mission for the small crew aboard. Thirteen days after departing their home port at 1418hrs *U21* missed a Royal Navy destroyer, initially claiming hits heard while submerged and retreating from the scene. It was otherwise a depressingly monotonous patrol.

Otto Kretschmer sailed from Wilhelmshaven at 1000hrs, the second combat mission following his first curtailed sortie. To frenzied waving from fellow sailors ashore, off duty soldiers and flower-throwing girls of this naval city, *U23* cruised through the estuary guided by *Vorpostenboote* escort. The final strains of a military band's marching song '*Wir fahren gegen England*' drifted towards those on the bridge as Kretschmer took his vessel into the North Sea. This time his mines were laid squarely in the shipping lanes of the Firth of Forth. Fortunately for his enemies, British minesweepers counteracted his efforts and the mines damaged no ships. On 14 September, during his return to Germany, Kretschmer launched an unsuccessful torpedo attack of a complete bow salvo plus one extra torpedo against a darkened steamer estimated at 2,000 tons and sailing under Allied escort. All four torpedoes missed their intended target. This was a particular disappointment to Kretschmer, the quiet skipper rated as the Kriegsmarine's best torpedo shot. His crew were also infected by the frustration of being yet to taste triumph. The analytically minded Kretschmer checked and rechecked his firing solution, holding an on-board conference with his officers and torpedo men. He surmised that his torpedoes had malfunctioned rather than been badly aimed, believing that the fickle 'eels' had run deeper than set, passing directly beneath the ship's keel. Kretschmer communicated his conclusion to Dönitz and continued the patrol. Six days later *U23* docked again in Kiel. Similar unsuccessful patrols were carried out by both *U13* and *U15*. The former returned to Kiel with the crew of a downed German bomber aboard, plucked from their dinghy in the North Sea.

On 24 September Kptlt. Udo Behrens' *U24* experienced a similar problem to Kretschmer, one that would soon plague Germany's submarine force. Eleven days into his patrol he was approaching a British destroyer unaware of the U-boat's presence in the Moray Firth. Lining his attack perfectly Behrens fired two torpedoes, periscope crosshairs squarely over their target. However, to his dismay both torpedoes passed straight through, or under, their target, which sailed onwards unconcerned. They had malfunctioned. Internal depth-keeping mechanisms appeared to have become unstable, somehow ruining any chance of success. Slamming the handles of the periscope upwards Behrens had no choice but to depart the scene at silent underwater 'creep speed'.

Other commanders had begun to report similar torpedo failures, initially given little notice by OKM, but soon to become a significant and far-reaching crisis for U-boat operations. Despite grave concern expressed by Dönitz on behalf of his officers the potential disaster of German torpedo performance received scant attention.

29 September: Kretschmer put to sea once more to patrol in the Orkney region. This time his orders were to operate directly against British Naval forces near the Shetlands. He scored the first victory for the Flotilla by torpedo with the sinking of the small 876-ton British steamer SS *Glen Farg*, stopping the ship with a burst of 20mm gunfire across the bows on 4 October 1939. Initially the small British ship had attempted to flee before more cannon shells raked the cramped bridge. Amidst much confusion her crew scrambled away from their scarred ship. Kretschmer allowed the panicked men to row clear before sending their ship to the bottom with a single torpedo. The tonnage that he could now claim was a small beginning for a personal score that would make him the leading 'Ace' and undisputed 'Tonnage King' of the U-boat service.

By this time the first month of war was over, and with it the first two U-boat casualties. Type IXA *U39* ('Hundius' U-Flotilla) and Type VII *U27* ('Saltzwedel' U-Flotilla) had both succumbed to depth charges during their maiden patrols. The former boat had been sunk first; Kptlt. Glattes was located and destroyed by escort destroyers after an unsuccessful attack against HMS *Ark Royal* on 14 September. Six days later Kptlt. Johannes Franz was found and destroyed by patrolling destroyers HMS *Fortune* and HMS *Forester* near the Hebrides. He had attempted to attack the British warships, but his torpedoes exploded prematurely, alerting his adversary to his presence. The crew were all rescued and spent the remainder of the war in captivity. More damaging was the capture of secret documents by a Royal Navy boarding party, able to snatch them from the commander's quarters before the submarine finally went under.

Maintenance work back at Kiel and Wilhelmshaven swung into high gear. Despite rigorous trials and months of combat exercises in the Baltic, U-boats quickly showed their weaknesses after actual war patrols. Engine mountings had frequently shaken loose due to vibration and depth charges had placed extra stresses on U-boats' pressure hulls. Engineers strove to keep the boats in action, working 24-hour shifts in the shipyards and docks.

Meanwhile enlistment continued unabated, and reserves of trained men without boats began to be deployed as 'U-Holding Companies' (*U-Stamm Kompanien*). This enabled the U-boat service to keep its recruits, despite possible efforts by other naval branches to 'steal' trained men for alternative Kriegsmarine duties. Officer candidates also continued to receive the same intensive preparation as before hostilities. During three months of training, candidates would learn submarine handling at a UAA (*Uboot-ausbildungsabteilung*) establishment, then techniques of torpedo use at the U-Commander's Torpedo Course (*Kommandanten-Schiesslehrgang*). Following these courses the student would accompany a serving U-boat on patrol as an officer aspirant for some initial operational experience.

Once commander and crew were ready for their submarine they were assigned a boat still under construction and undertook a period of 'boat familiarization' (*Baubelehrung*). During this process they would be present as their boat was built, becoming intimately familiar with its construction from the keel upward. This entire procedure, during which time the commander would be known as a *Baubelehrung* Commander, was undertaken under supervision of the Warship Construction Instruction Group (*Kriegsschiffbau-Lehrabteilung* or KLA).

1 October: A new chain of command for Germany's U-boat fleet was established. Two subcommands – Baltic and North Sea – divided the seventy-two available boats, spread between eight flotillas, both for combat and training.

Baltic command: HQ East, Kiel.
  'Weddigen' Flotilla – Kiel
  'Lohs' Flotilla – Kiel
  'Emsmann' Flotilla – Kiel
  'Wegener' Flotilla – Kiel
North Sea command: HQ North, Wilhelmshaven.
  'Saltzwedel' Flotilla – Wilhelmshaven
  4th U-boat Flotilla (training) – Emden
  'Hundius' Flotilla – Wilhelmshaven
  8th U-boat (training) Flotilla – Wilhelmshaven

17 October 1939: Kptlt. Harald Jeppener-Hattenhoff's *U17* was transferred to Danzig's U-boat Training School (*U-Ausbildungsflottille*). Her new commander, Kptlt. Udo Behrens, in exchange, handed over his previous boat *U24* of the 'Lohs' Flotilla to Jeppener-Hattenhoff. *U17* would carry out three more operational patrols during the first four months of 1940, before remaining purely on training duties until the war's end.

25 October: Kptlt. Karl Daublebsky von Eichhain took *U13* from Kiel at 0230hrs bound for the North Sea. Readjusting to the damp and mildew of a U-boat after the relative luxury of cabins aboard the tender *Saar* was surprisingly easy. There was a barely concealed excitement to be at sea again, coming to grips with the enemy. Five days later lookouts sighted the unmistakable smudge on the horizon of a convoy rolling through oily swells. Closing as rapidly as he could von Eichhain fired torpedoes and hit the 4,666-ton SS *Cairnmona* of convoy HX 5B, bound for Halifax, Nova Scotia. The large British steamer rolled over in flames and quickly sank. It was the sole victory of the patrol and the second torpedo sinking for the 'Weddigen' Flotilla. The remainder of 1939 found *U13* twice more at sea, during November and December. These last forays of patrolling and mine-laying outside the Firth of Tay were under the boat's new commander Kptlt. Heinz Scheringer. During the November voyage serious engine trouble developed and on the boat's return two Engine Room Petty Officers were awarded the Iron Cross Second Class for their difficult but successful onboard repair work.

October saw *U19* achieve remarkable success with further mine-laying. Kptlt. Hans Meckel made his last patrol aboard as captain, to the east coast of England. After laying his mines near the Inner Dowsing lightship on 17 October he plotted a return course to Kiel, arriving uneventfully the next day. His mines claimed three victims in rapid succession. On 21 the French 3,087-ton SS *Capitaine Edmond Laborie* was sunk two nautical miles east of the Inner Dowsing Lightship, followed by the Norwegian 3,295-ton MV *Deodata*. Three days later the Greek steamship SS *Konsyantinos Hadjipateras* added 5,962 tons to the grim tally. One further mission for the U-boat during 1939 under her new commander Kptlt. Wilhelm Müller-Arnecke sank the 6,371-ton Yugoslavian freighter SS *Carica Milica* by mine near Orfordness on 18 November.

8 November: Kptlt. Fritz Frauenheim returned to Kiel aboard *U21*. Returning from this, his third patrol, Frauenheim was again the object of attention by a British submarine. HMS *Sealion* missed *U21* with a complete bow salvo of six torpedoes before turning tail and retreating from possible retaliation. For his part Frauenheim had left his mark with the boat's first mine-laying mission. The small well-positioned field badly damaged British cruiser HMS *Belfast* in the entrance channels of Rosyth on 21 November and sank the 605-ton Naval net layer HMS *Bayonet* (ex-*Barnehurst*) on the same day. *Belfast* had been on gunnery exercise with HMS *Southampton* and two destroyers before her return to Rosyth. Her veteran skipper Captain Scott recorded the attack in his Log:

> '0800: Wind: SWF3
> Weather and Visibility: Blue skies, 7 miles
> Sea and swell: 7
> 0947: Passed through A/S boom
> 1005: Out paravanes
> 1058: Violent explosion felt in *Belfast*. Extensive damage.
> 1140: Taken in tow by *Krooman*.
> 1314: Prepare to abandon ship.'

The blast injured sixteen men and caused severe structural and machine damage. The full extent of her injuries was only apparent after the crippled cruiser had been towed to Rosyth dry dock. Her back was broken and she was only marginally considered repairable. She was out of the war until 3 November 1942.

Three days later the 2,266-ton SS *Royal Archer* was the last victim of this particular minefield. The damage suffered by *Belfast* was a considerable blow to the Royal Navy, compounded on 4 December by the battleship HMS *Nelson* being severely damaged by magnetic mines laid by the 'Saltzwedel' Flotilla's *U31* in Scotland's Loch Ewe. This natural harbour was an important northern anchorage for the British and host to many of the Royal Navy's capital ships once Scapa Flow had been evacuated, following Günther Prien's legendary attack and Luftwaffe bombing. Although both ships were towed away for repair and later re-entered service, the effect on British morale of sudden destruction in a 'secure' area was detrimental to say the least. Although the magnetic mine was not a technologically new development to warfare, it still shook British confidence. In his memoirs Winston Churchill wrote:

> 'During September and October nearly a dozen merchant ships were sunk at the entrance of our harbours, although these had been properly swept for mines. The Admiralty at once suspected that a magnetic mine had been used . . . Without a specimen of the mine it was impossible to devise a remedy.'

Fortunately for the British, the Luftwaffe, eventually released by Göring for mine-laying tasks, soon provided one such example. For three nights in November Luftwaffe bombers laid forty-one mines in the Thames, off the Humber and at Harwich. Between 2100 and 2200hrs on 22 November a German bomber was seen to drop a large object by parachute into the shallow mudflats near Shoeburyness. After delicate recovery and examination by four Royal Navy experts the magnetic trigger was discovered and counter-measures were slowly developed and put into operation.

Meanwhile another patrol yielded further victory for *U21* with the destruction of the 1,277-ton Norwegian steamer SS *Arcturus* on the first day of December. Following the U-boat's safe return and twelve days of rest and regeneration at Kiel, *U21* put to sea again for its final voyage of the year at 0300hrs on 17 December. Operating off the north-east coast of Scotland, Frauenheim sank two Swedish ships, the 1,474-ton SS *Mars* heading from Kopmanholmen to London and the 1,352-ton SS *Carl Henckel*, in the North Sea on 21 December. *U21* put into Kiel on Christmas Eve, where her crew received a well-deserved extended leave, proudly conscious of their status in Germany as men of the elite *Unterseebootwaffe*.

Kretschmer's *U23* made two more patrols before the New Year, the sole victory recorded as the destruction of the 2,400-ton Danish steamer SS *Scotia*, torpedoed in the first minutes of 8 December. The 290-foot ship took nineteen of her crew to the depths with her. Four nights later Kretschmer attempted an attack on a second ship 'approximately 2,500GRT' in Yale Sound, Shetlands, but to no discernible effect. Two torpedoes were fired at the unmistakable silhouette of a British cruiser lying at anchor. An enormous eruption displayed a direct hit although oddly there seemed no perceptible change in the target's attitude. In fact Kretschmer had launched a successful torpedo attack – on rocks bearing remarkable resemblance to a cruiser silhouette by moonlight. Despite fuming at the waste of a precious torpedo Kretschmer radioed BdU the tongue-in-cheek report:

> 'Rocks torpedoed but not sunk.'

This was not to be the end of the unfortunate mistake. On his return Kretschmer was somewhat mystified by the constant congratulations of fellow officers for his successful patrol, particularly as he himself considered it to have been rather barren of triumph. It was only after the customary briefing with Dönitz that the young skipper realized the reason for his congratulatory Flotilla-mates. The German word for rocks is 'felsen'. Somewhere in signal translation this had transformed into 'Nelson', the name of one of Britain's most powerful battleships and a target of prestige for the Kriegsmarine.

Recently arrived Flotilla-mate Kptlt. Peter Frahm made a single patrol in 1939, putting out as new commander of U15 on 14 November, replacing Kptlt. Heinz Buchholz. Laying mines near Lowestoft they accounted for a single British fishing boat, the 358-ton *Resercho*, on 28 December. The small vessel was virtually obliterated by the TNT warhead detonation, ample evidence that the magnetic triggers inside TMB mines were too sensitive.

TMB (*Torpedo Mine B*) had gradually phased out TMAs from mid-September 1939. These new weapons were specifically designed for submarine use. Again deployed via the torpedo tubes in the same manner as a torpedo, they were slightly smaller than TMA mines, measuring 2.31 metres, thereby allowing the submarine carrier to load even more into its confined storage space. Up to three could be fired from a single torpedo tube as a single shot. This was an unearthed 'ground mine' that utilized a magnetic firing pistol, activated by timer allowing the U-boat to depart before the mine became 'live'. It carried a 576 kg TNT warhead, twice that of period torpedoes. The mine, once laid on the bottom in shallow seaways, was detonated by the magnetic field generated by ships passing above. The explosive force beneath a ship's keel and carried by shock waves through incompressible water was usually more effective than a contact hit against a hull side, often snapping a vessel's spine and dooming her instantly.

These mines were originally ordered laid at a depth of 30 metres. However, questions arose as to the weapon's reliability at that depth and further trials were conducted. Following these it was established that 25 metres was a more suitable depth, and more likely to prove fatal to shipping above. It began to be noticed that often the magnetic trigger was itself overly sensitive and smaller ships were sunk than those intended, as was the case with the *Resercho*. U-boat crews subsequently began sowing their minefields in progressively shallower waters, also de-magnetizing them so as to reduce their sensitivity.[14]

During November the Flotilla was strengthened by the arrival of U24 transferred from the 'Lohs' Flotilla, which shared Kiel's harbour, and commanded

[14] A final torpedo mine – TMC – was designed after Dönitz' worries that the TMB's warhead might not be powerful enough to sink captial ships. Measuring 3.39 metres in length the maximum number of TMC that could be deployed per tube at one time was reduced to two. However, the TMC was packed with an explosive charge of 1,000 kgs, believed to be lethal from a depth of 36 metres.

by Oblt.z.S. Udo Heilmann. The boat had already made four operational war patrols as a Type IIB minelayer, claiming a single 961-ton victory. She lay dormant for the remainder of the year in Kiel.

There were further reinforcements with the December arrivals of two Type IIC boats: Kptlt. Jürgen Oesten's *U61* and Kptlt. Hans-Bernhard Michalowski's *U62*. The latter had only just been commissioned on 21 December and was still embarked on its gruelling shakedown trials. Oesten's boat had, however, been commissioned during the previous August and had already carried out two mine-laying missions. Its final sortie of the year began on 7 December and sought to supplement the successful field laid by *U21*, which had damaged the *Belfast*. Oesten was, however, unable to penetrate the inner defences of the Firth of Forth, now heavily patrolled by the British. He therefore laid his mines further out to sea, north of Saint Mary's in the Firth of Forth. The sole casualty was the 1,086-ton British SS *Ferryhill* sunk on 21 January 1940.

As 1939 drew to a close Germany's U-boat men had electrified the world with their courage and skill, invoking either admiration or fear and loathing. During October Günther Prien had made history by penetrating the supposedly impregnable Scapa Flow and torpedoing the aged but revered battleship HMS *Royal Oak*. While headlines were not bestowed on the men of the 'Weddigen' Flotilla, they nevertheless had taken the war to Britain's doorstep and contributed to the terror and respect generated among their enemies by the words 'U-boat'. Among the ranks of the Flotilla, operating the smallest of Germany's submarines primarily in the unglamorous role of minelayers, were men whose names were soon to become legendary. The baptism of fire was behind them and the Flotilla had operated without loss to themselves.

Karl Dönitz had been promoted to the position of Commander of U-boats (*Befelshaber der Unterseeboote* – BdU) on 19 September 1939, with an increase in rank to KA on 1 October. Immediately beneath Dönitz were created two distinct offices to handle the slowly expanding U-boat arm. *Kapitän* Hans-Georg von Friedeburg handled general organizational duties and preparation of U-boats in his capacity as BdU Org. (*Befelshaber der U-Boote Organisationsabteilung*), while actual U-boat operations were handled by KK Eberhard Godt as BdU Ops. (*Befelshaber der U-Boote Operationsabteilung*).

Further to the performance of the U-boats themselves was the gravitation towards unrestricted submarine warfare by German High Command. Following Hitler's 24 September cancellation of the order to spare French shipping, further slackening of operational limitations was announced. On 30 September strict observance of the Prize Regulations, which Hitler had insisted on at the war's outset, was removed in the North Sea. Two days later permission was given to attack any darkened ship sighted near the English and French coasts. By 4 October the rescinding of Prize Regulations observance had been extended from the North Sea into a zone as far as 15° west, further extended to 20° on 19 October. Also OKM gave permission to U-boat commanders to attack without warning any ships identified to be hostile within this area. Strong warnings were issued to neutral shipping to avoid travelling in these areas. Although Hitler forbade the use of the term 'unrestricted submarine warfare' this in effect had been established within two months of declared war. During the Great War it had taken two years to reach that point.

By the end of 1939 nine German submarines had been sunk, six by enemy warships, three by mines. This represented slightly more than 15% of the complete operational U-boat force. For this loss U-boats had accounted for a total of forty-one Allied and neutral ships in September alone, amounting to roughly 154,000 tons. By New Year these figures had risen to 114 ships totalling 420,000 tons sent to the bottom of the sea. Now that they had begun, 1940 would show the world that nothing could stop them. The scalpel was raised above Britain's jugular; U-boats of the Kriegsmarine were to bring it slashing down.

4.

FIRST BLOOD – VICTORY AND LOSS
1 JANUARY 1940 to 30 APRIL 1940

During January 1940 all six existing combat U-boat flotillas were reorganized into a more streamlined and effective structure. Coupled with the shuffling of boats and personnel came a redesignation of the flotillas themselves. No longer would the U-boat units be known by the illustrious names of First World War commanders; now they bore solely numerical designation. The entry dated 1 January 1940 bears the 'Weddigen' Flotilla's new title, *1.Unterseebootflottille*.

Into the ranks of 1st U-Flotilla came those men and boats that had been previously 'Lohs' and 'Emsmann' elements. Sharing Kiel with 1st U-Flotilla now was 7th U-Flotilla, the virtually unchanged order of battle of 'Wegener'. The final U-boat unit was 2nd U-Flotilla formed from an existing core of 'Saltzwedel' with additional 'Hundius' Flotilla boats.

January reinvigorated the veterans of the old 'Weddigen' ranks. To eight existing flotilla boats nine new additions had been transferred in order to bolster the small unit: *U9* from training duties, *U20*, *U22* (Type IIB) from the now defunct 'Lohs' Flotilla and *U56* (on patrol), *U57*, *U58*, *U59*, *U60* and *U63* – Type IIC – of the also defunct 'Emsmann' Flotilla. The latter boat was freshly commissioned on 19 January 1940 and took part in no operational missions during that month. Four weeks of gruelling shakedown in the frozen Baltic lay before them, handling trials under the instruction of officers of the Technical Training Group for Operational Submarines (*Agrufront – Technische-Ausbildungsgruppe für Front-Uboote*) followed by dreaded tactical exercises, including nearby depth-charging to accustom the crew to this uncomfortable experience. Only after these had been satisfactorily completed would her commander Oblt.z.S. Günther Lorentz take *U63* out to face the enemy.

4 January 1940: With New Year behind them, the first to emerge from the ice-encrusted harbour was *U19*. At 2300hrs shivering seamen on her conning tower kept the boat away from drifting ice and ensured they followed in the wake of their grey painted escort. Their new commander Kptlt. Joachim Schepke had recently transferred from *U3* of Neustadt's *Unterseeboote-*

sschulflottille following three war patrols despite the boat's status as a training vessel. During the last voyage he had sunk 2,348 tons of enemy shipping by a combination of torpedoes and scuttling charges. In impenetrable winter darkness the U-boat made its way through the Kaiser Wilhelm Canal, linking Kiel with Brunsbüttel, and into the North Sea bound for Scotland's north-east coast. After five days the sole victory of the patrol was finally recorded when Schepke torpedoed Norwegian freighter SS *Manx* within the proclaimed blockade zone. Leaving the Norwegian vessel burning and settling into the swell north-west of Kinnairds Head, *U19* spent the remaining three days of its patrol returning to port.

January developed into a familiar pattern of operations for the men of 1st Flotilla. Their chief designated areas were the north-east English and Scottish coast and further east past the Orkney and Shetland Islands. This was home ground for the Royal Navy and they became prime targets for U-boat men. The relentless pursuit of a tight blockade meant attacking any 'unfriendly' steamer as well as naval vessels. Many neutral ships were sent to the bottom in this crusade to sever Britain's trade lines. By sinking ships of any nation it was hoped to convince those countries still supplying Britain's needs that it was no longer worth their while to do so. Although mine-laying was still undertaken by 1st Flotilla boats, free-ranging patrols, primarily hunting Royal Navy ships, began to be regularly undertaken and commanders scoured their designated sectors for any targets deserving one of the precious six torpedoes that the Type IIs could carry. Despite the fact that Allied casualties to mines sometimes exceeded torpedo sinkings, particularly due to faulty torpedo weaponry, Dönitz correctly surmised that the carefully nurtured aggressive spirit of his men could not be satisfied by the unpopular task of mine-laying. Although enemy ships were sunk, victories from mines yielded no perceptible elation of success for submarine crews and were often thought to be unfairly credited when they did occur. Dönitz also considered torpedo attacks to have a far greater negative impact on the morale of the enemy than minefields. With a growing emphasis on ship-to-ship combat, the small coastal U-boats began to write their own legend.

8 January: Kretschmer was determined to add to his score during *U23*'s sixth war patrol. Departing Kiel at 2345hrs, destined for the Orkneys and the Royal Navy's backyard, he had aboard a complement of five torpedoes with which to leave his mark. Before departure he and his officers had noted the arrival of a new flotilla addition *U58* – late of the 'Emsmann' flotilla – returning from twelve days of patrol and flying two victory pennants from her periscope. After an uneventful transit through the Kaiser Wilhelm Canal during the night, *U23* emerged into the Elbe to meet the single *Vorpostenboot* escort that would accompany them during their initial transit into the North Sea. On the opposite bank of the river lay the low countryside of Altenbruch and the minesweeper port of Cuxhaven, disappearing behind as *U23* nosed forward towards the British Isles. A traditional 'Good Hunting' flashed from the armed trawler's bridge and she peeled away at nightfall leaving the U-boat to thunder forward into action following Kretschmer's barked '*Aüsserste Kraft voraus!*' (All ahead full!). Winter waters are not kind in the North Sea and soon those on the bridge were shivering in their sodden leathers, binoculars sweeping endlessly in search of prey. During the late afternoon of 11 January Kretschmer and his crew were rewarded with the sighting of a darkened steamer travelling solo through oily swells north-east of Kinnairds Head. Approaching cautiously, his eye pressed against the attack periscope, Kretschmer gave his order to fire, '*Los!*' In under a minute the cargo ship, identified as the Norwegian SS *Fredville*, was afire and sinking, her crew rushing to abandon ship. Early the following morning at 0650hrs fellow Scandinavian MV *Danmark* followed her to the bottom, ripped apart by torpedoes, her back broken as the tanker lay anchored in Inganes Bay, Shetland Islands. This latter ship of Det Danske Petroleum was the prize, a 10,517-ton Danish tanker laden with valuable oil bound for England and the largest sinking by the flotilla to date. Two pennants fluttered from her periscope as *U23* returned to Wilhelmshaven on 15 January. But the number of pennants belied the success of their patrol. In two attacks Kretschmer had accounted for 11,667 tons of shipping.

However, not all patrols managed to achieve such results. While Kretschmer had been at sea both *U60* and *U15* stalked the North Sea to no avail, the latter patrolling along the Downs and returning dispirited on 20 January. Kptlt. Peter Frahm, already with three confirmed victories from successfully laid minefields the previous year, whipped his crew back into enthusiasm for their next war patrol scheduled to begin at the end of the month.

15 January: As *U23* returned victorious to Kiel a further pair of 1st Flotilla U-boats slipped moorings and ploughed towards England. New arrivals to the flotilla, Type IIB *U22*, and Kptlt. Oesten's *U61* were both destined for the waters of north-east Scotland. At 0800hrs six-foot-tall Oesten gave the order to cast off from Tirpitz Mole. Once free of her berth the boat's electric motors disengaged and both diesels roared into life. Half speed (*Halbe Fahrt*) was ordered and the boat nudged out of the U-boat basin. The traditional military band and cheering crowd had gathered to see Oesten's U-boat on its way, many well-wishers waving from the decks of the moored *Saint Louis* and *Weichsel*, both former passenger liners, and from Kiel's seafront Hindenburg promenade.

Approaching Kiel's Holtenau Lock, eastern entrance to the Kaiser Wilhelm Canal, Oesten prepared to take on board the pilot who would accompany his boat through the deep inland waterway until they reached the final lock at Brunsbüttel. There the boat would pass into the North Sea and rendezvous with its escort for the first leg of its sea journey. *U61*'s fourth war patrol would last for fifteen days at sea, during which they would claim the sinking by torpedo of the Norwegian SS *Sydvold* east of the Orkneys on 22 January.

Aboard *U22*, formerly of the 'Lohs' Flotilla, Kptlt. Karl-Heinrich Jenisch already had an unconfirmed Polish submarine (in actual fact a missed torpedo attack on *Zbik* on 7 September 1939) and three freighters to his credit. After leaving Kiel at 2200hrs and transit through the canal he used the night to hammer through a rising sea towards new hunting grounds. Six days later while patrolling off Scotland's north-east coast, he chanced upon the British destroyer HMS *Exmouth* in the Moray Firth steaming ahead unaware of the U-boat. To attack a Royal Navy warship was a difficult proposition, rewarding if successful, often devastating if not. The large destroyer carried five 4.7" guns and a formidable array of depth charges. Her turbine engines were capable of carrying her quickly out of danger at a speed far in excess of the U-boat's surfaced capabilities. On this occasion fortune was with the German crew and the destroyer became Jenisch's fourth victim, hit and sunk with a small though devastating torpedo spread. All hands aboard the destroyer perished with their ship. Later the same day the Danish tanker SS *Tekla* added its 1,469 tons to his score. Jenisch returned victorious to Wilhelmshaven on 24 January, his one January patrol over.

The only mine-laying mission to begin in January for the 1st Flotilla left Wilhelmshaven at 2200hrs on 16 January. Kptlt. Claus Korth and his crew of *U57* were detailed to plant their field near the Orkney Islands in an attempt to disable more Royal Navy ships. Since Prien's attack on Scapa Flow the main British Fleet had moved to other stations, primarily Loch Ewe on Scotland's north-west coast. Increased defences and reinforced patrols in the Orkneys were sweeping the area of what had previously been considered a bay impenetrable by U-boat. Despite the lack of capital ships within the sound, Scapa Flow continued to function as a destroyer refuelling station until improved protection allowed the return of the main British fleet. Korth was well aware that his target area was still no easy meat for German submarines. En route to their destination *U57* encountered and torpedoed the Norwegian steamer SS *Miranda*, felt by the often superstitious sailors to augur good things for their mine-laying mission. Cheered by this effective start the crew deposited their mines near Invergordon on the night of 22 January. Despite regular Royal Navy minesweeping in this region, 8,240-ton Union Castle liner SS *Durham Castle*, under requisition to the Royal Navy as a stores ship, activated a mine and was sunk on 26 January, one day after *U57* had returned to Wilhelmshaven.

The success rate of the flotilla continued on its upward curve. As men settled into the routine of their own particular brand of warfare they developed a familiarity with their equipment and its operation. Life ashore in Kiel continued in much the same vein as before the war. The massive Allied bombing raids were years into the future and Germany rode high on a conquering tide. Men from all sections of the Kriegsmarine called the

29

city home, and bars and restaurants overflowed with blue suited sailors.

For crews of the Type II U-boat there were, however, some frustrations. Although the 1st Flotilla had moved onto a more free-ranging basis of operation as opposed to laying carefully designed minefields (particularly after Dönitz had persuaded OKM to suspend Type II mining operations at the end of December), a weapon load of five, perhaps six, torpedoes was hardly sufficient to carry the war to the enemy in an effective manner. An example of this problem can be seen in the operational log of *U9*, ordered to patrol offensively against enemy shipping around Kinnairds Head. Former law student Oblt.z.S. Wolfgang Lüth, previously second watch officer on *U27* and first watch officer of *U38*, took his small U-boat from Kiel at 2200hrs on 16 January. The conning tower was still adorned with its large peacetime metal Iron Cross, but now it was reduced to only the painted grey backing. The sharply defined black and white steel plating, a perfect bullseye for potential enemies, had been removed now that the boat was dressed for war.[15] Once through the canal Lüth proceeded towards his patrol area off the north of England. However, north-west of the West Frisian Island of Texel he sighted a darkened steamer within the prescribed blockade zone and immediately closed for an attack. Firing two precious torpedoes he managed to disable the Swedish cargo ship SS *Flandria*, the 1,179-ton ship later heeling over and sinking. With only three torpedoes left, he continued on his plotted route, sighting another darkened steamer within two hours. Again closing rapidly, he fired two torpedoes, striking the Swedish cargo steamer SS *Patria* and severely disabling her. As the crew scrambled to abandon ship he was forced to use his last eel to finish the ship. With all ammunition expended, Lüth set course for Wilhelmshaven, tying up in the harbour during the mid-afternoon of 22 January after only six days at sea. However, such short patrols could reap higher dividend. During eight days at sea, begun by Kptlt. Harro von Klot-Heydenfeldt's *U20* on 21 January, the small U-boat accounted for four ships, a total of 6,848-tons, all torpedoed during the night of 27 east of Wick, north-east Scotland.

29 January: The final sailings of January, *U15* and *U59*, both departed Wilhelmshaven for operations. Kptlt. Harald Jürst and his crew headed for the familiar waters of England's east coast, concentrating on the region of Cross Sands. During the next ten days they accounted for three British ships totalling 2,400 tons and including the small tanker SS *Creofield*.

U15, however, had a rendezvous of a different nature. Kptlt. Peter Frahm and his 24-man crew battered northwards through an agitated winter sea, separating from her armed trawler escort at nightfall on 29 January. The submarine was rolling uncomfortably, long shuddering vibrations rippling

---

[15] *U9* was the only U-boat to carry the emblem of the First World War Iron Cross, in honour of the original *U9* of 1914 captained by Otto Weddigen.

through her as she ploughed from crest to trough. Northern Europe was in the grip of one of the worst winters for 40 years and conditions in the North Sea were atrocious. Needless to say visibility was very poor and miserable lookouts huddled low in the conning tower, no doubt wishing for the relative warmth of the interior pressure hull. Sharing the same seas was small destroyer – *Torpedoboot* by Kriegsmarine designation – *Iltis* of the 6. *Torpedobootflottille*. An elegant light warship, *Iltis* was a Type 24 Wolf-Class *Torpedoboot* of 933 tons. Her 92-metre hull handled the difficult seas with greater ease than any small 250-ton submarine, although her 127-man crew would not have thought the passage comfortable. The following day dawned grey and featureless. Sky and sea merged in angry harmony, monotony of sight leading to a creeping lethargy among miserable bridge occupants. Finally night fell on the 30th, both ships suffering from the poor visibility, periodically reduced still further by squalls sweeping from west to east. In the expansive waste of the North Sea, Kptlt. Heinz Schuur's *Iltis* and *U15* converged on one another until by sheer coincidence their paths fatally crossed in the swept channel off Hoofden. Atop the conning tower of *U15* lookouts had barely a chance to shout any warning before *Iltis'* bow surged free of the darkness and smashed into the small U-boat. The *Torpedoboot*'s momentum drove her forward to the shriek of grinding metal, forcing the shattered U-boat beneath her. In seconds the small submarine flooded and she plummeted to the seabed. Of her 25-man crew there were no survivors for the frantically searching *Iltis* to rescue. The 1st U-Flotilla had lost its first casualty after 153 days of war.[16]

Flotilla Chief Kptlt. Hans Eckermann spent the end of January in Brunsbüttel. Transferring to Wilhelmshaven on 2 February, his diary entry records the unfortunate end of *U15*. Accompanying the U-boat number in his entry are words soon to become regular features in this document of the Second World War: *'Vermisst **'* or *'Vermisst zwei Stern'* (missing two stars). This phrase denotes the confirmed loss of a U-boat.

U-boat Command instituted a system of reference to the status of lost or missing U-boats once war was declared. When it was apparent that a boat was missing and yet could not be confirmed by hard evidence as lost, it was officially listed as *'Vermisst ein Stern'* (missing one star). Full investigation into cases of unconfirmed loss was undertaken, using any means of confirmation: information from other U-boats, Red Cross lists of wounded or captured crewmen, radio intercepts of Allied operational units or indeed Allied propaganda broadcasts. In the case of a loss being confirmed, the status of one star was removed and replaced with two. The loss of *U15* presented no particular mystery and she was immediately classified *'Vermisst zwei Stern'* in both the

---

[16] There is a certain repetitious irony to the fate of Peter Frahm's *U15*. The first U-boat to be lost in the First World War had been *U15*, rammed and sunk by cruiser HMS *Birmingham* on 8 August 1914.

Flotilla War Diary and U-boat Command's War Diary – the eleventh U-boat loss of the war.[17]

Meanwhile, German mine-laying was still posing an enormous problem for the Allies. Coupled with U-boat-delivered fields the Luftwaffe had stepped up its own mine-laying, particularly along England's heavily travelled east coast. Though it was true that recently developed British LL magnetic minesweeping equipment was being put into service alongside the technique of degaussing or 'wiping', there were considerable numbers of vessels and miles of coastal waters to be dealt with. Unfortunately for merchant shipping, an air of complacency still prevailed in the upper echelons of the British Admiralty regarding the extent of German minefields. What at first were thought to be small isolated pockets of U-boat mines fast became thick mine barrages; the U-boat-laid weapons bolstered by Luftwaffe drops and Kriegsmarine surface vessels made the most of cover provided by foggy winter conditions to dash into coastal English waters, lay mines and leave.

During September 1939 a total of twenty-six ships had been sunk by U-boat attack as opposed to merely two sunk by mines. In the first month of 1940 these figures were reversed, two ships (6,549 tons) sunk by direct U-boat attack and eleven ships (61,943 tons) sunk by mines along Britain's east coast. Though these figures are partially explained by severe weather making U-boat operations difficult at best, the problem of magnetic mines, now combined with acoustic devices, continued to plague Britain. Between October 1939 and 1 March 1940 the *U-Bootwaffe* helped considerably to place a strong cordon of mines around Britain, particularly in vulnerable entrance channels to the more vital harbours. The mine, for a while, became far more reliable than the rapidly growing number of defective torpedoes.

6 February: After overseeing his boat's final outfitting and provisioning Oblt.z.S. Wolfgang Lüth took *U9* to sea from Wilhelmshaven again. Lüth's small submarine slipped from the U-boat basin at 1000hrs beneath a dull sky. The comfortable routine of brief words from the flotilla commander, named 'the last rites' (*Letzte Ölung*) as a grim joke, the receipt of sealed orders, rousing marching music from Kriegsmarine bandsmen and crowds of boisterous well-wishers eased the crew back into their duties. *U9* was again bound for Scotland and the steep sided marine canyon of the Moray Firth. Nine mines were fired from *U9*'s tubes on 9 February to lay in silt below the U-boat's keel before she quietly eased away from British shores. Away from the rain-lashed coast Lüth ordered *U9* surfaced and directed north in search of targets for the only two on-board torpedoes, finding and sinking the 1,212-ton Estonian steamer SS *Linda* two days later. Again, despite strenuous British sweeping with both standard Oropesa sweeps and the newly developed

[17] For space reasons U-boat losses will generally be recorded only once, the second confirmation generally omitted.

LL magnetic sweep, not all of Lüth's mines were neutralized. Nearly three months later the British tanker SS *San Tiburcio* had her spine shattered by the compression wave of an erupting ground mine. Lüth had sent 5,995 more tons to the bottom.

8 February: Wilhelmshaven welcomed two returning U-boats. *U58* and *U59* both put in from patrols begun during the final week of January. Kptlt. Harald Jürst's *U59* boasted the higher achievement of three ships sunk.

Outward bound from the same harbour were two more 'canoes'. Kptlt. Jenisch's *U22* and Kptlt. Korth's *U57* made their way towards England. Jenisch was to suffer disappointment thirteen days later on 21 February during an attack on British fishing ship *Strathclova*. After nearly two weeks of frustrating nothingness, the torpedo run against the small ship was at least guaranteed to rid the crew of the mocking spectre of returning to port with a full store of torpedoes. The previous victors of 1st U-Flotilla's first Royal Navy sinking did not relish becoming the butt of endless jokes from their shipmates in the 'Patzenhofer' bar on Kiel's *Dreiecksplatz*, a favourite haunt of Kriegsmarine men. Jenisch crept towards his unsuspecting target and loosed a single torpedo which ran straight and true towards *Strathclova*. The First Watch Officer Oblt.z.S. Herbert Opitz counted away the seconds of the torpedo run until a dull rumble of detonation reverberated through *U22*. However, the muted cheers died away when Jenisch announced that the small steamer was still there and producing massive plumes of smoke from her funnel as her commander guessed correctly what had caused the unexpected explosion to port. *U22*'s torpedo was a *Frühzünder* – premature detonation. The U-boat slunk away, an air of frustration clouding her interior.

Aboard *U57* Korth and his crew operating between Bergen and the Shetland Islands had the satisfaction on 14 February of listening to the collapsing bulkheads of the 10,191-ton British tanker MV *Gretafield* while she plunged beneath the waves. Straggling behind the main body of convoy HX18, the heavily laden tanker was sunk in the early morning. Her flaming oil quickly died away in the frigid waters north-west of Wick. On the evening of the 21st Korth torpedoed SS *Loch Maddy* of Halifax convoy HX19 east of the Orkney Islands, striking the ship amidships with a single torpedo. This 4,996-ton ship, however, refused to die and simply settled low into the sea as her crew abandoned ship. *U57* had no choice but to depart the scene due to expended torpedoes and the danger of discovery by escort ships snapping at the heels of larger convoy members. There was neither time, opportunity nor torpedoes for a coup-de-grace and she was claimed as a 'probable'.

Seven hours after Korth's departure another U-boat chanced upon the burning wreck. Beneath a drab and drizzling sky *U23* had departed Wilhelmshaven on the morning of 9 February bound for the Orkneys. The U-boat benefited from poor marksmanship shortly after separating from her escort. Three British torpedoes brushed past *U23*'s hull from starboard, prompting a rapid crash-dive. After submerging, an anxious sweep with hydrophones revealed the faint trace of a swiftly departing submarine.[18] On the 14th it was Kretschmer's turn to stalk an unsuspecting prey and he sank SS *Tiberton* east of the Orkneys. However, four nights later he scored a particularly satisfying victory, sinking the flotilla's second British destroyer. Eight-year old 'Defender' Class HMS *Daring*, travelling through Kriegsmarine map reference AN1692, was escorting an HN convoy southeast of the Shetlands when Kretschmer's bridge watch spied the merchant column. While Kretschmer was making an approach to the convoy he was startled by the appearance of HMS *Daring* to starboard and closing. Brief flashes of blue light were discernible as the British crew passed through heavy blackout curtains along her companionways. Remaining surfaced, Kretschmer chose to retreat from a convoy attack and fired two defensive torpedoes at the destroyer before breaking away at full diesel speed. The 1,375-ton destroyer of 3rd DF Home Fleet staggered under the torpedoes' violent strike, her entire stern blown off. Within 30 minutes the ship had capsized and sunk, taking nine officers, including her captain Commander S.A. Cooper, and 148 ratings to the seabed. Accompanying submarine HMS *Thistle* picked up only five survivors, one officer and four ratings.

Kretschmer's third and final kill of that patrol wallowed into his crosshairs on 22 February. Seven hours after Claus Korth had devastated SS *Loch Maddy*, causing her crew to flee, the battered ship still stubbornly refused to go down. Kretschmer's final torpedo tore apart the steamer's hull, breaking her in two.

The grim toll harvested by 1st U-Flotilla steadily mounted during February as commanders demanded more from their ships and men; Oblt.z.S. Herbert Wohlfarth's *U14* sank four Scandinavian ships near Scotland within two days of blinding rain and heavy seas. Schepke was foiled by yet another torpedo malfunction on 20 February. After closing on his quarry, British tanker MV *Daghestan*, his torpedo ran straight for the enemy ship but exploded prematurely only metres short. Direct torpedo attack became the norm although mines were still occasionally hauled away by flotilla U-boats from Wilhelmshaven and Kiel to be laid in British silt.

Eckermann's two War Diary pages that tell of the comings and goings of the flotilla during February show regular widely spaced patrolling by his boats during that month. Weather conditions were, however, prohibiting frequent voyages and taking their toll on weary crewmen. Training in the Baltic was virtually at a standstill and new crews were delayed in commissioning their freshly launched U-boats.

Of recent arrivals to 1st U-Flotilla only *U63* had seen no action before

---

[18] This was probably HMS *Sturgeon* although Prof. Jürgen Rohwer's excellent *Allied Submarine Attacks of World War Two* gives the date of this attack as 14 October 1939 as *U23* was returning from her third patrol.

February. Commissioned into the flotilla on 18 January 1940, the U-boat had undergone six weeks of trials in the Baltic before transfer to the forward U-boat base on Heligoland. The small fortified island was unpopular with U-boat men, open to the elements and a confined target for British aircraft, while offering none of the traditional delights to be found in naval towns. During the previous war the military base, which occupied the island's southern portion, had provided a vital forward staging area for the Kaiser's U-boats, but, with the improved long distance weaponry of the Kriegsmarine, its strategic importance had faded during the Second World War. Here *U63* spent a further fortnight working up, although forced to return to port every night due to bad weather, which also curtailed the working up period to only eight days in total. The U-boat left Heligoland on 17 February at 1300hrs for her maiden patrol, carrying four electric torpedoes. In the tiny captain's cabin, separated from the rest of the boat by its green curtain, Oblt.z.S. Günther Lorentz, former commander of *U10*, pondered his boat's forthcoming baptism of fire. The crew were in high mettle despite an uncomfortable passage, the only peace being when the boat did its daily trim dive, the roaring of wind and diesels replaced by an eerie submarine silence broken only by the low hum of electric motors and occasional spoken commands from the control room. Most of the day was spent submerged easing the hardship of weather-induced rolling and providing cover from British attention. *U63* was ordered to operate against British naval forces between Bergen and the Shetland Islands. After nine difficult days the unmistakable smudge of distant smoke from multiple ships was sighted by the bridge watch on the early evening of 24 February. Following swift confirmation of their sighting by the captain, *U63* went to periscope depth. The gift of southbound convoy HN14E ploughing directly for the U-boat electrified the crew into action. Lorentz was aware that the destroyer escort remained a ticklish problem, but prepared his attack accordingly. During the next one and a half hours he carefully positioned his boat, the 24-strong crew tense and anxious for the action to begin. Finally he spoke the command and a single torpedo flew from number one tube. Seconds later the sea erupted alongside the Swedish SS *Santos* and she went down in minutes. The crew were jubilant; their target estimated at 5,000 tons (in fact 3,840 tons) was a good start to the boat's score.

Lorentz used the remaining minutes of light to observe the convoy's behaviour and ordered a fresh course, enabling *U63* to surface out of visible range and circle ahead at maximum revolutions for a new assault. A brief crash dive due to an unsuccessful British air attack reminded the crew that they were vulnerable while surfaced and lookouts remained galvanized at their posts once the U-boat resurfaced. The night seemed interminable, the submariners wide-eyed with anticipation of what morning would bring. For those few off duty there was no rest, minds churning while the boat vibrated and shook through rolling seas, the constant movement accompanied by the roar of diesels. Torpedoes were greased and received yet another overhaul to search for possible defects, a difficult task made no easier by the U-boat bucking wildly during the chase. All three tubes were eventually loaded, leaving one reload available.

A little after midnight Lorentz made a fresh attack, missing with a single torpedo aimed at an unidentified steamer. A third attack was launched at 0200 hrs, again missing its intended target. The curse of torpedo problems seemed to be with them. Another attack run was made, this time foiled by engine trouble as the convoy steamed on. Atop the conning tower the four-man bridge watch were glued to their Zeiss binoculars, invigorated by the same blinding spray which they had cursed only days before. *U63* began a high-speed run out of sight of the target to reposition for a final attack. Ahead lay the convoy and, with the dull light of dawn spreading in the east, smoke appeared on the horizon followed by mastheads and finally low silhouettes. Lorentz was placed where he wanted to be and prepared his ship for action at periscope depth. However, the fatigued bridge watch, due for relief after four hours duty, failed to notice the slender branch of a nearby periscope shadowing their own movements as they submerged. British submarine HMS *Narwhal*, part of the convoy escort, had observed the U-boat's approach at 0800 hrs, prior to her dive. The submarine was ostensibly present to counter a possible attack by the much-feared German surface raiders known to be at sea. It was not impossible for the submerged British submarine to stalk *U63*, but the U-boat was between him and the convoy, posing an immediate threat to the vital merchant ships. The captain ordered a hurried signal sent and aboard the destroyer escorts HMS *Escort*, HMS *Inglefield* and HMS *Imogen* action stations blared as the ships closed up for submarine action. The likely position of the submerged U-boat was plotted and the destroyers roared ahead to drop their first series of depth charges.

The sudden reversal from hunter to hunted momentarily threw Lorentz off balance. He swiftly recovered, ordering his boat deep with helm put full over. The Type IIC hurtled sharply downwards touching 395 feet, exceeding her rated shipyard depth. Water abruptly began to jet through diesel exhaust valves into the cramped pressure hull and Lorentz was compelled to take his boat up to 160 feet while propellers churned audibly above him. It was too late for *U63*, her movements plainly discernible to British hydrophone operators. Beneath the destroyers' keels all eyes aboard *U63* strained upwards as if to see their assailant. The ominous sound of multiple splashes made by heavy canisters was plainly heard and the men braced themselves for what would surely follow. Rolling from HMS *Escort*'s stern and set to explode at 150, 250 and 350 feet were the first in a planned pattern of depth charges. Seconds passed with a barely audible clicking until the thunderous roar of exploding canisters hammered the German crew. Their submarine reeled as gauges shattered and electrical systems failed, plunging them into darkness. For the men of *U63* there was no hope of staying submerged. Emergency lighting revealed a rapidly flooding bilge and little control over the boat's trim. The U-boat plunged downwards again, unable to maintain her depth with hydroplanes. *U63* crashed into the sand below, water entering the electric engines. There appeared to be no way of stopping the rising tide as her main bilge pump was out of commission. Lorentz ordered ballast tanks blown and *U63* began to rise, before halting and falling to the seabed again. With only 225 lbs of compressed air pressure ieft to raise his boat Lorentz had no choice but to use this last remaining chance to get his boat and crew to the surface. Of course the problem of survival would receive no cure on the surface. There was no hope of lasting long; the destroyer's cannon would tear their vessel apart. With bitter resignation Lorentz gave the order to surface and prepare to abandon ship.

In a heaving sea the grey hull of *U63* emerged from the depths. Already British small-calibre weapons began to fire toward the U-boat, although wildly inaccurate due to the ships' roll. Below decks Lorentz urged his men to escape. He ordered all secret documents swiftly bundled into a weighted bag and prepared to open the outer hatch. There followed what must have seemed a bizarre scene to the Royal Navy spectators. As Lorentz opened the conning tower hatch internal air pressure, built up while manoeuvering submerged and higher than external, suddenly rushed out, hurling the young commander from his submarine and into the sea. Lorentz' crew scrambled from their sinking U-boat, the Chief Engineering Officer, Oblt (Ing) Karl-Heinz Asbeck, being the last to leave, for it was his responsibility to ensure that seacocks and hatches were open and the boat would successfully scuttle.

Thus *U63* ended her first patrol south-east of the Shetlands, damaged beyond repair and sunk by her own crew. The U-boat's conning tower finally submerged at 0930 hrs on 25 February. Nearly her entire complement were rescued, only one crewman consigned to the deep with his boat. Günther Lorentz and the rest of his crew would spend the remainder of the war behind barbed wire.

Eventually it became obvious to BdU that *U63* was overdue from her patrol. Repeated requests to confirm her position went unanswered, though this in itself not conclusive evidence of loss. One month after her departure for patrol *U63* appeared in the 1st U-Flotilla War Diary again. The single entry: '*U63* – Vermisst*'

On the British side of the naval war, escort vessels for vulnerable convoys had become a top priority for Admiralty operational planning staff. First Sea Lord Winston Churchill suggested in his minute to the Director of Naval Construction on 11 September 1939 that Britain's naval shipbuilders concentrate on:

> 'An anti-submarine and anti-air vessel which can be built within twelve months in many of the small yards of the country . . . These will be deemed the 'Cheap and Nasties' (cheap to us, nasty to the U-boats).'

Thus were born the small corvettes of the Second World War in direct response to the burgeoning U-boat campaign. The Admiralty were ever mindful of the effect on Britain of the last war's submarine blockade. By the end of February, despite appalling conditions, the Allies had lost nearly 250,000 tons of merchant shipping, 60% of which was sunk by U-boat. On the other hand of the fifteen U-boats accounted for by Allied forces, convoy escort or mine had sunk most, Royal Navy anti-submarine patrols proving virtually a complete failure.

During the first days of March Dönitz prepared plans for a fresh wave of U-boat missions. At 1st U-Flotilla, boats in port were restocked with torpedoes, mines, food and water ready for the next round of Germany's ascending maritime war. However, on 4 March 1940 Hitler issued instructions to cease all U-boat operations, particularly in waters round Norway. He had decided to attack Scandinavia and wanted to divert attention from the region while his forces prepared for invasion.

New patrols were planned by OKM for the submarine units of northern Germany. While the logistics required for conquering Denmark appeared relatively simple, any invasion of Norway would require considerable naval transfer of men and equipment. Slow convoys of troop transports would make an inviting and easy target for enemy submarines. Therefore the majority of patrols undertaken by 1st U-Flotilla during March were anti-submarine patrols in the Skagerrak. British submarines were thought to be roving the narrow entrances to the Baltic Sea, although vigorous searching failed to find any. Kretschmer in *U23* carried out the initial search for these phantom enemies north of the Shetlands but found nothing except bleak empty seas.

14 March: Kptlt. Joachim Schepke took *U19* from Wilhelmshaven at 1630hrs to north-east England in search of British submarines or any target of opportunity. Earlier in the day at 1400hrs the mass sailing of *U7, U9, U20, U24, U56, U59* and *U57* had excited cheering Wilhelmshaven crowds to even greater enthusiasm than normal. All except the last boat were destined for fruitless scouring of the Skagerrak. Like Schepke, Kptlt. Claus Korth was ordered to take *U57* to the coast of Pentland Firth in a solitary roving mission. These two 'dugout canoes' were replacing larger Type VII boats which had been formed into 'attack groups' and transferred by Dönitz closer to Norway. Both of these patrols were successful, Korth sinking two ships for a total of 7,009 tons (both previously damaged by Luftwaffe attack), while Schepke destroyed four ships totalling 5,517 tons. Again, however, no enemy submarines were sighted.

20 March: *U22* slipped from Wilhelmshaven at 2000hrs, Kptlt. Karl-Heinrich Jenisch chafing to put to sea after nearly a month on land. Ordered to patrol near Cape Lindesnes near Norway's Kristiansand he and his boat disappeared, the final sight of them had by the men of their *Vorpostenboot* escort. It is probable that *U22* was a victim of extensive British minefields in the Skagerrak. It has also been suggested that French submarine *Orphée* sank her although the French deny this and there is no evidence to support the idea. There have been recent assertions in books based on U-boat operational histories that Jenisch may well have been sunk by collision with the Polish submarine *Wilk*. The events surrounding the *Wilk* incident, however, took place during the night of 20/21 June, too late to have been *U22*. The possibility remains that *Wilk* did collide with a U-boat, perhaps *U122* commanded by Hans-Günther Loof after his transfer to the 2nd U-Flotilla.

21 March: Kptlt. Wolf Stiebler eased *U21* away from Kiel's Tirpitz Mole at 1500hrs. His second voyage as commander was intended to patrol Pentland Firth, again in search of elusive British submarines. En route to his objective Stiebler received fresh orders to turn east in response to a reported sighting by Oslo's German Naval Attaché, KK Richard Schreiber, of major British naval activity near Egersund. The report later proved to have been incorrect and no enemy forces were found. Turning back towards his original destination on the night of 26 March, Stiebler's submarine grounded on Oddene, one of the most southern rocks on the Norwegian coast. There appears to be conflicting accounts of the reason for this grounding, the most likely being navigational error, perhaps compounded by poor depth-keeping. In Wolfgang Hirschfeld's outstanding book recording his experiences aboard *U109* and *U234* he recounts an exchange on 30 May 1941 between Dönitz and *U109*'s Chief Engineer Martin Weber (in 1940 the Chief aboard *U21*):

> 'The Admiral . . . slowly approached the front rank. He was slim, tall and serious looking.
>
> "Well, Weber, you always seem to be at the bottom of it when the shit starts flying."
>
> The Chief Engineer blushed bright red. "I could do nothing about it, Admiral," he protested.
>
> "You said that the last time." We all knew what Dönitz meant. Weber had been the Chief Engineer of a U-boat whose crew were interned after an unfortunate miscalculation of the trim had put the boat ashore on the Norwegian coast.'[19]

The U-boat could not manage to refloat herself using her straining diesels and remained wedged on the Norwegian shore. Unfortunately for Stiebler a local fishing boat observed the incident. In desperation the stranded Germans attempted to bribe the fisherman to help pull their U-boat off the rock, but the Norwegian departed for Mandal and informed naval authorities of *U21*'s presence. Within a few hours Norwegian warships and aircraft arrived and, as the U-boat had no legal reason for being in Norwegian waters, it was pulled into clear water and brought into Kristiansand to be interned at Marvika Naval Station in accordance with Norwegian neutrality regulations, despite German protests. Three days later the event made the front page of Norwegian daily newspaper *Aftenposten*.

---

[19] *The Secret Diary of a U-boat*, Wolfgang Hirschfield, p53.

Some days after, following talks held between Captain (*Kommandør*) Steen of the Norwegian Admiralty and the German Naval Attaché, the Attaché made it clear to Dönitz that Kptlt. Stiebler had handled the delicate situation in a 'very clumsy manner'. He could, for example, have claimed engine trouble or a similar reason for being inside Norwegian waters, thus avoiding internment.

This event proved a last-minute embarrassment to the German government, provoking a short-lived diplomatic confrontation. Fortunately for future operations Dönitz recorded that: 'The incident, however, had no unfavourable political repercussions', occurring too late in the day to foil German plans.[20]

On 1 March Hitler had issued the formal directive for German forces to prepare for *Weserübung* (Weser Exercise), the invasion of Denmark and Norway. This attack, launched after a European 'land war' that had consisted of months of inactivity, was in no small part due to pressure from *Grossadmiral* Raeder. During the First World War England had been able to bottle up the Imperial German fleet with the strong combination of a tight naval cordon from the Shetland Islands to Norway's coast and thick mine barrages. Raeder was determined to avoid a repeat of this, the most logical method of doing so being to secure Germany's northern flank with a subjugated Denmark and Norway, thereby securing the entrance and exit to the Baltic 'little pond'.

The role of the Kriegsmarine in the attack on Scandinavia was spelt out vividly in Hitler's secret directive detailing the forthcoming invasion, issued on 1 March:

> 'The part which the Navy and the Air Force will have to play, within the limits of their capabilities, is to protect the operation against the interference of British naval and air striking forces. . . .The numerical weakness will be balanced by daring actions and surprise execution. On principle, we will do our utmost to make the operation appear as a *peaceful* occupation. . . . If, in spite of this, resistance should be met with, all military means will be used to crush it.'[21]

While Hitler vacillated over implementing his decision to invade, Allied moves toward the region provided the final impetus he required for his decision. Russia's inexperienced and poorly led soldiers had attacked Finland on 30 November 1939 in the mistaken belief of their military superiority. The Finns, despite being overwhelmingly outnumbered, had managed to halt the Russian advances and inflict severe casualties. However, they faced a military machine of huge material resources and gradually the weight of their attackers

[20] *Ten Years and Twenty Days* Karl Dönitz p80.
[21] 'Nazi Conspiracy and Aggression', Office of the United States Chief of Counsel for Prosecution of Axis Criminality. Doc. No. C-174.

wore down Finland's courageous army. On 5 February the Allied Supreme War Council met in Paris to consider sending an expeditionary force to Finland to aid their sagging battle against Soviet aggression. Although this would have brought about the possibility of direct hostilities with Russia it would have secured for the Allies the rich iron-ore production of Scandinavia, while at the same time denying it to the Germans who depended heavily on this secure trade route for the Third Reich's hungry war machine. The Allied Expeditionary force would only be able to reach Finland after disembarking in Norway and moving through Sweden. As part of the Allied plan, the all-important Swedish Gällivare iron-ore mines were to be occupied by troops landed at nearby Narvik, under the guise of maintaining Allied lines of communication. Despite misgivings about a confrontation with Russia, particularly from the French, plans were put into effect and while the British forces gathered in Scotland French transport ships began to assemble in Brest and Cherbourg. Auxiliary cruisers, armed liners and cargo ships were given additional anti-aircraft weaponry and made ready to embark troops until, on 12 March, an exhausted Finland concluded an unexpected armistice with Russia. The mission was cancelled.

The Allies, however, were not finished with Scandinavia. To frustrate the unhindered flow of trade to Germany, British and French ships belatedly laid mines in neutral Norwegian waters, a logical though clear violation of neutrality as the gloves of diplomacy began to come off. This move to disrupt Germany's vital flow of raw materials had long been advocated by the First Lord of the Admiralty Winston Churchill who, in his inimitably humorous way, dubbed the operation, that he now considered too late and too small, 'Wilfred', ('so small and innocent'). Indeed the British military, although deprived of their Finnish pretext, were still quietly determined to send troops to occupy Narvik, whether they had to fight the Norwegians or not.

However, while Allied leaders haggled among themselves, Hitler's plan was executed. On 9 April 1940, while the war at sea gathered momentum, he made his sudden grab for Denmark and Norway to secure once and for all the Scandinavian iron-ore production for his war-machine that the Allies had coveted. Denmark was overrun instantly and, beneath the noses of the powerful British fleet, the Kriegsmarine was able to land assault troops at major ports, including Narvik, while *Fallschirmjäger* dropped for the first time into battle from their transport planes.

German submarines had put to sea in support of *Weserübung* during the beginning of April, U-boat activity planned and executed under the title 'Operation Hartmut', although they were as yet unaware of this, their sealed orders not to be opened until 6 April. This time the 1st U-Flotilla would sail without one of its rapidly emerging Aces. On 31 March, as the first wave of flotilla boats, *U13*, *U58* and *U59*, slipped from Wilhelmshaven, Otto Kretschmer was handing over command of *U23* to Kptlt. Heinz Beduhn

41

in Kiel. Kretschmer had been transferred to 7th U-Flotilla (sharing Kiel with the 1st U-Flotilla) as commander of Type VIIB *U99*.[22]

The core strength of the flotilla for Operation Hartmut was thirteen U-boats – *U9*, *U13*, *U19*, *U20*, *U23*, *U24*, *U56*, *U57*, *U58*, *U59*, *U60*, *U61* and *U62*. For the forthcoming operation training U-boats *U1*, *U2*, *U3* and *U4* had also been put under operational command of Eckermann's 1st U-Flotilla following their recall from the Skagerrak after *U21*'s potentially disastrous grounding.

Weserübung was to be the largest amphibious operation in German history. Virtually all of her surface fleet were off the coast of Norway in support of troop landings. Assisting the surface vessels of the Kriegsmarine and standing guard against interference from the Royal Navy were eight tactical groups of submarines, comprising the majority of operational boats of the *U-Bootwaffe*. Those included coastal boats (Type II A through D and Type VIIA), but also the bigger, ocean-going type (VII B through C, Type Is and the larger Type IX). Positioned from Narvik to the Orkneys were a total of thirty U-boats, one group deployed as far south as the English Channel.

Thus positioned, the *U-Bootwaffe* was prepared to intercept any British expeditionary force and severely cripple it before it had a chance to intervene in the battle for Norway. However, as events showed, the U-boat operation was a spectacular failure. Driven home with the customary élan and tenacity of the *U-Bootwaffe* the missions were defeated by faulty equipment; the German torpedo malfunction problem had reached crisis point.

3 April: *U19* departed Kiel's Tirpitz Mole at 1300hrs. Joachim Schepke had the same sealed orders that all 'Operation Hartmut' commanders had been given. Also, like the other commanders, he was under strict orders to remain unseen by the enemy. This meant long stretches submerged, the enforced idleness of the crew sawing at already raw nerves. Overhead it was obvious that something was afoot as frequent enemy armed trawler and destroyer patrols dropping random depth charge patterns made interminable submersion even longer. Despite the temptation to U-boat commanders to engage these ships, they had no choice but to dive deeper and creep away or lie still on the seabed and take the punishment. Aboard the U-boats life became difficult. The atmosphere inside quickly fouled and many crews resorted to using their Dräger potash-cartridge breathing equipment. Condensation streamed down metal walls, oxygen ran low and men drifted into a drowsy haze, all mental and physical exertion a trial. Brief though vital periods were spent either surfaced or with decks awash to allow invigorating

---

[22] It was in this vessel that Kretschmer would become famous to both German and Allies alike. 'Silent Otto' pioneered the technique of penetrating a convoy at night while surfaced and attacking with his 'one torpedo for one ship' motto.

fresh sea air to flood inside the submarines' rancid interiors and to charge depleted batteries. It was an arduous period for the U-boats.

4 April: Any doubts about the scale of impending operations must have been dispelled with the group sailing from harbours thronged with onlookers. At 0800hrs *U9*, *U56*, *U60* and *U62* glided away from Wilhelmshaven estuary, muddy Elbe water swirling about their flanks. Four hours later *U1*, *U2*, *U4*, *U5* and *U6* followed (*U1* later returned at 1800hrs due to engine problems, sailing again on the 6th). Crowds watched *U14* and *U57* sail at 1500hrs. Two days later, in the early hours of 6 April, commanders aboard 1st U-Flotilla boats, and other U-boats committed to the battle, opened their sealed orders. In them was explained the battle plan and their part in it.

When the Allied Expeditionary Force finally set out for Narvik on 15 April Naval High Command and BdU had a difference of opinions as to where exactly the British would disembark. High Command considered the fjords Lavangen and Gratengen to the north of Narvik most probable. Dönitz, however, believed that the site of disembarkation would be Bygdenfjord, also to the north of Narvik, but at greater distance. Consequently, he was proved right when late on 15 April Günther Prien of *U47* arrived at Bydgenfjord and spotted three large British transports (some 30,000 GRT each) and several smaller ones disembarking troops in fishing boats. Immediately the 'Bull of Scapa' fired eight torpedoes with impact pistols at the stationary and over-lapping targets – all of which missed.

U9, *U56*, *U60*, *U62* were ordered to join the 3rd U-boat Group (*Unterseebootgruppen*) operating off Bergen in support of troop landings from 9 April. *U13*, *U19*, *U57*, *U58*, *U59* were ordered to form part of 6th U-boat Group patrolling the seas between Pentland Firth and east of the Orkneys. The first 'Weddigen' boat to contact enemy forces was Schepke in *U19*. He sighted HMS *Zulu* on 9 April as the destroyer escorted HMS *Cossack* engaged on towing the damaged HMS *Kashmir* and *Kelvin* to Lerwick. At 1415hrs Schepke surfaced with the conning tower above water and decks running awash. As he attempted to gain an advantageous firing position he was spotted by *Zulu* which promptly charged the small U-boat, *U19* submerging as the destroyer was barely 600 yards distant. Schepke wildly loosed off a salvo of torpedoes at the speeding destroyer, which narrowly evaded the oncoming 'eels' before the inevitable depth-charge attack. Severely shaken and with minor damage, *U19* survived the onslaught and was able to creep away with battered dignity when *Zulu* was forced to return to her escort duties one and a half hours later.

Meanwhile *U23* and *U24* carried out solo patrols around Bergen during the invasion. The two boats had been initially held in Wilhelmshaven in preparation for *Fall Gelb*, the proposed invasion of Western Europe, but released into action after 13 April as the German hold on Narvik appeared to be slipping. The oldest U-boats of the *Unterseebootwaffe*, now training ships, featured briefly in the 1st U-Flotilla War Diary, their deployment limited to the southern-most areas of Norway due to the boats' limited radius of action and crews' inexperience. Each received differing orders. *U2* was instructed to join 8th U-boat Group in action off Lindesnes to engage British naval forces. However, her presence was not required for long and she soon received her recall to Wilhelmshaven, effectively ending her operational career. *U3* was recalled before attaining her patrol sector, engaging British submarine HMS *Porpoise* with no result during her return journey. *U4*, as part of 4th U-boat Group, operated off Stavanger in response to rumours that British forces were planning to mine the waters around Skudenes. On 10 April Oblt.z.S. Hans-Peter Hinsch sighted and attacked an unidentified British submarine. Launching a torpedo spread at his target, Hinsch claimed a hit and target destroyed. Although never confirmed, the British 1,090-ton Triton Class submarine HMS *Thistle* was in the same area when she disappeared, the last report radioed to her headquarters on 9 April. *U4* returned to Wilhelmshaven to resume her training duties, reaching port on 14 April. Another submarine ordered to join 4th U-boat group off Stavanger was Kptlt. Jürgen Deeke's *U1*. It never arrived. The premier U-boat of the Third Reich's *Unterseebootewaffe* had disappeared to the north of Terschelling after 6 April, the victim of either British minefield number 7, or the British submarine HMS *Porpoise*, which reported torpedoing an enemy submarine off Egersund, Norway, on 16 April.

9 April: By 0200hrs in Kristiansand the Captain, one officer and fifteen men from *U21* had been placed under Norwegian Army guard as disturbing news of unidentified ships entering Norwegian harbours reached Marvika Naval Station. At 0730hrs a solitary British plane made a low-level flight overhead and opened fire at the moored *U21*, which suffered several machine gun and cannon hits to its conning tower. Norwegian patrol boat *William Barents*, lying close by undergoing repairs, was also slightly damaged. The confinement of Kptlt. Stiebler and crew was nearly over.

Heading toward Kristiansand was Kriegsmarine *Gruppe 4*, including the light cruiser *Karlsruhe*, three *Torpedoboote* and several *Schnellboote*, and carrying 1,100 men of 310 Infantry Regiment, *214 Infanterie-Division*. Kristiansand was the location of one of Norway's five primary naval fortifications, huge artillery batteries and naval surface and submarine vessels. Initially, the Norwegian batteries, aided by destroyer escorts in the harbor, repulsed the first two German attempts to land troops and take the city and in so doing damaged the *Karlsruhe*. However, later in the day a third attempt proved successful and the town was captured, liberating the crew of *U21* and their boat. After repairing minor damage to the submarine, Stiebler departed for Kiel at 1500hrs on 16 April arriving four days later, whereupon *U21* was placed in dry-dock for extensive repair to hull damage suffered during her grounding. Her operational days were over. Stiebler then had the unpleasant duty of facing his Commander-in-Chief. 'The Lion' could be a daunting prospect for any of his men whom he considered had performed poorly.

11 April: *U61* slipped from Kiel to operate off Trondheim, an uneventful though uncomfortable passage through blinding rain and snowstorms. During the night of 18th/19th she refuelled from a German tanker supply ship in Bergen. Following this she patrolled in the North Minch before returning empty-handed to Kiel on 7 May.

Results achieved by U-boats during the Norwegian campaign were abysmal. Although Royal Navy targets were found and engaged by several U-boats there were very few successes. After the return of the 'Operation Hartmut' boats and intense investigation of commanders' reports Dönitz discovered beyond any doubt that the problem lay not in the mode of operation but the weaponry with which it was undertaken. During March 1940 the U-boat service had received new armaments with which to take the war to its next level. G7e (TII) electric torpedoes with improved magnetic-proximity firing pistols (*Magnetzündung Pistole* or MZ-Pi) were shipped by truck to operational flotillas as replacement for the compressed air powered G7a (TI) model. These latter pre-war torpedoes were unsatisfactory in combat in no small part due to the trail of bubbles behind them, pointing out for any observant escort where the U-boat could be found. The G7a was retained but only released for use at night so as to negate the danger of its visible trail. Also during the previous months commanders had repeatedly experienced premature detonation of the G7a torpedo, hopefully something remedied by the newly developed G7e magnetic weapon.

There were of course complicating factors. The practice of degaussing British ships had apparently negated the probability of a magnetic firing pistol activating the torpedo warhead due to little or no magnetic field around the target. Weapons developers attempted to remedy this by increasing the sensitivity of the magnetic pistol. Unfortunately this then made the weapon liable to interference from the Earth's magnetic field with the result that a deep-running torpedo might explode prematurely or indeed not at all. Detonation had become a primary problem.

As early as 11 April Dönitz distributed new orders to the boats participating in operation *Weserübung* that reflected an accumulation of torpedo failures over the previous two days. At that point it seemed to U-boat command that only impact fuses (*Aufschlagzündung* or AZ) were successful against warships, although this conclusion was later disproved through subsequent combat experiences. Consequently Dönitz ordered his commanders to rely primarily on impact pistol torpedoes. Although the Torpedo Department (*Torpedo Versuchs Anstalt* or TVA) had assured BdU that the proximity of the North Pole in the so-called 'Zone O' (northern Norway) should not affect the efficiency of magnetic pistols, torpedo failures continued at epidemic proportions.

45

Dönitz threw his considerable energy into discovering the reasons for these torpedo disasters. After an emergency conference with officers of OKM and the TVA, Dönitz concluded that magnetic interference from the fjords did, after all, affect magnetic torpedoes. It was also found that an essential problem with the impact-pistol torpedo Mark G7e was that its depth-keeping gear was faulty, causing the torpedo to run as much as 2.7 metres deeper than its set depth, passing harmlessly beneath its target. Thus, wrote Dönitz:

> 'We found ourselves equipped with a torpedo that refused to function in northern waters either with contact or with magnetic pistols.'

A compromise decision was to use magnetic firing Mark G7a torpedoes except when near to northern fjords where the strength of the Earth's magnetic pull caused premature detonation. It later transpired that the problems encountered in torpedo depth-keeping had been known to testers of the TVA who dismissed it as of no great importance during development of the new magnetic firing pistols.

A commission was set up in mid-April to investigate the case thoroughly. Their comprehensive report issued in late July placed considerable blame on the Torpedo Department. This department, it was found, had supplied new, and faulty, magnetic firing pistols with four-blade propellers after undergoing only two test runs during peacetime. In Dönitz's own words this could 'only be described as criminal'.[23] Depth keeping continued to prove a huge problem, one that was not fully explained until February 1942 when the crew of *U94* made an unauthorized on-board examination of their torpedoes whilst on Atlantic patrol. The cause of the problem transpired to be another design and construction fault.

During long periods of submersion, frequent releases of compressed air were essential aboard a U-boat to maintain stability. Thus a considerable excess pressure accumulated inside the boats. Normally, no excess pressure accrued within torpedoes stored aboard U-boats. Situated inside the torpedoes' balance chambers was a hydrostatic valve controlling the depth at which the 'eel' travelled. This valve rests at 'normative atmospheric pressure'. However, many balance chambers were later found not to be airtight. The resulting alteration of internal pressure within the balance chamber as it equalized with increased atmospheric pressure within the U-boat adjusted the hydrostatic valve thereby changing the torpedo's depth-keeping after it had been fired. This discovery, added to magnetic influence from the Norwegian fjords, largely explained the stunning failure of boats during 'Operation Hartmut'. Many of them had remained submerged for up to twenty hours daily, accumulating considerably higher atmospheric pressure aboard. After BdU's final computations were made, it was found that between 30 and 35% of torpedo attacks during the Norwegian campaign had been complete

---

[23] Dönitz memoirs.

failures. Consequently, key personnel of the Torpedo Experimental Institute responsible for this disaster were court-martialled and sentenced to prison terms.

Following the results of their investigation a furious Dönitz noted in his War Diary:

> 'It is my belief that never before in military history has a force been sent into battle with such a useless weapon.'

The high spirits and peak efficiency of the U-boat arm sagged considerably. Handicapped by barely functional weaponry, U-boats were about to pit themselves against the might of the Royal Navy in the savage waters of the Atlantic in all-out assault on merchant convoys. The Battle of the Atlantic was about to begin.

5.

FIRST TASTE OF THE ATLANTIC
1 MAY 1940 to 15 JUNE 1941

Following the depressing failure of most 1st U-Flotilla boats during the Norwegian campaign KK Eckermann devoted considerable energy to reviving the spirits of his men. Winter was fading fast and, despite the U-boats' poor performance, Denmark had fallen instantly to German Armed Forces while the Battle for Norway still raged. As crews returned despondently to their home ports, opinion was divided among Naval Command as to whether they should be sent back into combat equipped with faulty weaponry. Dönitz remained adamant and during 15 May 1940 he recorded in the BdU War Diary:

> 'I cannot leave the boats idle without causing incalculable harm to the *Unterseebootwaffe*. As long as there is the smallest prospect of hits, operations must continue.'

Meanwhile changes to 1st U-Flotilla composition had occurred during April. Type IIB *U8* (Kptlt. Georg-Heinz Michel) had transferred from *U-Abwehrschule* (Anti-Submarine School) to the Flotilla, essentially to be used as a training boat for newly inducted men. *U19* departed on 30 April, seven days after its return from 'Operation Hartmut', to be transferred to Danzig's U-training flotilla (*U-Ausbildungsflottille*). Her commander, Joachim Schepke, also transferred to 7th U-Flotilla and command of Type VIIB *U100*. Like Kretschmer he would go on to greater heights in his new command, becoming the tenth highest-scoring 'Ace' of the U-boat service.[24]

2 May: *U17* arrived in Kiel after fruitless patrolling between Bergen and Stavanger. Her commander Kptlt. Udo Behrens had passengers aboard, grateful to be in Kiel but nonetheless ready to leave the confines of the small U-boat. On 26 April Behrens had plucked the ditched aircrew of a Luftwaffe

---

[24] A favourite of the German propaganda machine Schepke with his blond hair, blue eyes and easy smile embodied to many the very essence of a U-boat captain. His fame continued long after his death on 17 May 1941, crushed in the conning tower of *U100* after she was rammed and sunk by destroyer HMS *Vanoc* Southwest of the Faroes.

bomber from Norway's freezing waters. This was the last operational patrol for *U17*, returning to the training duties which she had left to take part in 'Operation Hartmut'. On 21 May she joined the Anti-Submarine school.

U13 also returned to Kiel at 0900hrs, four hours after Behrens had docked. Oblt.z.S. Max Schulte had performed the most effective patrol of the flotilla during the grim month of April: as part of 6th U-boat group he had claimed two ships damaged and two sunk by attacks, using three electric and two compressed air torpedoes. On 16 April Schulte claimed an unidentified British destroyer hit and damaged with one of his electric G7e torpedoes, while the following evening he hit and sank 4,935-ton British 'Q-ship' SS *Swainby* 25 miles north-east of Muckle Flugga. Following a refuelling stop in Bergen, from *S-Boote* depot ship *Carl Peters*, he proceeded to sea again, claiming a merchant ship sunk near the mouth of Loch Eriboll on the 26th and definitely damaging the British tanker SS *Scottish American* north-east of Kinnairds Head at 2336hrs two days later. In a month of depression for the German submariners, Schulte's 11,934 tons gave some measure of consolation and provided a reason to toast something in Kiel's bars and cafes. Jubilant crewmen received the Iron Cross Second Class, Schulte the higher award of the Iron Cross First Class. While their weathered boat was taken into the yard for a refit, her crew were granted home leave in Germany.

5 May: Oblt.z.S. Wolfgang Lüth, aboard *U9*, the boat that Schulte had commanded until December 1939, gave the order to fire diesels at 1700hrs after his U-boat had eased from Tirpitz Mole. Fresh hunting grounds lay ahead, the Dutch and Belgian coasts south of Dan Helden being Lüth's destination. On the 'other side of the hill' Allied submarines were also patrolling this region. Despite his rather thinly veiled hatred of the British Empire, French Admiral Darlan had agreed to the transfer of two 600-ton submarine divisions from Bizerta and Brest to Harwich, to be placed under the command of British Vice Admiral Horton (C-in-C Submarines). Horton exercised tactical control over the French submarines though they answered directly to their own divisional commander Lieutenant Commander (*Capitaine de Corvette*) Belot. From 7 April submarines *Thétis*, *Calypso*, *Circé* and *Doris* began a series of unsuccessful patrols along Holland's West and East Frisian Islands. This sphere of duty was expanded to include the north of Heligoland Bay following hostilities in Norway in an attempt to intercept shipping bound to and from Hamburg and Wilhelmshaven. Again the French patrols were unsuccessful.

On 9 May *Capitaine de Corvette* Favreul aboard submarine *Doris* was traversing the eastern approaches to the English Channel surfaced. He was heading for Harwich and due to dock within four days. Oblt.z.S. Lüth's lookouts spied the high conning tower, which they immediately recognized as hostile although erroneously identified as British. Diving to periscope depth Lüth made his approach and fired a single torpedo at *Doris* at 0014hrs. It proved devastatingly successful, the thirteen-year-old French submarine exploding in a brilliant ball of flame. Literally ripped apart she sank in seconds. None of her 42-man crew survived.

Regarding the aftermath of the *Doris* sinking Lüth later wrote:

> "Poor fellows,' said my Watch Officer, 'they were only U-boat sailors like us.'
>
> But war drives feelings like these into the background. It is either you or me. If we hadn't sunk them they would have sunk us or one of our comrades.'[25]

He was of course correct. There was little room for sentimentality towards enemy naval vessels while waging total submarine war, and they would have received little from their opponents. For bald-headed Wolfgang Lüth there were but two true loves: his ship and his crew, to both of whom he was devoted. No act seemed too much effort for Lüth if it was of benefit to his men, and despite his somewhat priggish lifestyle and overbearing manner those who served aboard his U-boats regarded him highly and served him with great loyalty.[26]

Buoyed by success, although mistakenly claiming a British submarine sunk, the crew of *U9* went on to sink two merchantmen near Ostend (a combined tonnage of 3,838 tons) before returning to Wilhelmshaven for rapid refuelling and replenishment on 15 May, and to receive the Iron Cross First Class for Lüth, putting to sea first thing the next morning. By such means Lüth effectively extended his patrol, haunting the same area that he had recently left. His persistence reaped dividends on 23 May when north-west of Zeebrugge, home to the First World War's U-boats, he torpedoed and sank SS *Sigurds Faulbaums*, a 3,256-ton German ship captured and taken as prize by the Royal Navy and returning to England with a small British crew aboard.

By then the invasion of the Low Countries was in full swing and British and French naval activity had intensified in Lüth's operational area. Sure enough during the early morning of 24 May *U9* was located by roving destroyers and subjected to an intense depth-charge attack lasting several hours and causing severe damage to the small boat. Aboard *U9* there was an air of tension as she attempted to escape the noise of thrashing propellers and roar of near misses. Finally the attack from above ended and *U9* was able to limp home to Kiel, her battered hull emerging from Holtenau Lock and into the Kiel Estuary at 1400hrs to a thunderous welcome from comrades ashore. They had survived.

10 May: Further transfers had taken place from Kiel. The short-lived tenure of *U8* was over and she and *U20* were posted to the strength of training estab-

---

[25] *Boot Greift wieder An* Wolfgang Lüth and Klaus Korth, p 96.
[26] For a fuller picture of the enigmatic Wolfgang Lüth see *Lone Wolf* by Jordan Vause.

lishments in Danzig, departing Kiel on 10 May, a day of great significance to Germany and to her enemy, England. Earlier that morning the forces of the Third Reich had begun the conquest of Western Europe (*Fall Gelb*), while in Britain Winston Churchill entered 10 Downing Street as Prime Minister of a newly formed National Government.

In Holland German armoured forces of Field Marshal Fedor von Bock's Army Group B, supported by intense Luftwaffe bombing and paratrooper (*Fallschirmjäger*) landings, ripped through thinly held defensive lines. The Wehrmacht delivered stunning body blows to the Low Countries using their astounding Blitzkrieg to devastate opponents still mired in defensive ways of thinking not much changed for thirty years. Field Marshal Gerd von Rundstedt's Army Group A poured through the 'impassable' woods of the Ardennes to outflank a bewildered Allied front line. Eckermann noted the transfers of *U8* and *U20* in his War Diary, writing underneath the somewhat understated words 'Fighting in Holland and Belgium'.

The effect of Germany's assault on the Low Countries during May was also felt in Norway's grim struggle against the Wehrmacht. With the perilous position that Allied forces in Holland and Belgium found themselves, Norway became a drain on what were fast becoming endangered resources of Allied men and material. The decision was made to evacuate Norway despite Allied troops finally wresting control of Narvik from General Dietl's mountain troops (*Gebirgsjäger*) on 27 May.

26 May: Max Schulte, *Weserübung*'s most successful 1st U-Flotilla commander, took *U13* towards the Kaiser Wilhelm Canal's western lock at 1500hrs, after four days of sea trials following refitting. His orders were to return to the North Sea, there to harass with his five-torpedo load what appeared to be British naval forces retreating from Norway. Schulte set course for the western edge of the North Sea immediately upon emerging from the Elbe at 2200hrs. This time, however, his fortune deserted him. The patrol started badly, a wireless defect forcing a return to Heligoland for two hours of repair before continuing.

At 2230hrs during the night of 29th one of *U13*'s diesels broke down, engine room artificers sweating for 19 ½ hours to repair it. Then Schulte's luck appeared miraculously to change as he sighted and began to shadow convoy FN 84 east of Lowestoft. However, he was detected and immediately attacked by escort HMS *Weston* on 31 May. Slammed mercilessly by five depth-charge attacks, the boat became unstable, starting to take serious water on board, some of which leaked into battery cells cracked during the onslaught. Men began suffering from creeping chlorine gas and the crew, their eyes streaming from the effect of noxious fumes, broke out emergency breathing equipment. As lighting failed and chaos took hold aboard the crippled submarine, high-pressure hoses leading from compressed air storage bottles fractured, raising the boat's internal pressure and causing further pain and discomfort to the men aboard. By this time there was so much water flooding the bilges that Schulte was faced with either inevitable sinking or attempting to blow tanks and regain the daylight world above. Opting to try and save his crew, *U13* burst from the depths 400 yards ahead of their attacker which immediately opened fire. The British destroyer did not have sufficient speed to ram *U13*, although damage to the conning tower was caused by at least one 4" shell hit. Schulte and his men abandoned their vessel, which they believed was going down. The Chief Engineer and a single rating remained below decks to ensure that their submarine sank, both men successfully escaping from the U-boat, which went under in two minutes. In a mass of bubbles her hull slid stern first beneath the waves as the victorious English rescued her entire crew. However, the wreck lay in comparatively shallow water and within the range of military divers. Following *U13*'s sinking a Royal Navy salvage team managed to retrieve several Enigma rotors and operating instructions, although the Enigma itself had been successfully ditched.[27] Three days before Schulte's capture Eckermann recorded the '*Kapitulation der Belgium*' in his Diary.

30 May: *U9* transferred from Kiel to Danzig's 24th U-Flotilla (training). German success in Western Europe was largely done without the aid of U-boats. During the period of the invasion of Norway, up until the end of May, the Kriegsmarine had suffered catastrophic losses: heavy cruiser *Blücher*; two light cruisers *Karlsruhe* and *Königsberg*; gunnery training ship *Brummer*; destroyers *Wilhelm Heidkamp, Anton Schmidt, Hans Ludemann, Georg Thiele, Bernd von Arnim, Wolf Zenker, Erich Geise, Erich Köllner, Herman Kunne, Dieter von Röder*; torpedo boat *Albatross*; and U-boats *U1, U13, U22, U44, U49, U50, U54* and *U64* had all been sunk by Allied forces or minefields. In addition to these the majority of the remaining surface fleet was under repair from damage sustained during the invasion.

By the end of June 1940 the entire active German Fleet at operational readiness numbered one heavy cruiser, two light cruisers, four destroyers and nineteen torpedo boats. U-boats that had been temporarily withdrawn from Atlantic operations were still largely used to ferry supplies and equipment to exhausted troops in Norway, whose government finally surrendered to Germany on 7 June. First U-Flotilla's boats were involved in these supply missions, but to little effect due to their small cargo capacity. On the morning of 7 May Raeder had raised the subject while in conference with Hitler. The minutes taken from this meeting record:

[27] Also recovered were a set of orders from Dönitz ordering his men not to rescue torpedoed crewmen. Although introduced as evidence at Nuremberg against Dönitz the charge was rebuffed as a necessary way of safeguarding the lives of U-boat men who put themselves at risk during such rescue attempts.

'It is proposed to release from transport duties the small boats having little cargo space, and to continue using the remainder until the railway at Trondheim is again in operation. . . .The Führer agrees.'

Further minutes from Raeder's meetings with Hitler betray the certain knowledge that a protracted war lay before the Wehrmacht. On 21 May Raeder recorded:

'The C-in-C Navy asks how long the Führer believes the war will last. Would we be justified in sending all training submarines out on operations now, in the hope that the war will be decided quickly, or would it be better to assume that the war will last some time, and therefore to organise a long term programme for submarine training and construction?

'The Führer decides on the second course, which is also recommended by the C-in-C Navy.'

Minimal patrolling was carried out by the 1st U-Flotilla in both the preparation for and during the German assault against Holland and Belgium. It was not until 24 May 1940 that Hitler gave Raeder permission to lift restrictions on U-boat activity around Britain and France (with the proviso to spare all US shipping and 'friendly neutrals' such as Italy, Spain, Japan and Russia. The hugely reduced and somewhat lacklustre U-boat assault recommenced.

2 June: *U62*, commanded by Kptlt. Hans-Bernhard Michalowski, docked in Wilhelmshaven after a patrol carried out against the backdrop of Dunkirk in flames. The bulk of the British Expeditionary Force had been caught unprepared by the skill of German armoured thrusts and Belgium's rapid collapse. After a bloodstained retreat the BEF were penned into a pocket surrounding Dunkirk, backs to the wall and dependent on naval evacuation. The now-legendary 'Operation Dynamo' lifted 338,000 British and Allied men off wide sandy beaches before the Germans finally closed their escape route. During this evacuation, one of the largest and most successful in history, the Luftwaffe failed in its attempt to deny the Allies their escape route. They, in conjunction with the Kriegsmarine, nonetheless exacted a high price; destroying six British and three French destroyers, damaging another nineteen and accounting for eight troop ships sunk and nine damaged. The cost in 'little boats' has never been determined.

On 29 May *U62* was surfaced near Kwinte Buoy north-west of Ostend. Ahead, Michalowski and his bridge lookouts could see the low silhouettes of evacuation shipping making its way along what the Allies knew as Route Y, from Dunkirk to Kwinte Buoy, then west to Ramsgate. While Michalowski pondered an interception route the night sky was abruptly lit by the blinding impact of a torpedo against one of the distant ships. In fact *Schnellboot S30*, racing from the darkness and disappearing again at full throttle, triple Daimler-Benz engines thundering into the shadows, had just torpedoed HMS *Wakeful*. Within 15 seconds the British destroyer was gone, taking nearly 700 men with her.

Ships began to converge on the horrific scene to assist where they could. Minesweepers *Gossamer* and *Lydd*, Scottish drifter *Comfort*, motor drifter *Nautilus* and destroyer HMS *Grafton* all rushed to aid men struggling in the water. Aboard *U62* Michalowski saw his opportunity, closing swiftly on the scene with crew at battle stations.

Aboard HMS *Grafton* Commander Charles Robinson was well aware of his ship's perilous position. Two questions kept repeating in his mind; who had torpedoed *Wakeful* and where was the assailant now? It was 0230hrs and lifeboats were put out from all vessels to rescue any survivors still struggling in the water. At that moment Robinson noticed on his port quarter a small, darkened vessel making directly for him. Assuming it to be *Comfort* he ordered an Aldis lamp to flash the message: 'Close and pick up survivors'. However, the newcomer made no answer.

Michalowski knew that he would soon receive a harsher challenge. He resisted the temptation to attempt buying time by answering in gibberish and continued closing upon his victim. At 0250hrs he ordered tubes one and two '*Los!*' Both torpedoes streaked away and Michalowski brought his submarine swiftly about, retreating at full speed still surfaced, exhausts gurgling as the boat heeled over. The first torpedo hit *Grafton*'s wardroom, slicing through her hull plates and killing thirty-five men. The second smashed against the stern ripping it apart with devastating force. Commander Robinson and three crewmen lay dead in her bridge, now a twisted shambles. Soldiers believing themselves free of Dunkirk's hell were again confronted by screaming, wounded men and all order was lost aboard the stricken ship.

Ironically, vessels closest to HMS *Grafton* opened fire on a darkened ship that they believed to have been the attacker, sinking the British minesweeper *Comfort* with concerted machine-gun and cannon fire. The destruction of the small drifter was completed in minutes, adding to the mass of bodies floating in the Channel swell beneath Kwinte Buoy, which continued to throw its bleak flashing light over the carnage. *U62* had made good her escape. Her victim HMS *Grafton* refused to die, the battered hulk burning and forlorn until finally sunk by three shells from fellow destroyer HMS *Ivanhoe* as dawn crept into the eastern sky. Initially BdU believed that Michalowski had sunk French transport ship *Douaisia* until Allied reports intercepted by *B-Dienst* and *U62*'s War Diary laid bare the identity of her victim.

5 June: The unsteady French front line stretching from the mouth of the River Somme to Switzerland was ripped apart by the second phase of Germany's invasion of France. In the 1st U-Flotilla War Diary Eckermann initially noted no special activity, before adding in bold '*U13*'. She was acknowledged as being overdue. Within two days a further entry was devoted to this U-boat: '7 June: *U13 Vermisst*.*'

The 1st U-Flotilla continued to patrol both the North Sea and Norwegian waters. Now that British and French forces had evacuated Norway there continued a drudgery of supply missions for U-boats to run, although the small Type IIs had been virtually absolved of this responsibility following Raeder's conference with Hitler. During 10 June Eckermann noted in his Diary the entry of Italy into the war on the Axis side, a cynical leap into supposed easy spoils by the dictator Mussolini.

17 June: During the mid-afternoon Kptlt. Herbert Kuppisch brought *U58* to rest once more against Kiel's Tirpitz Mole. A single victory pennant fluttered at the periscope alongside the U-boat's commissioning ribbon and Kriegsmarine battle ensign. Bearded Kuppisch and his crew wearily acknowledged the welcoming crowd, taking the salute from Eckermann, while the ship's First Watch Officer Oblt.z.S. Günther Reeder docked *U58*. Their single victory on 1 June had accounted for 8,401-ton British SS *Astronomer* north-north-west of Kinnairds Head. The 483-foot ship had been requisitioned by the British Admiralty to act as a boom carrier, and took four crew and several naval ratings to their deaths. Following this successful torpedo attack *U58* had crash-dived to evade closing British destroyers bent on vengeance.

During the next 43 hours depth charges hammered at the iron hull, venting the frustration of hunting an elusive foe. Alternately lying stationary and motoring quietly in an attempt to slip the cordon of swirling propellers above, Kuppisch was unable to shake his pursuers. Battery power and oxygen reached critical lows, the crew sprawled on sweating deck plates in the stupor of men resigned to probable death. But the urge for survival remained strongest. Emergency potash breathing equipment kept haggard men functional until miraculously the propellers above began to fade away. Nearly two full days after the torment began Kuppisch swept an empty sea with his periscope before surfacing and throwing the hatches open for cool fresh sea air, sweeping away the stench of 43 hours of fear.

On land the war against France was rapidly nearing its conclusion. Paris had fallen on 14 June, victorious Wehrmacht troops marching along the Champs Elysées. France's government collapsed and elderly defeatist Field Marshal (*Maréchal*) Pétain became head of state. Allied troops remaining in western France had been rapidly evacuated by 'Operation Aerial' covered by a feeble French rearguard, which fell easily before the onrush of victorious German troops. Brest capitulated to the Wehrmacht on 19 June on the orders of French Admiral Traub. Lorient was declared an open city and surrendered by Admiral Hervé de Penfenténuo de Kervériguin two days later, the first German troops entering sullen outskirts at 1400hrs.

The official end of active fighting in France came with an armistice, signed on 22 June 1940. Eckermann's entry in the War Diary reflects the U-boats' order to spare all French shipping from that date. Despite isolated areas not fully submitting for several weeks, hostilities were effectively over as of 0135 hrs on 25 June and German occupation began immediately. A partitioning line was established that allowed south-eastern France nominal self-government under Pétain's newly established Vichy régime.[28] However, Hitler demanded that while France could maintain garrisons and naval bases along the Mediterranean coast, Germany must have control of the Atlantic coast and areas which encompassed the bulk of French industry occupied during the advance. German troops of all services immediately moved to their new garrisons. Within Brittany men of General von Pragen's XXV Army Corps took up their occupation posts during December 1940, its headquarters in the beautiful resort area of La Baule.

Brittany, lying along France's north-western seaboard, had developed into a strategically important marine centre to the French Navy during centuries of maritime conflict. Brest had been the home port to some of the proudest ships of the fleet. Founded in Roman-Gallic times as a military outpost, the settlement's strategic value was first recognized as a potential naval base in 1631 by Cardinal Richelieu who had the first wooden wharves constructed. These humble beginnings were augmented by masonry constructions jutting into the *Rade de Brest*, built under orders of Jean Baptiste Colbert, *Minister de la Marine* to King Louis XIV. By the Twentieth Century the harbour was a stronghold of fortifications and facilities added to over the intervening centuries. Around its harbour and along the winding River Penfeld, Brest had contained some of the most sophisticated repair and docking facilities for *la Marine Nationale* or '*la Royale*', as the French Navy was still sometimes known. It was, and still is, also the site of an imposing building, overlooking the harbour, which housed the Naval Academy, engaged in producing young officers for their large fleet. An elegant city with architecture that could be traced to medieval times, and often beyond, Brest had begun life as a fortified camp before Roman occupation. Now it was to become a fortified camp once more.

The strategic importance of bases on France's western seaboard was not lost on the Kriegsmarine High Command. In order to range into the Atlantic, where Dönitz knew the convoy war must be fought, U-boats previously had needed to make the time-consuming journey around Scotland or the more perilous English Channel dash, both areas dominated by the Royal Navy. Small Type II U-boats had not the range to journey into the Atlantic from Kiel or Wilhelmshaven. However, based in France all Germany's operational U-boats in Western Europe would be able to begin the convoy onslaught. It was imperative to make the French bases operational and Kriegsmarine

---

[28] This state of affairs was destined to end when the entire country was occupied two years later, after the successful November 1942 Allied landing in Vichy-held North Africa.

personnel raced through smouldering villages and roads choked with demoralized French prisoners to survey the damage and begin repairs.

In Brest the Army requisitioned the Hotel Continental for their *Kommandantur*, recently host to French Military Authorities. Kriegsmarine officials took charge of the Hotel Moderne, only a short time ago vacated by the English, while the *Kriegskommandantur* took control of the Caserne Guépin. The next day, in the name of the German Navy, KA Lothar von Arnauld de la Perière took command of the Brest Arsenal as Marine Commander Brittany (*Marinebefehlshaber Bretagne*). De la Perière harboured a strong feeling of kinship with the new breed of submariners, having served as a U-boat commander during the First World War. In the course of his service between 1914 and 1918 he became the highest scoring U-boat 'Ace' of the war, sinking 194 ships for a total of 453,716 GRT and being awarded the famous Prussian 'Blue Max' medal in October 1916.

The potential of existing French Navy bases at Brest and Lorient as forward staging areas for the Kriegsmarine, particularly the U-boat arm, was obvious and moves were made to survey their condition immediately following occupation. Many vessels had been scuttled in France's ports during the chaotic retreat and the Kriegsmarine raised a number either to clear channels, for scrap, or for rehabilitation as a member of the German Navy. In addition to the two existing French military bases the industrial and commercial ports at Saint Nazaire, La Pallice (within the city of La Rochelle) and Bordeaux were judged suitable for expansion as Kriegsmarine bases. Convoys from Germany began rumbling along roads still littered with the rubble of *blitzkrieg*, carrying torpedoes and equipment to enable rapid use of the newly conquered ports. In June *Kapitän* Robin Schall-Ernden was named overall commander of the Kriegsmarine in Western France, excluding Brittany, (*Marinebefehlshaber Westfrankreich*, later the title modified to *Marinebefehlshaber Atlantikküste*), with headquarters in Royan, near Bordeaux. This new post augmented the *Marbef Bretagne* (Marine Commander Brittany) that von Arnauld de la Perière had established in the Brest Arsenal. Originally the new command only covered from the River Loire to the border of Spain, but it was enlarged to include Brittany in December 1940, absorbing *Marbef Bretagne* under its umbrella. At that point de la Perière took over from Schall-Ernden. His tenure was to be brief, however. Von Arnauld de la Perière was killed in an aircraft crash at Le Bourget between Paris and Strasbourg on 26 February 1941. He had been travelling to take up a new appointment as Admiral Commanding Southwest Europe.

The captured French ports rapidly began to be garrisoned by units essential to the smooth running of a naval presence:

Hafenkommandant and *Hafenkapitän*
(Hako and Haka – Port commandant and captains respectively, responsible for all port operations and with attached company of marines – the former holding greater authority than the latter.);

Kriegsmarinearsenal
(Naval arms depots);
Kriegsmarinedienststelle
(Personnel services);
Marine-Artillerie-Abteilungen
(Coastal artillery, both heavy and light);
Marine-Flak-Artillerie-Abteilungen and *Marine-Flak-Brigaden*
(Naval flak artillery);
Hafenschutzflottillen
(Harbour patrol boats – small lightly-armed fishing boats);
Marine-Kraftfahr-Abteilungen
(Naval transport units);
Marine-Funkmess-Abteilungen
(Naval radio detection units);
Marine-Nebel-Abteilungen
(Smoke laying units).

Brest also saw the creation of a *Kriegsmarinewerft* (Naval Shipbuilders), outside of *Seeko* control, when the 'Deschimag' company of Bremen began construction of vessels and marine engines in November 1940 within the old French Arsenal. KK August Vollheim took initial command of this unit that eventually incorporated several varied construction services, torpedo supply and repair and personnel services. Lorient too had a *Kriegsmarinewerft* installed during August under the direction of KK Waldemar Seidel, commandant of the Lorient Arsenal, as did Saint Nazaire and other German military ports further to the south. Units of *Netzsperrflottille West* provided thick steel nets for protection from submarine attack at both both Brest and Lorient. Anchored in place and suspended from large buoys, these thick steel mesh anti-submarine nets stretched across the entrance channels to both ports, moved aside by steam tugboats to allow vessels free transit between port and open sea.

On 28 June 1940 Dönitz had sent KK (*der Reserve*) Helmut Brümmer-Patzig and Kptlt. (*Ing*) Hans Looschen of his staff to Lorient to scout for possible locations for BdU headquarters and reconnoitre the newly conquered French ports. Now that the war was evolving in the Atlantic he felt too far removed in Kiel. After a successful search Dönitz opted for a group of villas at Kerneval opposite Port Louis at the entrance to Lorient harbour. The Kerneval nerve centre, christened 'Berlin' by those within, became a veritable fortress with underground bunkers, artillery and machine-gun emplacements, an anti-tank ditch and continually increasing anti-aircraft installations. (Indeed the first RAF bombs fell on Lorient's Scorff River installations on 2 September 1940.) The U-boat war had moved west and the staff of the 1st U-Flotilla received notification that following reorganization of their flotilla they would be transferred to Brest.

29 June: *U56* sailed from Wilhelmshaven to patrol the Minch area. Oblt.z.S. Otto Harms cruised for nearly a month before being the first boat from 1st U-Flotilla to dock in a French port. In the early morning of 21 July he tied up at Lorient to take on fuel and supplies. His arrival came only 15 days after Kptlt. Lemp's *U30* of 2nd U-Flotilla had been the first German U-boat to dock in Lorient. During the coming summer six Type II U-boats would operate from this port as a base for Atlantic patrols.

11 July: Emerging from Kiel's repair yards *U21* again put to sea, damage to her systems and hull from her Norwegian grounding repaired. She would, however, see no more action. Beneath the warmth of the afternoon sun, Kptlt. Stiebler sailed her east to join Pillau's 21st U-Flotilla where she would remain as a training ship. The small U-boat made easy weather of the Baltic Sea, thick ice and driving rain of winter now months behind. Stiebler himself returned to 1st U-Flotilla to briefly take command of *U61* between August and November.

That same day a new commander for 1st U-Flotilla put to sea. Former First Watch Officer aboard Herbert Sohler's *U46*, Oblt.z.S. Erich Topp took *U57* from Bergen bound for the North Channel. The U-boat had undergone only one structural alteration due to her new commander – a waterproof box had been welded inside the conning tower to hold Topp's tobacco pipe when it was not in use. During June the U-boat had been used to transport stores to Norway, as well as for training duties within the 1st U-Flotilla. The young commander, leaving Bergen nine days after his 23rd birthday, had transferred from Kiel in a voyage begun the previous Friday. Topp recalled:

> ' "Never start sailing on a Friday" is an old rule among sailors, and knowing that sailors are superstitious, Admiral Dönitz made an order of it. But not to lose one day we tried to cheat 'Hob Goblin!' We left the pier in Kiel at Thursday evening. A band was playing, our friends waving, but we went only on the other side of the bay to take over torpedoes, and left harbour on Friday morning.'

On the first day of the voyage *U57* became mired in swirling fog. Suddenly a floating mine appeared dead ahead, bumping against the grey steel hull several times before miraculously drifting away. After a refuelling stop in Bergen *U57* sailed west and barely escaped the unmistakable bubble tracks of two torpedoes sweeping barely alongside its hull as the U-boat passed the Norwegian lighthouse of Marstän. There was no trace found of the attacker. Topp began his career as a U-boat commander well, torpedoing two ships from Halifax convoy HX 55 during 7 July, one in early morning the second that evening – SS *O. A. Brodin* and SS *Manipur*. He returned to Bergen on 20 July.

22 July: A day after Oblt.z.S. Harms' *U56* entered Lorient Oblt.z.S. Heinrich Schonder's *U58* followed her into the French port. Schonder's initial patrol as captain had resulted in a claimed hit on MV *Scottish Minstrel* and the confirmed sinking of Norwegian SS *Gyda* north-west of Ireland's aptly named Bloody Foreland. Replenishment at Lorient would take a full week during which Schonder and his crew were able to savour the delights of summer in Brittany as members of a conquering army. The Hotel Beau Séjour on Place Lorraine had been commandeered for officers of 2nd U-Flotilla who accordingly extended the use of these facilities to those officers of the 1st U-Flotilla stationed in Lorient during refitting.

Within Lorient's *Port de Commerce* workers of the M.A.N. *Maschinen Fabrik* had arrived to begin work on strengthening existing slipways for U-boat use. It was found that even after this work had been completed the only submarines the slipways could accommodate were Type II U-boats, all other classes exceeding the absolute maximum weight of 400 tons allowable. Although 2nd U-Flotilla's Type VII U-boats were soon to make Lorient their permanent home, only Type II submarines like those of 1st U-boat Flotilla were able immediately to make use of the slipways for maintenance and careening. Above the slipway six stations fed by a huge turntable were created where the U-boats could rest during their time out of the water. RAF attention was not long in coming to the French ports and Kriegsmarine Command ordered the creation of two huge arched bunkers – 'Dombunkers' or cathedral bunkers – at two of the dry stations, enabling two U-boats to be sheltered in each. Long-term planning was soon taken in hand for the creation of separate U-boat pens for Kriegsmarine vessels.

The presence of newly positioned British mines and submarines in the approaches to France's Atlantic ports did not escape the notice of Dönitz. Royal Navy attempts at interference with U-boat entries and exits had yielded little result so far, but, combined with an increased RAF mine-laying schedule, posed significant potential for problems if not countered immediately. Dönitz requested the transfer of heavy *Sperrbrecher 'Rostock'* from Germany to Brittany during the summer to bolster an overworked minesweeper service. Following the arrival of KK Friedrich Plate's *Sperrbrecher* the effectiveness of this converted merchant ship became obvious and later, in July 1941, an entire flotilla (6th *Sperrbrecherflottille*) was formed in Nantes before transferring to Concarneau where they were frequent shepherds for U-boats and surface craft sailing to and from Brest or Lorient.

The advent of the *Sperrbrecher* (barrage breaker) was a rather unusual method employed to combat the menace to German shipping posed by Allied mines. These vessels were converted cargo ships designed primarily for clearing passages through minefields, though not as a traditional minesweeper. The technique employed in the early stages of the war was simply to sail the ship into the suspected minefield to contact and explode any mines in its path. With cargo holds filled with buoyant material (usually cork) it was reasoned that the *Sperrbrecher* would be difficult to sink, and some of the explosive impact would be absorbed. Early barrage breakers, understandably, suffered heavy casualties; often no amount of impact-absorbing material could prevent the ship's spine snapping in two. With the introduction of magnetic and acoustic mines new, more sophisticated techniques were introduced, no doubt to the relief of *Speerbrecher* crews.

Two days after returning from his first patrol as commander, Erich Topp took *U57* to sea once more. This time a brief patrol north of the British Isles resulted in the sinking of the 2,161-ton Swedish SS *Atos* on 3 August. Following an unsuccesful aircraft retaliation *U57* silently crept away to head for its new port of Lorient, arriving on 7 August.

24 July: At the pier side of Kiel's Deutschewerke shipyard Oblt.z.S. Robert Bartels and his crew saluted the raising of their battle flag and commissioning pennant as their boat *U139* entered service for training duties within the 1st U-Flotilla. Her tenure would be brief, three months before transfer to the 21st U-Flotilla.

25 July: Oblt.z.S. Otto Harms slipped from Lorient at 2000hrs. *U56* eased her way from the harbour in the wake of her escorting auxiliary minesweeper. From the nearby dockside comrades and wellwishers cheered the boat on its way. Now the military band romped through new music with which to stir both crew and crowd. As well as the traditional *Deutschlandlied* and the Anglophobic *Englandlied* came the addition of 'We'll Hang Out The Washing On The Siegfried Line', played by German bandsmen with an overt sense of irony.

Atop *U56*'s bridge Harms and his watch crew, accompanied by men taking their final cigarette, gazed at the expanse of the Bay of Biscay stretching before them. Summer was in full bloom along France's western edge and a gentle haze lay low over the horizon. But for the dull grey military colours and incongruous heavy weapons of war on her bow platform the armed trawler leading *U56* could have been putting to sea to fish the abundant Breton waters. A final 'Good Hunting' flashed from her bridge and the escort vessel reversed her course for Lorient. *U56* glided through smooth calm seas towards a horizon stained crimson by the setting sun. All too soon the order was given to submerge and *U56*'s hydroplanes tilted downwards as she slid under for the first trial dive of the patrol.

The 1st U-Flotilla was now involved in Germany's war against Atlantic convoys, the small Type IIs' range constraints aided by operating from forward bases in Brittany. This benefit was to be relatively short-lived, however, when successful Luftwaffe attacks on convoys during July (as the opening of what became known as 'The Battle of Britain') forced the British Admiralty to divert their merchant shipping north, in effect closing the Western Approaches to shipping. Despite the increased distance required to intercept British shipping (now a similar mileage from Wilhelmshaven as from Lorient), the advantage of not having to traverse difficult and heavily mined

Skagerrak waters still made a move to France worthwhile by BdU's reckoning. During July Type II 'canoes' alone accounted for twelve ships totalling 64,600 tons.

After nine days at sea reports were received aboard *U56* of westbound convoy activity in sector AM north-west of Eire's Malin Head. Late in the evening of 4 August Harms attacked and sank the British SS *Boma* of convoy OB 193. Firing a two-torpedo fan shot at the steamer, one torpedo missed while the other detonated after a nail-biting run of 7 minutes and 25 seconds. Remaining within this area for the following week Harms scored the largest success so far for 1st U-Flotilla. During the darkness of early morning and in an ugly sea *U56* torpedoed and sank the 16,923-ton British Armed Merchant Cruiser HMS *Transylvania*. This 16-year-old ex-Anchor Line passenger ship was severely damaged in the attack, losing two officers and twenty ratings. Trawlers took off the remaining 300 of her complement, lifeboat launching being too hazardous to attempt in the rough seas. Taken in tow by accompanying ships she quickly foundered and went under.

8 August: *Grossadmiral* Raeder visited Lorient to inspect for himself the situation within the port, crucial for the forthcoming Atlantic war. He appeared satisfied with what he saw, agreeing with Dönitz on the urgency to start construction of new larger U-boat bunkers.

14 August: *U56* entered Lorient to military bands and cheering crowds, a scene familiar from the days at Kiel. As Harms made his triumphant return Oblt.z.S. Topp was ready to put to sea for his first patrol from France. Destined for the seas of western Scotland he ran into eight days of gale-force winds before disaster struck:

> 'Alarm! Plane attack! At 20 metres a bomb exploding very close to the hull. The boat is bottoming at 60 metres. As a result of the explosion the foundation of one diesel is broken.'

Aboard the crippled submarine officers held a brief conference to discuss their options. Both Topp and his First Watch Officer Kurt Reichenbach-Klinke proposed that the patrol be continued rather than heading back with a full load of five torpedoes. The boat's Chief Engineer Herbert Pankin was alone in his view that the risks entailed with only one diesel and reduced surface speed were too great for continuing. The boat sailed for Liverpool estuary.

U57 found rich pickings from convoy OB 202 and then HX 65. Forty-two minutes after midnight on 24 August Topp charged into action, attacking and sinking SS *Cumberland* and SS *Saint Dunstan* for a combined tonnage of 16,620 tons. Also in the same attack on OB 202 he damaged British steamer SS *Havildar*. Immediately after firing the second of his three-torpedo assault an escort destroyer located the charging U-boat and turned at high speed towards her. Topp dived, but with the bottom at only 50 metres the ensuing crescendo of depth charges was dangerously effective. Amid shattering explosions all pumps, instruments and lights were immediately put out of action. Water cascaded into the narrow pressure hull and soon the boat became stuck fast to the seabed, pinned by tons of extra water. Topp recalled the nightmare ordeal that followed:

> 'The crew is moving the water by hand bucket to correct the trim and to press it out of the boat by air. No result. We can't move the boat during the whole day, in intervals, depth charges. Water in the boat is rising slowly. Suddenly a bump! Something is skidding, gliding outside the hull. They are searching for us with ropes! Everybody feels put to the rack.
>
> 'After unnumbered depth charges and twenty-six hours at the bottom, at midnight we tried to surface. I say we tried. The water was still covering the floor. We succeeded in making a rough and ready repair with the main pump. One hour before midnight again depth charges . . . then silence. The listening device received some propeller noise far away.
>
> 'I order the crew to move fore and aft to disengage from the bottom. Seconds seem to be hours. Suddenly a light vibration! The boat is rising slowly and then faster and faster. The boat comes up like a shot. We reach the surface and the hatch is opened – darkest night (sea state six). Starboard side, 500 meters distance, the shadow of a destroyer. We turned the boat with the lowest speed to show the small silhouette.'

Creeping away to freedom the German crew celebrated their 'rebirth'. The magnetic compass and gyro were out of commission as the crew worked feverishly to reload tubes with their two reserve torpedoes. That evening *U57* located and sank HX 65 straggler MT *Pecten*, the tanker's burning oil throwing a macabre light against the reflective steel of *U57*'s sleek hull and its two dancing red devils painted on either side of her small conning tower (an emblem inherited from Claus Korth's period as commander). The 'Anglo-Saxon Petroleum' transport ship took forty-eight of her fifty-seven-man crew with her to the sea floor, including skipper Captain H.E.Davies. Topp was displaying the kind of ruthless and vigorous determination that would later take him towards the Knight's Cross and label of U-boat 'Ace'. Despite suffering further depth-charging the U-boat escaped and her crew prepared for their homeward journey, all torpedoes gone. The cook prepared a ritual '*Bergfest*' (mountain festival), as they had 'reached the summit of the patrol and her bow was now homeward bound.'

It was, however, to be the submarine's final operational patrol, stopping in Bergen at 0030 on the second day of September for refuelling. The final leg would take the weary *U57* south to the Baltic and her new scheduled career in training grounds.

During the same day at Kiel *U140*, a Type IID boat from the *Deutschewerke* yards, was commissioned into 1st U-Flotilla with Oblt.z.S. Hans-Peter Hinsch in command. Hinsch, recently the commander of *U4*, gave the traditional perfunctory speech to his men as the crew mustered on the stern deck. Following the parade all hands went below to begin feeling their way around their new boat, preparing for the months of training that would follow.

20 August: German *B-Dienst* intelligence received an unforeseen setback. Guessing correctly that their codes had been broken by Germany, the British Admiralty introduced a brand new code system. The German Listening Service (*Beobachtung Dienst* or *B-Dienst*) had been able to decipher and read British Royal Navy codes since 1936. In the OKM buildings of Berlin's *Tirpitz-Ufer* fifty men under *Kapitän* Kupfer worked diligently to provide Dönitz with the latest up-to-date information on signals received from convoys and escort, giving routes, times and rendezvous areas. This somewhat alleviated the deficiency felt in German air reconnaissance over the Western Approaches to England. Thanks to this priceless intelligence U-boats had enjoyed months of well-coordinated attacks against Allied convoys, though results were occasionally still marred by defective torpedoes.

21 August: Another Type IID was commissioned into the flotilla. Oblt.z.S. Heinz Otto Schultze performed the customary commissioning duties aboard *U141*, launched 27 July 1940. During the months of September to November eight more Type IIDs were commissioned into the flotilla, *U142* to *U150*, all used solely for training and eventually transferred from the 1st U-Flotilla to other training units during December 1940.

2 September: Oblt.z.S. Topp had been ordered from Bergen to proceed to Kiel on 1 September. Following a rapid and uneventful voyage south he was bringing his U-boat towards the thick sliding right-hand lock gate of the Kaiser Wilhelm Canal at Brunsbuttel on electric motors in early evening. A crowd and military band had assembled to welcome the returning U-boat and her crew who felt they had glimpsed the very face of death while trapped at the mercy of British depth charges. Suddenly the huge bows of Norwegian ship SS *Rona* loomed over *U57*'s conning tower. The tramp steamer had emerged from Brunsbüttel Lock as Topp approached, and was unexpectedly caught in a tidal eddy, swinging her bow towards the small U-boat. Aboard *U57* Topp bellowed for both engines *Ausfahrt Zurück* (full astern), realizing instantly that his boat's electric propulsion could not generate enough power to escape collision. Bowing to the inevitable, Topp ordered his men to abandon ship moments before impact. A rending shriek of steel plates grinding together and Topp knew his boat had been rammed immediately abaft of her conning tower. She rapidly filled with water, dragging the shattered hull below with seven members of his veteran crew still trapped inside. One of the submerged survivors managed to escape before two others became wedged in the conning tower hatch, effectively sealing the only available exit. It was a tragic end for *U57* and six young submariners.[29] Later in September the hulk was raised, but she was never made operational again, serving the remainder of her life as a training ship of 22nd U-Flotilla in Gotenhafen and then 19th U-Flotilla, Pillau. Her sole remaining moment of glory was on 5 May 1941 when Hitler toured the U-boat as part of an inspection visit to Gotenhafen. This was probably only the second time that Hitler, who suffered from violent seasickness, had set foot aboard a submarine.[30] Topp himself now left the ranks of 1st U-Flotilla, transferred to Kiel's 7th U-Flotilla to work up new Type VIIC U-boat *U552*, eventually commissioned on 4 December 1940.

Two commanders in new Type IIDs made outstanding first patrols with their fresh U-boats. Oblt.z.S. Wolfgang Lüth, previously of *U9*, took his boat *U138* to sea on 10 September from Kiel. During his transit to Lorient Lüth sank four ships in the course of a three-hour surface attack on westbound convoy OB216 west of Islay, Hebrides. His remarkable achievement added 34,644 tons to his score, 13,801 tons of which was from the torpedoing of the British tanker SS *New Sevilla*. Aboard *U137* Oblt.z.S. Herbert Wohlfarth, four days behind Lüth, despatched three ships from another westbound convoy, for a total of 12,103 tons sunk and a further 4,917 ton damaged after hitting SS *Ashantian*. Wohlfarth arrived in Lorient on 29 September, three days after Lüth. On 1 October Wohlfarth received the Iron Cross First Class from Dönitz.

11 October: 32-year-old Kaptlt. Hans Cohausz became Flotilla commander. Cohausz had briefly held the post during 1936 before becoming a Staff officer for FdU. In September 1939 he had then taken command of his third U-boat *UA* (previous boats being *U15* and *U30* during pre-war years) until October 1940 and his resumption of 'Weddigen' Flotilla leadership. KK Hans Eckermann left Brest to take command of Cohausz' boat *UA* in which he remained until January 1942.

16 October: BdU transferred from temporary headquarters in Paris' Boulevard Souchet 18 to Kerneval, Lorient. The interim Paris location had been occupied during September while the possibility of 'Operation *Seelowe*'

[29] Erich Topp was cleared of any responsibility for the disaster in a subsequent investigation. The majority of his crew were transferred to his new boat, a request that the survivors had made to Topp as they assembled ashore at Brunsbuttel the morning immediately after the loss of their submarine. As Topp recalled, 'It was perhaps the only time that my eyes became wet, before I had turned and slowly walked away, thinking of our departure on Friday against the rule.'

[30] Hitler had inspected the 'Weddigen' Flotilla when the unit was still embryonic, touring *U7*'s interior.

(planned invasion of Britain) being implemented was still alive and the distances from Sengwarden near Wilhelmshaven considered too great to exercise operational command. In Lorient Dönitz kept his small and highly efficient staff around him and a few other essential personnel.

The 1st U-Flotilla continued to add its strength to escalating Atlantic combat. With France defeated, much of the Royal Navy's destroyer and corvette strength was withdrawn from convoy escort duties to protect England against feared invasion, merchant shipping thus becoming increasingly at risk to U-boat attack. Spirits among men of the 1st U-Flotilla began to rise again after the slump suffered following the abortive Norwegian operations.

During *U137*'s second patrol, her first from Lorient, newly promoted Kptlt. Wohlfarth torpedoed and seriously damaged the British Armed Merchant Cruiser HMS *Cheshire* on 14 October. Within the U-boat force, the fast-rising star Herbert Wohlfarth was well known by his nickname '*Parsival*'. After a radio message to BdU, reporting this latest success with his 'dugout canoe' against the British AMC he received the following praise from Dönitz:

> '*An Wohlfarth: Gut gemacht!*' (To Wohlfarth: Well done!), to which Wohlfarth replied; '*An Löwe von Parsival: Ja, ja, diese kleinen Boote!*' (To Lion from Parsival: Well, well, these small boats!).

24 October: Following his second patrol as commander of *U138* and a further 5,327-ton ship sunk and 6,993 tons damaged, Lüth was awarded the coveted *Ritterkreuz*, Knights Cross of the Iron Cross, the only Type II commander so honoured and the first for a commander operating as part of 1st U-Flotilla. Dönitz had credited Lüth with a personal score of 87,236 tons plus French submarine *Doris*.[31] Lüth's career had also undergone a radical turn. Four days previously he had been transferred to Lorient's 2nd U-Flotilla to command Type IXA *U43* recently arrived from Bergen and undergoing refit.

22 December: Kptlt. Hans-Peter Hinsch brought *U140* safely home to Kiel from another Atlantic patrol. Having departed on the morning of 20 November from Tirpitz Pier the U-boat called initially at Bergen for refuelling before proceeding westwards to face the enemy. Three weeks at sea resulted in 15,800 BRT claimed sunk by Hinsch. In fact he had sent to the bottom two British and one Finnish cargo ships (SS *Victoria City*, SS *Ascrest* and sailing vessel *Penang*) for a total of 12,388 tons. *U140* had been obliged to refuel in Bergen again on 17 December, departing for Kiel two days later. The tonnage war continued to gradually take its toll on Allied war efforts.

---

[31] In fact Lüth had sunk thirteen ships for 57,192 tons. Generally the Knight's Cross was awarded for 100,000 tons of enemy shipping, or for conspicuous gallantry in combat.

This was to be the most successful period of the war for German submarines. Between July and December 1940 U-boats sank 285 merchant ships, amounting to 1,470,388 tons, for the loss of just eight U-boats[32]. It is possible that the main reason for Britain surviving this period was simply the small number of U-boats available to Dönitz. The so-called 'Happy Time' saw Kretschmer and Schepke among others make their names household words in newspapers of both friend and foe alike. Although during this period U-boats did not have things as easy as post-war mythology would have us believe, the age of the 'Aces' was born and Knight's Crosses began to adorn the throats of many commanders.[33]

Dönitz and his BdU staff had started to refine their groupings of U-boats in Atlantic attacks, using newly established Kriegsmarine charts. By dividing featureless ocean areas into small squares U-boats were able to gather with greater precision at any location instructed over the radio. As far back as 1935 Dönitz had been preparing his crews for the *Rüdeltaktik* style of group operations, the next year would see the chance properly to implement his idea, long remembered as the 'Wolf Pack'. During initial pack attacks Dönitz had used a tactical commander in one of the boats involved to co-ordinate the assault, but mediocre results gained using this method persuaded Dönitz to co-ordinate the gathering of U-boats himself at BdU headquarters.

Of course the key to successful synchronization between the centre of operations and front-line boats was an efficient radio system. A small van accompanied BdU wherever he was, powerful transmitters crammed into every inch of the vehicle's interior. For an additional range boost there was also the possibility of routing signals through the massive 'Goliath' station near Magdeburg capable of transmitting to all corners of Atlantic U-boat operational territory.

Those U-boats of the 1st U-Flotilla that operated in the Atlantic added valuable weight to the small number of operational submarines at BdU's disposal. They were, however, found to be essentially unsuited to the rigours of Atlantic battle. Type II U-boats were small by any standards, tossed around like toys in harsh weather and capable of only moderate underwater and surfaced speeds. Comfort was not possible for the crew of a Type II boat, not that their larger Type VII cousins enjoyed much more. Primarily, of course, their limited range and torpedo capacity hampered their contribution. Torpedoes and fickle magnetic fuses themselves also continued to be a problem. In desperation many commanders used only contact fuses and set

[32] *Histoire Générale de la Guerre Sous-Marine*, Leonce Peillard, p93.
[33] The myth of the 'Happy Time' has been debunked by such leading U-boat veterans as Otto Kretschmer, stating correctly that although Allied defences were still in early stages of development, damage to U-boats and permanent losses steadily mounted, leaving few boats available for combat at any one time.

their torpedoes for extremely shallow running, a necessity somewhat negating the effectiveness of this erratic weapon.

British aircraft and submarines attempted in vain to interfere with German use of Lorient. Mines were laid and several torpedo attacks recorded by U-boats entering and leaving port. *U58* was attacked with torpedoes on 20 September, the following day *U138* missed by another four-torpedo spread. Submarines leaving Lorient began to rely heavily on escort vessels. Either *Sperrbrecher* or minesweepers (*Minensuchboote*) shepherded U-boats between the port entrance and continental shelf, sometimes joined by additional *Vorpostenboote* (coastal defence ships) or *U-Boot Jäger* (submarine hunters) until four or five miles from the coast, whereupon the U-boat would proceed alone. Flotillas of such support vessels were raised or transferred to the ports of Brest and Lorient (among others) immediately following the capitulation of France and organized into Security Divisions (*Sicherungsdivisionen*).

The region of Brittany fell under the control of 3rd *Sicherungsdivision*, responsible for the coast from Saint Malo to Lorient. Formed on 17 February 1941, its headquarters was originally at Trez-Hir (near Brest), but moved to Nostang (near Lorient) on 28 April 1942. Often the ships used for the flotillas of the *Sicherungsdivisionen* were not 'regular' naval boats, i.e.; they were not built by or for the Navy, but were requisitioned and converted into 'auxiliary' warships by addition of armour and weapons. The composition of the nine units which comprised the Kriegsmarine's 3rd Security Division was typical for this type of formation, and carried the everyday regional workload of the German Navy in what remained an unglamorous branch of naval service.

During the final months of 1940 two foreign submarines were added to the ranks of 1st U-Flotilla. On 21 November *UD1* was formally commissioned into the Flotilla at Kiel. She had been taken in prize by the Germans at Den Helder following Holland's 1940 capitulation. Originally built by Canadian Vickers, Montreal, she had been christened *S6* of the Royal Navy, launched in August 1915. During her service in the First World War she had an unfortunate accident, running aground at Schiermonnikoog on 18 January 1916, her entire crew being captured and interned by the neutral Dutch. Later purchased by the Netherlands Navy she became Dutch submarine *O8*. Finally in 1940 her third change of name and flag brought her to the ranks of 1st U-Flotilla and under the command of KK Hermann Riegele. She remained on the flotilla's strength as training and experimental boat until transferred to 5th U-Flotilla in April 1941.

The second foreign vessel was the only enemy submarine to be captured at sea by the Germans during the Second World War, and by the Luftwaffe. British 'Porpoise Class' submarine HMS *Seal*, built in Chatham dockyards and launched on 27 September 1938, had been engaged on a mine-laying mission (designated FD7) near Gothenburg while part of Gosport's 6th Submarine Flotilla. Spotted by enemy aircraft, she had undergone a short though effective aerial attack, which resulted in some damage to her pressure hull on 3 May 1940. The following day she suffered further injury by depth charges of ships belonging to *12.Unterseeboot Jäger Flottille* in an attack lasting for eight hours and sending her crashing to the seabed at 1900hrs on 4 April. Conditions aboard *Seal* were deteriorating rapidly and, after several failed attempts at overcoming the suction of the thick mud seabed, her commander, Lieutenant Commander Rupert Philip Lonsdale, finally managed to break his vessel free and she resurfaced to find the sea bare of enemy forces.

The powerless minelayer wallowed listlessly in a slight swell while her damage was assessed. It was discovered that, as well as partial flooding, her rudder was jammed, both electric motors out of action and only one of her diesels semi-functional. Lonsdale radioed their dire position to the Admiralty and stated his intention to limp towards neutral Sweden. Almost inevitably the ambitious attempt at escape was unsuccessful. At first light the following day an Arado 196A-3 floatplane piloted by Lt. Günther Mehrens appeared above *Seal*. After receiving no reply to its semaphore message 'K' – 'stop immediately' – Mehrens proceeded to attack with bombs and machine-gun fire, the British crew replying with a single Lewis gun. Luftwaffe reinforcement of a second Arado piloted by Lt. Karl Schmidt followed by a Heinkel 115 from Aalborg then roared into view and Lonsdale knew his position was hopeless, casualties mounting under the lash of aerial machine-gun fire. Hoisting a white tablecloth on the submarine's periscope HMS *Seal* surrendered. The two Arados landed nearby, taking Lonsdale and Petty Officer Cousins hostage. As the aircraft lifted off, one of *Seal*'s original antagonists, *U-Bootjäger UJ128*, hove into sight, removed the remaining crew and took the battered submarine in tow for Frederikshaven, and later on to Kiel where she was pulled into harbour by the tug *Seeteufel*.

After months of refit at the Germaniawerft yards she was restored and commissioned into the Kriegsmarine as *UB1* on 30 November 1940, commanded by FK Bruno Mahn. She served as training and experimental boat within 1st U-Flotilla at Kiel until transferred to 3rd U-Flotilla in May 1941.[34] One of the greatest finds aboard the huge minelayer was the German discovery of her torpedoes' efficient contact firing pistol. Dönitz ordered immediate copies to be made as a desperate attempt to help remedy the continuing shortcomings of German torpedoes.

By the end of December 1940 the strength of the 1st U-Flotilla had been reduced to two foreign boats and six Type IID German U-boats, *U140*, *U143*, *U146*, *U147*, *U149* and *U150*, the remainder having been posted from the flotilla to training units, mainly 22nd U-Flotilla, during the previous months. On 1 October OKM had passed a ruling that all Type IIs were to be relegated

---

[34] Commander Lonsdale was court-martialled on 10 April 1946 after his return from captivity. Charged with the premature surrender of his vessel he was honourably acquitted after three days of testimony and deliberation.

solely to training roles so that the Kriegsmarine could cope with the large influx of volunteers for U-boat service. The first to depart were *U56* to *U62*, the remainder soon following, as 1941 saw the men of 1st U-Flotilla receive larger Atlantic boats of the Type VII series.

Christmas leave was granted to most of the flotilla's sailors and they journeyed to all corners of Germany to enjoy the second Christmas of the Second World War glorying in being part of the still ascending U-boat arm. On 27 December Kaptlt. Cohausz himself departed for holidays over the New Year.

1941

7 January 1941: Hitler provided a boost to U-boat operations by ordering twelve *Kondor* aircraft of KG 40 near Bordeaux placed under BdU command. Ex-sailor Lieutenant-Colonel (*Oberst-Leutnant*) Harling Hausen's *Kampfgeschwader 40* (Bomber Group 40) equipped with imposing four-engine Focke Wulf 200 *Kondor* bombers and the already successful Junkers 88 would now be devoted to U-boat reconnaissance and convoy harassment. The large and graceful *Kondor* aircraft would play a significant role in the forthcoming convoy war. Able to fly over 1,500 kilometres into the Atlantic from their advanced base in France to attack shipping that lacked any kind of air support in the war's early stages, they harried many ships to their doom, as well as occasionally providing invaluable reconnaissance information to BdU enabling U-boats to form forward patrol lines (*Vorpostenstreifen*) in a convoy's path.

Initially under Luftwaffe command, there had been only a tenuous and difficult relationship between these aircraft and the Kriegsmarine during their early days of service in France. Following a protocol established in February 1939 maritime reconnaissance was the domain of the Kriegsmarine, although the actual material, i.e. the aircraft, still had to be supplied by the Luftwaffe. By December 1940 a shaky relationship had been fostered between U-boat Command and the BV 138s of Brest's Reconnaissance unit *Gruppe 406* (stationed at Lanveoc-Poulmic), KG 40, and occasional assistance from other aircraft of Luftflotte 5. However during that month all Brest's BV 138s were grounded by technical faults, reducing Dönitz's aerial reconnaissance virtually to nil.

Despite the obvious advantage of long-range reconnaissance designated specifically for the U-boat service and therefore greater numbers of ships intercepted and sunk, it took prolonged lobbying to OKW by Dönitz and Raeder to break the squadron free of *Reichsmarschall* Herman Göring's grasp. Hitler held Göring in high esteem at this stage of the war, the corpulent Luftwaffe chief then being probably at the height of his power. A veteran of the First World War, Göring had led the famous 'Flying Circus' Squadron following the death of Baron Manfred von Richthofen, becoming involved in politics following the war. He was one of the original Nazis. Placed in command of the newly established Luftwaffe in the years leading toward war the vain and arrogant *Reichsmarschall* would loudly proclaim, 'All that flies over Germany belongs to me!' He continued to obstruct any plans for the separate Kriegsmarine Air Arm envisioned by Raeder, or allow Kriegsmarine control over any elements of the Luftwaffe. Indeed at a later stage of the war Dönitz reported to Raeder that Göring had remarked:

> 'As long as he [Göring] lived and did not resign from his post, *Grossadmiral* Raeder would not get his Naval Air Arm.'

Dönitz travelled to Berlin in exasperation to enlist Raeder's and Field Marshal Jodl's aid in a personal approach to the Führer. Finally on 6 January 1941, after the attack by Condor aircraft on the 4,427 ton British steamship *Temple Moat* bound from Oban to Buenos Aires which resulted in heavy damage but no sinking, Hitler decreed KG 40 to be placed directly under Kriegsmarine control. Reason and sound military judgment, traits that became rarer and rarer in the following years, had finally won the day for Dönitz.

Notably, while Hitler had been in conference with Dönitz and had agreed to his request, Göring was absent, enjoying the hunting season. On his return he was furious to discover that his jealously guarded power had been usurped and boarded his personal train bound for Lorient. On arrival he arrogantly demanded to see Dönitz who received him stiffly at his Kerneval head-quarters. Göring, one moment ranting the next conciliatory, attempted every way he could to persuade Dönitz to reconsider the arrangement and return KG 40 to Luftwaffe control, but to no avail. Even the thinly disguised invitation to share a meal with Göring and 'discuss matters' fell on deaf ears, and they parted company on bad terms.[35]

15 January: Kaptlt. Hans Cohausz recorded the progress of work at Brest in order to receive 1st U-Flotilla boats:

> 'Preparations for Brest U-Support station (*U-Stutzpunktleiter*) in full swing. The Flotilla's head of U-Support is sending a large portion of specialist personnel to Brest to join the holding company (*Stamm-kompanie*) in training there. Head of U-Support station Brest is *Kapitän* von Schmidt.'

19 January: 1st U-Flotilla lost its final Type II boat when *U140* departed for the 22nd U-Flotilla. Her combat days with 1st Flotilla were over as she sailed east for Gotenhafen and her new unit. The U-boat offensive in the Atlantic lost much of its momentum during the New Year. Appalling weather con-

---

[35] Dönitz's hold over KG 40 became gradually more tenuous over the months that followed until eventually there were no aircraft left under his command.

ditions not only made patrol work extremely difficult but also curtailed much training in the ice-shrouded Baltic.[36] U-boat construction still had received no priority from OKW, now engaged on planning an assault against Russia. The *Unterseebootwaffe* would have to manage with what they had. On 21 January Dönitz recorded in the BdU War Diary his thoughts on increasing British effectiveness at avoiding his patrol lines:

> 'New information indicates that the enemy is more successful now than at the beginning of the war in taking bearings on radio reports and short weather reports of U-boats. This surmise must be given the most careful attention. In view of the small number of craft in areas where U-boats concentrate, bearing signals reveal that the enemy is bypassing attack areas. It is noteworthy that:
>
> 1. In all cases we make sure that radio is used only when it is important in an operational sense. All other radio messages, position reports, etc, are to be transmitted only when an exact bearing on the U-boat no longer matters, that is to say when her presence has been discovered by other means.
> 2. Weather boats are to be so used that the other boats will not be jeopardized.'

During the end of 1940 and the opening weeks of 1941, 1st U-Flotilla, now devoid of U-boats, adopted the role of U-boat Support Flotilla (*U-Stutzpunktflotilla*) for use as a personnel reserve. On the orders of BdU Org. a War Staff (*Kriegstab*) was created within the 1st U-Flotilla for the chief of Kiel's naval base. Here was formed a pool of trained men and auxiliary staff personnel specifically for the U-boat service. Cohausz recorded:

> 'As per decision of the BdU.Org, a War Staff for the Head of Support Kiel is created for 1st U-Flotilla. The purpose of this section is:
>
> 1. Support for all boats leaving Kiel on enemy patrol – regardless of the flotilla of origin. Monthly numbers estimated at around 15 to 19 boats . . .
>
> As it stands, the support section is not capable of fending for itself; it works with and within the capabilities of the flotilla . . . . The support Section of the Head of U-Support Kiel finally starts operating on 1/2/41.'

On that same date, 1 February 1941, Hans Cohausz received his promotion to Korvettenkapitän after 16 years in the German Navy.

25 January: At 1100hrs Oblt.z.S. Adalbert 'Adi' Schnee, veteran of 1st U-Flotilla combat aboard Kretschmer's *U23* and his own *U60*, assembled his

---

[36] *U140* carried out two combat patrols while with 22 U-Flotilla in the Baltic. On 21 July 1941 she torpedoed and sank Soviet submarine *M94*.

crew on the stern casing of *U201* for her commissioning ceremony from the yards of Germaniawerft, Kiel. As recorded in the flotilla War Diary:

> '*U201* . . . attended by members from all parts of the flotilla, commissioned at 1100hrs as the first of the 500t series of 'Frontboats'.'

U201 was indeed the first Type VIIC U-boat inducted into the flotilla in preparation for transfer to its front-line port of Brest and the savage battles in the Atlantic. Beneath the grey drizzle of a north German winter the crew, drawn up in three ranks, listened to Schnee deliver his address, followed by the raising of the blood-red Kriegsmarine battle ensign on the submarine's conning tower flagstaff. Once the ceremony was completed her crew scrambled below into the U-boat, her interior still carrying the smell of fresh paint and new machinery.

The 1st U-Flotilla continued to receive newly commissioned boats during the first months of 1941:

U556 (Type VIIC) commissioned at Blohm & Voss, Hamburg, 6 February, commander Kptlt. Herbert Wohlfahrth,

U83 (Type VIIB) commissioned at Flenderwerfte, Lübeck, 8 February, commander Kptlt. Hans-Werner Kraus,

U651 (Type VIIC) commissioned at Howaldstwerke, Hamburg, 13 February, commander Kptlt. Peter Lohmeyer,

U557 (Type VIIC) commissioned Blohm & Voss, Hamburg, 14 February, commander Oblt.z.S. Ottokar Paulshen,

U203 (Type VIIC) commissioned against Tirpitz Mole, Kiel, 17 February, commander Kptlt. Rolf Mützelberg,

U558 (Type VIIC) commissioned at Blohm & Voss, Hamburg, 20 February, commander Kptlt. Günther Krech,

U559 (Type VIIC) commissioned at Blohm & Voss, Hamburg, 27 February, commander Kptlt. Hans Heidtmann,

U204 (Type VIIC) commissioned Germaniawerft, Kiel, 8 March, commander Kptlt. Walther Kell,

U561 (Type VIIC) commissioned at Blohm & Voss, Hamburg, 13 March, commander Kptlt. Robert Bartels,

U79 (Type VIIC) commissioned at Bremer Vulkan, Vegesack, 13 March, commander Kptlt. Wolfgang Kaufmann,

U371 (Type VIIC) commissioned at Howaldtswerke, Kiel, 15 March, commander Kptlt. Heinrich Driver,

U562 (Type VIIC) commissioned 20 March at Blohm & Voss, Hamburg, commander Oblt.z.S. Herwig Collman,

U202 (Type VIIC) commissioned 22 March at Germaniawerft, Kiel, commander by Kptlt. Hans-Heinz Linder,

U563 (Type VIIC) commissioned at Blohm & Voss, Hamburg, 27 March, commander Oblt.z.S. Klaus Bargsten (delayed by repair work after Bargsten rammed the Scharnhorst Brücke during demagnetising on Kiel's deperming range),

U331 (Type VIIC) commissioned at Nordseewerke, Emden, 31 March, commander Kptlt. Hans-Dietrich von Tiesenhausen,

U564 (Type VIIC) commissioned at Blohm & Voss, Hamburg, 3 April, commander Oblt.z.S. Reinhard Suhren,

U80 (Type VIIC) commissioned at Bremer Vulkan, Vegesak, 8 April, commander Oblt.z.S. Georg Staats,

U565 (Type VIIC) commissioned at Blohm & Voss, Hamburg, 10 April, commander Oblt.z.S. Johann Jebsen,

U401 (Type VIIC) commissioned at Danzigerwerfte, 10 April, commander Kptlt. Gero Zimmermann.

Korvettenkapitän Hans Cohausz' War Diary entry on 10 April culminated with the satisfying words: '20 Flotilla U-boats in service'. By the end of April that number would be raised by four more – *U566, U372, U81, U84*. During March the 1st U-Flotilla Chief journeyed to Brest in order personally to inspect preparations for his unit's scheduled movement. Deputizing for Cohausz was the soon-to-be 3rd U-Flotilla Chief KK Hans Rösing.

With flotilla strength burgeoning time was taken up by strenuous shake-down cruises throughout the Baltic. The flotilla's new U-boats moved east, away from the traffic lanes of Kiel, where their commanders began to put both machines and men through their paces. Training had lost none of the harsh-ness that Dönitz had insisted on six years previously and at the end of gruelling months of drills and rehearsals the boats looked weather-beaten and rust-stained, the fine texture of their military grey paint roughened by exposure to wind and sea. Their crews had also had their shine removed, replaced by the confidence needed to survive an escalating U-boat war.

During the month of March Winston Churchill had named the all-impor-tant struggle of Britain's convoy war, a name that was used by men on both sides of the conflict:

'I said to [Admiral Sir Dudley] Pound, 'We have got to lift this business to the highest plane, over everything else. I am going to proclaim 'the Battle of the Atlantic'. This, like featuring the Battle of Britain nine months earlier, was a signal intended to concentrate all minds and all departments concerned upon the U-boat war.'[37]

Thus it was that on 6 March 1941 Churchill penned his now famous directive, read before House of Commons on 25 June. The first few lines outline the essence of its message:

'In view of various German statements, we must assume that the Battle of the Atlantic has begun. . . .We must take the offensive against the U-boat and the Focke Wulf wherever we can and whenever we can. The U-boat at sea must be hunted, the U-boat in the building yard or in dock must be bombed.'[38]

Correspondingly, March had been a grim month for the U-boat service. Three of Germany's greatest commanders had been lost in battle against the British. The first casualty was one of the most shattering. Although not announced to the German public by Goebbels' *Rundfunk* news service until 23 May, *U47* and Günther Prien had been lost at sea. Believed for years to have been sunk by depth charges from HMS *Wolverine* it is now thought that *Wolverine* in fact was engaged against *UA* and the fate of Prien and his crew remains unknown, lost on or about 7/8 March. Confirmed beyond any doubt, however, were the losses of Kretschmer and *U99* on 17 March, captured after his boat was sunk by *HMS Walker*, and Schepke aboard *U100* also on 17 March, the handsome blonde commander crushed and then severed in two within his conning tower, sent to the deep with thirty-seven of his men after being rammed by HMS *Vanoc*. Both latter commanders had been engaged on attacks on convoy HX112, paying the ultimate price demanded by an increasingly effective escort presence. The Royal Navy received a boost in morale at the expense of Germany's three underwater heroes and the edge had been taken of the Kriegsmarine's sword. In retrospect it could be said that this marked the beginning of the decline in U-boat warfare. Despite brief periods of success and victory over the Allies during coming years, the *Unterseebootewaffe* never truly regained the ascendancy of the 'Happy Time'.

5 April: Oblt.z.S. Schnee had completed his demanding months of *U201*'s shakedown, the boat sailing from East Baltic training grounds past the Kiel lightship and tying up alongside the tar-coated wooden pylons of Tirpitz Pier. Rust repair was scheduled in Kiel's shipyards in preparation for a maiden war patrol, although only critical works could be undertaken due to already stretched dockyard resources and facilities. While the U-boat's officers began to transfer their personal effects aboard the 5th U-Training Flotilla tender

---

[37] *The Second World War*, Winston Churchill, Vol. III, p105.
[38] *The Second World War*, Winston Churchill, Vol. III, p105.

Lech where they would be billeted they were joined by two other U-boats, *U556* and *U557*, also having completed their arduous Baltic training.

Oblt.z.S. Paulshen's *U557* was listed for a complete refit. During transfer from Königsberg to Kiel in preparation for departure to the Atlantic, a routine practice dive had gone tragically wrong. As the U-boat submerged her Chief Engineer had been unable to close outboard air induction valves causing the boat to plummet downwards out of control, water jetting inside the pressure hull. After crashing into the silt of the Baltic's floor the induction valves were finally closed but not before several tons of water had flooded in. During the chaotic tumble *Machinist* Eckstein had been killed in the aft torpedo room, his head split open by the impact of a collision with the stern tube. After twenty harrowing hours Paulshen managed to free his trapped boat from the bottom. Following gruelling redistribution by bucket of stinking oily water flooding his bilges and rocking the U-boat free with crewmen running backwards and forwards the length of the ship, the suction of metres of sticky mud was overcome and *U557* floated free. It was later found that a spanner had become lodged in the outside air induction valve, nobody aboard knew how.

7–9 April: While U-boats prepared for their routine repairs and refitting in preparation for sea, large English bomber formations numbering an accumulated total of 389 aircraft attacked Kiel and her important shipyards for two consecutive nights starting late on the evening of 7 April. Under a full moon, bombs rained down, devastating the suburbs of Gaarden and Hellingdorf. The huge shipyards of Deutschewerke and Germaniawerft suffered a dramatic fall in output and corresponding drop in U-boat maintenance schedules for several days. *U201*, *U556* and *U557* all had their rust treatment or refit delayed by the severe air raids. Alongside maintenance work, German submarine production could ill afford any delays and the RAF raids added to an already heavily burdened industry. Training U-boats were moved east while combat ready submarines prepared to depart the smouldering port installations, the naval arms depot continuing to burn for two days after being hit.

On 8 April BdU was forced to order two U-boats to recommence Luftwaffe weather reporting duties, an unpopular and monotonous duty for U-boat commanders and crew. More importantly, weather reporting duties for the benefit of Germany's air force removed two valuable U-boats from the Atlantic front line at a time when U-boat strength was barely enough to keep a constant operational presence against the Allies.

11 April: Cohausz' War Diary entry recorded the loss of a cadre of men from his flotilla staff:

> 'With effect from 10 April the officers of the U-base Commander Kiel, which has been Chief of Staff since 1 December 1940, and the 1/II

auxiliary staff of the 1 U-Flotilla, are transferred to the 3rd U-Flotilla, KK Rösing commander.'

The reformation of the 3rd U-Flotilla, previously the 'Lohs' Flotilla, was completed, using a cadre of experienced men from 1st U-Flotilla staff, many of whom had originated from 'Lohs'.

15 April: Flotilla Chief Cohausz spent fourteen days between 16 and 30 April on leave, deputizing Chief in his absence again being 3rd U-Flotilla commander KK Rösing.

In Kiel much repair had been completed on the battered shipyards and work recommenced with a vengeance on construction and servicing. *U201*, *U556* and *U557* were finally able to receive their scheduled refurbishment. Over the course of the following weeks leave was granted for the three crews while their U-boats received their fitting out and any repairs deemed necessary. At the end of their periods ashore, crews assembled again in Kiel, eager to put to sea for what was to some their first war patrol. Fresh paint covered the grime built up from harbour mooring and systems aboard were put through final checks with routine trim dives in Kiel Bay. A brief voyage to the arsenal saw torpedoes loaded aboard, a time-consuming and strenuous task. The following day U-boats took food and deck weapon ammunition aboard. Fuel was delivered, the heavy diesel disappearing into cavernous tanks. The day before departure fresh water, bread, eggs and vegetables were crammed into the last remaining spaces aboard. The U-boats were ready for war.

22 April: *U201* eased from Tirpitz Mole at 1330hrs and began its long passage to the western edge of France and front line service (*Fronteinsatz*). Schnee travelled easily through the Kaiser Wilhelm Canal, then proceeding north, skirting the hazardous waters of northern England. During the evening of 2 May he stumbled upon the smouldering hulk of British tanker MV *Capulet*, the 8,190-ton ship carrying 11,200 tons of fuel oil. Owned by Bear Creek Oil and Shipping Company, the tanker's crew had abandoned her four nights previously after suffering torpedo damage during a convoy attack made by Erich Topp's *U552*. At 2114hrs, firing the boat's first torpedo in anger, Schnee sent the wreck to the bottom.

Six nights later *U201*'s radio operator received a call to rendezvous with *U110*, shadowing convoy OB 318 east-north-east of Cape Farewell. One unsuccessful torpedo attack against an 'unidentified passenger liner ' estimated at 6,000 tons was recorded in the U-boat's War Diary, at 1547hrs on 8 May before the successful rendezvous.[39]

---

[39] Although Schnee recorded seeing the torpedo hit the ship without detonating, German historian Jürgen Rohwer has stated that the French liner *Kervegan* was possibly sunk by this attack, reported missing after 5 May.

The following day, 9 May, both U-boats struck the convoy, *U201* sinking the 5,802-ton British ship SS *Gregalia* and severely damaging SS *Empire Cloud* during the afternoon. However, Schnee was not to have the battle all his way and he and his crew suffered the hell of depth-charging from escorts HMS *Nigella* and HMS *St Apollo*. Thunderous detonations rocked *U201*, a steady rain of depth charges (*Wabos* or *Wasserboms*) exploding around them. With a British corvette and anti-submarine trawler tenaciously hounding the U-boat, Schnee opted for retreat, eventually shaking the pursuers from his trail. Proceeding towards his original destination the rocky coast of Brittany eventually appeared on *U201*'s port bow during 18 May. After the rust-streaked U-boat had docked at Lorient, Schnee, surrounded by a welcoming crowd, was able to report the claimed sinking of 26,000 BRT.

30 April: Hitler's birthday was toasted in cramped wood-panelled wardrooms aboard 1st U-Flotilla's boats. All except *U203*, transferred to Kiel's shipyards for minor repairs following an underwater collision with 2nd U-Flotilla's *U68*. Training in battle-like conditions continued in the Baltic as the 1st U-Flotilla and new boats of other combat units prepared for their baptismal patrols.

1 May: '*23 Boote in Dienst*' (23 boats in service). *U556* began her passage from Kiel to the North Atlantic. The status accorded to Japanese-born Wohlfarth was demonstrated by Rösing's comment noted in the War Diary on this day:

> 'Motto: It is the First of May and Parsival is sailing'

Ordered to patrol west of the British Isles, Kptlt. Wohlfarth passed close to the Arctic Circle during 5 May, the next day attacking and sinking with gunfire the small Faeroese fishing vessel *Emanuael* west of its home port. The following day *U556* surfaced and, rolling heavily in high seas, began receiving beacon messages transmitted by nearby *U94* closing upon convoy OB 318 south of Iceland. Wohlfarth ordered a new course laid and within three days was able to make out myriad smokestacks of the slow convoy. The 'Grey Wolf' nosed under and prepared to attack. *U556* launched three separate assaults. The first at 0442hrs sent two torpedoes streaking towards heavily laden SS *Aelybryn* and SS *Chaucer*. A single roar of detonation erupted against *Aelybryn* although she refused to go down, limping into Reykjavik seven days later. The second torpedo missed and Wohlfarth disengaged, seething at the waste of an 'eel'. His second attack was more successful sinking SS *Empire Caribou* for 4,861 tons, the third assault sending SS *Gand* to the bottom, bulkheads exploding underwater, the terrible sound of a dying ship reverberated through the steel walls of *U556*. On the convoy's opposite beam *U94*, having sent two ships under, had been lightly damaged by four hours of depth-charging from escorts HMS *Amazon*, HMS *Bulldog* and HMS *Rochester*. She finally slunk away to effect whatever temporary onboard repairs could be made after the British escorts were forced to depart, searching in vain for *U556*.

Wohlfarth's boat and *U94* now became part of an organized patrol line, collectively known as *Westboote*, strengthened by the arrival of six more U-boats. Again *U94* was the contact ship for a new convoy HX126 in grid square AJ 6636, the train of Allied shipping heading north at eight knots. The line formed up for an attack as *U94* continued transmitting its brief homing signal every 30 minutes. *U556* made the first assault in devastating style after mist and strong hailstorms had reduced visibility to less than one mile, prompting Dönitz to order U-boats in pursuit to attack individually rather than wait for the group to form. On the stormy afternoon of 20 May torpedoes lanced from the U-boat's bow damaging the 13,037-ton tanker MV *San Felix* and sinking the 8,470-ton MV *British Security* and the 4,974-ton MV *Darlington Court*.

The crew and commander were jubilant. Further to the success of their mission a message was received aboard *U556* during the 20th of an award for her commander. In the 1st U-Flotilla War Diary for that day Cohausz recorded:

> 'Wohlfarth of *U556* has been awarded the Knight's Cross. Having sunk with previous U-boats 61,000 BRT plus one destroyer and with *U556* 49,900BRT during this mission! In total 110,900 BRT!!'

In fact Wohlfarth had sunk a total of 23,577 tons, damaging 17,023 tons more, during *U556*'s maiden patrol, but this in itself was still a figure to be reckoned with. His was the seventieth Kriegsmarine Knight's Cross, thirtieth for the *Unterseebootwaffe*, but second to be awarded to a member of 1st U-boat Flotilla.

Beginning their return to base on a blustery 24 May, some of the edge was taken off celebrations aboard as urgent messages emanated from BdU's headquarters. The first, received and translated by Senior Telegraphist Schlupp (scheduled to face court martial for selling his uniform in order to finance a heavy alcohol intake), lifted spirits aboard the boat:

> 'Battlecruiser *Hood* sunk this morning in Denmark Strait by *Bismarck*. Heavy cruiser shadowing *Bismarck* and *Prinz Eugen*. *Bismarck* attempting to draw shadowing forces across *Westboote* line.'

The *Bismarck*, commanded by Admiral Lutjens, and *Prinz Eugen*, commanded by Kapt. Helmuth Brinkmann, had left Gotenhafen on 18 May for 'Operation *Rheinübung*', a mission intended to attack Allied convoys in the North Atlantic. However, the raiders met with disaster. After a promising start, the storied sinking of HMS *Hood*, the two formidable ships were harried and hunted by a large British naval squadron intent on their destruction in one of the most important naval pursuits of the war.

The second message received by Wohlfarth and the other *Westboote* submarines crushed all euphoria aboard as BdU reported that *Bismarck* had taken a hit in the rudder and was unable to steer. Swordfish aircraft launched from HMS *Ark Royal* had managed to disable the steering of the great ship and she made way in huge lazy circles, manoeuvring by propellers alone. Aboard *Bismarck* Admiral Lutjens ordered his accompanying cruiser *Prinz Eugen* to dash for Brest (which she reached five days later on 1 June). Shortly thereafter a further urgent transmission was received in the small U-boat radio room:

'To all Biscay boats. Whoever has a torpedo, go to the protection of the *Bismarck*.'

Wohlfarth lost no time. Ordering diesels to maximum revolutions, he stayed atop the bridge as breakers crashed and foamed around the tower. The boat had expended all its ammunition during the convoy attacks, but at least could still join the search. Vision was terrible in angry sea, conditions continuing to deteriorate. *U556* gradually crept toward the last recorded position of *Bismarck*, observing the flash of distant cannon fire and transmitting the necessary homing signal for other boats to converge. Wohlfarth was granted a final frustration while trying to close upon *Bismarck*. Unable to offer assistance to the distant ship he could only gaze in silent fury as HMS *Renown* and *Ark Royal* hove into view converging on their German quarry. Wohlfarth's War Diary entry vents his frustration:

'May 26, 1941. Position 640 miles west of Land's End. Wind NW, force 8, Sea 5. Weather clear, slightly overcast. Visibility medium to Good.
1948hrs. Alarm. A battleship of the King George class and an aircraft carrier, probably *Ark Royal*, came in right through the mist from astern, travelling at high speed. Bows to the right, inclination 170°. If only I had a few torpedoes! I would not even have had to manoeuvre, I was just perfectly placed for an attack. No destroyers, no zig-zagging! I could have stayed where I was and got them both. Torpedo-carrying aircraft observed operating from carrier. I might have been able to help the *Bismarck*.
May 27. Wind NW. Force 8. Sea 5. Intermittent rain squalls. Visibility medium. Night very dark.
0000hrs. Surfaced. What could I now do to help *Bismarck*? Observed star shells and *Bismarck* returning enemy's fire. It's a horrible feeling to be so near and yet not be able to do anything.
0400hrs. Sea now running higher than ever. *Bismarck* still putting up a fight. Sent in weather report for Luftwaffe and at 0630hrs made last signal giving position.'

No boats with torpedoes were within range as the drama was finished with further flashes along a wild horizon. A final message was received from the doomed battleship, relayed to all U-boats through BdU:

'We fight to the last shell. Long live the Führer! Long live Germany!'

The pride of German sea power was sunk in the morning of 27 May. Wohlfarth had been unable to attempt reaching the ailing ship in order to retrieve her War Diary, defeated by worsening weather and low fuel. This last desperate act was undertaken by the approaching *U74* of 7th U-Flotilla. Following the final explosions of the dying ship *U556* was left powerless to assist in a sea stained with the warship's thick oil.

Wohlfarth continued his homeward journey, arriving in Lorient on 31 May. As the battered U-boat came to rest beside the rusting hulk of the sailing ship *Isere* her bearded crewmen wore weary smiles, their periscope flying 49,900 tons' worth of victory pennants. Adorning the front of the conning tower was a stick-man caricature of a knight (*Parsival* himself) sinking a merchant ship with his thumb while pulling a U-boat by its lead with the other hand, the tonnage number 49,900 written below. Dönitz strode immediately aboard, shaking hands with the fatigued Wohlfarth and slipping the ribbon of the Knight's Cross over his battered white-topped captain's cap and around his neck, five days before his 26th birthday.

One of the U-boat war's most crucial events had taken place during May 1941. The early success of Germany's U-boats had relied heavily on secure and instant wireless communication between BdU and his boats. By this means Dönitz, receiving daily and detailed decrypts of intercepted Royal Navy signals traffic during the war's early months, was able to direct his commanders to the best hunting grounds and most likely areas in which to encounter convoys. This secure system revolved around the Enigma machine, the Kriegsmarine version of which was known as *Schüsselmaschine M* (Code writer M). These electronic coding devices, resembling a small portable type-writer, relied on a variable internal wiring and rotor system to provide an incredible 6,000,000,000 variable code settings, changed daily.

While British code-breakers at Bletchley Park's top secret Government Codes and Cypher School had managed to begin penetration into Luftwaffe and Heer Enigma ciphers, the more complex Kriegsmarine system defied all attempts at penetration.

The first break for British crypto-analysts came with the capture of an intact Enigma machine and rotors from auxiliary supply/weather reporting ship *München* by a boarding party from destroyer HMS *Somali* near Jan Mayan island on 7 May. While this enabled the brilliant team of mathematicians at Bletchley Park to crack the low-grade weather code, it still did not give access to the far more complicated naval code system used by combat units such as destroyers and U-boats.

The final breakthrough was not long in coming. On the night of 8 May *U201* of the 1st U-Flotilla had homed in on signals sent by Kptlt. Lemp's *U110*, from Lorient's 2nd U-Flotilla, who had been shadowing convoy OB 318. The following morning the two U-boats attacked independently, Schnee aboard *U201* achieving success before departing for Lorient. Lemp on the other hand suffered mixed fortune. Firing three torpedoes into the dense convoy, *U110* sank two British ships, the third 'eel' passing wide of its mark. Inside the U-boat torpedo men frantically attempted to free a fourth 'eel' that had failed to leave the tube. As his sweating crew laboured in the forward torpedo room Lemp lined up another attack, this time on a 15,000-ton whaling ship, when he saw to his horror that escort corvette HMS *Aubretia* was cleaving swiftly through the sea toward him. Crash diving, the U-boat was shaken by accurate depth charges causing considerable damage to the still shallow boat. As Schnee disengaged from the action on the convoy's opposite beam all Allied attention focused on Lemp, destroyers HMS *Bulldog* and HMS *Broadway* dropping further charges, disabling the U-boat's hydroplanes, rudder and electric engines. Choking gas from flooded batteries filled the boat and she seemed unable to stop her downwards plummet to oblivion. Inexplicably the U-boat's rapid fall ceased and she gradually began to rise, her crew rushing to abandon ship as *U110* came under concentrated fire after coming to the surface. HMS *Broadway* rapidly bore down on the stricken boat as if to ram her. Aboard *Bulldog* Commander Baker-Cresswell saw an alternative and ordered *Broadway* to veer away at the last moment, though the destroyer still struck *U110* a glancing blow. Lemp and his crew had meanwhile abandoned ship, the bearded commander having set scuttling charges himself. Aboard the stationary *Bulldog* boats were lowered and struggling Germans rapidly pulled from the water and into captivity, while other boats raced for *U110* intent on boarding her. Lemp, now alone in the gentle swell, saw with despair that his scuttling charges had failed to detonate and realized the obvious implications. He or his panicked men had not thrown their Enigma and vital code books overboard in weighted sacks during their hasty escape; they remained on the radioman's small desk. Although exact details of what followed are obscure, it appears that struggling through the water towards his floundering ship Lemp attempted to hoist himself aboard the slippery wet casing but was seen by one of the boarding party and shot dead. He was the fourteenth crewman to die during the attack.

Sub-Lieutenant D.E.Balme, leading the boarders, gingerly lowered himself through the conning tower hatch and stumbled through the wrecked interior to recover an intact Enigma, spare rotor wheels, current daily rotor settings, patrol signals and diary. The U-boat war was about to be transformed.[40]

The Enigma and all its paraphernalia arrived at Bletchley Park and began to be mastered by the British in an operation code-named ULTRA, one of the best-kept secrets of the war. The Kriegsmarine never knew that this event had taken place and continued to assume that their Enigma coding was

---

[40] HMS *Bulldog* took *U110* in tow but she eventually foundered and sank on the morning of 10 May. The German prisoners were secured below decks and had no idea of the events that had transpired.

impenetrable. Though not always capable of continuous code penetration, as Kriegsmarine settings were frequently altered, enough intelligence was gathered to enable Commander Roger Winn, head of the British Admiralty's Submarine Tracking Room, to use interpreted signals combined with 'intuitive guess-work' to evade or intercept U-boats on patrol with ever increasing accuracy.

1 June: *U558* slipped from Kiel at 0400hrs to traverse the shallow heavily mined Skagerrak en-route to the North Atlantic and ultimately Brest, followed on 4 June by *U559*.

During the ensuing week remaining 1st Flotilla U-boats began their arduous journey to France where the facilities of the captured ports were now operational. During 5 June *U79*, *U203* and *U371* all started the journey from Kiel. Two days later at 1330hrs locomotives loaded with fifteen wagons of supplies and the 'train' of 1st Flotilla departed for France. The move was relatively smooth as Cohausz recorded:

> 'Various difficulties, including repeated mis-shunting/derailing of rail cars, have been overcome. Each section has sufficient supplies so that the Flotilla can in essence remain half a year without resupply. This is an appropriate principle and is recommended for the next Flotillas.
>
> 'Transportation of the Flotilla in one train; or in two in France. Flotilla operations of boats remaining in the Fatherland, including lists and overview, have been transferred to U-Support Station Kiel.
>
> 'Flotilla with secondary staff [*Unterstab*] and spares [*Ausfallzuschlag*] by rail to France, Flotilla staff and Engineers section travels ahead with Ju 52 to make preparations.
>
> *1330hrs: Grosse Flottillen Abmarsches nach Brest.*'

12 June: *U574* received her commissioning ceremony beneath the summer sun at Hamburg's Blohm & Voss yards. After photos taken with representatives of the shipbuilding yard Oblt.z.S. Dietrich Gengelbach eased into the control room for the customary celebration. Months of training were to come, but at the end of it the young crew knew that they were destined for France and the Atlantic war.

During the course of the day final movement of the 1st U-Flotilla took place from Kiel to Brest. In Cohausz' diary entry the move from *Deutschland* to *Frankreich* was recorded as taking only four days. The flotilla's operations staff flew in to Guipavas aerodrome, a short distance north-east of Brest aboard Ju52 transport aircraft on 13 June.[41] The green-painted corrugated-skinned

---

[41] Guipavas was home to German fighter aircraft of Major Oesau's 8th and 9th Staffeln, JG2.

aircraft circled first over the port city affording to most the first glimpse of their new home.

> 'After making good time, Flotilla transport arrives evening of 15/VI in Brest; 15 wagons, the rest to follow next day from Saint Brieuc. Moving in and setting up at the support station.'

14 June: *U559* at sea in the Denmark Strait on her maiden patrol radioed BdU to report ice damage to her periscope. After requesting permission to proceed to Bergen for repair Kptlt. Hans Heidtmann received fresh orders to proceed to grid reference BD33 and thus Lorient, due in large part to a lack of optical repair facilities in Norway. During his transit Heidtmann was directed to grid references BD20 and BD30 in search of elusive convoys. Although constrained to an enforced impotence by day he was deemed capable of having an impact on operations in progress if able to attack surfaced at night.

Another of the Flotilla's patrolling boats *U557*, out for her maiden operational voyage, radioed BdU:

> 'Have been attacked by British submarine in CC 36. Enemy escaped.'

While traversing sun-drenched seas in grid square CC3656 alert lookouts had sighted tell tale tracks of three torpedoes streaking towards them. Ordering full speed and rudder hard to starboard Kptlt. Paulshen attempted to drag his submarine around and 'comb' the incoming torpedo tracks. *U557* was too sluggish, however, and impact appeared inevitable. To the disbelief of the stunned bridge watch two of the three incoming 'eels' ran against the U-boat's side and straight beneath her keel to continue ineffectually to the end of their run. The contact-fused torpedoes had been set to run too deep, sparing the U-boat certain destruction.

Atop his conning tower Ottokar Paulshen made out the launching point, betrayed by an uneven swell on otherwise calm water. Racing into attack, Paulshen ordered his boat submerged and prepared for an underwater duel. Hydrophones detected propeller noises and the U-boat moved to attack, bow caps open and tubes flooded. However, it was not to be; the enemy's propeller noises grew fainter as they hauled away from *U557*. Moments before the noise of blowing tanks was detected aboard *U557* Paulshen ordered his own boat surfaced and prepared to give chase on diesels. In the distance could be seen a silhouette of what the U-boat's officers took to be a 'Thames' class submarine, probably HMS *Thunderbolt*, making off at high speed.

6.

TRANSFER 16 JUNE 1941 to
31 DECEMBER 1941

The first U-boat to use Brest harbour had been *U65* of 2nd U-Flotilla on 22 August 1940, though only for six days of repair.[42] Nearly a year later the 1st U-Flotilla, commanded by KK Hans Cohausz, arrived from Kiel for permanent stationing in the port. Between 12 and 16 June 1941 their headquarters were established in huge granite buildings of the French Naval Academy crowning a hill on the city's western edge, immediately behind the military harbour. Officers were billeted inside the ornate building while enlisted men lived on the compound in separate buildings. Soon the Flotilla insignia adorned the central archway of the Academy's face, from where officers were able to gaze over the expansive harbour and *Rade de Brest* towards the Crozon Peninsula.

No luxury was spared for Brest's U-boat men. A resort area for relaxing officers was established in the requisitioned Hôtel des Bains situated on the beautiful expanse of Trez-Hir beach near Le Conquet. Here commanders and their officers could unwind and refresh themselves before preparations for their next patrol while looking out across the sea past Fort Bertheaume towards Camaret. In Brest itself the Hotel Café Astoria, among other Breton establishments, quickly became a social centre for U-boat men.

Naval activity was constant in these waters, much as it had been before German occupation. The headquarters of the Kriegsmarine's 3rd *Sicherungsdivision* was located at Trez-Hir for a brief period, responsible for the day-to-day operations of its various naval units in the region. These included two flotillas stationed directly in Brest itself, *7. Vorpostenflottille* and *40. Minensuchflottille*, both of whom U-boat men would become very familiar

---

[42] Following an unsuccessful attempt to land two Irish agents near Smerwick Harbour, County Kerry, KK Hans-Gerrit von Stockhausen had put in first of all to Lorient on the 19th, transferring to Brest three days later for minor work to be completed aboard his boat. The espionage operation had been aborted after General Sean Russell, Chief of Staff of the IRA, died aboard the submarine enroute on 14 August 1940 from a bleeding stomach ulcer. His partner Frank Ryan returned to Germany.

with as the patrol boats and minesweepers escorted German submarines in and out of Brest harbour. Further leisure facilities, nicknamed the 'U-boat meadows', were initially provided at Kerguillo north-west of Brest before relocation to the estate of Château de Trévarez, inland among rolling Breton farmland overlooking the small town of Châteauneuf de Faou. This red brick structure, built in the late 19th and early 20th century by then-Member of Parliament Marquis de Kerjégu, towered over sumptuous grounds that again allowed the opportunity for submariners, and more often than not their lady friends or 'wives', to unwind in more pleasant surroundings than naval barracks. Similar facilities were also provided in the beautiful Château de Rosmorduc, situated on the water's edge near the small village of Logonna, south of Brest on the small Daoulas Peninsular. Paul Helmchen, *EObermaschinist* (Senior Electric Motor Artificer) aboard *U441*, remembered:

> 'For we submariners the stay in Brest, both in the French naval instal-
> lation and at the so-called 'U-boat meadows', was quite agreeable.
> These 'submarine meadows' were used by the personnel for a period of
> recuperation after combat trips, and were in beautiful houses under the
> best care, often by French personnel.'

As Germany's U-boat men began to operate from Brest their boats were hidden from British aerial reconnaissance beneath large camouflage nets at the base of the winding Penfeld River. With originally only seven or eight U-boats to contend with, these mooring facilities had proved adequate, but could not cope indefinitely. Coupled with expanding flotilla strength was increased attention from RAF Bomber Command. During December 1940 Brest had played host to heavy cruiser *Admiral Hipper* attracting unwanted air raids on the port and city.

One week after her departure Brest harbour was host to two more large warships. Escorted by three *Sperrbrecher* and two *Torpedoboote*, the battleships *Scharnhorst* and *Gneisenau* arrived after a successful raiding patrol in the North Atlantic. These two majestic ships, commanded by Kapt. Kurt Caesar Hoffman and Kapt. Otto Fein respectively, had sunk twenty-two enemy vessels (totalling 115,622 BRT) during their fruitful mission 'Operation Berlin'. *Gneisenau* was first to arrive, passing Pointe de Petit Minou at 0700hrs on 22 March 1941. For routine maintenance she carefully manoeuvred into Basin Number 8 at Lanninon. Later that afternoon her sister-ship, suffering from recurring engine trouble, also steamed into the *Rade de Brest*.

The British Admiralty finally discovered their whereabouts on 27 March with the aid of a coded message from newly recruited French Resistance member Jean Philippon, code-named 'Hilaron'. Philippon had previously been the second officer on French submarine *Ouessant*, scuttled before the Germans' arrival, at Post 4 in the Penfeld on 18 June 1940. Following the occupation, he continued to work under the armistice arrangements within the confines of the Arsenal and so had access to exact locations for the

German ships, and, by extension, so did the RAF. British bombers began a long series of heavy air raids against the two battleships, one of which resulted in an unexploded bomb lying malevolently beneath the docked *Gneisenau*. The decision was made to move *Gneisenau* from her perilous position, so she was temporarily moored in the harbour, without the benefit of extensive torpedo net protection. It was a target too tempting for the British to miss. On 6 April 1941, Coastal Command's 22 Squadron, based at St Eval in Cornwall, ordered six aircraft to attack her with a mixture of torpedoes and mines.

However, the elements conspired against the British and only a solitary Beaufort, flown by Flying Officer Kenneth Campbell, reached Brest. In a suicidal attack that resulted in the death of aircraft and crew the *Gneisenau* was hit by torpedo and severely damaged by a breach in the stern hull, flooding generator and turbine housings.

The capital ships' presence in Brest had caused more complications to Dönitz's U-boat operations than just Allied bombing. In order to repair the initial problems suffered during 'Operation Berlin', and bomb damage during subsequent raids, over 800 U-boat maintenance personnel had been transferred to Brest from the Atlantic ports in order to start work on the powerful surface ships. Dönitz protested strongly, but ineffectually, to OKM regarding this redirection of manpower. His words went unheeded and consequently refitting and repair of front line U-boats suffered long delays. The number of boats available for patrols fell alarmingly.

Movement of the damaged *Gneisenau* from harbour to dry dock for extensive renovation triggered further heavy Allied air raids launched against the port. As a result of one such raid on 11 April, made by a combined force of Blenheim, Wellington and Manchester aircraft from eight different squadrons, a bomb again hit the ship, killing seventy-eight sailors and causing further ruin on board.

During the spring of 1941 another heavy cruiser appeared in Brest. The *Prinz Eugen*, commanded by Kapt. Helmuth Brinkmann, had left Gotenhafen on 18 May, with the battleship *Bismarck*, for the disastrous 'Operation Rheinübung'.

The presence of three large warships in Brest during June 1941 provoked a renewed surge in bombing of the city just as the first U-boats began to arrive. The *Prinz Eugen* was next to be hit, killing fifty men and immobilizing her for repair. Only the *Scharnhorst* was able to leave Brest during July, for exercises near La Rochelle. However, she was not to remain unscathed and returned to Brest suffering a 7° list to starboard after being hit in a bombing attack, codenamed 'Operation Sunrise', by nine RAF 35 Squadron Halifax bombers.

The cumulative effect of these escalating raids against Brest military harbour was the confirmation of the necessity to provide shelter for boats of the 1st U-Flotilla or risk needless damage and operational problems. The decision to build safe enclosed bunkers for anchorage and maintenance work was hurried into effect. These bunkers were huge construction projects, involving hundreds of *Organisation Todt* workers and French labourers, which took years to finish. They provided safe docks and points of repair for the German submarines, as well as a constant target for the Allied Air Forces. Oddly the British made no real effort to attack the bunkers during their vulnerable construction process, but then expended considerable energy making ineffectual attacks after their completion.

Brest's U-boat pens began construction on the seafront of Lanninon at the beginning of 1941 before the arrival of 1st U-Flotilla. Positioned on what had once served as a seaplane base for the French Navy, Base des Quatre Pompes, this single huge structure would eventually measure 333m long, 192m wide and 17m high, covering a total of 5,200 m². The first stage of its construction included thirteen pens, the westernmost five coded from A to E, the remainder 1 to 8. Those pens with a letter designation were able easily to enclose two submarines: pens A through C were 115m long by 17m wide; the remaining two pens were each only 96m long. The enclosures with a numeric designation were dry docks (96m long and 11m wide) where repair and inspection of U-boats could safely be conducted. The final addition to the pen complex came with two larger dry docks, labelled 9 and 11, each 114m long by 14m wide. The completed U-boat bunkers' energy needs were supplied by electricity from generators housed beneath yet more thick concrete immediately on the ridge behind the pens.

Carved into this granite ridge to the bunker's rear were subterranean stores for various services: marine artillery maintenance and servicing was in the hands of FK Bruno Glüer; the *Marineoberbaurat* (Ing) Witt, Kaye and Ehrenberg handled naval construction; while torpedoes were the domain of Kptlt. (T) Walter Elbe, chief of *Torpedo-Kommando Brest*. Further underground areas west of the pens atop a small rounded hillock functioned as fuel reservoirs, store depots for torpedoes and mines and command bunkers. The first portions of the actual U-boat bunker itself were operational by the end of 1941, though it was only completed after 1,562 Organisation Todt workers and 8,458 French labourers had poured an enormous 256,950m³ of cement, over the course of two years.

19 June: Cohausz recorded with some satisfaction the state of his Flotilla in Brest:

> 'Flotilla Chief reports completed move and operational readiness at Brest to *Vizeadmiral* Dönitz, BdU. Base is completely ready; for the time being the dock can only take two boats, then up to seven boats after running in machinery in the extra shifts.'

Meanwhile, in Lorient *U556* departed for the North Atlantic on its first patrol from France. Rested and refreshed, the crew dressed in gleaming new leathers took the salute of their comrades and nearby Staff Officers in the grounds of Dönitz's headquarters villa before their diesels took them out into Biscay.

22 June: On land in central Europe the war exploded horrifically to a new level of violence. With dawn beginning to edge its way onto the eastern horizon, morning's crystalline peace was shattered by the blast of massed artillery and thundering aircraft. 'Operation Barbarossa, Hitler's long cherished attack on the Soviet Union, was unleashed. He had always stated that his U-boats were Germany's 'first line of *defence*' allowing land forces to proceed with the 'necessary' destruction of Bolshevism. This statement in itself reveals something of the attitude that Hitler had toward his U-boat arm. In truth the U-boat was an offensive weapon and perhaps held Germany's greatest chance of victory against the Western Allies if allowed sufficient strength in which to assault enemy convoys. Had Hitler concentrated on achieving this goal before turning his attention to the east, the war's outcome could conceivably have been very different. As it was, from the massive manpower and material pouring from German recruiters and construction yards, U-boats again did not receive the priority they had been promised and so desperately needed. Dönitz, and his superior, Raeder, knew that above all else they must have more submarines. Irrespective of the failure to obtain them, however, his men fought on.

U83, 1st U-Flotilla's sole Type VIIB U-boat, under the command of Kptlt. Hans-Werner Kraus finished its Baltic shakedown. Moored again in Kiel, final adjustments and treatment for rust would take over a month to complete before she was ready for her first combat patrol (*Feindfahrt*). Secured nearby was Kptlt. Hans Heidtmann's *U559*, which three days later slipped from Kiel to begin her active service. Destined eventually for the North Atlantic Heidtmann was initially ordered with *U79* to support the breakout attempt through the Denmark Strait by the German cruiser *Lützow*. The latter U-boat had been at sea since 5 June, her commander Kptlt. Wolfgang Kaufman cruising for little reward in the North Atlantic. Ordered to join *U559* she journeyed back toward Denmark.

Both boats were relieved of this mission after *Lützow*'s attempt at running the tight Allied blockade failed during the night of 12/13 June. Kaufmann's *U79* then proceeded to sink an opportune steamer target west of Reykjavik on the 12th, the Norwegian SS *Havtor*'s 1,524 tons opening *U79*'s score, which Kaufmann endeavoured to increase as part of a four-day operation against convoy HX133, 450 miles south of Greenland's Cape Farewell. On 27 June, during the course of this convoy interception, *U79* caused heavy damage to the Dutch tanker *Tibia* with a single torpedo strike after which the crash-diving U-boat was subjected to a short sharp hunt by destroyer HMCS *Ottawa* and corvette HMCS *Chambly*. Kaufmann abandoned his attack and sailed for home. Early the following month, on 5 July, *U79* put into her new base at Lorient. The same day, miles to the south,

U559 sailed into Saint Nazaire's harbour, brown waters from the Loire washing around her hull. Heidtmann had achieved no victories during his cruise.

26 June: Kptlt. Walter Kell approached his new port of Brest while a low haze of summer dust hung above precipitate cliffs crowned with flat land and occasional small whitewashed houses. Ouessant Island passed to the port of the submarine and Pointe Saint Mathieu glided into view, marking the outer part of the Brest entrance channel. The boat glided onwards, acknowledged by waving troops stationed alongside either channel face in new concrete artillery emplacements. Kell rested easy in his conning tower, quietly observing his men for any lapses of concentration as they began to unwind from the rigours of patrol. Finally Brest and the Penfeld River anchorage hove into view. Ordering his crew to assemble on the stern casing apart from those involved in mooring or duties below deck, Kell watched critically as the First Officer docked his boat. Ashore, a crowd of fellow officers, uniformed female auxiliaries and nurses waited to greet the U-boat's crew. *U204*, her hull streaked and dirty, adding natural colours to her daubed camouflage paint, tied up against the old French submarine mooring posts beneath the ancient walls of *la Château de Brest*. The battered U-boat flew only a single pennant marked with the number 8,000. Kell's claim was very close to the mark, his sinking of the Belgian SS *Mercier* rated at 7,886 tons as part of the *Kurfürst* Wolf Pack the sole victory of *U204*'s first sortie. Three days after his arrival Kell stood before Dönitz for BdU's customary debriefing. By personally interviewing his commanders and asking explanation for each entry in the U-boat's War Diary, Dönitz was able to form an accurate picture of how his men were faring in action. He was also constantly searching for anything that betrayed a lack of aggressiveness on behalf of a commander, anxious to maintain a high fighting spirit in the U-boat service.

27 June: The War Diary of 1st U-Flotilla recorded the inaugural use of its facilities:

> 'The U-Support Station of the 1st U-Flotilla in Brest has received its first Front boat and hence fulfilled its actual purpose. The base, as it stands, is ready for 15 U-boats, the dock currently for two to three boats, thereafter six, and then more later.'

1 July: The 1st U-boat Flotilla continued to settle into its new Breton surroundings. Facilities were being arranged for the billeting of its personnel.

> 'Division Reimer assigns, as a new replacement for Huelgoat [previously occupied billet], U-boat quarters for the 1st U-Flotilla at: Grand Hotel, Cape Coz near Beg Meil.
> Thus on 1/VII, the Flotilla has:

1. Quarters/Brignogan with 1 Hotel, 5 houses and 1 warehouse for supplies
2. Quarters/St Anne with 5 houses
3. Quarters/Locronan with 1 Hotel (*L'Auberge St Renan*) and Annexe
4. Quarters/Gormodet with 1 Hotel
5. Quarters/Cape Coz with 1 Hotel
6. Warehouse for supplies in Le Bourget.'

U371 arrived during the mid-afternoon, sailing into Brest's military harbour after nearly a full month at sea. It was the second Flotilla boat to dock in Brest and had been delayed due to poor visibility near the coastline. Her crew tied their U-boat's ropes under the attentive eye of Kptlt. Driver. Their first patrol had been rewarded with two ships sunk, claiming 17,000 BRT. (There is still no confirmation of their first victim, recorded in Driver's War Diary as a 'large ship' sunk on 12 June, while their second was from convoy HX133, the Norwegian SS *Vigrid* of 4,765 tons). In fact *U371* had sunk a further vessel from this convoy, though having been unable to confirm its destruction only claimed the ship as damaged.

Two days later when Driver made his report to Dönitz at Lorient he received a stern reprimand, not the expected congratulations. In his eagerness for combat Driver had travelled to his operational area surfaced and at high speed. So when *U371* engaged convoy HX133 her fuel bunkers were already seriously depleted. Driver was compelled to disengage prematurely and carry home most of his torpedoes when what fuel remaining for combat had been exhausted and only enough for the return journey remained. While displaying an aggressive spirit, this action lacked elementary common sense, a vital component in a U-boat commander's character. The young captain returned to Brest considerably chastened by his Commander-in-Chief.

Further south another of 1st U-Flotilla's submarines eased into Saint Nazaire during the course of the day. Her commander, Kptlt. Rolf Mützelberg, claimed 24,000 BRT sunk from convoy HX133 during this, his first patrol as commander. His boat had, more significantly, come very close to upsetting the delicate balance of power between increasingly aggressive American warships and U-boat commanders eager to attack them.

The United States of America had been treading a wary path through pro-British neutrality. During the previous April President Roosevelt had extended the so-called American Security Zone in the North Atlantic to include waters west of 26° longtitude. This effectively put US warships in places where U-boats operated against convoy shipping. Although strictly bound by international law, their presence was a definite threat to German submariners. Frequently American ships that had detected a U-boat would shadow the submarine while directing British forces towards its location. On 21 May 1941 *U69* of 7th U-Flotilla torpedoed and sank SS *Robin Moor*, the first American merchant casualty of the Second World War. The U-boat's commander had made a careful decision after stopping the ship and examining her papers. Carrying a load of arms and aircraft parts to Allied Cape Town she was a legitimate target and once all crew had evacuated the ship *U69* sank her. President Roosevelt consequently froze German and Italian assets in the USA. During July US troops relieved the British garrison stationed in Iceland and began running American supply convoys, escorted by US warships from the States, to this new outpost. Of course an invitation was extended to other ships that they may join the convoys if desired. The line between neutrality and belligerence shrank even further. The 'Neutrality Patrol' of large cruisers and destroyers roved over America's Security Zone virtually inviting challenge. On 20 June it received one.

Kptlt. Mützelberg (previously Watch Officer of Schepke's *U100*) was patrolling Germany's proclaimed 'free-fire' zone between Iceland and Greenland when he sighted a large cruiser surrounded by destroyer screen. In heavy Atlantic swell *U203* crept closer to the ships, zigzagging at least 10 miles within the blockade zone. Mützelberg finally was able to identify his quarry as the American cruiser USS *Texas*, darkened and steering a hostile course as if on war patrol. He deliberated for some time on this unexpectedly delicate situation before ordering his navigator to plot an intercept. He would close to attack. *Texas* was within sea-space where all 'non-friendly' shipping risked attack and destruction. What's more she appeared to be adopting a warlike posture with her course and escorts. Still it was not a decision to take lightly and Mützelberg ordered a message sent to BdU:

> 'Have sighted U.S. battleship *Texas* in blockade area. Ask permission to shoot. *U203*'

Other U-boats having intercepted the message waited in anticipation of the answer. America's increasingly aggressive warships were a constant threat to U-boats on patrol and opinion was generally in favour of an attack. There was no immediate reply and *U203* continued the chase. After 16 hours and 140 nautical miles Mützelberg attempted to contact BdU again, this time generating an instant response:

> 'By order of the Führer all incidents with United States ships must be avoided in the coming weeks. Until further notice, attacks may not be made on battleships, cruisers and aircraft carriers unless definitely identified as hostile. Warships steaming at night without lights are not necessarily hostile.'

This order was relayed to all U-boats and U-boat commands. By clamping such a restriction on commanders at sea, U-boat attacks on unidentified darkened warships were no longer permissible until absolute confirmation of the opponent's identity was ascertained. While this may appear logical in a conference room, in the rolling North Atlantic swells it was exceedingly difficult at best.

Mützelberg broke off his attack approach in mounting seas and proceeded west to his original patrol area. So far his journey had proved disappointing. However, in early morning darkness of 23 June *U203* encountered convoy HX133 south of Greenland. During the next two days he stalked and attacked the lumbering convoy torpedoing four ships for a claimed 24,000 BRT (in fact *U203*'s definite victims were MV *Solöy*, MV *Kinross* and SS *Schie* for a total of 11,325 tons). As Mützelberg was debriefed by 'The Lion' at Lorient on 29 June, Dönitz sternly lectured the commander about his 'attempted attack' on USS *Texas*. Also, although Dönitz was satisfied with *U203*'s patrol he noted what he considered to be Mützelberg's precipitate withdrawal from action against convoy HX133. While acting as contact boat for the convoy Mützelberg had prematurely attacked the convoy despite standing orders to wait until a group had assembled and had been authorized by BdU to make a concentrated attack. Despite sinking two freighters, Mützelberg was forced early on to abort with damage to a muffler valve, leaving Dönitz fuming in Kernavel at the loss of his contact boat during the critical period of pack assembly. However, on 1 July Mützelberg, who had at least displayed a thirst for combat, was presented with an array of decorations: Iron Cross First and Second Class and his U-boat combat badge (*U-Bootskriegsabzeichen*).

2 July: '*U331* leaves from U-Support Station Kiel for front-line service'

Kptlt. Hans-Diedrich von Tiesenhausen began what turned out to be an unsuccessful patrol from Kiel to Lorient. The twenty-eight-year-old commander, who had accompanied Kretschmer on three patrols aboard *U23* as First Officer, was now embarking on his first combat patrol in command of a U-boat. Following a failed attempt to intercept convoy OB 346, sighted by a KG40 *Kondor* on 17 July, *U331* proceeded to Spain where she crept into Cadiz harbour during the night of 1 August. Moored in the neutral anchorage was a German ship that had been interned by Spanish authorities. In actual fact her internment had been a deliberate Kriegsmarine act, the ship *Thalia* carrying supplies of food, fuel and ammunition for U-boats. Von Tiesenhausen cautiously moored alongside *Thalia* and under cover of darkness began recharging his boat.

The remainder of *U331*'s patrol passed with neither serious mishap nor victory. Repeated attempts to attack Gibraltar convoy HG 69 were driven off by strong escort counterattack. Finally on 19 August *U331* secured her lines in Lorient where she was temporarily placed under the command of 2nd U-Flotilla.

6 July: Brest suffered from further heavy Allied air raids. During the night 6/7 July RAF bombers attempted once again to hit the three large German warships in harbour. Headquarters of 1st U-Flotilla received bomb damage from two direct hits while Kell's *U204* also suffered from the effects of two hits on her immediate dockside.

Flotilla vessels continued to come and go at France's Atlantic bases throughout July. This was the mid-point in what many consider the second phase of the Battle of the Atlantic. Dönitz's *Rüdeltaktik* had begun to take effect, BdU directly coordinating large packs of U-boats by wireless transmission against convoys anticipated from aerial reconnaissance or *B-Dienst* intercepts. Finally there were nearly enough U-boats operating from France for large groups to be formed as advanced patrol lines across the expected merchant route. Luftwaffe *Kondor* aircraft began to attack enemy shipping and direct U-boats to sightings, although with less success than hoped for. Exact navigation was required from aircrews as well as instant notification of sightings. Often *Kondor* crews were as much as 80 miles out from their reckoned position and sometimes only radioed ship sightings to BdU after departing the area completely. Submarine conning towers were not high enough to provide a distant horizon line of sight to make up for these errors.

Italian submarines of the BETASOM base in Bordeaux had begun to operate within Biscay. U-boats were ordered to ensure that suspected British submarine sightings were confirmed before attacking (Italian and British submarines bore a striking resemblance from a distance), while at sea warships also had to be clearly identified for fear of attacking an American ship. America, though having edged ever closer to open hostility with Germany, still failed to take the final step.

However, sinkings by U-boats had tailed off in July. Although U-boats were moving out from Kiel to reinforce front-line boats, using Dönitz's own theory that only one third of operational boats could be at sea at any one time, the remainder in repair or resupply, there simply were not enough available for a full onslaught against British shipping. War with Russia ensured that this situation would not alter in the immediate future. On 15 July Dönitz recorded in the BdU War Diary:

> '*U201* is returning. The boat has been assigned an unlimited operational area since 29 June and has sighted nothing. The problem of finding the enemy is always the most difficult one. Only when the number of boats is larger and there are more of them to keep a lookout, will the situation become more favourable.'[43]

A harsher judgement was conferred by BdU on ObltzS. Hans-Heinz Linder on 24 July, the day following his arrival in Brest with *U202*, freshly transferred from Kiel. Dönitz's brief notation within the BdU War Diary stated:

> 'ObltzS. Linder made several tactical errors on this his first operation. He sighted little and had no success.'

[43] Schnee's *U201* had been part of the disastrous attack on HX133 until 28 June when he was driven off after having made no attacks. His U-boat achieved nothing in five weeks of patrol.

27 July: KK Hans Cohausz was finally able to enter good news into his War Diary. Amid U-boat arrivals with no victories and escalating air raids on Brest he refers to *U564*'s arrival as 'a sunbeam in these bleak times!' Indeed Oblt.z.S. Reinhard Suhren's first patrol from Kiel to Brest had claimed four ships for 21,500 BRT. Sailing into Brest harbour at 2000hrs *U564*'s crew received a rapturous welcome from the banks of the Penfeld. Cohausz was first aboard, grasping Suhren's hand in congratulations at his success. In fact *U564*, with a single bow salvo on 27 June, had sunk SS *Maasdam*, MV *Malay II* and damaged MV *Kongsgaard*, all from convoy HX133, as well as sinking two days later SS *Hekla*, sailing independently. This totalled a respectable 18,678 tons sunk and a further 9,467 tons damaged for the U-boat's first patrol. Within the Naval Academy headquarters there were celebrations at last. Following Dönitz's meeting with Suhren he recorded in the BdU War Diary that regarding *U564*'s patrol, the commander had 'carried it out with skill and courage'.

The following day Cohausz departed for a meeting with BdU Ops regarding the suspected sinking of both *U556* and *U651*. In his brief absence Mützelberg returned on 31 July from a second patrol in *U203* with another 31,000 tons strung in pennants from his periscope. His patrol and action against southbound OG69 convoy west of Ireland was recorded in the flotilla's War Diary as:

> 'One of the most successful boats out of the flotilla at yesterday's convoy (30/VII) when 76,000t were destroyed.'

The added honour of being the first U-boat to officially enter the Saint Nazaire pens was also bestowed upon Mützelberg and his crew. Following a stirring speech from Dönitz, made in the presence of several ranking Kriegsmarine officers and Fritz Todt, *U203* motored gently into its concrete basin with pennants flying. While the commander celebrated his continued success other boats were consigned to more mundane times: Oblt.z.S. Herwig Collman's *U562* docking in Lorient with heavy *Wabo* damage and a poetically disgusted line against its name in the War Diary:

> 'No smile from the God of War for this boat either, *Keine Tonnen!*' ('no tonnage!').

The War Diary entry records that the boat was literally 'showered with depth charges'. On the same day of Collman's entry to Brest, in the frigid waters of Norway *U84* transferred from Bergen to Trondheim for minor rust treatment before her maiden patrol.

The sphere of operations was now extended for 1st U-Flotilla. In the frozen wastes of the Barents Sea *U566* and 3rd U-Flotilla's *U451* became the first German submarines to patrol the Kola coast. This was the future battleground of the Arctic convoys and marked the northern front line against Germany's new foe, Russia. There were no immediate results and lookouts suffered freezing conditions in their vigil for enemy shipping and icebergs.

1 August: Kptlt. Robert Bartels completed his first war patrol as commander of *U561*. Slipping into Brest harbour Bartels claimed 16,000 BRT sunk (in reality only the 1,884-ton SS *Wrotham* from convoy OG 69 west of Ireland). The return of the U-boat was cause for celebration as 1st U-Flotilla's War Diary continued its poetic flow with more references to the God of War:

> 'Mars has shown us his countenance again.'

3 August: Resting inside the pages of the War Diary are many slips of paper cabled from BdU for 1st U-Flotilla's commander's attention. This date marks the first of them. Clear and concise it reads:

> '*U401 zwei Stern. Totalverlust.*' (*U401* two stars. Total loss).

From summer 1941 onward BdU would forward its own summary of U-boat losses for inclusion in the flotilla's War Diary, continuing to use the one and two star system. This particular reference had arrived at 1st U-Flotilla head-quarters on 11 November 1941 and been retrospectively attached to the corresponding date of loss. *U401*, commanded by Kptlt. Gero Zimmermann, had departed Trondheim on 9 July bound for the North Atlantic and in due course Brest. Their first patrol lasted into August, Zimmermann and fifteen other boats unsuccessfully attempting to intercept convoy OB 346. On 1 August *U401* and seven others were directed to the location of convoy SL 81 by flotilla mate *U204*. This particular convoy had a strong escort and on 3 August as Zimmermann approached he was quickly located by ASDIC and depth-charged out of existence by destroyers HMS *Wanderer* and HMS *St. Albans* teamed with frigate HMS *Hydrangea*. There were no survivors. The German U-boat was last seen by *U205* while under its final attack from above. Convoy SL 81's effective escort ships managed to keep the circling U-boats at bay until 5 August when they finally penetrated the defences and sank five ships before being driven off. It was a hard-won score for the U-boats.

The presumed loss of Kptlt. Wohlfarth's *U556* was also finally acknowl-edged. Knight's Cross holder Wohlfarth had departed Lorient on 19 June for the North Atlantic. Aboard the U-boat was prospective commander Kptlt. Franz Rolinck accompanying Wohlfarth in order to gain experience for his own future command. While converging with other boats on convoy HX133 south of Greenland, *U556* was located and attacked on 27 June. The U-boat's final assault had begun in dense early morning fog, when lookouts atop her conning tower heard but could not see their quarry. Following a bearing toward their suspected prey, the mist suddenly parted to reveal columns of freighters nearly on top of the U-boat. *U556* dived rapidly and continued her approach.

Convoy HX133 comprised forty-three ships grouped in nine columns, making approximately 8.5 knots in a heavy swell. A ten-corvette escort prowled the convoy's flanks in search of danger. By the morning of 27 June two ships had already been lost from the convoy and at least three U-boats were believed to be in contact. In fact ten U-boats were briefly in contact at one time or another, *U71*, *U79*, *U201*, *U371*, *U552*, *U556*, *U562*, *U564*, and *U651*, all guided to the lumbering Allied ships by Kptlt. Mützelberg in *U203* before his rash decision to attack. At 0735hrs 'Flower' class corvette HMS *Nasturtium*, stationed on the convoy's port quarter, attained an ASDIC contact 1,200 yards to starboard, only 500 yards from the convoy flank. Investigating, Lt Cdr R.C. Freaker ordered two charges dropped on the suspected contact. Visibility was approximately 2,000 yards as the corvette returned to its station. Less than an hour later Freaker's ASDIC operator reported contact regained, stronger and more definite this time. HMS *Nasturtium* raced again to the attack, dropping all her remaining charges set for 100, 150, 250, 350 and 500 feet. The U-boat in question, *U556*, was rocked by the accurate explosions and all lighting immediately failed. Emergency lighting aboard *U556* bathed the submarine in an eerie glow, augmented by phosphorous paint applied to many surfaces on board. Wohlfarth knew he had been detected and believed that couplings from his port motor, unsatisfactorily adjusted before departure from Lorient and knocking loudly, had betrayed his presence. During the U-boat's previous overhaul in Lorient the cooling system had been poorly repaired and, since commissioning, diesel cylinder heads and jets had given constant trouble. It now appeared that mechanical problems had been the U-boat's undoing. Wohlfarth ordered the knocking electric motor stopped but water entered the still-turning starboard motor following their savage depth-charging, causing a short circuit. Wohlfarth had little choice but to restart his port motor.

Above Wohlfarth HMS *Nasturtium* could only circle in frustration, empty of depth charges after expending her full complement of forty-one. Freaker summoned two other corvettes of the convoy escort and despite their having no contact with their own detection systems, HMS *Celandine* and HMS *Gladiolus* were led over *U556* by HMS *Nasturtium* in further attacks.[44] Freaker's ship indicated the aiming point by applying full rudder when over the target. Aboard the two other corvettes there was some doubt about the reported contact. Lt Cdr H.M.C. Sanders aboard *Gladiolus* radioed:

'Are you sure about contact? It seems strange we cannot get anything.'

To which a definite and confident Freaker replied:

'Wish you could see my recorder trace.'

[44] HMS *Gladiolus* was the first 'Flower' class corvette to be launched by England, reaching the water on 24 January 1940.

At 1100hrs *Celandine* dropped a ten-charge pattern rewarded with traces of oil drifting to the surface. Aboard the struggling U-boat, panic began to grip the crew. According to Allied Intelligence reports regarding the U-boat sinking and reportedly gleaned from German survivors, two wild-eyed men rushed into the shattered control room demanding that they surface before being driven back to their posts by an armed Midshipman (*Fähnrich zur See*).[45] The stern torpedo room began to take on water through the tube and hope faded in a creeping cloud of chlorine gas. Wohlfarth decided in desperation to go to periscope depth either to launch an attack against his tormentors or, if possible, run for it surfaced.

Finally, aboard HMS *Gladiolus* a firm ASDIC contact was obtained at 2,000 yards and she raced to attack with ten charges set at 150 and 385 feet. Amidst the churned water huge pools of oil began to gush from below. *U556* was doomed. As the corvette turned for another attack the crippled submarine broke surface at a steep angle under her starboard bow; Wohlfarth had lost control of his ascent. She surfaced so close to the corvette that one depth charge hit her casing and rebounded into the sea. Immediately coming under intense fire from two of the attacking corvettes, the crew abandoned ship.[46] During the helter-skelter evacuation a single 4' shell penetrated the conning tower, killing one of the fleeing crewmen. *Matrosengefreiter* Peter Wimmer, one of the last men to leave *U556*, remembered:

> 'Quickly I climbed up to the hatch. I knew the way by heart. This was my territory. Many times I had ascended those two ladders or, during an alarm, slid down them. After me two others followed. The helmsman was one of them. I propped myself against the iron hatch. I almost had the feeling I was the captain. Normally this was his duty. But I could only open it a small crack. A heavy object must have been laying on it. Together, with all our might, we were able to push the object to the side. It was the body of one of the diesel engine mates, who was hit waist high by a projectile from a cannon which ricocheted from the shaft of the telescope. Good for him he was dead, because we would have removed him by any means, no matter how loud he would have moaned from pain.'

HMS *Nasturtium* was by this time closing to ram the U-boat, although her commander realized that this was no longer necessary and veered away at the final moment. *U556* slowly began to settle by the bow as she sank, her battered conning tower disappearing beneath a calm Atlantic sea moments after a

---

[45] This has not been confirmed by other sources. *Matrosengefreiter* Peter Wimmer remembers nobody carrying a pistol aboard the U-boat and nobody by the name given for the Midshipman (Urbanski) in the Allied Anti-Submarine Warfare Report.

[46] On board a U-boat the captain was the first to ascend to the bridge when abandoning ship, but often the last to actually leave the boat after having assured all his men were off.

British boarding party had abandoned their attempt to enter the U-boat. Only minutes after surfacing the boat was gone, sliding under from a ruptured hull and leaving forty-one men bobbing in the cold Atlantic. The victors picked up Wohlfarth and his surviving crew. Through positive confirmation via the International Red Cross of which crew members had been rescued, BdU surmised that five men went to the bottom: her engineering officer Oblt. (Ing) Körner, Petty Officer (*Obermaat*) Linow, and three seamen, Leading Seaman (*Obermatrose*) Freitag, Seamen (*Matrose*) Faust and Winkelmann. (One of the men had lived for several hours aboard his British captor's ship but died as a result of lung damage from chlorine gas). In subsequent Allied intelligence reports the British surmised that the majority of Wohlfarth's crew were 'poor material', although it is now difficult for researchers to determine to what level wartime bias was allowed within these reports, as they bear no resemblance to the recollections of those aboard the U-boat. Officers were similarly found to be 'relatively inept, with reliance on experienced Chief and Petty Officers'. However, the ship's First Watch Officer Lt.z.S. Hans Schaefer was described as a 'thoroughly efficient' officer.

The battle of HX133 was not over, however. Following *U556*'s sinking the Canadian-controlled escorts departed to be replaced by British Escort Group 12. U-boats continued to give chase. During the early morning of 29 June Kptlt. Peter Lohmeyer aboard *U651* launched his attack. Closing at periscope depth he fired two torpedoes after penetrating the destroyer screen, hitting and sinking the convoy commodore's ship SS *Grayburn* laden with 10,000 tons of steel. Within four minutes the 6,342-ton ship had gone. Unfortunately for Lohmeyer a brief lapse of concentration allowed the next ship in the convoy column, tanker *Anandara*, to ram the stern of the still submerged U boat, throwing her momentarily out of control and weakening her structurally, although not rupturing the tough welded pressure hull.

Escorts, destroyer HMS *Scimitar* and minesweeper HMS *Speedwell*, began randomly dropping charges before gaining a firm contact on Lohmeyer and concentrating their attack. Bursting depth charges pulverized *U651*; her number three ballast tank was damaged, water began penetrating the aft torpedo room, depth gauges burst showering the control room with water and glass and all lighting failed. Lohmeyer's boat was paying the price for her weakened hull following the collision with *Anadara*. The U-boat began to flood quickly and slid to a terrifying 525 feet before slowed by both electric motors racing at full speed. This strain on the crippled submarine drained her batteries and Lohmeyer had no choice but to blow main ballast and rise.

As *U651* burst free of the surface she was some distance from her attackers and Lohmeyer ordered diesels started in an attempt to run. As the engines roared into life they emitted their customary burst of thick bluish-black smoke, sighted by destroyer HMS *Malcolm* five miles distant. The British Senior Officer's ship closed at high speed and could soon make out the thin conning tower of *U651*. Both A and B turrets roared their challenge as the destroyer opened fire. Soon HMS *Speedwell*, *Northern Wave*, *Arabis* and *Nasturtium* joined *Malcolm*, all five ships racing towards the fleeing U-boat with guns blazing. Slowly *Malcolm* drew ahead, closing the distance to *U651*. Cease-fire was ordered aboard the other hunters for fear of accidentally hitting the British destroyer, Cdr C.D. Howard Johnston's ship propelled to new speeds by an over-zealous Engine Room Artificer aboard who opened every valve in sight during the excitement. Aboard the running U-boat Lohmeyer recognized that there was no chance of escape from her attacker and gave the order to abandon ship and scuttle. At 1,500 yards the bridge watch of *Malcolm* could plainly see Lohmeyer's crew abandoning ship and at 0537hrs the conning tower, adorned with the words '*Heia Safari!*', disappeared for the final time. All forty-five U-boat men were rescued.

The convoy battle had been disastrous for Dönitz's men. Unbeknown to U-boat Command a contributing factor in HX133's successful defence was that British Western Approaches Command had been aware of the impending U-boat attack thanks to the newly captured and broken Enigma codes. Intercepted German U-boat radio traffic was finally able to be deciphered by British intelligence. Once the Admiralty became aware of the U-boats' dispositions, orders were issued and the convoy's route changed at the same time that ships of two separate westbound convoys received strengthened escorts. Coastal Command air patrols were directed to cover the convoy's flanks and attacking U-boats constantly forced to dive to escape bombardment, hampering their ability to assemble for a group attack. Once the attack was launched U-boats were staggered by the ferocity of their opposition and the whole operation had only resulted in six merchant ships sunk for the loss of two U-boats from a loose group of ten. The war against Germany's 'Grey Wolves' had changed irrevocably.

13 August: Kptlt. Heinz-Joachim Neumann brought *U372* into Brest after completing his transit from Trondheim via the North Atlantic. During this first operational voyage Neumann had sunk two ships from convoy SL81, SS *Belgravian* and SS *Swiftpool* totalling 8,341 tons, for a claimed 12,500 tons.

21 August: Three boats (*U86*, *U208* and *U374*) were transferred to 1st U-Flotilla from their training unit, Kiel's 5th U-Flotilla, after completing their tactical excercises. This raised the strength of 1st U-Flotilla to twenty-eight boats, three having been lost since the year's beginning (*U556*, *U651* and *U401*)

22 August: A pair of 1st Flotilla boats returned in triumph after hammering convoy OG 71. Following the dramatic failure to disrupt convoy HX133 spirits were raised when *U204*, commanded by Kptlt. Kell, and *U559* under Kptlt. Heidtmann claimed 28,000 BRT plus one destroyer, and 16,000 BRT (two steamers) respectively.

Kell had spent exactly one month on patrol, his first victory scored on 5 July when he managed to torpedo the British SS *Kumasian* from convoy SL 81 before being driven off. The escorts' ferocious tenacity prevented further success for Kell and he retreated shaken by near miss depth charges. Flotilla-mate Oblt.z.S. Adalbert Schnee aboard *U201* had transmitted homing signals from 17 August as he began to shadow OG 71 southbound from England to Gibraltar and originally spotted by a KG 40 *Kondor*. *U559* was also closing on Schnee's signal, diesels pounding the boat through rising seas. Two other U-boats approached the unwieldy convoy, *U564* of the 1st U-Flotilla one day into its patrol and 7th U-Flotilla's *U552* captained by the familiar Erich Topp.

In the early hours of the 19th *U201*, *U204* and *U559* opened the attack. Schnee torpedoed the 3,255-ton British steamer SS *Aguila*, Kell sank the 1,809-ton British steamer SS *Ciscar* and the Norwegian destroyer *Bath*, conforming to a new directive from Dönitz to attack the escorts of the Gibraltar convoys first. The Norwegian-crewed ex-American 'four-stacker', given to the Royal Navy under the Lend-Lease agreement, disintegrated rapidly beneath the hammer blow of Kell's torpedo blast. Meanwhile Heidtmann sent the 1,584-ton British steamer SS *Alva* to the deep, claiming one more sunk and another damaged. The sea south-west of Ireland was stained red with an inferno of sinking ships.

For *U204* and *U559* this was the end of their action and they began the return slog to France. The day following this first devastating attack contact was lost with the convoy and only Schnee aboard *U201* remained to doggedly search the tumbling sea. Outbound *U564* and *U552* finally reached the area and assisted in the hunt, Oblt.z.S. Suhren aboard *U564* at last glimpsing on 22 August the matchsticks of masts on the horizon and drawing his two companions in for the kill. Suhren re-opened the battle once evening had fallen. Racing into attack on the surface he torpedoed the 484-ton steam tug *Empire Oak* and 1,203-ton SS *Clonlara*. Early the next day Schnee destroyed two more ships, MV *Stork* (787 tons) and SS *Aldergrove* (1,974 tons) before breaking off to return to Brest. Suhren continued his onslaught, sinking corvette HMS *Zinnia* and damaging SS *Spind*, later finished off by Topp, as well as claiming two more unconfirmed sinkings. The concentrated *Rüdeltaktik* attack had been a spectacular success.

On the return of U-boats involved in the attack on convoy OG 71 there were mammoth celebrations held by 1st U-Flotilla in Brest. Kell brought *U204* past the majestic walls of *la Château de Brest* and under the *Recouverance* bridge, pennants flying from the periscope. Crowds gathered to watch, lining both Brest's ancient walls and nearby *Vorpostenboote* moored opposite *U204*'s berth beside the old French Armoury. A customary Kriegsmarine honour guard and band were drawn up to welcome the bearded crew and their U-boat, her conning tower painted with an enormous 'V' and the words '*on les aura*'. The boat was battered but intact as her engines spluttered to silence.

On 25 August as Schnee brought his rusty boat alongside its Penfeld dock he was greeted with exultant crowds and an equally jubilant Cohausz. Easing into his mooring near the Jean Bart gate over the Penfeld River, Schnee and his fatigued crew felt ready for their forthcoming period of leave. The rust smudges added their own layer to an already tatty camouflaged conning tower. Grey paint along the U-boat's hull was flaked and peeling, suffering from the harsh combination of abrasive Atlantic salt and enemy attack. Flanking either side of the tower were the coats of arms of the German town of Remscheid, official sponsors of *U201*. Special attention was given to Oblt.z.S. Schnee. Cohausz' War Diary lists his achievements as a personal total of 95,000 BRT sunk, 40,000 BRT while in command of the Type II *U60* during that boat's service within 1st U-Flotilla between January and November 1940.

27 August: *U564* returned from the slaughter of convoy OG 71 claiming seven ships sunk, including a corvette. The U-boat sailed into harbour to an enthusiastic reception, seven pennants, all decorated with tonnage numbers and the familiar '3 X Black Cats' logo streaming from the periscope. Suhren's reputation soared. He already wore the prestigious Knight's Cross, earned from his days before the 1st U-Flotilla.[47]

The results from the attack on convoy OG 71 reaffirmed faith among the U-boat arm in Dönitz's views of bold group attacks, prompting the 1st U-Flotilla War Diary to record:

'From conclusions drawn regarding the convoy battle in which *U201*, *U204*, *U564* and *U559* were involved, the following have proved effective:
   a. The group tactics of BdU
   b. The boats' tactic of punching into the convoy at a weak point and just as quickly retire after emptying all tubes in fan or individual shots aimed at a wider target group. The number of ships sunk is important, less so the exact tonnage.'

28 August: Dönitz arrived in Brest on his first visit to the Flotilla since its relocation to France. Two days later Schnee received notification of his award of the Knight's Cross for his considerable achievements – another 'Ace' for the 1st U-Flotilla. Schnee's was not the only decoration given. Dönitz lifted

---

[47] This award had been received on 3 November 1940 while serving as First watch Officer to Kptlt. Heinrich Bleichrodt aboard *U48*. Bleichrodt, due to be awarded his Knight's Cross on 24 October 1940, refused to wear the decoration unless Suhren received one. He correctly pointed out that as U-boat Executive Officers handled the firing of torpedoes during surface attacks Suhren had sunk over 20,000 tons of shipping during his long service aboard *U48*. Dönitz concurred and Suhren received his award.

his men's spirits by awarding several Iron Crosses First Class to men of the 1st U-Flotilla. The BdU invited his officers to exchange views and information about U-boat operations, allowing free rein of ideas to be exchanged. He galvanized his men to greater heights and provided an electric feeling of belonging to one of Germany's elite forces. During his meetings with officers, KK Hans Cohausz made his official report as Flotilla Chief. He stated that since the beginning of the war:

> 'The Flotilla, according to relevant documents, sunk more than 1,000,000 BRT, and three- quarters of this tonnage was sunk with small 250t boats.'

1 September: *'U556 Vermisst **, U651 Vermisst **'* – confirmed losses. The official record was now completed.

Further complications added themselves to Atlantic U-boat operations. During September thick fog smothered not only Brittany's ports but also hampered visibility at sea. *U83* was one of several boats that spent up to seven weeks at sea with no sightings or successes to report. Dispirited by both weather conditions and what appeared to be stronger escorts in the Atlantic, Dönitz concentrated his boats on the Greenland coast where he believed more and more Allied convoys were passing, often under American escort. On 4 September *U652* of Kiel's 3rd U-Flotilla attacked destroyer USS *Greer* after some provocation. The American promptly dropped depth charges on the orders of US Destroyer Division 5's commander. Although neither side suffered casualties the incident caused a further escalation of American-German tension. On 11 September Roosevelt declared that US Naval units would protect all Atlantic convoys and added in a national radio broadcast:

> 'In waters we deem necessary to our own safety American warships and planes will no longer wait until Axis submarines lurking under the water, or Axis raiders on the surface of the sea, strike their deadly blow first.'

Following this broadcast USS *Bellknap* began to keep a War Diary, the first ship of the United States Navy to do so and four months before war was declared.

Roosevelt's words clearly had an effect on both Raeder and Dönitz. They flew to Hitler's East Prussian headquarters at Rastenburg on 17th September to attempt to persuade Hitler to remove restrictions on engaging American shipping. The Führer was not to be budged. He firmly believed that his Russian campaign would reach a climax in mid-September and refused to lift his order until mid-October at the earliest.

Despite this rebuff Dönitz prepared a fresh North Atlantic offensive before the harsh winter made operations difficult. Seventeen U-boats were strung between Greenland and Iceland combing the sea for expected convoy HX150. The fifty-one heavily laden ships managed to slip through the cordon thanks to earlier ULTRA intercepts but, due to bad weather conditions and a sudden, but routine, change in Kriegsmarine Enigma ciphers requiring time to crack, sixty-four ships of the following convoy SC 42 were neither able to reroute or evade waiting U-boats of the freshly deployed *Markgraf* pack. *U85* of the 3rd U-Flotilla provided an initial homing signal after sighting SC 42 sixty miles from Cape Farewell. BdU immediately began to coordinate a pack attack scheduled for that night for six U-boats of the fourteen-strong pack within striking distance. Dönitz exhorted his commanders by radio from Kerneval:

'This convoy must not get through. U-boats pursue, attack and sink.'

In the days that followed sixteen ships were sunk by the boats, including 1,980-ton Swede SS *Scania* on 11 September by *U202*. Kptlt. Hans-Heinz Linder took his U-boat into Brest harbour on 17 September flying two pennants from the commander's flagstaff, one for his Swedish victim (claiming 2,000 tons) and one for the British fishing vessel *Lady Love* torpedoed on 27 August.

Kptlt. Heinz-Otto Schultze's *U432* on her first war patrol also formed part of the *Markgraf* group. When the battle was over and Schultze sailed into the placid waters of the Penfeld on 19 September *U432* flew four pennants from her periscope, 10,778 tons of enemy shipping, and carried only one remaining torpedo. Alongside *U432* at 1400hrs was a further U-boat from the battle. *U81* finished her second patrol with a single sinking from convoy SC 42, 5 591-ton SS *Empire Springbuck*. Dönitz claimed success for his boats and again for the strategy of flexible Wolf Pack patrol lines. He intensified his attacks, now concentrating on the Gibraltar convoys in Biscay.

14 September: Kptlt. Wolfgang Kaufman departed Lorient for a special mission (*Sonderunternehmen*). His command *U79* was the first of the *Goeben* group destined for the Mediterranean. In North Africa Rommel was engaged in his struggle against the British Eight Army. His fragile supply lines stretched across the crystal blue Mediterranean to Italy and were constantly interrupted by British naval units stationed in both Malta and Alexandria. Royal Navy aircraft carriers were contributing aircraft both for the defence of besieged Malta and attacks on German supply convoys. Hitler's decision was to transfer U-boats to a newly established base at Salamis, Greece, as part of 23rd U-Flotilla. Dönitz on the other hand was despondent over the loss of yet more of his U-boats. Coupled with his belief that the naval war could only be decided in the Atlantic was the knowledge that every submarine lost to the Mediterranean theatre would never return to Atlantic operations again. To attempt the dangerous eastern passage through heavily guarded Straits of Gibraltar was risky enough, but in reverse there was virtually no chance of success. Fierce currents running into the Mediterranean could assist an entry passage but ensured that any attempt at exiting would be virtually impossible in the course of a single night.

Furthermore the Mediterranean did not offer good conditions for U-boats. Allied air power was considerable, the sea often clear enough to detect shallow-running U-boats by sight alone. Dönitz himself had bitter memories of his own capture by Royal Navy forces in the Mediterranean at the end of the First World War. However the choice was not his to make and with heavy heart he eventually authorized the transfer of fifteen U-boats to the virtually land-locked sea, the vanguard group comprising *U75, U79, U97, U331, U371* and *U559*. *U79* was delayed in joining the group, her commander, Kptlt. Kaufmann, receiving an order to rendezvous and escort German supply ship *Kota Pinang* during her transit south towards the South Atlantic (Kaufmann waited in vain not knowing that *Kota Pinang* had already been sunk by HMS *Kenya*). He eventually made his difficult passage between Gibraltar and Algeria on the night of 4/5 October, announcing his arrival with the torpe-doing of a small barge near Tobruk on the 18th and gunboat HMS *Gnat* on 21 October. *U79* put into her new base two days later passing out of the 1st U-Flotilla.

Three other boats from 1st U-Flotilla were to follow as part of the *Goeben* group. *U371* left Brest on 16 September, slipping past Gibraltar on the night of 21/22 September, also to operate against shipping between Alexandria and Tobruk. *U331*, the last of the *Goeben* boats to leave Brest, made the same passage eight nights later. Despite the dwindling of his U-boat strength in Atlantic operations Dönitz continued his Pack operations when U-boat numbers permitted.

20 September: *U203* and *U559* departed from Sainte Nazaire for opera-tional patrols, the latter en route for Salamis and transfer to 23rd U-Flotilla as the final Goeben boat from Cohausz's flotilla. In Brest, *U204* slipped away for its third patrol. Kptlt. Kell's U-boat was the fifteenth to have been refitted in Brest's yards since the arrival of Cohausz' flotilla.

22 September: Kptlt. Horst Uphoff entered Lorient in *U84*, returning from his first war patrol, one steamer claimed as sunk. Uphoff had fired four torpe-does at ships of convoy SC 42 while operating as part of the *Markgraf* group on 12 September. Diving away in the early morning darkness a single detona-tion was heard and a sinking assumed. In fact the torpedo had exploded harmlessly, possibly a premature detonation or exploding in a ship's wake. The fact that Uphoff had returned to Lorient not Brest was due to overcrowding in the northern port, as recorded in the War Diary entry for 22 September:

'Dock capacity in Brest is only six U-boats. In addition due to the lack of dock capacity in the west, boats of the 3rd and 5th U-Flotillas are being assigned to Brest which means the Flotilla sees even less of its own boats.

'From the point of view of management these circumstances are not viable in the long term because the times for providing feedback (to BdU) from the flotilla are already few and far between.'

The following day Dönitz again visited 1st U-Flotilla. At 1600hrs, to celebrate the first 'quarter year' at Brest, an impressive Flotilla celebration was held. During this event Dönitz awarded three service medals and participated in the unveiling of five traditional plaques at the U-boat base. All the plaques were named after U-boat officers who had fallen to the enemy in action during either World War:

Weddigen – above the *Deutschlandhalle*;
Prien – above the officers' mess;
Looff – above the former administrative quarters, known from then on as *Haus Looff;*
Fresdorf and Fraben – in the departure yard for U-boats.

Following the unveiling and lunch BdU spent the afternoon in informal talks with all flotilla officers. Finally, in a formal ceremony, he awarded Iron Crosses to men of *U81*, *U432*, *U558* and *U85*.

During the course of the day at the U-boat bunker, still smothered in a cobweb of scaffolding, 3rd U-Flotilla's *U85* was the first U-boat to trial dock inside a completed dry-dock pen. Later the following month, at 1100hrs on 13 October, an operational U-boat used the first completed 'wet' pen, Kptlt. Neumann bringing *U372* back from its second war patrol and only small success as part of the *Brandenburg* pack.

24 September: Kptlt. von Tiesenhausen departed Lorient as part of the *Goeben* group transferring to Salamis. Passing through the Straits of Gibraltar during the night of 29/30 September, he proceeded to take *U331* towards the British shipping lanes between Tobruk and Alexandria. He engaged enemy forces while surfaced on 10 October, exchanging gunfire with three British lighters in the Gulf of Sollum. During the brief combat Petty Officer (*Bootsmann*) Hans Gertenich was killed while manning an anti-aircraft weapon, and *U331* dived in retreat. Later the submarine surfaced for the Captain to carry out a burial at sea, Gertenich's flag-draped body consigned to a sailor's grave. *U331* passed out of the 1st U-Flotilla on 11 October as she docked in Salamis as part of 23rd U-Flotilla.[48]

October found Dönitz concentrating his energy against Gibraltar's convoys. KG 40 *Kondors* operating within this theatre finally began employing

[48] *U331* was later involved in commando operations in Libya, and torpedoed and sank the battleship HMS *Barham* on 25 November 1941. On 17 November 1942 she was depth-charged and unable to dive. After raising a white flag of surrender the U-boat was torpedoed by Albacore aircraft, this time sinking. Her commander and sixteen men were all that survived.

more successful technique. The large aircraft now circled convoys that they had located while simultaneously transmitting homing signals for U-boat groups. Allied air cover was sparse at this stage of the war and the four-engine bombers were able to operate with relative impunity. After the beginning of this new offensive, convoy HG 75 was mauled in October, prompting the British Admiralty to suspend the Gibraltar route until stronger and more effective escorts could be provided. It was a small success for the Kriegsmarine.

On the opposite side of the English Channel British views of the war against German submarines received expression through Winston Churchill's 'Review of the War' speech to the House of Commons on 30 September 1941, culminating in a thinly disguised reference to American aid:

> 'Certainly the Germans have used an ever-larger force of U-boats and long-range aircraft against our shipping. However, our counter-measures, which were undertaken in good time on the largest scale, have proved very successful. . . . The losses from enemy action of British, Allied and neutral merchant ships during the quarter July, August and September have been only one-third of those losses during the quarter April, May and June. During the same period our slaughter of enemy shipping, German and Italian, has been increasing by leaps and bounds.
>
> 'We must expect that the enemy U-boat warfare, now conducted by larger numbers of U-boats than ever before, supported by scores of Focke Wolves, will be intensified. The U-boats will be beaten, and kept beaten, only by a corresponding intensification of our own measures and also, to put it very plainly, by that assistance which we are receiving in increasing degree from other quarters'[49]

25 October: In the late afternoon, at 1700hrs, one-time Luftwaffe pilot and First Watch Officer on Schepke's *U100*, Kptlt. Günther Krech gave orders to secure the lines of *U558* in Brest. His torpedo compartment was empty of 'eels' and from the periscope fluttered five pennants totalling 24,000 BRT and one escort ship. Krech had begun his third patrol by sinking the inde-pendent sailing Canadian freighter SS *Vancouver Island* (ex-German ship *Weser*) three days after slipping from Brest. This fortuitous attack had been during Krech's approach to convoy SC48, homing in on beacon signals from shadowing contact boat *U553*. The single 'four-stacker' destroyer and seven corvettes of the mainly Canadian convoy escort were aware of the gathering U-boats thanks to Bletchley Park Enigma intercepts but had scattered during a mid-Atlantic storm. During 16 October the escort received welcome rein-forcement from five 'neutral' American ships of the US Navy Task Unit 4.1.4 and two British destroyers with two British and one French corvette arriving

---

[49] British Library of Information.

later, detached from other convoy duties. Next morning in pitch darkness five U boats began their attack.

Krech, aboard *U558*, scored two important victories during his run toward the convoy: the 9,552-ton tanker SS *W C Teagle* and 6,595-ton tanker MV *Eriken* both sunk amidst boiling flames. As chaos erupted inside the convoy with torpedoes exploding among the fifty-strong convoy and escorts firing random starshells, Krech made another successful attack. Pinpointing one of the corvette escorts he launched a torpedo at HMS *Gladiolus*, victor over Wohlfarth's *U556*, blowing the small corvette to pieces with her veteran crew. His third merchantman kill, the 1,369-ton Norwegian freighter SS *Rym*, was also sent to the deep soon afterward.

Daylight dawned with SC 48 convoy shattered and confused. Krech and his fellow U-boats clung grimly to the tattered merchant ship procession, but there were no further successes for *U558*. After expending all her torpedoes she turned for home. Convoy SC 48 had suffered nine merchant ships (including three valuable tankers) and one corvette lost, while two destroyers were damaged (HMS *Broadwater*, fatally holed by *U101*, later also sank). Amid the pandemonium another attacking U-boat, *U568* of 3rd U-Flotilla, had torpedoed USS *Kearny*, first American casualty of the Atlantic war. Hitler's determination to avoid incidents with America had inevitably failed. During the confused group attack on convoy SC 48, and believing her to be British, Kptlt. Joachim Preuss fired three torpedoes at the ship. One torpedo ripped through the starboard engine room while the deck above and wing on the bridge were obliterated. With great skill Lieutenant Commander Anthony L. Davis nursed his crippled ship to Iceland, escorted by USS *Greer*. On board the shattered destroyer eleven men were dead and twenty-four injured; the military had lost its first men as a result of enemy action. (American merchantmen had long been under fire, the first casualties coming when SS *City of Rayville* was sunk by a mine in Australia's Bass Straight on 8 November 1940.) The final day of that month saw the sinking of USS *Reuben James* as she was torpedoed by Erich Topp's *U552*. Escorting convoy HX156 the *Reuben James* was hit just forward of the forward funnel by a single torpedo. Only forty-six survivors were rescued, leaving 115 dead American sailors. Admiral Stark wrote:

> 'The Navy is already at war in the Atlantic, but the country doesn't seem to realise it. Apathy to the point of open opposition is evident in a considerable section of the press. . . . Whether the country knows it or not we are at war.'

29 October: *Sperrbrecher Rostock*, accompanied by two *Vorpostenboote* of Saint Malo's 2nd Vp-Flotilla, escorted Schnee's *U201* and Guggenberger's *U81* from Brest harbour at 1400hrs. The procession steamed west from

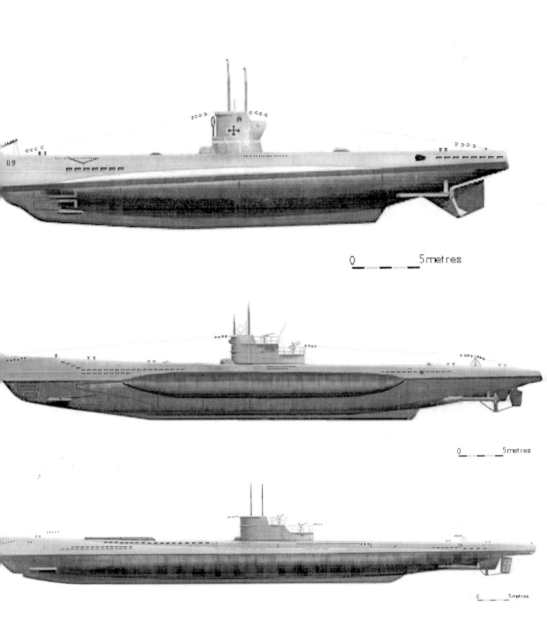

1. U-Boats operated by the 1st U-boat Flotilla. Top: Type II; centre: Type VII; bottom: Type XB. See Appendix for details.

2. Hitler's state yacht *Grille* (Cricket) in attendance as U-boats of the 'Weddigen' Flotilla and the Neustadt U-boat school pass in review, May 1936.

3. U-boats of the 'Weddigen' and 'Emsmann' Flotillas alongside the tender ship *Lech*.

4. 'Weddigen' U-boats undergoing maintenance. The boat in the foreground is so far unidentified but appears to be a Type IID; the background boat is Wolfgang Lüth's *U9* with its distinctive 'Weddigen' Iron Cross tower marking.

5. The Kriegsmarine battle flag and commissioning pennant are hoisted during the commissioning ceremony of Type II *U139*, Kiel, 24 July 1940.

6. The commissioning of *U139*. Immediately behind the small Type II U-boat is Kiel's famous Blücher Bridge.

7. Provisions being stored aboard a Type VII at Kiel.

8. Korvettenkapitän Hans Cohausz, Flotilla Commander.

9. Kapitänleutnant Schnee, aboard *U201*, exercises his musical skills.

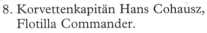

10. Dönitz inspects men of the 1st U-Flotilla before their Naval Academy headquarters in Brest. The polar bear cap emblem worn by many of the recently returned crewmen in the foreground would seem to indicate that this is the crew of *U566*, later scuttled near Spain in October 1943.

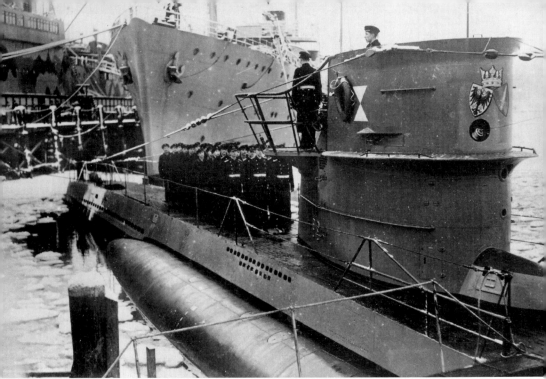

11. *U203* is commissioned at Kiel, 18 February 1941. The crest of the sponsoring town of Essen adorns the front of the conning tower. On the starboard side the white triangles represent UAK markings, these specifically for 21 Germaniawerft U-boats, painted on between launching and final acceptance into Kriegsmarine service.

12. Not all crossings were difficult – an early model Type VIIC U-boat at sea.

13. Matrosengefreiter Peter Wimmer beneath the caricature of 'Parsival' on the front of *U556*'s conning tower in Lorient. The 49,900 tons of claimed tonnage is written below the smiling knight.

14. Kapitänleutnant Herbert 'Parsival' Wohlfarth aboard the hulk *Isere* in Lorient, 30 May 1941, at the end of *U566*'s first operational patrol. The young commander of *U566* received his Knight's Cross from Dönitz shortly after this photo was taken.

15. The slim hull form of a Type VIIC can be appreciated by this view of *U372* approaching the Goulet de Brest, 1941.

16. On 13 October Kapitänleutnant Hans-Joachim Neumann brought *U372* back from its second war patrol to be the first operational U-boat to use a completed 'wet' pen of the Brest U-boat bunker. The crest visible on the conning tower is based on Viersen's coat of arms, sponsoring city of the boat.

17. Kapitänleutnants Rolf Mützelberg and Adalbert Schnee receive their Oak Leaves from the Führer, 8 August 1942.

18. Flotilla commander Kaptlt. Heinz Buchholz decorates a crew-member of *U564* with the EKII and the coveted U-boat service badge. On the right is *U564* commander Kaptlt. Reinhard Suhren.

19. Suhren celebrates the award of Oak Leaves and Swords to his Knight's Cross and promotion to Korvettenkapitän, 1 Septembe 1942 on *U564*'s stern deck. The three 'piston rings' on his sleeve that denote his new rank were cu from tin cans for the ceremony.

20. Kapitänleutnant Mützelberg dives from the conning tower of *U564* during a rendezvous between Suhren's boat and *U203* (glimpsed at right) on 23 July 1942. Suhren later wrote: "My hair stood on end and I said to him, 'What did you do that for? You wouldn't catch me doing that!'...but he laughed and told me he did it quite often."

21. Kapitänleutnant Walter Kell brings *U204* into the Penfeld River, Brest, 22 August 1941. It was the second and final time that *U204* would safely return – she was lost with all hands less than two months later.

22. Maschinistobergefreiter Wilhelm Schmidt receives the EKII from his commander Günther Krech *(U558)* in front of the Naval Academy.

23. The straw that broke the camel's back – Mexican tanker *SS Petrero del Llanko* lies in flames after being torpedoed by the Suhren's *U564* on 14 May 1942. Mexico declared war on Germany eight days later.

24. The Bay of Biscay became extremely dangerous for U-boats to traverse as Allied air power smothered German naval movement. U-boats were ordered to proceed in groups on the surface in a vain attempt to fight back.

25. Repairs at sea were the domain of all crew members. Here a commander assists his radio operator in maintenance of the antennae that travelled along the U-boat's jumper wire.

26. The eyes of the U-boat – heavily muffled bridge watch scour the horizon for targets or danger.

27. U-boat men were treated with great respect by Germany's people, politicians and miltary. Here an unidentified crew leave the Reichs Chancellery preceded by their officers and SS Leibstandarte guide.

28. Oberleutnant zur See Herbert Werner aboard *U230* as First Watch Officer. In the background can be seen the escort Sperrbrecher *Sp 9 Lüneburg* (6th Sperr. Flotilla) clearing possible mines for the U-boat as they approach Brittany. Werner later went on to command *U415*.

29. A close view of the impressive weaponry aboard *U441* after conversion to her role as *Flakfalle*. Ultimately, of course, it became obvious that U-boats were an unsuitable choice as an anti-aircraft weapon platform.

30. *U564* approaches Brittany in the company of a Patrol Boat from the 7th *Vorpostenflottille*, 18 September 1942.

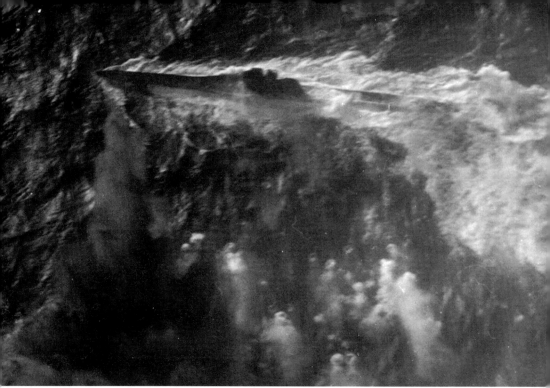

32. *U584* desperately twists in an attempt to shake off Avenger aircraft from *USS Card* on 31 October 1943. Shortly after this photo was taken Kapitänleutnant Kurt Nölke ordered the boat dived where she was destroyed along with all fifty-three hands by a 'Fido' torpedo.

33. A U-boat Obersteurmann (navigator) takes his sextant reading. Navigation was an exacting task at any time, but particularly essential for the formation of effective patrol lines and wolf packs. In the foreground can be seen the torpedo targeting device for surface firing.

34. Château de Trevarez, the red brick *U-Bootheim* inland from Brest that was used for rest and relaxation for unwinding U-boat crews after patrol. The impressive building was later targeted and bombed by Mosquitoes of the RAF.

35. The Château de Rosmorduc near Logonna, another relaxation centre for U-boat crews, this time on the Plougastel Peninsula near Brest.

36. Endless vigilance was demanded of a U-boat's bridge watch. These men are identified as belonging to *U558* due to their distinctive conning tower emblem (*Holzauge, sei wach* – "Wooden eye, stay alert"), partly visible. Sharp eyes did not save the forty-five men of Kapitänleutnant Günther Krech's crew when their boat was sunk by air attack on 20 July 1943.

37. Korvettenkapitän Werner Winter, final commander of the 1st U-Flotilla and captured by Amercan troops at the fall of Brest, September 1944.

38. The War Diary (, or, KTB) of 1st U-Flotilla.

Pointe Saint Mathieu until the 200-metre contour was reached and both U-boats dived away.

Two days after leaving Brest bound for the Mediterranean *U81* returned. Spotted while surfaced by a 209 Squadron Catalina 250 miles north-west of Brest, the U-boat was shadowed while a Hudson of 53 Squadron raced to the scene. Both aircraft dived onto Kptl Friedrich Guggenberger's boat, dropping depth charges on the swirl left behind after *U81*'s hasty crash dive. Although seriously shaken by the attack, *U81* suffered only minor damage, although Guggenberger judged it sufficient to return to base for repair.

Alongside the battered *U81* Kaptl Hans-Werner Kraus' *U83* also sailed into Brest harbour. Having departed for patrol a month earlier on 28 September Kraus had been directed against convoy OG 75 by a Kondor sighting. *U83*, joined by *U71*, made contact and began to shadow the Allied convoy. Eventually weather conspired to defeat the two boats and contact was lost in heavy seas on 8 October.

Four days later Kraus stopped and boarded the Portuguese steamer SS *Corte Real*, sinking her by torpedo after discovering contraband aboard. Meanwhile spies in Spain and Morocco had noted the safe arrival of convoy OG 75 and the imminent departure of HG 75 for England. While awaiting the expected convoy Kraus sighted a naval task force comprised of British aircraft carriers HMS *Argus* and *Eagle* (engaged in flying off aircraft for Malta), cruiser HMS *Hermione* and a single destroyer. Firing four torpedoes at the carriers Kraus missed but mistakenly believed that he had hit the screening destroyer.

Dönitz immediately began to organize a pack to meet the expected target. Named *Breslau*, it comprised *U83*, *U204*, *U563* and *U564* of 1st U-Flotilla and *U71* and *U206* of 7th and 3rd U-Flotillas respectively. Reinhard Suhren took *U564* into Cadiz harbour, along with Kell in *U204*, to take on fuel from *Thalia* while the *Breslau* pack began to form.

Again using Enigma interceptions, the Royal Navy became aware of the *Breslau* group and attempted to dislodge the waiting menace with daily anti-submarine patrols. Kell, aboard *U204*, was destroyed after sinking the tanker *Inverlee*, but the remaining *Breslau* boats waited for their target to sail. Finally the seventeen ships of HG 75 put to sea with a massive thirteen-ship escort (four destroyers, one sloop, seven corvettes and the fighter catapult ship HMS *Ariguani*) on the evening of 22 October. Contact was established by the U-boats during the convoy's first night although escorts managed to keep the Grey Wolves at bay.

During the convoy's second night at sea U-boats managed to penetrate the defences. Ex-merchant mariner Klaus Bargsten (who had also served as a Midshipman aboard Hitler's state yacht *Grille* prior to the outbreak of war and later as First Watch Officer aboard Kretschmer's *U99*), in command of *U563*, made the first kill, missing his intended freighter target but hitting

'Tribal' class destroyer HMS *Cossack*. The destroyer had her bows blown off by the torpedo impact and later sank while under tow. Reinhard Suhren, aboard *U564*, waded into attack, firing eleven torpedoes altogether and claiming six steamers sunk (in reality SS *Carsbreck*, SS *Ariosto* and SS *Althama* were his three victories for 7,198 tons).

The U-boats continued to harass OG 75 and on the morning of 26 October Kraus in *U83* fired his three remaining torpedoes at three different ships, all of which he claimed sunk. In fact only the 6,746-ton fighter catapult ship *Ariguani* was hit. Abandoned by her crew, she refused to sink and was later towed by tug back to Gibraltar. *U83*, all torpedoes gone, headed for Brest in the wake of *U71* and *U206*. This left only *U563* and *U564* to continue their fight against the slow-moving Allied convoy.

Dönitz had in the meantime vectored KG40 *Kondors* on to the convoy, as well as Italian BETASOM boat *Ferraris* (which was promptly located, surrendered and sunk on 25 October by HMS *Lamerton*). Finally on 26 October *U563* and *U564* expended all but one torpedo against the convoy, claiming several hits whereas in actual fact all torpedoes missed. Bargsten's boat *U563* underwent the indignity of an air attack from Luftwaffe aircraft before reaching port. Intercepting the Luftwaffe pilot's report of 'one British submarine sunk' in his area, Bargsten ordered his own signal transmitted explaining that the number of the British submarine was *U563*!

Dönitz felt that a great victory had been won by his men, based on his commanders' reports – one destroyer and thirteen freighters sunk, with *U204* missing (actually sunk in the action) and the Italian submarine *Ferraris* confirmed sunk. The truth was more modest – one destroyer and four freighters destroyed and one fighter catapult ship damaged. On 1 November *U563* returned to Brest flying four pennants and *U564* to Lorient with six. The latter would spend weeks in the shipyard for rust treatment and work on her diesel engines. The British Admiralty confirmed their decision to suspend Gibraltar sailings in the face of continual losses. Larger and more effective escorts would have to be found.

1 November: The same day that Bargsten and Suhren returned from the battle against convoy HG 75 the 9th U-Flotilla was created in Brest under Kptlt. Jürgen Oesten (formerly commander of *U61*). They were housed in separate quarters to 1st U-Flotilla, the grounds and buildings of Brest's *Hôpital Morvan*, an imposing structure whose entrance gates were later crowned with the soon-to-be adopted 'laughing sawfish' flotilla emblem.[50] The hospital had not yet become functional when the Germans arrived, being still under construction in June 1940, although still occupied at the time by

---

[50] This famous flotilla emblem came into being after 9th U-Flotilla's second commander, Lehmenn-Willenbrock, brought it with him from the conning tower of his last combat boat *U96*.

British troops. Over the months that followed the building complex was completed by Kriegsmarine-controlled workers specifically to house U-boat crews.

3 November: 1st U-Flotilla lost yet another U-boat to the Mediterranean. Oblt.z.S. Johann Jebsen took *U565*, heavily painted in dark grey splinter camouflage, from Lorient to join the *Arnauld* group about to run the gauntlet of Gibraltar. The following day at 1700hrs *U81* slipped from Brest also as part of this four-boat transfer (the remaining U-boats were 3rd U-Flotilla's *U205* and *U433*). Kptlt. Guggenberger took his freshly repaired *U81* through the Straits of Gibraltar surfaced during the night of 11/12 November. The day after his arrival in Mediterranean waters he made his presence felt after sighting the powerful British Task Force H. Centrepiece of the naval group, HMS *Ark Royal*, had already narrowly escaped a three-torpedo attack by the newly arrived *U205* during the morning. Later that day Guggenberger sighted the Task Force steaming directly for him at 19 knots and carefully moved into a suitable submerged attack position. At 1629hrs in unruffled seas Guggenberger lined the periscope crosshairs on both the carrier and the battleship HMS *Malaya*. He fired a bow salvo of four torpedoes, two at each, at the same moment that *Ark Royal* manoeuvred into the wind to retrieve Swordfish aircraft still searching for *U205*.

Forced by an approaching destroyer to plunge deep, the crew of *U81* heard two detonations after a run of six minutes and six seconds and seven minutes forty-three seconds, and hits were assumed on *Malaya* and an unknown target. *U81* then underwent a severe depth-charge attack by Task Force destroyers before going deeper still and retreating from the scene. In fact Guggenberger had mortally wounded the *Ark Royal*. The crippled carrier finally sank at 0613hrs on 14 November, for the loss of one man killed by the initial torpedo strike. Dönitz awarded Guggenberger a *Ritterkreuz* after his arrival in La Spezia and Cohausz recorded in the 1st U-Flotilla War Diary on 15 November:

> '*Ja die Deutschen sind im Mittelmeer!*' (Yes, the Germans are in the Mediterranean!)

Despite this success for a recently transferred Mediterranean boat Dönitz was dismayed at the constant whittling away of his Atlantic force by OKM 'special missions'. During November the attacks against Atlantic convoys virtually ground to a halt. Escort missions for prize ships and raiders, for which a U-boat was completely unsuited, vulnerable to enemy aircraft if surfaced and often too slow underwater to prevent enemy surface attack, weather reporting duties for the Luftwaffe and Mediterranean 'sideshow' missions all sapped valuable U-boat strength from the fight against British Atlantic merchant shipping. To cap it all, eight U-boats (including 1st U-Flotilla's *U574*) were then detailed to support a proposed breakout of the pocket battleship *Admiral*

Scheer from the Baltic into the North Atlantic. Dönitz wrote in frustration on 10 November:

> 'In connection with four boats already carrying out reconnaissance duties in the north, Naval War Staff has now requested four more boats for weather reports, including one boat (*U574*) off Jan Mayan if possible combined with submarine operations. So once again the departure of one ship will interfere with submarine warfare.'

11 November: Dönitz's headquarters in Kerneval became fully operational on this auspicious date, Armistice day.

In Brest Oblt.z.S. Unno von Fischel, son of First World War U-boat commander Hermann von Fischel, completed his first operational patrol in command of *U374*.[51] Departing Kiel on 29 September, he participated in *Mordbrenner* group operations sinking a single 5,120-ton freighter MV *King Malcolm* (claimed as 6,000 tons) during the morning of 31 October near Cape St Francis, Newfoundland. The freighter disappeared in less than 30 seconds. Within a few hours convoy SC 52 heaved into view and von Fischel began to shadow, transmitting homing signals as contact boat for the newly formed *Raubritter* group. Canadian corvette HMCS *Buctouche* of the convoy escort located the boat south of Greenland while von Fischel attempted to take advantage of a dense fog bank and launch his attack, subjecting the new U-boat to a short six-depth-charge attack. Von Fischel escaped by going deep, reaching the seabed at 305 feet and waiting for the Canadian's fury to subside. Low on fuel, a shaken *U374* headed to Brest.

12 November: Another *Mordbrenner* boat on its maiden patrol from Kiel, *U208* commanded by Oblt.z.S. Alfred Schlieper, entered Brest. From his conning tower also fluttered a single pennant. Claiming 7,000 tons sunk, Schlieper had in fact accounted for the 3,872-ton British steamer SS *Larpool* on 2 November east-south-east of Cape Race. Like the other boats of his group, their progress against Allied shipping was constantly hampered by thick Atlantic fog. The day following its single victory *U208* laid course for Brest.

Kptlt. Rolf Mützelberg also eased up to a Penfeld dock in Brest during the day. After nearly a month at sea *U203* had participated in two pack operations, unsuccessful attacks on convoy SL 89 west of Ireland and then as part of the fourteen-strong *Raubritter* group homing on convoy SC 52. In drifting fog Mützelberg had followed the homing beacon transmitted by von Fischel's *U374* closing on the slow thirty-six-ship convoy with several other *Raubritter* boats.

---

[51] *Vizeadmiral* Hermann von Fischel subsequently became commander of Kriegsmarine forces along France's Channel coast, *Marinebefelshaber Kanalküste* between 17 February 1941 and 21 April 1943.

Another 1st U-Flotilla boat, Kptlt. Hans–Heinz Linder's *U202*, opened the attack by torpedoing two ships north-east of Notre Dame Bay, Newfoundland, 2,022-ton SS *Flynderborg* and 4,586-ton SS *Gretavale*, mistakenly claiming a third also hit and sunk. *U203* then made its move. Mützelberg streaked inside the nine Canadian escorts and torpedoed SS *Empire Gemsbuck* and SS *Everoja* for a combined total of 10,456 tons. He was then driven off by sharp depth-charging attacks from frantic escorts. The damage to this convoy, however, had already been done.

In the fog and confusion two ships ran aground while trying to evade their attackers. With swelling panic taking its own toll on the shattered convoy, the British Admiralty made an unprecedented and never-repeated move when they aborted the convoy, sending the battered merchantmen back to Sydney, Nova Scotia. The price paid for failure – five ships sunk for 20,400 tons.

Following this success, Dönitz then withdrew his U-boats from Newfoundland waters. Both *U202* and *U203* returned to Brest, each boat running on only one diesel to conserve their sparse fuel. Mützelberg was the first to arrive, Linder following next day.

Dönitz was again in Brest to welcome his returning crews. On 14 November he spent the afternoon talking to his men in Brest's U-boat support base, followed by a brief ceremony where he awarded commanders of *U202*, *U208* and *U374* the Iron Cross First Class, while crewmen also were decorated. In the words of Cohausz this was followed by 'a highly appreciated feedback period in the smoker's salon' of 1st U-Flotilla's headquarters.

18 November: '*U204 Vermisst ein Stern.*' Kell's U-boat was listed as 'missing in the Gibraltar Strait'. The U-boat's third war patrol had begun on 20 September with escort duty for 6,062 BRT German blockade runner *Rio Grande*, embarking on the perilous voyage from Bordeaux to Osaka, Japan. The two vessels parted on 29 September, Kell heading for his patrol region south-west of Ireland. It is believed that he sank small Panamanian vessel SS *C Jon* before proceeding south to Cadiz and refuelling from supply ship *Thalia*. From there Kell and his crew sailed for Morocco to join the *Breslau* pack, directed by Abwehr spy reports to intercept convoy HG 75 preparing to sail from Gibraltar. British Enigma decrypts had alerted the Admiralty to six waiting U-boats and the convoy was delayed for nearly a week. There were still targets to be had while the German commanders bided their time. Kell sighted and attacked the 9,200-ton British tanker MV *Inverlee* on 19 October, sinking her with torpedoes. However, this successful attack told the sloop HMS *Rochester* and the corvette HMS *Mallow* of the daily British anti-submarine sweeping force the area in which to hunt for *U204*. There followed a thunderous depth-charge attack resulting in a pool of oil and debris from the U-boat's torpedo room. Kptlt. Kell and his men were no more, although claimed as only a 'probable' by the Allies pending further proof.

113

Cohausz recorded forlornly:

> 'It is hoped that a large number of the crew have been rescued, no news yet from the International Red Cross.'

On a happier note the War Diary stated that on the same day:

> 'BdU arrives in the afternoon to award the Knight's Cross to Kptlt. Mützelberg for his exceptional performance on the last enemy patrol and for his overall service.'

Elsewhere the war ground on. *U84* returned from a barren patrol to Brest. The following day *U557* departed from Lorient, while *U562* put into the port to take on fresh supplies for its attempt at slipping through the Straits of Gibraltar. Far to the north *U654*, having departed Kiel for its maiden patrol and transfer to 1st U-Flotilla on 16 November, was forced to divert to Bergen. Arriving on the 19th commander KK Hans-Joachim Hesse was immediately hospitalized, suffering from scarlet fever. Hesse was replaced by Oblt.z.S. Ludwig Forster, but although the boat later transferred to France and operated from Brest in the ensuing months it never passed out of the operational command of Bergen's 11th U-Flotilla.

26 November: Kptlt. Robert Bartels arrived at Brest from his third war patrol. During *U561*'s voyage he had sunk two straggling Panamanian ships in the central North Atlantic from convoy SC 53, the 5,592-ton SS *Meridian* on 11 November and 2,939-ton SS *Crusader* on the 14th, the last two sinkings by 1st U-Flotilla for the month. These were the only successes for Bartels who finished his patrol as escort for German raider *Komet* returning to Biscay from its successful South Atlantic cruise.

During November the 1st U-Flotilla suffered further dissipation of its Atlantic force. Recently commissioned *U584*, commanded by Kptlt. Joachim Deecke, had completed its three months working up in the Baltic. Instead of transferring to the front line west of France he departed Kiel for his first patrol on 27 November to be stationed in the inhospitable Arctic seas. Operating against Murmansk convoys Deecke and his crew contended with extreme hardships aboard their Type VIIC submarine. On the opposite end of the same problem, three U-boats were ordered by OKM transferred from Brest to the Mediterranean, *U562*, *U557*, *U558* (although the latter boat aborted its transfer after *flibo* and *wabo* attack by Fleet Air Arm Swordfish from 812 Squadron, recently of HMS *Ark Royal*, operating since the carrier's loss from Gibraltar). The U-boat campaign in the Atlantic had fizzled to nothing. All boats ready for operations were earmarked by OKM for possible use in the Mediterranean in support of Rommel's land war.

Dönitz had calculated the following allocation of his U-boat arm's meagre forces on 10 December: 86 operational U-boats, with the following deductions: 4 in the Western Mediterranean; 5 west of Gibraltar; 4 in Salamis;

2 in La Spezia; 16 on their way to either the Mediterranean or Gibraltar; 55 remaining. From this 55 a further 14 would be needed to keep the previously listed regions at the necessary operational levels, reducing the number of available boats still further to 41. Of this remaining figure, 3 were in the Arctic, 5 returning from the South Atlantic, leaving 33. Of only 33 U-boats the majority were in dockyards and repair facilities. Using Dönitz's 'rule of thirds' regarding operational patrols (one third on duty, one third in transit to their stations, one third in shipyards undergoing routine maintenance) this left a paltry 10 operational U-boats with which to throttle England and take on the might of America's shipbuilding industry in the Atlantic, Dönitz's *Schwerpunkt* (centre of operations). It painted a depressing picture. Dönitz was more firmly convinced than ever that the only way of preventing America from deploying its overwhelming military might in Europe was an intensive sustained attack on the Atlantic supply lines.

Coupled with this was the concern of KK Cohausz at the decline in returns for U-boat operations. Despite often savage weather conditions in patrol areas, Cohausz believed that there were more prosaic reasons for this loss of efficiency. At the end of November he recorded with some satisfaction the implementation of his ideas on extended internal flotilla training, endorsed by BdU Ops. for the entire western U-boat force:

'For all western flotillas a so-called basic military training has been in place since 1/XI. One third of the crew of each boat take part at a U-boat quarters (at present Cap Boz).

Goal: to give the newcomers the general and improved basic training that is necessary, and at the same time to raise the performance level of all ranks which has fallen considerably.

'I made the proposal for this measure in August/September on the basis of experience, at first it received no official support from command and is now being implemented in all western flotillas according to voluntary agreement.

'In my opinion, this measure lags half a year behind what military necessities require, as is demonstrated in the noticeable drop in performance throughout the ranks.

'For next spring it is planned to provide so-called training and relaxation quarters; the latter is for soldiers who are not due for training and instead wish to take a rest break at quarters.'

3 December: Oblt.z.S. Alfred Schlieper's *U208* slipped from Brest during the day and proceeded out toward open sea. Following his minesweeping escort past Fort Berthaume and Pointe Saint Mathieu the bridge watch huddled low against a biting breeze, the bay dull beneath a pale and watery winter sun. Diesel exhaust left long trails of steam behind them as they finally reached deep water shedding their escort and preparing for an initial trim dive to check for potential problems.

U208's destination was an operational area west of Gibraltar. Three days into the patrol Schlieper was handed a Top Secret triple-enciphered transmission by his Second Officer, ordered decoded by the Captain only. It contained new instructions – proceed through the Straits of Gibraltar for operations in the Eastern Mediterranean. Traversing the narrow strait was no easy prospect. Constant and heavy Royal Navy patrolling had stiffened yet further following the successful voyage of several U-boats and the sinking of such notable ships as *Ark Royal* and *Barham*. As Schlieper's boat departed the Bay of Biscay it radioed a final status report, and was never heard of again. During the night of 7 December destroyers HMS *Harvester* and HMS *Hesperus* of Gibraltar's constant anti-submarine patrols obtained a firm ASDIC trace and attacked the contact with depth charges. The trace vanished and with it all forty-five men aboard *U208*. It was the third boat lost attempting the passage and the first from 1st U-Flotilla.

In Lorient Oblt.z.S. Klaus Bargsten brought severely damaged *U563* into port. The U-boat had been depth charged by Flying Officer W.W.Cave's 502 Squadron Whitley on 1 December on its fourth day of patrol while bound for the North Atlantic. Severely damaged, *U563* was forced to the surface where machine-gun fire from the circling British bomber wounded three men, including Bargsten, hit twice in the shoulder. Creeping home to Brest, Bargsten was dismayed to find no room in the crowded port and his boat was rerouted to Lorient for repairs.

7 December: Japan attacked American ships moored in Pearl Harbor during the early morning. There seemed little doubt that a declaration of hostilities would rapidly follow between Germany and what was probably the most powerful industrial nation on earth. As Cohausz recorded in 1st U-Flotilla's War Diary: 'The war has become the Second World War'.

9 December: Oblt.z.S. Adalbert Schnee brought *U201* into harbour at Brest with nothing to show for over a month on patrol in the North Atlantic. In appalling weather he had participated in two group operations that found no trace of their elusive enemy. Despite Luftwaffe sightings of convoys OS11 and OG77 the U-boats encountered nothing but mountainous seas and freezing salt spray. Severe icing-up of the U-boat's deck gun and conning tower, the extra weight destabilizing the submarine as she sailed, compounded the difficulties of operating surfaced in ferocious seas. Only by constantly submerging could the warmer salt water slowly rid the U-boat of its unwelcome burden and provide any measure of comfort for the crew.

Four days after returning to Brest, as if to add insult to this abject failure, a battery explosion during maintenance work aboard the rusty submarine killed Firemen (*Maschinenobergefreiter*) Josef Zander and Wöllner, and

116

injured two others. The year was ending badly for men of Brest's *Unterseebootwaffe*.

11 December: During a belligerent *Führerede* (Leader's speech) Hitler declared war on the United States of America. The sham of non-aggression was finally over. In Brest Cohausz recorded the lifting of restrictions against US shipping: '*U-Boote gegen U.S.A. Schiffe.*'

Within the text of a carefully worded statement handed to United States government officials in both Washington and Berlin the events that had taken place in the Atlantic during previous months received pride of place:

> 'On 11 September 1941 the President of the United States publicly declared that he had ordered the American Navy and Air Force to shoot on sight at any German war vessel. . . . Acting under this order, vessels of the American Navy, since early September 1941, have systematically attacked German naval forces. . . . The German Government, consequently, discontinues diplomatic relations with the United States of America and declares that under these circumstances brought about by President Roosevelt Germany too, as from today, considers herself as being in a state of war with the United States of America.'

16 December: '*U557 Vermisst zwei Stern. Totalverlust.*' Kptlt. Ottokar Paulshen's U-boat had passed from 1st U-Flotilla's operational control into the hands of La Spezia's 29th U-Flotilla during the first week of December. Still Cohausz recorded her fate. After sailing from Messina on 9 December Paulshen attacked and sank the 5,200-ton British light cruiser HMS *Galatea* west of Alexandria on the 15th. Heading back to her base *U557* was passing 15 miles from Crete's western edge in the early evening when the Italian MTB *Orione* sighted the submarine and, mistaking her for British, attacked with machine guns blazing. Closing rapidly on the surprised U-boat, *Orione* rammed, damaging her fatally. As the MTB drew away from the collision barely afloat, *U557* sank beneath her almost immediately. The Italians only realized their error after claiming victory the next day. Luftwaffe air patrols in search of survivors failed to find any trace; forty-three Kriegsmarine sailors lay on the sea floor in the second U-boat loss within the Mediterranean.

Further U-boats continued to leave for the Mediterranean arena. Cohausz' flotilla lost *U81*, *U372* and *U374* during December to the 29th U-Flotilla at La Spezia. *U202* aborted its transfer attempt after damage from Gibraltar's 812 Fleet Air Arm Squadron's Swordfishes, returning to Brest for repair. As the flotilla commander noted bitterly: 'Eight veteran boats out of nine are now in the Mediterranean flotilla.'

The same evening that *U557* was destroyed by 'friendly' forces, RAF bombers again raided Brest's docks, aiming principally at *Prinz Eugen*, one of the three capital ships still penned inside the harbour confines.

30 December: The final sortie of the year launched by 1st U-Flotilla began in Kiel. At 1200hrs Kptlt. Johannes Oestermann sailed for his maiden patrol destined for the waters of Eastern Canada. Commissioned on 28 August 1941 at Kriegsmarinewerft, Wilhelmshaven, *U754* had undergone nearly four months of exhausting shakedown in a Baltic Sea now once again shrouded with ice.

The year 1941 had started with great promise for German U-boats but ended with little combat activity of any use to Dönitz's war plans. What meagre resources had been scraped together from an undersized U-boat arm were dissipated by futile 'special missions' and operations in the peripheral theatres of the Arctic and Mediterranean. Losses had begun to mount as Allied convoying and improved anti-submarine weaponry came into being, used by the Germans' opponents with greater experience and confidence. The naval Enigma codes had been broken, although this was unknown in Germany. Dönitz and many of his officers voiced suspicions regarding the possibility of the British Amiralty being able to decode vital U-boat radio traffic but were confidently reassured by German Naval Intelligence that this was an impossibility.

U-boats of the 1st U-Flotilla, now firmly established in Brest, had accounted by German reckoning for a confirmed 481,523 BRT of enemy merchant shipping during the previous seven months. The facts were less impressive. Over-claiming by U-boat commanders, whether deliberate or in genuine error, formed a more optimistic picture of actual successes against Britain's convoys.

However, beginning at 1800hrs, New Year celebrations began in individual quarters throughout the Flotilla. Cohausz made his official report to Kptlt. Karl Daublebsky von Eichhain (*Admiralstabsoffizier (A2)* – BdU's Second Staff Officer):

> 'From May to November 1941, sinking of 481,523 BRT and 13 steamers of unknown type, plus an aircraft carrier, two destroyers and numerous small craft. A further eight armed ships hit.
>
> 'Despite lack of dock space, a total of sixty-one U-boats were made ready for action at the front.'

Festivities continued into the night. More cause for toasting and drinking among the men of the Flotilla was provided when Oblt.z.S. Reinhard Suhren received the Oak Leaves for his Knight's Cross, the subsequent day also celebrating his new promotion to *Kapitänleutnant.*

7.

THE BATTLE OF THE ATLANTIC
1 JANUARY 1942 to 31 DECEMBER 1942

1 January 1942: The strength of 1st U-Flotilla on the first day of 1942 rested at fifteen boats:

U84 – Oblt.z.S. Horst Uphoff, en route to the Mediterranean on his third war patrol.

U86 – Kptlt. Walther Schug, six days into a voyage to the Newfoundland Bank on the boat's second war patrol.

U201 – Oblt.z.S. Adalbert Schnee, stranded in Brest's shipyard for repairs following an explosion in the U-boat's batteries after their sixth patrol.

U202 – Kptlt. Hans-Heinz Linder, also in Brest's yards after damage sustained in an air attack during an aborted attempt at entering the Straits of Gibraltar on their fourth war patrol.

U203 – Kptlt. Rolf Mützelberg, assembling as part of the *Seydlitz* pack near the Azores on his sixth patrol as commander.

U558 – Kptlt. Günther Krech, laid up for repairs in Brest after aircraft attack in the Straits of Gibraltar during their fifth war patrol.

U561 – Kptlt. Robert Bartels, having completed his boat's refitting in Brest and preparing for his fourth patrol.

U563 – Oblt.z.S. Klaus Bargsten, returned to Lorient following an unsuccessful third patrol, hunting in the wastes of the Atlantic, with damage sustained during an attack by an RAF Whitley of 502 Squadron on 1 December.

U564 – Kptlt. Reinhard Suhren, his boat undergoing rust treatment and maintenance in Lorient following their third patrol and action as part of the *Breslau* pack.

U566 – Kptlt. Dietrich Borchert, also in Lorient as his boat underwent maintenance after transfer from Kristiansand.

U582 – Kptlt. Werner Schulte, preparing for his first operational patrol from Trondheim, bound for the Newfoundland Bank.

U584 – Kptlt. Joachim Deecke, at sea in the extremely cold and stormy waters of the Arctic Circle as part of the three-boat *Ulan* group. His sole success from their mission was soon to come with the torpedoing and sinking of 250-ton Russian coastal submarine *M175* on 10 January.

U653 – Commissioned on 26 May and fresh from working-up trials, Kptlt. Gerhard Feiler, roving the mid-Atlantic during his first patrol in a vain attempt to fool the British into believing a hefty group of U-boats remained operational in the Atlantic. Attempting to disguise the relocation of the majority of U-boats to Gibraltar, Dönitz ordered 32-year-old Feiler to broadcast dummy radio messages in an effort to simulate large-scale U-boat presence. The British, however, were not taken in by the ruse and had correctly surmised from Enigma intercepts that there was only a group of 'five or six' U-boats heading for the Newfoundland area. Feiler's boat suffered in savage weather conditions, culminating with the loss overboard of Petty Officer (*Bootsmaat*) Heinz Wendler on 22 December. The boat spent exactly one month at sea putting in to Brest on 13 January.

U656 – Kptlt. Ernst Kröning, finishing working up exercises in the Baltic after the U-boat's September commissioning into 5th U-Training Flotilla.

U754 – Kptlt. Johannes Oestermann, two days into his first operational patrol bound for Newfoundland.

The first official duty of the New Year took place at 1100hrs when a memorial plaque was unveiled within the 1st Flotilla compound for Kptlt. Gero Zimmermann and his crew, lost on 3 August 1941. With work on U-boats continuing in the harbour the RAF made an unwelcome appearance in the skies above Brest. Cloaked in early winter darkness bombers thundered overhead, sirens sounding at 1846hrs and not shrieking the 'All Clear' until 2114hrs. One sailor from harbour-mates 9th U-Flotilla was killed during the raid.

3 January: *U654*, *U582* and *U561* all put to sea for operational patrols. Hesse, aboard *U654*, took his boat from Brest destined for the Newfoundland Bank and the eastern seaboard of the United States. Werner Schulte also took his boat *U582* towards Canadian waters, slipping from Trondheim during the day. Ten Type VIICs were being concentrated around Newfoundland in an effort to support the five 2nd U-Flotilla Type IXs of 'Operation *Paukenschlag*' – the assault on America. Dönitz had lobbied in vain for a stronger group of long-range Lorient boats for the attack against America. His frustration was compounded by an almost immediate order from Hitler to then send eight more boats to the defence of Norway, the Führer's pet paranoia. Desperately

Dönitz grasped at sending smaller Type VII boats to Canadian waters in an attempt at pinning Allied forces in those inhospitable waters. The Type VII at this stage was still considered to not possess a sufficient range to partake in activities against the United States.

The third 1st U-Flotilla boat *U561* was making its final departure from France. Kptlt. Bartels began transferring his boat to the Mediterranean's 24th U-Flotilla and new hunting grounds. He passed through the treacherous Straits of Gibraltar during the new moon period of 14/15 January, docking at Messina on 22 January after an uneventful voyage.

6 January: '*U574 Vermisst seit 19 Dezember 1941. Vermisst ein Stern.*' (*U574* missing since 19 December 1941)

Oblt.z.S. Dietrich Gengelbach had taken his new Type VIIC *U574* from Kiel for her first operational patrol on 8 November 1941. The U-boat had been one of those assigned to reconnoitre the area south of Iceland in support of the proposed breakout of battleship *Admiral Scheer* from the Baltic.

After that operation's cancellation Gengelbach took his boat south to join five other U-boats of the *Steuben* pack, formed off Newfoundland. Ten days of fruitless patrol found the boat tossed by heavy seas, many of her inexperienced crew suffering severely from seasickness. Conditions aboard the pitching U-boat rapidly deteriorated. First Watch Officer Eckart Joost remembered:

> '[We] travelled through the North Sea, north of British Isles in the North Atlantic, with Newfoundland the target. Journey was made against severe north-westerly storms, partly hurricane force, with permanent heavy breakers crashing over the boat. During this at least two crewmen were injured – broken ribs, broken wrists, grazes, bruises among other things. Then news reached us of our new orders for the destination at the end of November 1941 'Turn back – new destination (set course for Gibraltar.'

U574 turned south-east and began the long leg to Gibraltar, contacting convoy OS12 en route but unable to launch a single attack due to atrocious weather conditions. Strong anti-submarine forces were present near the Straits of Gibraltar and Gengelbach was compelled to remain submerged for long periods. Morale aboard had slumped due to the severe northern Atlantic weather, a frustrating inability to engage their enemy and enforced idleness of waiting near Gibraltar. The crew believed that they would soon be proceeding to their new port of Brest for a Christmas in France, the fuel bunkers aboard *U574* depleted to the point of an enforced return. The boat was only able to limp along at 5 knots on a single diesel.

Spirits aboard were lowered even further when, after receiving up-to-date sealed orders from BdU via *U434* on 2 December, Gengelbach revealed that they were to refuel in Vigo from an interned German tanker before embarking on six more weeks of patrol. During the night of 11/12 December at 2200hrs *U574* slipped into Vigo harbour and tied up against the seaward side of German supply ship *Bessel* to begin refuelling and replenishment of stores under cover of darkness. As *U574* made her way clear of the harbour at 0330hrs the control room was cluttered with bunches of bananas and Spanish fruit in every nook and cranny.

Dönitz had decided that Gengelbach would participate in his proposed pack attack on convoy HG 76, reported by spies to shortly be putting to sea. The six-strong *Seeräuber* group (including 7th U-Flotilla 'Ace' Engelbert Endrass aboard *U567*) was directed to intercept the expected convoy on 16 December following a *Kondor* sighting two days after it had sailed. Visibility was poor and contact only brief, but *U574* and the other *Seeräuber* boats raced to intercept with diesels hammering. Gengelbach made contact during the night of 16th/17th and began to shadow. The convoy wallowed slowly on its course, thirty-two ships arranged in nine columns and only making an average 7.3 knots, the escort of seventeen warships prepared for impending action. Although *Abwehr* intelligence had accurately reported the size of the merchant convoy they had understated the escort strength as 'three destroyers, a submarine and some corvettes'. In fact it comprised three destroyers, four sloops, nine corvettes and the escort carrier *Audacity* carrying four Martlet fighter aircraft. Command of the escort forces was in the hands of tough and experienced Captain Frederick J. ('Johnny') Walker, ex-head of Portland's Anti-Submarine Warfare School.

The ensuing battle was disastrous for the U-boats. On the morning of 17 December contact boat *U131* was scuttled following damage from air attack and approaching destroyers. Next morning *U434* was sunk, forced to the surface and scuttled by her commander. With this inauspicious start, the four remaining U-boats regrouped for another attack on 18 December. Gengelbach's *U574* fired two torpedoes at corvette HMS *Convolvulus* missing with both and undergoing a terrifying two-hour hunt by her one-time target and fellow corvette HMS *Penstemon* accompanied by destroyer HMS *Stanley*.

By next morning several of Walker's escorts had departed from the convoy, the final remaining destroyer ex-American 'four-stacker' HMS *Stanley*. Aboard *U574* Gengelbach had received fresh instructions from Kerneval to attack escorts first, with the aim of punching a hole through to the vulnerable merchantmen. Early that morning in slight swell and beneath a fine but cloudy sky that masked the moon from casting its revealing light, Gengelbach made his second combat approach, this time remaining surfaced as he had been unable to spot the convoy through his periscope. At 0413hrs HMS *Stanley* urgently reported sighting the approaching U-boat. Walker, aboard HMS *Stork*, promptly ordered the destroyer to fire flares. Atop *U574*'s tower, Gengelbach realized at once that he had been located as blinding flares arced into the heavens. Spying *Stanley* on his port bow at 1,100-metres, he fired two torpedoes before beginning to retreat at full diesel speed. A further panicked message followed from *Stanley*, 'Torpedoes passed from astern' and suddenly the aged destroyer erupted in a 'sheet of flame several hundred feet high'. *U574* had made its first and last kill before crash diving to escape retribution.

HMS *Stork* immediately altered course to port and ordered the commencement of 'Operation Buttercup' astern of *Stanley*'s final position.[52] Speeding towards the area of the U-boat's sighting at 15 knots the British ship proceeded to drop single depth charges. At 0424½hrs ASDIC contact was made aboard *Stork* with submerged *U574* at 700 yards distance and Walker recorded:

> 'Movement was very slight and the U-boat's position suggested that she was waiting for a ship to stop and pick up *Stanley*'s survivors, thus providing her with another victim.'

At 0426 five charges set to explode at 50 feet were dropped. These were the most damaging to Gengelbach's boat. The charges exploded immediately above *U574*, putting both electric motors out of action and starting a small fire in the banana-filled control room due to an electrical short circuit. Loud explosions from several bottles of compressed air that had split open startled crewmen and water began to jet inside the pressure hull due to a fractured supporting rib. The boat began to sink and chaos erupted aboard.

On the surface Walker had lost contact after the multiple blasts, his ship's dynamo affected by the explosion. It was only a matter of minutes before contact was regained, however, the U-boat lying 900 yards away. Ten charges were dropped over her position, set to explode at 50 and 140 feet. Once more the dynamo failed for several minutes, but again contact was eventually re-established. Aboard *U574* there was no hope of keeping the ship stable with both motors out of commission. Gengelbach realized that there was no chance of escape for *U574* and resigned himself to death. According to survivors, he took little interest in any further attempts to saving his ship. The boat's Chief Engineer Oblt. (Ing) Erich Lorenz (painfully suffering from an ulcerated stomach) made his way through the devastated smoky interior to come face to face with the silent commander and demanded that they surface. He confronted Gengelback, apparently saying: 'Either you leave the boat or I do, I cannot take any more responsibility'. A heated dispute then ensued between the two men as the crew struggled to maintain some semblance of control over the crippled U-boat. Finally Gengelback bowed to his Chief's wishes and ordered the boat surfaced and scuttled. He instructed all his crew to don life-saving equipment and prepare to abandon ship as soon as she broke surface.

The boat had sunk to 180 metres when the captain commanded all tanks

---

[52] 'Operation Buttercup' was a pattern attack devised by Walker for the location of recently submerged U-boats by methodical deduction of their likely position, dropping depth charges while lighting with searchlights and flares the likely avenues of surface escape for a U-boat.

blown, *U574* plummeting still further to 240 metres before beginning her uncontrollable climb. Above them Walker was preparing for a new attack when his hydrophone operator reported a strong effect heard at 500 yards. At 0438hrs the U-boat broke surface 200 yards ahead, her diesels roaring instantly into life, although both rudders were jammed hard to port. The crew began to charge helter skelter from her conning tower into the sea while their boat gathered momentum in its directionless charge.

Walker immediately ordered speed increased and preparations made to ram. A ten-charge pattern was primed, set for 50 and 150 feet, and all guns opened fire as blinding white snowflakes illuminated their target. Walker recorded:

> 'The ensuing chase lasted 11 minutes and I was surprised to find later by the plot *Stork* had turned three complete circles. The U-boat appeared to be turning continuously to port just inside the *Stork*'s turning circle at a speed of only two or three knots less than the latter's best. . . . Some 4" was fired from the forward mountings, until the guns could not be sufficiently depressed, after which the gun crews, reduced to fist shakings, roared curses at an enemy who several times seemed to be a matter of feet away rather than yards . . . the prettiest shooting was made by my First Lieutenant (G.T.S. Gray DSC RN). With a stripped Lewis gun over the top of the bridge screen, he quickly reduced the conning tower to a mortuary.'

Leutnant zur See Eckart Joost, having survived the hail of bullets as he plunged from the U-boat, remembered the bizarre situation of nearly being run down by his own circling boat, a stream of escaping Germans trailing behind her as the U-boat surged onward with *Stork* in dogged pursuit. Aboard *U574* the Engineering Officer Lorenz, after opening the valves to enable scuttling, drew his service pistol and shot himself in the head. Gengelbach, having ensured that he was the last man aboard still alive, remained standing in the ruins of *U574*'s shattered control room and prepared to sink with his ship.

Before the U-boat went under the two circling opponents collided at 0448hrs and *U574* was rammed slightly aft of her conning tower at a 20° angle. The wrecked U-boat hung on *Stork*'s bow and then ASDIC dome before scraping with a nerve-rending screech of tortured metal to the corvette's stern where she received the final ten shallow depth charges. What remained of *U574* disappeared in a fountain of dirty water as did several swimming escapees from the doomed submarine. Joost and many of the Germans still alive in the sea remembered the terror of being under what they perceived was a direct attack, unable to see that their U-boat lay slightly astern of Walker's corvette:

> 'The *Storck* (sic.) fired from all barrels and launched more depth charges, which we, swimming in the water, thought were meant for the survivors. Only later did I learn that *U574* was still nearby and afloat.'

HMS *Stork* later plucked five shocked German survivors from the water, including Joost, while HMS *Samphire* rescued eleven more. In order to positively identify their target the dazed German survivors were threatened with abandonment unless they told their rescuers their ship number and commander's name.[53] Thirty men died with their boat, some as an unfortunate result of depth-charge explosions while lying helpless in the sea.

At 0528hrs Walker signalled to his commander:

> '*Stanley* sunk by U-boat, U-boat sunk by *Stork*.'

For Joost and his comrades their ordeal was not yet over. Of the five shocked survivors aboard *Stork*, two more were to die after an accidental ramming by HMS *Deptford* of the escort group. The bow of the old British sloop had smashed its way into the port side of *Stork* during the early morning of 22 December missing the vital engine room and steering gear. However as Walker reported

> '*Deptford*'s stem had walked straight into the prison of survivors and two of the five Boches had been pulped, literally, into a bloody mess.'

The convoy battle dragged on for one further German casualty, Engelbert Endrass killed aboard *U567* with his entire crew. The number of surviving 'Aces' was dwindling rapidly. Dönitz was appalled at the scale of the disaster and on 22 December called off any remaining U-boats. He calculated that one aircraft tender and three small freighters (in reality two) had been sunk for the cost of five U-boats including, Endrass. The gloom in which 1941 ended deepened considerably.[54]

15 January: *U566* slipped from Lorient under the command of Kptlt. Dietrich Borchert for its first North Atlantic patrol. Previously active in the Arctic, reflected in the boat's mascot of a polar bear, worn on every crew member's headgear, Borchert had yet to make a sinking, his sole action being in September 1941 when he unsuccessfully attacked submarine HMS *Trident*.

The same day that Borchert put to sea Cohausz recorded another loss for the 1st U-Flotilla during the previous December: '*U208* missing since 12 December, '*Vermisst ein Stern*' – presumed lost.

16 January: *U656* sailed on her first operational voyage. Slipping her mooring lines at Kiel she began an uneventful patrol, cut short by Dönitz who ordered her commander Kptlt. Ernst Kröning to head directly to Brest in preparation for operations against Canada and the USA.

---

[53] *Neither Sharks nor Wolves*, Timothy Mulligan. Whether or not the British ship would have actually carried out this threat is of course pure speculation.

[54] In reality only four U-boats were sunk during the battle as the fifth boat *U127* had been lost in a separate engagement.

Dönitz's 'Operation *Paukenschlag*' attack on American East Coast shipping was four days old, five Type IX 2nd U-Flotilla U-boats savaging American merchant shipping within sight of the coastal lights.

In the French port new regulations had been issued regarding U-boats' entry and departure. Reflecting the growing attention and confidence of RAF anti-submarine attacks the regulations noted in the flotilla War Diary contained the following stipulations:

> Boats were to proceed during the night at high speed through Brittany's coastal waters (from the 200-metre curve inwards) and take on a local pilot at sunrise. When entering the port it was no longer considered necessary to use a high tidal state.
>
> Departures should be scheduled for the evening so that the U-boat is released by its *Vorpostenboote* escorts near point 30 or 32 at dusk.
>
> Test dives were only to be conducted seaward of the 200-metre curve.
>
> The reasons given by BdU for these new instructions were:
>
> 'The already existing danger from the air as well as the recent and considerably growing threat of mines in the region of the 200-metre line. These pose greater threat to the boats than entering the Atlantic ports at low tide.'

Indeed the increasing attention of enemy bombers had begun to show regularly in War Diary entries. Cohausz recorded that by 16 January there had been a three-day pause in 'persistent English air attacks'. Previous to that, multiple air raid warnings had been sounded daily, often followed by the delivery of high explosive bombs and myriad incendiaries. Although there was no discernible drop in Flotilla operations, Cohausz did acknowledge setbacks due to some bomb damage and its knock-on effects, such as hours of disrupted sleep for his men. Although U-boats rated high on the Allied target list there was a firm conviction that Brest's unwanted bomber attention was in no small part due to three huge and potentially powerful warships languishing in the harbour. *Scharnhorst*, *Gneisenau* and *Prinz Eugen* continued to suffer periodic damage at the hands of the RAF and appeared powerless to change the situation. Camouflage netting strung across the ships had little effect.

20 January: Kptlt. Siegfried Strelow took *U435* from Kiel on its first active patrol. Transferring from 5th U-Flotilla, Strelow's was the first of the new induction of trainee boats from late 1941 to ship from the Kiel training Flotilla.

21 January: In Lorient *U563* prepared to depart for Hamburg. After preliminary repairs it was decided that the heavily scarred boat must return to Germany for a total refit. Oblt.z.S. Bargsten, himself bearing the scars from their brush with a Whitley the previous December, began the first leg of his journey directed initially to Bergen. The voyage, made entirely surfaced as *U563* was unable to submerge while moving, was not without incident.

126

Approaching Bergen, Bargsten could not locate the entrance to Bergen Fjord, inquiring of a local fisherman met at sea the correct access channel. This Norwegian patriot promptly sent the U-boat 40 miles in the wrong direction. In increasingly bad humour Bargsten took the next fisherman he came across on board and eventually they reached their destination on 3 February. While in Bergen, Klaus Bargsten and two officers from other ships in harbour were invited to the German consulate for drinks. After the evening drew to a close Bargsten and his two colleagues made their way to their respective ships. One of the other officers, captain of a Vorpostenboot, arrived during a small celebration aboard his ship held by several crewmen from both his own ship and *U563*. Unfortunately at that moment one of *U563*'s Petty Officers was toying with a service pistol that went off, wounding the captain in the foot. The Petty Officer was later punished for carrying an illegal weapon and shooting an officer.

Proceeding from Norway to Hamburg shipyards via Heligoland *U563* and its icebreaker escort became stuck fast in thick pack ice, freed later by a second escort vessel. Finally on 11 February *U563* reached its destination where Bargsten, convinced that the boat would never sail again, transferred to 2nd U-Flotilla and the new Type IXC *U521*. His shabby U-boat sailed into its berth at the Blohm & Voss shipyard to begin its rebirth. Following the completion of repairs she would serve briefly as a training boat under new command before returning to Brest and front-line duties despite Bargsten's predictions.

29 January: Rolf Mützelberg docked *U203* in Brest after over a month at sea. Originally ordered to the Mediterranean, he had received new instructions to patrol the Newfoundland Bank as a part of the ten-boat concentration around that area on 2 January. In savage weather he attacked and sank the Portuguese fishing vessel MV *Catalina*, the Norwegian SS *Octavian*, the American patrol craft *Rosemonde* and damaged the Canadian MV *North Gaspe*. His claimed score of 18,000 BRT rates as the largest return so far that year for a 1st U-Flotilla boat.

1 February: Two new submarines were transferred to 1st U-Flotilla. The Type XB minelayers *U116* and *U117* passed into the unit while still in Kiel undergoing trials. *U116* had been commissioned on 26 July 1941 under the command of KK Werner von Schmidt while her sister ship had reached the water on 25 October of the same year, under the command of KK Hans-Werner Neumann. Both U-boats were undergoing difficult conversion work from minelayer to transport submarine. Von Schmidt's boat would not be fully operational until April while Neumann's was expected to take even longer, not fit for duty before September.

4 February: After hasty replenishment Kptlt. Ernst Kröning took *U656* from Brest bound for the North Atlantic. Kröning's orders were to rendezvous with blockade-runner *Osorno* on 20 February, the German ship laden with 6,796 tons of goods from Kobe, Japan. However, the escort duty proved somewhat unnecessary due to Kapitän Hellmann bringing his 6,951-ton ship through the muddy Gironde River to Bordeaux on 19 February. *U656* continued outwards to Newfoundland to join fourteen other boats on station. Kröning radioed a final report to Kerneval on 24 February and was never heard from again. Unknown to BdU, on 1 March an Argentina-based VP 82 US Navy Hudson bomber, piloted by Ensign William Tepuni, spotted the U-boat approximately 60 miles south of Cape Race. Immediately attacking the crash-diving submarine, Tepuni dropped depth charges onto the submerging stern of Kröning's boat. Oil and bubbles were observed on the surface, a tell-tale trail moving away from the area. Tepuni was forced to break off his surveillance to refuel, but returned with two other Hudsons to deposit further depth charges ahead of the oil track. A thicker gush of oil was observed following the devastating explosions and destroyers were summoned to ensure the German sunk. During the next 24 hours thirty-three depth charges were dropped sporadically, ensuring that Kröning and his forty-four-men were killed. *U656* was the first confirmed U-boat destroyed by American forces and the first sunk in American territorial waters, which had recently witnessed the opening carnage of Type IX driven 'Operation *Paukenschlag.*'

February yielded meagre pickings for Brest's U-boats, hampered by a lack of unit strength and vile weather conditions in the Atlantic. *U582* returned from patrol with a single claimed 6,000 BRT (5,189-ton SS *Refast* sunk from convoy ON 56 south of Cape Race) while *U754* docked with 16,000 BRT claimed (MV *Belize*, SS *William Hansen*, SS *Mount Kitheron* and SS *Icaron* for a combined 11,386 tons, all sunk off the Newfoundland Bank area). *U86* accounted for 8,627-ton British SS *Toorak* and damaged the tanker SS *Dimitrios G Thermiotis* before returning to Brest with a rescued German aircrew aboard, plucked from their life raft in Biscay. Meanwhile, others came into port empty-handed. U-boats began to use the first completed cells of the massive concrete bunker below the Naval Academy as Allied air attacks intensified against the city, its port and the three warships still anchored in Brest harbour.

11 February: The position of the large German ships bottled in Brest, under constant observation and air-attack, was becoming untenable and it was decided by Hitler to withdraw them to Germany. Raeder, as head of the Kriegsmarine, argued strongly that they should instead head into the Atlantic on new raiding missions to keep the pressure on Britain's struggling supply artery, but the dictator's decision was final. His increasing paranoia over the possible loss of these vessels and his lack of understanding concerning naval warfare were combining to end the operational lives of his large warships. In Hitler's words, the situation that the mighty German warships were in was that of 'a patient with cancer who is doomed unless he submits to an operation'. Also, Hitler nursed the strong belief that British and American troops were planning to invade Norway, turning his northern flank and upsetting the flow of raw materials from Scandinavia to Germany. He reasoned that by returning the three warships trapped in Brest to Germany it placed a powerful naval squadron within striking distance of any Allied landing attempt. This obsession with the idea of an impending Allied attack against Norway would in the long run have disastrous consequences on an already overstretched Kriegsmarine. The culmination of Hitler's mood of despair was a daring, almost suicidal, plan to send the three German ships dashing up the English Channel to Germany with strong Luftwaffe and Kriegsmarine escorts, right under the noses of the British, and in broad daylight.

Many among the Kriegsmarine command were aghast at the prospect of the almost certain destruction of these ships, but Hitler was inflexible, and on 11 February 1942 the three warships broke out of Brest and raced towards Wilhelmshaven, strongly escorted by a dense screen of smaller surface vessels, led by *Z29* carrying Kapt. Erich Bey (*Führer der Zerstörer*). Commanding this audacious move was Admiral Otto Ciliax, C-in-C of German battleships and one time captain of the *Scharnhorst*, now a passenger aboard his old ship. For the first time the Luftwaffe worked in close liaison with the Kriegsmarine and provided strong air support under the control of the 'Ace' fighter pilot Oberst Adolf Galland, and with a Luftwaffe liaison officer, Oberst Max Ibel, aboard the *Scharnhorst*. Overhead, Luftwaffe pilots provided an umbrella of Me109, Me110 and Fw190 fighters, ferociously attacking any approaching threat. 'Operation Cerberus', as it was known, worked spectacularly well, with the British caught napping by the daring move. Feeble, badly co-ordinated, though bravely handled, British air and sea attacks on the Germans produced no tangible results, the only hint of disaster being when the *Scharnhorst* struck a mine near her destination. While Ciliax was transferred to an accompanying *Z29* to continue his role as operation commander, the battleship, with damage to her turbo-electric motors, was able to reach its goal with assistance from escort ships after 34 minutes of nerve-wracking immobility. *Gneisenau* also activated a British mine but with less detrimental effect. She was consigned to dry dock for an anticipated three weeks, however, after striking a submerged wreck upon entering harbour. It was to be here that the majestic ship suffered her cruellest blow. On the night of 25/26 February RAF bombers attacked the docked ships, hitting *Gneisenau*'s forward magazine and wrecking her completely. In France, Brest was now left to the smaller ships of Germany's *Sicherungsdivisionen*, *Zerstörerflottillen* and the *Unterseebootwaffe*.

14 February: KK Hans Cohausz departed from his post as commander of 1st U-Flotilla. He left to resume command of the ex-Turkish *Batiray*, re-designated *UA* since being taken over by the Kriegsmarine. In Cohausz' absence from the U-boat during his period as flotilla chief previous commander of the 1st U-Flotilla KK Hans Eckermann had commanded *UA*.

The large submarine had undergone conversion to the role of refuelling U-boat, soon to become a vital link in the deployment of Type VIIs against the American coast. Replacing Cohausz as temporary acting flotilla chief was 32-year-old Kptl. Heinz Buchholz, ex-commander of Type IIB *U15* for two years from October 1937.

1 March: Kptlt. Hans-Heinz Linder slipped his U-boat from her Brest mooring at 1730hrs. *U202* purred gently sternwards on electric motors until clear of the dock when her diesels exploded into life. The crowd of well wishers cheered them on their way after listening to the brief speech of their new flotilla chief and the rousing march played by Kriegsmarine bandsmen. Flowers were thrown at the waving crew and their boat nosed gently forward to rendezvous with its *Sperrbrecher* escort near Pointe des Espagnols. The anti-submarine net was moved aside and the journey along the narrow *Goulet de Brest* began. Once free of the coastline, the boat headed for new hunting grounds in America as part of the fourth wave of boats sailing against the United States. He was soon to be joined by flotilla-mate Mützelberg aboard *U203*, sailing from Brest on 12 March. Back inside 1st U-Flotilla's compound, still awaiting the overhaul of his boat to be completed, Adalbert Schnee received welcome notification of his promotion to Kapitänleutnant.

3 March: '*U656 Vermisst ein Stern*' – presumed loss.

6 March: Returning from Newfoundland Kaptlt. Reinhard Suhren claimed a single sinking during *U564*'s patrol. After operating in disgusting meteorological conditions near Canada's eastern seaboard Suhren ventured southwards, conscious of his fuel limitations aboard a Type VIIC. Opposite the glittering waterways of New York, lit as if still peacetime, *U564* attacked and sank the Canadian 1,141-ton tanker MV *Victolite* north-north-west of Bermuda on 11th February, recovering a calendar and ensign from the luckless tanker before she went under.

Suhren was now critically low on fuel and radioed Dönitz at Kerneval for instructions and a possible refuelling rendezvous. *U564* was ordered to take fuel from Type IXB *U103*, then beginning its voyage home. However, due to severe weather and bad navigation, the two submarines failed to meet. Suhren was next directed to refuel from another Type IXB, Kplt. Harald Gelhaus' *U107*, on 13 February. This time the two U-boats met as planned and devised a strategy to begin the difficult process of transferring fuel oil from one to another. Unfortunately for the two U-boats, disaster struck without warning in the heaving swell as *U564* was thrust against *U107*, ramming Gelhaus' boat and rupturing his starboard fuel tank. There was worse news for Suhren:

> 'Gelhaus of course swore good and proper, since he now had to turn back, and wouldn't be able to do anything more. The one with reason

130

to swear was in fact me; I swore away at myself and would happily have jumped overboard, for in the collision I had bent the doors of all four torpedo tubes and wouldn't be able to fire them any more.'[55]

Both boats were forced to abort and headed in company for France, creeping through the Atlantic on single engines to conserve their precious fuel. Frustratingly they then encountered a northbound convoy and were forced to let it pass. Three days after the accidental ramming Suhren caught sight of another tanker, the British MV *Opalia*, and engaged it in a high sea with his deck cannon. The struggling gunners scored several hits but caused little damage, their quarry escaping into the distance. The battered *U564*, instantly recognisable by its '3 X Black Cats' painted on her conning tower, a legacy of Suhren's service aboard *U48*, limped into Brest for a month of difficult repairs. However, Suhren's patrol had proved to Dönitz that by careful route planning and husbanding of fuel it was possible for Type VII U-boats to spend up to ten days off America's east coast. The decision was taken to direct these smaller boats south from their accustomed Newfoundland hunting grounds against the United States, previously the domain of other flotillas in large Type IX ocean-going boats, instead of the less productive and naturally hostile Canadian waters.

7 March: Two 1st U-Flotilla boats took to the seas, *U754* from Brest at 1730hrs bound for Canadian waters and *U405* from Trondheim in support of heavy German surface units moving south along the Norwegian coast. The latter U-boat was one of nearly twenty German submarines tied to Norway by Hitler's obsession with Allied designs on that country. Over a year previously, on 24 January 1941, Hitler had remarked to Vice-Admiral Fricke his 'absolute conviction that Britain and the United States are determined to affect the war's course decisively by an attack on northern Norway'. While Dönitz was desperate for strength in the Atlantic and for consolidating the gains of '*Paukenschlag*', twenty boats of various flotillas battled their way through Arctic seas for virtually no result.

11 March: *U558* sailed into Brest to a rapturous reception after completing one of the most notable convoy attacks of the Atlantic war. Having departed for the North Atlantic on 10 February Kptlt. Günther Krech received reports from *U155*, shadowing convoy ONS 67 westbound along the Great Circle shipping route. The lumbering convoy consisted of thirty-five merchant ships, including many valuable tankers travelling in ballast, and escorted by only a single Canadian corvette and four American destroyers, two old and two new. Trailing behind was the rescue ship *Toward*, equipped with new HF/DF

---

[55] *Nasses Eichenlaub*, Reihard Suhren.

(High Frequency Direction Finding – 'Huff-Duff') radio detection sets for locating the point of origin of radio messages or beacon signals transmitted by stalking U-boats. *U155* opened the attack by sinking two ships, a tanker and freighter, and by late evening on 23 February seven U-boats were homing on the merchant convoy.

The next boat to attack was Krech's *U558*. In the darkness of early morning, on 24 February, Krech launched three separate assaults over a five hour period against the convoy, sinking three tankers, SS *Inverarder*, MV *Anadara*, MV *Finnanger*, and the British freighter SS *White Crest*. He rounded out his successful onslaught by damaging the Norwegian tanker MV *Eidanger*. These initial attacks had claimed a total of 27,503 tons destroyed. Later that afternoon he again closed to fire torpedoes and this time sank the ailing *Eidanger* adding a further 9,432 tons to his score, for a total of 36,936 tons. After firing all but one of his torpedoes the jubilant Krech set course for Brest and a hero's return.

Credited by German reckoning with destroying 40,432 tons Dönitz and the German press lavished much praise and attention on captain and crew, and on 15 March Dönitz was at 1st U-Flotilla headquarters to decorate Krech and his men with Iron Crosses First and Second Class.

The boats that remained in contact following Krech's departure mauled the convoy. In total the devastated merchant formation lost a total of eight ships sunk, including six precious tankers and one tanker damaged. Despite the US Navy decorating the escort group's commanding officer and praising his 'outstanding' work, it was an Allied disaster. Dönitz rated the battle as extremely 'satisfactory' and further vindication of what a powerful group attack could achieve. Within a week of Krech's return, flotilla mate *U582* departed Brest for its second war patrol in the Atlantic battleground. On 24th March, finally repaired and ready for action, *U201* also sailed from Brest at 2030hrs for her sixth war patrol with Schnee in command.

28 March: The flotilla War Diary entry for this date marks another crucial event on France's western coast:

'0400: *Rheinland Appell.*
0600: *Landung englischer Streitkräfte in Saint Nazaire.*'

The milestone commando attack 'Operation Chariot' took German forces completely by surprise in the naval port of Sainte Nazaire. Christened by the British 'Operation Chariot' this audacious plan involved ramming an obsolete destroyer, the ex-American flushdecker HMS *Campbeltown* (ex-USS *Buchanan*), packed in the bow with explosives, into the gates of Saint Nazaire's dry dock. By disabling these facilities the Germans would be deprived of the only dock large enough to accommodate the battleship *Tirpitz*, a lingering threat to the Royal Navy. The small assault force set out from Falmouth at 1400hrs on 26 March 1942. In a flotilla comprising *Campbeltown*, *MGB 314*, *MTB 74*, sixteen Motor Launches (MLs) and offshore escorts of HMS *Tynedale* and HMS *Atherstone* were 345 Royal Navy officers and men, 257 commandos, four medics, three liaison officers and two journalists. Despite many hair-raising brushes with the enemy before the attack began, the British carried their mission through to its objective, and ultimately, success. Although only three of the Motor Launches returned from the battle, and 169 British men were killed with a further 200 captured, the raid was judged to have achieved its desired result. Huge essential, but vulnerable, dry-dock pumps were disabled by Commandos during fierce combat, often hand-to-hand, although the nearby U-boat bunker remained untouched. After the gunfire had died away and all those British troops that could escape had, Kriegsmarine infantry rounded up any survivors and examined the British destroyer impaled on Saint Nazaire's massive dry-dock gates. HMS *Campbeltown* exploded at 1135hrs as German troops were exploring their prize with some bewilderment. Forty-two Germans were killed and 127 wounded during the initial battle against the English. One hundred and fifty more perished as *Campbeltown* exploded.

As a result of this courageous operation, defences before other vulnerable harbour installations along the French Atlantic coast were ordered thickened by a shaken *Marinegruppenkommando West*. Along the waterline fringe of the Goulet de Brest's southern shores were constructed solid concrete bunkers. Inside these impregnable shelters torpedo tubes were manned by Kriegsmarine artillerymen, ready to repel any possibility of seaborne attack. Facing them, the northern shores had no such suitable site for construction at the water's edge. To counter this problem requisitioned French vessels, armed with similarly formidable torpedo tubes, were grouped together to complete the last line of defence before the submarine pens. This rather motley collection of small French boats and barges, again manned with Kriegsmarine men, was situated in small bays on the northern Goulet de Brest coast.

Dönitz was compelled by his superior Raeder, with Hitler's agreement, to leave his command post at Kerneval during May 1942 and relocate to Paris, his new headquarters located in the *Avenue Maréchal Maunoury*. This was another of the long-term and far-reaching effects of the British raid on Saint Nazaire. With Allied commandoes becoming bolder in their attacks, often as intent on capturing Germans for intelligence reasons as destroying installations, there was real fear that Dönitz would be a target for such a raid. It was a blow to Dönitz who preferred the 'hands on' approach to managing his men, and also was felt amongst his commanders and crews. To the men of the U-boat service 'The Lion' gradually became more distant, although still managing to command unconditional loyalty and respect from his subordinates.

4 April: *'U116 ausgelaufen zur Unternehmung über Heligoland.'* KK Werner von Schmidt's Type XB tanker *U116* began its first transfer from Kiel to Heligoland. Slipping through the Kaiser Wilhelm Canal in the course of a single afternoon the huge boat then travelled overnight to the bleak forward base on the rocky outcrop that was Heligoland. Arriving at 1330hrs, *U116* was to spend six days undertaking minor repairs and adjustments. A further journey to Bergen for refuelling and *U116* began its voyage to Lorient, finally arriving on 5 May, ready for Atlantic operations.

5 April: Hitler had sent more U-boats to fight within the Arctic Circle in increasing paranoia regarding a possible Allied invasion of Norway. So, by April 1942 there were twenty-five U-boats operating in this inhospitable region, including *U405*, *U435* and *U584* of 1st U-Flotilla. Local command was handled by *Konteradmiral* Hubert Schmundt aboard the *Schnellboote* tender *Tanga*, moored in Kirkenes, later moving his headquarters aboard Hitler's luxury yacht *Grille* moored in Narvik harbour.

The main target for these boats which were operating in conditions of extreme difficulty, compounded by nearly 24-hour darkness of an Arctic winter, was the interception of the PQ or QP convoys. The Arctic battle-ground was not an easy one for either combatant. U-boats were rewarded for their harsh existence with meagre sinkings and a creeping rate of attrition in the face of growing numbers of Allied destroyer escorts. To be sunk in the Arctic was certain death, whether by drowning or rapid freezing in an unforgiving ice-cold sea.

During the morning at 0900hrs Kptlt. Siegfried Strelow brought *U435* from patrol into Kirkenes. On 16 March Strelow had left Trondheim for operations following rust treatment to the U-boat's hull. Five days later convoy PQ13 sailed from Murmansk headlong into a massive Arctic storm, which scattered the twenty merchant ships over hundreds of square miles of bleak ocean. During the morning of 27 March *Kondor* aircraft sighted several of the disarrayed ships and proceeded to attack while transmitting beacons for approaching U-boats and nearby Kriegsmarine destroyers.

During the extended running battle that followed, attacking *Kondors* sank two ships, and three of the four approaching U-boats sank three, including the 6,421-ton American steamer SS *Effingham*, torpedoed by *U435* north-east of Kola Inlet. For their part the Kriegsmarine lost one attacking destroyer.

Sensibly, both *U405* and *U435* later passed from the strength of 1st U-Flotilla to that of the local Bergen-based 11th Flotilla during June 1942. *U584*, on the other hand, departed the frozen north for Germany on 28 February 1942, and ultimately Brest during May, having achieved no victories to that date.

12 April: The now famous Krech ordered *U558*'s diesels fired at 2000hrs, sailing again for the waters of America for his seventh patrol.

25 April: At 1200hrs Kptlt. Oestermann took *U754* into Brest harbour. His triumphant report to Flotilla Chief Kptlt. Buchholz culminated in a claimed

35,000 tons of merchant ships sunk. Seven weeks of patrol off Newfoundland and the east coast of the United States had resulted in eight confirmed sinkings, including three tankers. On 23 March he had opened his attack by torpedoing the 8,620 ton British tanker MV *British Prudence* south of Canada's St Pierre Island. Moving south along the US coast to balmy Virginia Oestermann sank the 441-ton tugboat *Menominee* and two 914-ton barges, damaging a third. Finally between 1 and 6 April he sank the American tanker SS *Tiger*, the British freighter *SS Otho* and the Norwegian tanker MV *Kollskegg* with torpedo attacks, an exceptional patrol resulting in 31,578 tons of enemy merchant shipping sunk.

His was not the only successful sortie against America for Type VIICs of the 1st U-Flotilla. Kptlt. Linder in *U202* arrived in Brest at 110hrs on 26 April claiming 16,000 tons sunk. He had spent a number of frustrating days at the voyage's outset in an unsuccessful search for the German blockade runner *Germania*, ordered to escort the 9,851-ton converted merchant ship into Bordeaux. After release from this fruitless duty he finally arrived off the United States as part of 'Operation *Paukenschlag*'s' fourth wave.[56] Linder then sank the 8,882-ton British tanker MV *Athelviscount* on 22 March and then 5,249-ton MV *Loch Don* eight days later.

Ritterkreuz-holder Mützelberg also returned during April. Docking at 1130hrs in Brest on the last day of the month he claimed 41,000 tons sunk; in fact he had sunk two ships for 14,232 tons, damaging another two for 16,164 tons. Mützelberg's *U203*, Linder's *U202* and Horst Uphoff, engaged in a mammoth two-month cruise off the United States in *U84*, had needed to refuel from *UA* during their long patrols, rendezvousing with their ex-flotilla commander Cohausz west of the Azores.

The addition of Type VIIC U-boats to 'Operation *Paukenschlag*' reaped enormous dividends for the Kriegsmarine. From all combat flotillas, twenty of these smaller U-boats sailed for America, sinking a confirmed total of forty-six ships (including twelve tankers) for a staggering 242,000 tons. However, in hindsight this can be seen as the high point reached by the smaller submarines in American waters. The initial '*Paukenschlag*' attack had been mounted by a mere five Type IX ocean-going U-boats against an American mainland woefully unprepared for aggression by experienced German crews. By April, despite still sinking a considerable quantity of Allied shipping, the trend was diminishing. The US Navy was recoiling from its previous mistakes in dealing with U-boat attack and preparing to go on to the counter-offensive. To the men of the 1st U-Flotilla, however, all that was immediately apparent was that their boats were still successfully sinking ships in distant American waters.

---

[56] Author's note: This term has been used with some (hopefully forgivable) creative licence here. Technically only the opening attack was code-named 'Paukenschlag'.

26 April: Kptlt. Siegfreid Strelow ordered his battered *U435* tied alongside Kiel's Tirpitz Pier at 1900hrs. He had been involved in an attack on convoy QP 10 sailing from Kola Inlet on 10 April. Strelow had attempted to torpedo escort destroyer HMS *Punjabi* to no avail before successfully attacking and sinking the Panamanian SS *El Occidente* and the Russian SS *Kiev* east-south-east of Bear Island. The addition of this 11,831 tons to the 6,421-ton SS *Effingham* sunk from convoy PQ 13 during the previous month made him tonnage-leader in Arctic operations.

5 May: Massive *U116* finally arrived in Lorient, putting into the Scorff River and beginning preparations for her first operational sortie into the Atlantic. Her sister-ship *U117* was still working up at the U-boat Support Station at Königsberg. Kl Werner von Schmidt's boat needed only minor refit and complete replenishment before facing the rigours of an Atlantic patrol. Brief dry-docking within Lorient's enormous pens was required, maintenance men crawling over *U116*'s stout hull for their innumerable tasks.

13 May: '*Richtfest der U-bunker.*' The imposing concrete bunker constructed by hundreds of Organisation Todt workers in Brest received its own form of commissioning ceremony. In the presence of several dignitaries, including *Direktor* Borsch of Berlin's Organisation Todt office and BdU staff officers headed by KK Günther Hessler, the bunker was declared fully operational. Portions of the mammoth shelter complex and its storage facilities were actually in full use already. Now, however, the base was totally operational and U-boats began to enter and leave the pens instead of proceeding up the winding Penfeld River.

14 May: Kptlt. Uphoff returned *U84* from its two-month sortie, feeling frustration at his lack of success. Uphoff claimed a paltry two ships for 9,200 BRT sunk; confirmed sinkings of the Yugoslavian SS *Nemanza* and Panamanian SS *Chenango* amounted to a combined 8,240 tons. It was a meagre showing for so long at sea. He sailed his boat quietly into one of the great concrete 'wet' pens at 1430hrs. Met by the Flotilla Chief, obligatory band and various off-duty Kriegsmarine men, the U-boat crew were at least happy to be among friends again. Brief speeches followed before the boat began to be de-stored and her ammunition unloaded. *U84*'s Chief Engineer Oblt. (Ing) Fritz Brüggeman held a short conference with the Flotilla engineers and presented his defect list for future work to be undertaken on the boat. The deck plating had attained the greenish tinge of an algae coating while bright red undercoat showed through worn paintwork.

Horst Uphoff was fondly remembered by his flotilla mates for his sense of humour. Not least of all for his habit of telling obscene, but apparently very amusing, jokes about the hierarchy of the Third Reich. As the war progressed this may have become a risky pastime, although Uphoff never paid a penalty for his actions. His penalty would come, but it would be much higher.

Meanwhile, that evening, after the luxury of a hot bath and shave, there was the traditional celebration banquet held inside the Naval Academy Flotilla headquarters. The following day leave was granted to at least half of the U-boat's complement, their rosters prepared while still at sea approaching Brest and tension from two months on patrol began to be released.

While the majority of the crew were absent on home leave *U84* transferred on electric engines to a 'dry' pen, where she was lifted from the water for work to begin in earnest. Guards were posted in the vicinity and no French workers allowed to board her; sabotage had become a problem of late to this Flotilla and others. She would receive fresh paint at the end of her dry-dock before being returned to a 'wet' pen and restocked for sea. British bombers were no longer a concern to the pace of work in Brest's U-boat yards, particularly since the departure of *Scharnhorst, Gneisenau* and *Prinz Eugen* and construction of the virtually impregnable U-boat bunker.

16 May: *U116* departed for the North Atlantic and her first voyage as supply ship. Following the new directive from BdU regarding optimal sailing times, she slipped from harbour at 2000hrs in the wake of her *Vorpostenboote* escort.

21 May: *U201*'s sixth war patrol ended at 0830hrs as Schnee brought his 'splinter camouflaged' boat into Brest's military harbour. Pennants fluttered again from the submarine's conning tower, this time adding up to 30,200 tons claimed during Schnee's part of the fifth wave of boats in 'Operation *Paukenschlag.*'

He had mounted his first attack as the sun began to set on 17 April. Stalking a solitary tanker, Schnee fired two torpedoes striking the ship and putting her into an immediate list. Unfortunately, and embarrassingly for the Germans, it was an Argentinian, the 7,417 ton MV *Victoria*. After Schnee had departed the scene American destroyers arrived and rescued the crew, which had prematurely abandoned their ship. The *Victoria* refused to sink, however, and her crew reboarded the damaged tanker, sailing her under American escort to a nearby port where the ship was confiscated by United States Naval authorities. A diplomatic uproar ensued as pro-German Argentina complained bitterly to both protaginists equally at the U-boat attack on their ship and its subsequent confiscation in America.

Further south, off Cape Hatteras, *U201* sank the Norwegian 2,227-ton steamer SS *Bris*. The following morning Schnee continued his streak of success by torpedoing the 6,069-ton American SS *San Jacinto*, finishing the burning ship with his 8.8cm deck gun after a brief exchange of gunfire with the American crew. Schnee waited until the passengers had left the ship before opening fire with his gun. Aboard the doomed passenger liner Captain Hart refused to leave the bridge and went down with his ship. Later that morning he claimed his final victory, sinking the 7,127-ton British SS *Derryheen* with a devatating bow salvo.

A further month was spent cruising the American east coast, but to no effect. Schnee frustratingly glimpsed fast moving liner *Aquitania* heading for New York and troop transport duties, but stood no chance of catching her with the U-boat straining to do any more than 17 knots.

24 May: Much to Dönitz's chagrin, and that of his U-boat commanders, OKM were still assigning special missions to boats of the 1st U-Flotilla. After departing Brest on 19 March, *U582* returned from two months at sea, Kptlt. Werner Schulte having spent the first three weeks in an unrewarding search for German blockade-runner *Rio Grande*. Despite U-boats being impotent in the role of escort, *U582* had been ordered to escort the laden ship to Bordeaux. The rendezvous scheduled for 3 April never transpired, *Kapitän* von Allwörden's *Rio Grande* being delayed off West Africa. On 7 April the mission was abandoned and *U582* proceeded to the sea north-east of Bermuda for equally pointless patrolling before returning to Brest.

Two 1st U-Flotilla boats were assigned a more exotic, but equally unsatis-factory, special operation. At 2100hrs Kptlt. Joachim Deecke's boat *U584* slipped from Brest U-boat bunker bound for the American coast. As well as the normal clutter and crew, aboard the crowded Type VIIC U-boat were four extra passengers dressed in Heer infantry uniforms – Edward J. Kerling, Herbert Haupt, Werner Thiel and Hermann Neubauer. These men repre-sented the first of two teams of agents bound for America's east coast in an undertaking named 'Operation Pastorius'.

Shortly following Hitler's declaration of war on the United States, he autho-rized a sabotage mission to be carried out inside the borders of the United States. Wanting to demonstrate that Americans were not safe within their homeland, various manufacturing installations and civilian targets were allo-cated for clandestine attack. *U584* only carried half of the complete team. Two nights later at 1945hrs Kptlt. Linder took *U202* from its pen to the open sea and ultimately America. Like Deecke's U-boat, there were four extra men aboard *U202* – Georg J. Dasch, Heinrick H. Heinck, Richard Quirin and Ernest P. Berger. Linder later recounted:

> 'Four men wearing infantry uniform came aboard; they brought with them shovels, explosives, a large sum in dollars and civilian clothes; which they later put on.'

Dasch and his team were to destroy the hydroelectric plants at Niagara Falls, the Aluminium Company of America factories in Illinois, Tennessee and New York. A cryolite plant in Philadelphia and the locks on the Ohio River between Louisville and Pittsburgh were also to be bombed. Kerling's team were sched-uled to blow up the Pennsylvania Railroad station in Newark, the famous horseshoe bend section on the railroad near Altoona plus other vital railroad parts. They were also to attack the lock and canal installations at St. Louis and Cincinnati and the water supply system for New York City. Both teams

138

were to plant bombs in Jewish-owned stores and in locker rooms at major passenger railroad stations to spread fear and panic. Their training had been undertaken between 10 April and 26 May at the *Abwehr* sabotage school near Brandenburg, under the watchful eye of Leutnant Walter Kappe. As planned by *Abwehr* these were only the first two teams of many being sent to America. When fully operational Kappe would join his men and lead their activities.

Aboard the U-boats there was considerable speculation from crew members as to the identities of their mysterious passengers and the contents of four small waterproof crates each team carried (three filled with explosives and the fourth containing fuses, wire and acid). Crew men were awake to the special nature of their mission, not only by the presence of strange passengers, but also by the removal at flotilla headquarters of any references to their boat or Field Post numbers within their pay books. However, of the U-boat crews only Deecke and Linder were aware of their U-boats' destinations and details of the agents' disembarkation. Anything else was considered unnecessary and they did not ask, nor were they told. Neither U-boat commander was pleased to have the agents aboard their ship. They felt that the men were neither motivated by patriotism nor a belief in their mission. Captured, they may well betray all that they knew about the U-boats and their method of operation. However, their opinion on the merits of their passengers was militarily irrelevant and the two boats began their crossing of the Atlantic. Linder had already made a patrol to the American coast as part of the fourth wave of 'Operation *Paukenschlag*' while Deecke was making his initial sortie from Brest, his previous four war patrols having ben in the Arctic.

First to make landfall was *U202* after fifteen days at sea. In heavy mist and fog the U-boat inched close inshore of the eastern end of Long Island near Amagansett. Two U-boat crew members launched a small rubber dinghy into which the agents and their four watertight containers were placed. With dinghy tethered to U-boat their small rubber inflatable made its way through the surf line to the beach where all four agents swiftly disembarked. Giving two tugs on their tether line, signalling to be pulled backwards to safety, the apprehensive seamen were returned to *U202*. Unfortunately for Kptlt. Linder, his trials were not over. During the seemingly endless minutes spent transferring the *Abwehr* agents to shore, his boat had settled onto a shallow sandbar where it remained stuck fast in glutinous wet sand.

Despite the danger of being overheard, Linder gave the order for both diesels to be put full astern, but to no effect. He then attempted to 'sally ship', i.e. get his boat to rock out of its position by a combination of rapid engine thrusts with frantic rudder movements, but again to no avail. Dawn had begun to creep into the eastern sky and, fearing the worst, Linder prepared to scuttle his U-boat. Luck, however, had not abandoned the tense Germans. Thick fog lingered over the stranded *U202*, providing precious time during which the tide rose and eventually her iron-grey hull shifted slightly in its sandy prison. Linder dumped a quantity of fuel from his outboard tanks in a last effort to lighten ship and *U202* broke free. Silently nosing outward on electric motors Linder heading for deep water and safety below the waves.

Following their escape, Linder radioed BdU the successful completion of his part of 'Operation Pastorious', receiving orders to patrol the seas off Cape Hatteras. During June he attacked and sank a neutral, the 4,864-ton Argentinian SS *Rio Tercero*. Linder rescued the skipper who angrily protested his sinking, claiming that thirteen Argentinian flags adorned his ship. The U-boat commander attempted to mollify his angry guest by offering him shoes and brandy, but was forced to break off talks with the raging captain due to approaching American destroyers and aircraft. He dived and sped away, leaving the irate neutrals behind. As the U-boat submerged aircraft bombs fell ineffectually around the boat, a barrage augmented later by a US Navy blimp's bomb load. The US Navy subsequently helped the Argentinian crew reboard their ship and escorted it to an American port where it was confiscated. The last freighter to fall to *U202*'s tubes was the American SS *City of Birmingham* on 1 July, sunk east of Cape Hatteras. Linder decided to head for home, and after taking fuel from *U460* a few days later, arrived at Brest on 1700hrs on 25 July.

The other four agents landed for 'Operation Pastorious' were disembarked from *U584* near Ponte Vedra, south of Jacksonville, Florida. The *Abwehr* men's transfer passed without incident during the early morning of 17 June. Like Linder, Deecke was subsequently ordered to patrol near Cape Hatteras but with no success. Deecke's only 'achievements' were to have fired eight torpedoes at various targets, three of which were faulty and the remainder missed. Plagued by mechanical breakdowns in its diesels, the boat finally neared France after also refuelling from *U460* during the homeward journey. Deecke and his crew reached Brest 2200hrs on 22 July.[57]

6 June: Kptlt. Reinhard Suhren docked *U564* inside the concrete U-boat shelter at Brest at 0930hrs. The scuffed paint work and weary crew revealed the rigours of two months at sea.

Near tragedy early in the patrol had resulted from a moment of carelessness on behalf of the veteran commander. Three days from Brest on 7 April in weather rated as 'still endurable' for Biscay – west-south-west force 6

---

[57] In bizarre circumstances the FBI arrested the entire eight-man espionage mission. Dasch informed the Americans as to the whereabouts of his seven co-agents and they were all subsequently rounded up, the last arrests being made on 27 June in Chicago. Fourteen accomplices and relatives were also arrested. Following a military commission ordered by Roosevelt, Dasch was sentenced to 30 years in prison, Burger life at hard labour (both sentences later commuted by President Truman in 1948) and the remainder death by electrocution, the sentences carried out on 8 August 1942. They were buried in a paupers' graveyard in Blue Plains, Washington, DC.

winds, swell of 4 metres – the First Watch Officer Lt.z.S. Hans-Ferdinand Geisler had enquired from the bridge watch on duty what was causing a loud and regular banging noise from the U-boat's upper deck. Believing it to be either a loose hatch cover or contraband beer stashed beneath the deck grating, Kptlt. Suhren ordered *Bootsmann* Heinz Webendörfer to proceed along the U-boat's slippery casing in search of the cause, which transpired to be a damaged hatch cover. Webendörfer was harnessed to the conning tower jumper wires as he began the perilous task, the U-boat frequently inundating him with rolling green water. While the unfortunate man clung to the bucking deck in search of the problem, Suhren arrived on the bridge to oversee the operation, without lifejacket or safety harness, and made the rash decision to go and help his struggling crewman.

As the commander peered over the conning tower rim in preparation to descend to the deck the U-boat struck a towering wave, Webendörfer, below on deck, hanging on for dear life as the steel hull was temporarily submerged. Suhren, however, was not quick enough and as the conning tower broke free of the swirling water the cry of *'Kommandant über Bord!'* echoed into the control room. Both engines were thrust into full reverse as Suhren, now several metres away, desperately kicked off his cumbersome leather jacket (with heavy binoculars and Mauser pistol in its pockets), trousers and sea boots in an effort to stay afloat. Fortunately the young commander was retrieved from the water, clinging to a life-ring thrown from the U-boat's bridge. The only casualty of the event was Suhren's pride.

In a bizarre example of paper-driven military bureaucracy there was an official enquiry held into the event and the loss of equipment from *U564*. Suhren's list of items included:

> '1 rain jacket (Sou'wester), 1 three-quarter-length leather jacket, 1 pair leather trousers, 1 pair U-boat boots (with cork soles), 1 Mauser pistol (7.65mm calibre), 1 artillery stopwatch, 1 pair of sunglasses in case, 1 artillery torch.'

Suhren's official statement – made in the inimitably tongue-in-cheek style that Suhren was famed for – that accompanied similar statements from Webendörfer and *Stabsobersteurmann* Limburg (IIWO) for the enquiry culminated with:

> 'One cannot blame *Bootsmann* Webendörfer that the commander climbed down onto the upper deck to help repair the damaged hatch cover. Further more I do not consider *Bootsmann* Webendörfer to be responsible for what the commander carries in his pockets. All efforts to retrieve the lost items remained unsuccessful and I should like to request that the lost items be replaced. Signed: Suhren.'

Everything but the pistol and stop watch were replaced by Brest's quartermaster department.

141

The remaining patrol passed without serious mishap. Most successful of May's Type VII missions, Suhren claimed 35,000 tons of shipping sunk (over-claiming due to two of his believed sinkings, the tanker SS *Eclipse* and freighter SS *Delisle* only being damaged and later towed to repair yards). Probably his most unfortunate and significant victim was the 4,000-ton Mexican tanker SS *Potrero del Llano*, attacked and destroyed with torpedoes near Sands Key, Florida, during the night of 14 May. Suhren maintained that the ship had been travelling under armed escort and blacked out, whereas the Mexican Government were adamant that brilliant searchlights had been blazing on her superstructure where huge Mexican flags were painted. Deploring the loss of thirteen men from the ship and protesting Germany's violation of her neutrality, the pro-Allied government declared war against Germany on 22 May. Dönitz subsequently opened season on Mexican shipping in the warm waters of the Gulf of Mexico.

19 June: Kptlt. Oestermann eased *U754* free from her moorings at 2120hrs in Brest. The U-boat had undergone extensive maintenance and was departing on her third operational patrol, this time bound for the Western Atlantic. '*Paukenschlag*'s pace had faltered and operations against the American coast were being phased out by Dönitz following a sharp rise in anti-submarine effectiveness and relative drop in sinkings. *U754* was to be one of the last seven U-boats to patrol there.

The voyage started well for Oestermann. Ten days out of Brest *U754* attacked and sank the British 12,435-ton MV *Waiwera* in mid-Atlantic, north-north-west of the Azores. The U-boat proceeded toward Cape Hatteras, but saw no targets in what had once been an area of rich pickings. Heavy anti-submarine presence were reported by other U-boats in the area and after fears regarding the loss of two of their number and heavy damage to two others, Dönitz ordered his remaining functional boats north to Canadian waters.[58] On 28 July Oestermann surfaced and attacked with his deck gun the 260-ton American trawler *Ebb* south of Halifax. The shelling killed five fishermen and wounded seven, sinking the small vessel in minutes. It was to be the final victory for Oestermann's U-boat.

Cruising surfaced near Cape Sable on 31 July, *U754* was detected by the newly developed land-based HF/DF network while transmitting routine position references to France. Oestermann's was not the only U-boat that day tracked by this method, though his received the most devastating air attack. Scrambled from nearby airfields, Canadian Hudson bombers of 11 and 113 Squadrons began searching for the German raiders. In fine weather Squadron Leader N.E.Small brought his 113 Squadron RCAF Hudson towards the last

---

[58] BdU wrongly surmised that *U215* had been sunk (out of contact with radio faults), but correctly that *U701* had. However, Dönitz was unkowingly correct that two U-boats had been lost – *U576* had also been destroyed.

reported contact coordinates of *U754*. At a range of three miles Small sighted the slim 'Grey Wolf' proceeding surfaced and dived his bomber to attack. Approaching from out of the sun, he was not seen by the bridge watch until the last moment, Kriegsmarine men tumbling through the conning tower hatch as Oestermann attempted to crash dive to safety. The U-boat was too late and Small released four shallow-set depth charges onto the swirling whirlpool left behind *U754*'s submerging stern.

Despite massive explosions and small amounts of oil spotted, the U-boat did not reappear for nearly a full hour, at which time Small roared towards the crippled boat spraying her conning tower with machine gun fire. The U-boat sank below the surface again and as Small circled above in frustration, his depth charges exhausted, there was an unexplained explosion from where *U754* had submerged. Large pools of oil and unmistakeable debris floated to the surface. Oestermann and his forty-two-man crew were dead, the first U-boat destroyed by a Canadian aircraft.

21 June: *U558* docked at 0915hrs in Brest, some members of her crew still showing small traces of suntans acquired in the Caribbean. Claiming 23,000 tons sunk Kptlt. Krech had sunk six ships, including 913-ton anti-submarine trawler HMS *Bedfordshire*, and damaged one more during a voyage that took *U558* as far south as Jamaica.

As the boat sailed into Brest seven pennants were strung from her periscope. In contrast to the Kriegsmarine battle ensign hoisted on the conning tower staff, an oil-stained American flag hung from the conning tower's front, plucked from the sea following the destruction of American freighter SS *Jack* on 27 May south of the lush tropical island Haiti.

25 June: New flotilla boat *U379* commanded by Kptlt. Paul-Hugo Kettner sailed from Kiel after six months of working up, bound for the North Atlantic. Two days later at opposite ends of Europe two 1st U-Flotilla boats put to sea. Kptlt. Eberhard Bopst departed Kiel at 0700hrs for *U597*'s first war patrol into the North Atlantic, while Schnee slipped *U201* from Brest at 2100hrs bound for the central Atlantic. The conning tower decoration of Schnee's boat had altered considerably, the Remscheid town crest, previously either side of the slim tower, now solely adorning the conning tower's front. In its place each side sported fresh paintings of a large snowman, an allusion to the German word '*schnee*' meaning snow in English. Further south, in Lorient, *U116* began her second operational sailing after 18 days of refit. Like *U201*, the U-boat's conning tower had received new decoration, this time an aptly humorous depiction of a sow and her suckling litter.

1 July: 1st U-Flotilla officially lost two of its strength to Norway's 11th U-Flotilla. Kptlt. Siegfried Strelow's *U435* and KK Rolf-Heinrich Hopman's *U405* had both only ever operated from either northern Germany or Norway, so were felt more as administrative losses than front-line Atlantic boats transferred. The following day, in France, *U86* put to sea. Schug's U-boat sailed at 2100hrs from Brest to join the *Wolf* pack forming 600 miles west of the North Channel.

6 July: *U653* arrived in Brest at 0900hrs. Little results were to show from Kptlt. Feiler's voyage, 9,000 tons being claimed from two sinkings, the 6,225-ton MV *Peisander* and 840-ton American seaplane tender USS *Gannet*. Both ships had been sunk during Feiler's prowl southwards well offshore of the United States' east coast. *Gannet* and another unidentified patrol vessel were attacked twice by Feiler on 7 June, north of Bermuda. His initial approach had failed, but the second torpedo attack left *Gannet* sinking in flames, while its companion vessel suffered a hit astern, debris blown skywards in a pyrotechnic display of destruction. Feiler's claim of the second vessel damaged has never been substantiated by Allied records.

15 July: In one of his final entries as Flotilla commander Kptlt. Heinz Buchholz recorded the awarding of Oak Leaves to the Knight's Cross to both Mützelberg on *U203* and Schnee aboard *U201*, respectively the twelfth and thirteenth U-boat men to receive this decoration. By German reckoning the two commanders had added sufficient tonnage to their existing scores to pass the 200,000-ton mark required for the prestigious decorations. Both skippers were notified of their honours by radio from BdU and celebrations rang through the confined interiors of the two U-boats. The 1st U-Flotilla's leading 'Aces' continued to add to their already considerable reputations.

Mützelberg's victories had been gained in an independent voyage as far south as Trinidad. During the seven-week patrol he sank five ships for 32,985 tons (including the 10,013-ton Panamanian tanker SS *Stanvec Palembang*) exhausting his entire torpedo supply. This was the third most successful Type VIIC cruise in these waters of the entire war. While en route for Brest and home *U203* rendezvoused with Suhren's *U564* to embark a man suffering from severe rheumatism, the incapacitated crewman having to be helped aboard the transfer dinghy. The two boats spent several hours in company, long enough for a swimming break to be given to men of both U-boats. Mützelberg's return to Brest on 29 July, in a U-boat festooned with oak branches, caused an uproar of celebration within the Kriegsmarine port, his Oak Leaves toasted by Kriegsmarine men from all branches of service in the city.

U201 had begun its latest tally of enemy ships on 6 July en route to its patrol area by torpedoing the huge solo-sailing British freighter SS *Avila Star*, the 14,443-ton ship going down east of the Azores. Proceeding on his course, Schnee joined the six strong *Hai* pack (*U116, U136, U201, U572, U582* and *U752*) assembling for a searching sweep southwards between meridians 20° and 25° west. Sharp-eyed veterans in *U201*'s bridge watch first sighted their quarry on 10 July as convoy OS 33 passed the extended patrol line also heading south into warmer waters. That night a group of ships disengaged from the main convoy and set course for South America's mainland. Schnee, aboard *U201*, and von Schmidt's *U116* chose to pursue those vessels and over the next 72 hours launched a series of devastating assaults. By the end of the engagement Schnee had sunk the British ships SS *Cortone*, SS *Siris* and SS *Sithonia* by a combination of torpedo and cannon attacks. Two days after the convoy battle had broken off on the 13th *U201* claimed its fifth patrol victory by sinking British tanker SS *British Yeoman* bringing Schnee's mission score to 40,491 tons.

The U-boat was left with only one torpedo and a small number of shells for her deck gun. Schnee requested permission to return to base but was refused on the grounds that his boat could undertake valuable reconnaissance near Freetown. Unhappily the skipper complied. Conditions aboard the submarine grew unbearable, temperatures of 120 degrees endured by sweating men inside the iron hull while their U-boat rode surfaced. Relief came only when submerged, and then all too briefly. *U201* expended its final torpedo in sinking the British anti-submarine trawler HMS *Laertes* 180 miles south-south-west of Freetown on the evening of 25 July. Finally Schnee received permission to return to Brest and a hero's welcome on 8 August. As the U-boat entered its harbour enclave the conning tower was adorned with oak branches to celebrate the commander's award. As well as Schnee, the ship's mascot had also received his Knight's Cross with Oak Leaves, a carefully painted decoration adorning the snowman's throat. A single tattered life preserver swinging from the conning tower antennae jumper wires marked 'HMS *T137*' recalled the destruction of HMS *Laertes*. An elated Dönitz was persuaded by the remarkable success of the *Hai* pack to send further U-boats and their U-tankers to the seas between the Azores and Sierra Leone.

17 July: Kptlt. Heinz Buchholz left the post of Flotilla Commander to return to duty as captain of Type IXD-1 *U195* during its working up period within Stettin's 4th U-Flotilla. His replacement in Brest was 30-year-old veteran commander Kptlt. Werner Winter.[60] Winter had captained both the 'canoe' *U22* and larger Type IXB *U103*, the latter boat part of 'Operation *Paukenschlag*'s first devastating wave in January 1942. A little over a month before arriving in Brest to take command, Winter had become the bearer of the Knight's Cross for his successes in battle. Between these two operational commands Winter had also served on Dönitz's staff as *Admiralstabsoffizier* (*A5*), proving himself an able administrator as well as combat U-boat commander. In the words of Claus-Peter Carlsen, captain of *U732* from October 1942, he was:

> 'a former highly decorated and famous U-boat commander, an ideal superior, consequently tolerant, friendly, reliable and communicative.'

---

[60] Buchholz was killed on 6 February 1944 when his next boat *U177* was sunk 540 miles west-south-west of Ascension Island.

At 1630hrs the available officers and staff of Brest's 1st U-Flotilla mustered in the gravel courtyard outside their Naval Academy headquarters to bid farewell to Buchholz and welcome to Winter.

19 July: Dönitz withdrew the last remaining '*Paukenschlag*' boats from American waters in the face of growing counter-attacks and diminishing returns. They were again to concentrate on increasingly daunting convoy attacks in the North Atlantic, the key to success in blockading Britain, and peripheral operations against Freetown's West African convoys.

29 July: '*U203* 1600hrs; Mützelberg arrives. Celebrations for the new Flotilla Oak Leaves holder.'

5 August: *Grossadmiral* Raeder appeared in Brest for a brief sightseeing tour of 1st U-Flotilla headquarters at 1600hrs. While the C-in-C inspected his flotilla, Kptlt. Gerhard Feiler took *U653* to sea for its fourth patrol. Trailing behind one *Sperrbrecher* and three minesweepers, the U-boat headed for open seas and the mid-Atlantic. The following day *U566* also followed a similarly heavy escort out of Brest. Accompanied by a single *Sperrbrecher* and two minesweepers, Oblt.z.S. Gerhard Remus began his first patrol as the boat's commander, heading for Freetown as part of Dönitz's new commitment to the West African area.

8 August: Schnee and *U201* made their triumphal return to Brest. The usual uproarious crowd as well as KA Ernst Schirlitz, *Seekommandant Bretagne* since June 1942, greeted the new Oak Leaves holder. Claiming 42,386 tons sunk Schnee later joined Mützelberg for their journey to Berlin and Hitler's formal presentation. After the joint ceremony within the Reich Chancellery both U-boat commanders were offered staff posts by Dönitz.[61] Mützelberg did not want to leave his combat command and fatefully elected to remain with his boat. Schnee, on the other hand, accepted an offer to become *Admiralstabsoffizier operativ* (*A I op*) convoy staff officer ('*Geleitzugs-Asto*'), a newly created post within Dönitz's BdU staff. 'Adi' Schnee began his new duties in October, Oblt.z.S. Günther Rosenberg taking command of *U201*.

11 August: Kptlt. Werner Schulte brought *U582* into her concrete bunker at 1730hrs. As well as four victory pennants claiming 32,000 BRT of shipping sunk while part of the *Hai* pack (in actual fact a confirmed 30,644 tons), and sub-

---

[61] This was a standard procedure among the U-boat service and other branches of the armed forces. By rotating highly decorated commanders to staff or training duties new recruits benefited from their experience and the possibility of a severe blow to morale in the event of the hero being sunk was averted. However, the choice remained in the hands of the commander himself.

sequently near Freetown in independent operations, the U-boat carried two prisoners. Schulte's final sinking had been the 6,801-ton American freighter SS *Stella Lykes* on 27 July, but the large American refused to die easily. Schulte attacked her with torpedoes and gunfire, causing her to flounder to a halt and take on a severe list. As her crew abandoned ship the U-boat deck gun fell silent, barking into action again once lifeboats were clear. Six and a half hours after the original attack Schulte realized that the freighter was merely exhausting his ammunition and she was sunk after U-boat men clambered aboard and set demolition charges in her holds. Before departing the scene, *U582* cruised among the American survivors and took on board both the captain and engineer as prisoners. This too was a new order emanating from BdU. By depriving the enemy of skilled masters and technical personnel, strangulation of Allied merchant shipping effectiveness appeared one step closer. There was also perhaps a certain intelligence value to be obtained from such prisoners, an insight into convoy operations that could provide a vital edge to U-boat controllers.

13 August: Kptlt. Uphoff docked in Brest at 1800hrs. Operating as part of the *Endrass* pack against HG 84, Uphoff experienced an initial frustrating lack of success, no doubt the spectre of previous unsuccessful sorties hauntingly present. However, his luck changed after breaking off from the *Endrass* group and proceeding to the Azores independently. Between 23 June and 12 July *U84* sank three ships and damaged a fourth between the Azores and Cuba. Claiming 44,000 BRT sunk (in fact a confirmed 21,382 tons including the damaged 7,176-ton American SS *William Cullen Bryant*) Uphoff finally had reason to celebrate. Nevertheless, three ships sunk after nearly two months at sea were not high returns. Moreover, there was a sinister new development noted by Uphoff. While cruising the Florida Straits near Havana he reported to BdU strong air and surface anti-submarine forces present both by day and night. He surmised that the Allied aircraft operating at night were equipped with ASV radar, a dangerous turn of events in the U-boat war. U-boat command, however, issued a sharp rebuke stating in flat terms that there 'is no confirmation of radar' in operation anywhere along the United States coastline. They were, of course, seriously mistaken.

22 August: Three days after German troops had bloodily repulsed the mainly Canadian landing at Dieppe, Brazil declared war on Germany. After repeated German U-boat sinkings of Brazilian merchantmen, the country threw in its lot with the Allies, providing airfields for U-boat hunting bombers. The Allies now firmly controlled the narrow 'waist' of the Atlantic. Those airbases opened in Brazil to Allied anti-submarine aircraft were soon to have a seriously debilitating effect on Caribbean U-boat operations.

23 August: *U116* docked in Lorient at 1600hrs after her second successful mission. As well as refuelling three U-boats west of Freetown, KK Werner von Schmidt had accompanied Schnee in *U201* on his convoy attack against ships of OS 33. During the action von Schmidt had torpedoed SS *Cortona*, later finished off by Schnee, and sunk 4,284-ton British SS *Shaftesbury* on 12 July. After the ship had keeled over and gone done, *U116* approached the survivors' lifeboat and took *Shaftesbury*'s captain on board as a prisoner.

27 August: A grinning Kptlt. Rolf Mützelberg eased his boat out from Brest at 1800hrs. Amid familiar sounds of cheering and band music *U203* followed her escort into the *Goulet de Brest*. The small procession surged through Brest's entrance channel, past waving artillerymen from casements occupying commanding positions along the rugged Breton shoreline, and gradually out to sea. Mützelberg was enjoying his first patrol since receiving the Oak Leaves and his crew revelled in their status as men of a leading U-boat. A month of leave and recreation lay behind them and they prepared for the recommencement of their war.

31 August: At 1630hrs beneath a clear summer evening sky *U653* docked in Brest at the conclusion of a frustrating and tragic patrol. While part of the Azores area *Blücher* pack *U653* attempted to attack convoy SL118 after sighting the merchant ships' smoke on 16 August. Kptlt. Gerhard Feiler began to shadow and transmit homing beacons for the rest of the *Blücher* group to congregate before attempting his assault.

For four days and nights the seven-strong pack tried to penetrate the convoy's defences, sinking four ships by 20 August. During these relentless assaults strong escorts equipped with 'Huff-Duff' counterattacked with great energy, causing damage to *Blücher* boat *U333* and driving other assailants away, most before they were able to launch their torpedoes. Land-based Coastal Command aircraft joined the fray causing further headaches for the attacking Germans. On 18 August, as U-boat efforts were at their height, B24 Liberator 'F' of 120 Coastal Command Squadron located *U653* and attacked the surfaced boat with six depth charges and two bombs. In shattering detonations the weapons exploded close to *U653*'s hull, hurling Seaman Second Class (*Matrosengefreiter*) Willi Pröhl from the bridge. While Feiler crash-dived to escape, his floundering crewman was left behind, in all probability already dead from the shattering effect of multiple depth-charge blasts. In any event, he was never seen again. Feiler reported to BdU that he had lost a crewman and suffered severe damage during the attack and was ordered to abort his patrol. After transferring spare fuel to *U406* and *U566*, the U-boat limped back to Brest. By the end of *Blücher*'s attempted attacks on convoy SL118 four of the seven U-boats had been forced to abort with damage. Dönitz, aghast at his losses, cancelled the assault. After arrival and a relatively low-key welcome the boat was transferred to a dry pen where she remained for nearly two months while work on her considerable damage was undertaken.

'*U654 Vermisst zwei Stern.*' The 11th U-Flotilla boat, prevented from entering the ranks of the 1st Flotilla by the illness of its commander Hesse, was lost in the Caribbean. Directed by BdU to depart a barren patrol station off Panama, the U-boat was sighted east-south-east of Isla de San Andrés by a radar-equipped USAAF B18 of the 45th Bombardment Group. Pilot Lieutenant P.A. Koenig charged at the surfaced boat, dropping four shallow-set Torpex-packed depth charges which straddled the boat. Within four minutes *U654* and her forty-four-man crew had disappeared below the surface, never to reappear.

Dönitz had become increasingly aware of the problems posed by Allied aircraft. At a Paris conference on 16 June 1942 BdU and various OKM department heads held consultations to discuss U-boat anti-aircraft strategy for the future. Development and testing of radar detectors was given top priority, followed by increased and improved weaponry, particularly flak armaments. The order to attach an additional conning tower kiosk aft of the existing flak station was also issued, once construction materials became available. From this meeting was spawned the *Wintergarten* addition to U-boat superstructures.

The first shipment of newly developed Metox sets had also arrived at front-line U-boat bases in France. Heralded as the answer to attack by radar-equipped aircraft, the Metox system was believed to be capable of picking up incoming radar pulses, providing enough warning for the U-boat to submerge out of harm's way. Named after its Paris manufacturers, the Metox (officially titled *Funkmessbeobachter 1 Metox R 600*) took the simple form of a flimsy wooden cross, around which was wrapped antennae wire, connected to a receiver mounted below decks. Known by crews as the '*Biscayakreuz*' (Biscay Cross) it initially proved highly effective against British ASV1 radar. There were, however, drawbacks.

The cross itself was mounted on the conning tower rim, a rudimentary directional capability given by hand turning the device within its simple mount. Any radar signal detected was represented on the receiver by an audible tone, the differing pitch reflecting differing signal strength. Unfortunately some of the tones were beyond the range of human hearing, somewhat negating its warning value. The cross was also connected to the U-boat's interior receiver by a long cable that ran through the open conning tower hatch. Closing the hatch became something that was no longer an auto-matic reaction if under attack, moments often lost while retreating sailors were compelled to consider the cable's integrity before slamming the hatch shut. The wooden cross had to be taken down as the U-boat submerged, thrown down into the control room when crash-diving, usually being subsequently destroyed by several pairs of heavy sea boots landing on top of it. Fortunately, by its very flimsy nature it was easy to repair in the event of breakage.

At Lorient on 2 September *U128* of the 2nd U-Flotilla sailed on an exper-imental eight-day voyage. Aboard were five specialist radar engineers led by Dr Robert Karl. Also aboard the U-boat was the new flimsy wooden and wire that was Metox. Deemed satisfactory by Karl and his four associates during the eight-day sea trial it was ordered operational and immediately issued to U-boats of the Atlantic Front. Despite its shortcomings Metox did help in threat detection and managed briefly to arrest the high casualty rate among Biscay U-boats. However, in the course of time, German dependence upon this flimsy construction would lead directly to the loss of many boats from air attack.

1 September: *U440* transferred from Kiel's 5th U-Flotilla to Winter's 1st U-Flotilla after eight months of trials and working-up exercises. The U-boat, commanded by Kptlt. Hans Geissler, began her first operational patrol and relocation to Brest. During the 20-day voyage *U440* participated in attempted attacks on convoy SC99 as part of the *Lohs* group. All attacks failed due to fierce escort opposition and *U440* arrived in Brest dispirited and damaged on 21 September at 1830hrs – '*Keine Tonnen*' (No Tonnage).

On the third anniversary of the outbreak of war Kptlt. Reinhard Suhren of *U564* was awarded the Swords to his Oak Leaves and Knight's Cross by radio. The eighteenth Wehrmacht officer to receive this exalted decoration and the third in the U-boat service after Topp and Kretschmer. Coupled with his new decoration came promotion to the rank of *Korvettenkapitän*. Aboard the U-boat a brief ceremony was held on the stern deck, Suhren proudly sporting the three rings, cut from empty tin cans by the engineering crew, of his new rank on each cuff.

2 September: Two entries denoted a run of disaster for 1st U-Flotilla:

> '*U754 Vermisst ein Stern.*
> *U379 Vermisst ein Stern*' – presumed lost.

The loss of Oestermann's *U754*, depth-charged by the Royal Canadian Air Force, was assumed. The U-boat had left from Brest on 19 June; there was no way she could still be at sea. Kptlt. Paul-Hugo Kettner's *U379* was also missing having sailed from Kiel for the U-boat's maiden patrol on 25 June. Kettner, described unflatteringly by his crew as lazy, inefficient and over-bearing, had formed part of *Wolf* group in mid-July but had achieved nothing. The captain was noted for barely ever rising from his green-curtained bunk to exercise control over the boat. During the vast majority of time First Watch Officer Lt.z.S. Martin Stoll and Chief Engineer Kptlt. (Ing) Karl Lang (described conversely by crew members as 'wonderful') saw to the U-boat's smooth running while Kettner remained in bed. Moved by BdU to a refuelling area south of the Azores, *U379* joined a new patrol line named *Steinbrinck* and closed to attack convoy SC94 on 8 August. In misty conditions the U-boats attacked the 30-ship convoy, nine days into its voyage from Sydney, Cape Breton, to Britain. With ships arranged in nine columns, escorted by one Canadian destroyer and five Anglo- Canadian corvettes, the convoy was only able to average seven knots. As U-boats converged stealthily on the herd of lumbering ships the stage seemed set for a potential Allied disaster.

Kettner attacked during the afternoon of 8 August, torpedoing the American SS *Kaimoku* and the British SS *Anneburg*, the latter suffering serious damage but refusing to sink. The wallowing British freighter was finished off after evacuation by escort corvette HMS *Dianthus* that evening. Bedlam erupted amongst the stumbling convoy as U-boats darted in to attack, the water criss-crossed with torpedoes, many of which however missed or malfunctioned.

Immediately following the despatch of Kettner's victim *Anneburg*, mast-head lookouts aboard the corvette HMS *Dianthus* spotted two U-boats at six miles moving close to each other surfaced. The corvette's commander Lieutenant Commander C.E. Bridgeman recorded in his log:

> '2045: Selected left hand one (U-boat), fired 12 HE at 12 000 yards, one shot falling within a yard of conning tower.'

Shaken by the near miss, Kettner ordered *U379* dived. By 2126hrs *Dianthus* had reached the diving position and began a slow ASDIC sweep, obtaining no contact. Bridgeman continued his search until nearly 2300hrs, whereupon he perceptively decided to sweep back towards the convoy. At 2308hrs a British signalman aboard the corvette spied a 'dark object', triggering Bridgeman to order eight star shells fired, although their effect was nullified somewhat by a heavy mist hanging low over the ocean. Kettner, startled by the British flares, made his fatal mistake and dived instead of running surfaced and making clean his getaway. Once submerged, *U379* was immediately located by the corvette's ASDIC. Aboard the U-boat, Kettner's hydrophone operator reported propellers closing rapidly. Kettner, perhaps feeling the strain and realizing the full implications of his inept escape attempt, flew into a rage saying that the hydrophone man was 'talking nonsense', prompting the exasperated crewman to remove his earphones and toss them aside in disgust.

At 2345hrs five deafening explosions rocked *U379* as the hydrophone operator's 'imaginary' corvette dropped five depth charges set for 100 feet. The shallow U-boat was thrown upwards by savage and powerful blasts as switches, gauges and lighting all failed inside the jumbled chaos *U379* had become. Within seconds the U-boat's trim had been shattered and she broke surface near to *Dianthus*.

The British corvette immediately framed Kettner's stricken submarine with her searchlight and began firing all available weapons. Six more depth charges were prepared and *Dianthus* turned to ram. Aboard *U379* the Chief Engineer blew all tanks to regain boat stability while the boat was ordered abandoned. Kettner was remembered by survivors to have 'fumbled with the hatch' after which the boat's Chief Petty Officer, Theodor Klaßen, intervened and calmly opened it. As the first crewmen climbed outside, *Dianthus* struck *U379* forward of her conning tower, riding over the crippled U-boat with a shrieking of tortured metal. When *U379* had fallen astern Bridgeman ordered his six

151

prepared depth charges dropped, all set for shallow detonation. The devastating explosions hurled crewmen and debris aloft as *Dianthus* turned to ram again. After the fourth corvette impact *U379* lifted from the water, her battered hull smashing against *Dianthus*'s starboard forecastle as if in final feeble defiance, before crashing back into the water, capsizing and sinking by the stern. By 0050hrs five German survivors had been rescued, all of them enlisted men. With growing concern at his own damage – the corvette's First Lieutenant and Chief ERA below attempting to shore up her crumpled bow – and the possibility of further U-boat attacks, Bridgeman suspended the search for survivors. Dropping a life raft overboard for any who remained, the corvette departed. No more men were recovered.

5 September: A smoke-blackened and devastated *U566* staggered into Brest's harbour at 0815hrs. Oblt.z.S. Gerhard Remus claimed 19,000 tons sunk during his patrol. However, as Remus was engaged in the attack on convoy SL119 she was rammed while submerged by a charging escort. The impact smashed the U-boat's bridge and flattened her periscopes. There was no choice but to disengage. Once clear of the raging action and the annoying presence of land-based bombers, Remus ordered the worst areas of jagged metal cut away using acetylene torches so that his boat could travel easier while submerged. In this sad state the U-boat set course for home. The severe damage was to put *U566* out of the Atlantic fight until late October.

6 September: Side by side *U201* and *U202* put to sea from Brest at 0815hrs. *U201*'s new commander, Oblt.z.S. Günther Rosenberg, had previously commanded Type VIIC *U351* while attached to Baltic based 26th and 24th Training Flotillas. His first operational command was aboard the prestigious *U201* and he determined to continue to add to the boat's formidable reputation gained by Kptlt. Schnee. *U202* also travelled under new command, Hans-Heinz Linder having transferred to a staff post at the conclusion of his patrol in March. Fresh commander Kptlt. Günther Poser had previously captained 22nd U-Flotilla's Type IIC *U59* while training in the Baltic. Trailing their minesweeping escorts through Brest's entrance channels the two boats proceeded to sea and the baptisms of fire for both commanders.

12 September: In sombre tones KK Werner Winter recorded a death within the ranks of the flotilla:

> 'At 2215hrs the body of Kptlt. Rolf Mützelberg was buried at sea at the coordinates 36° 14' 56" N, 31° 21' 2" W.'

Mützelberg had been the victim of a freak accident. While stationed in the warm Atlantic waters south-west of the Azores, and judged safe from enemy air patrols, Mützelberg and several of his crew were relaxing on the U-boat's casing and swimming in the sea, a common occurrence in the days before

Allied air power saturated the Atlantic skies. Enjoying temporary peace during the boat's seventh war patrol Mützelberg attempted a dive off the conning tower at the same moment as the U-boat rolled suddenly in the long lazy swell. Mützelberg struck the saddle tank with his head and shoulder and, after his crew had recovered him in great pain, he was rushed below to his bunk. Alerting BdU of their predicament, *U203*'s Watch Officer, Oblt.z.S. Hans Seidel, was ordered to rendezvous with the *Milchkuh* supply boat *U462* which carried a doctor. However, by the time the two boats met it was too late. Rolf Mützelberg died early on 12 September 1942. The U-boat then set course for Brest.

Three days later the daily forces' newspaper *Wehrmachtsbericht* printed Mützelberg's obituary:

> '*Kapitänleutnant* Rolf Mützelberg, U-boat commander, bearer of the Knight's Cross with Oak Leaves, lost his life on patrol. The U-boat arm has lost an outstanding commander and a successful fighter. The boat continues her patrol under the command of the senior watch officer.'

16 September: Returning to Brest Kptlt. Günther Krech celebrated the sinking of 26,421 tons of shipping in the Caribbean. His *U558* was the only Type VIIC to make two patrols within the confined waters of the Caribbean and following his recent successes he had accumulated a confirmed tonnage total of 104,593 tons of shipping (fifteen ships). While still on patrol on 16 September he was awarded the Knight's Cross for reaching the magic number required. His was the sixtieth U-boat *Ritterkreuz*. Winter recorded the award on the day of its confirmation 17 September:

> '*U558 Krech wid durch Fukspruch das RK zum Eisern Kreuz verliehen.*'

The day after Krech's award a subdued *U203* arrived in Brest minus its familiar smiling commander. Docking at 1800hrs, the U-boat was accompanied by Suhren's *U564*, returning from patrol with a recorded claim of 60,000 tons of enemy shipping sunk. In fact Suhren himself had made no such assertion. His radio report to BdU as he headed for Brest was that he had sunk only five ships for 35,000 tons, and damaged four others for an additional 26,000 tons. BdU's confusion over this message resulted in the logging of 60,000 tons sunk and the official record was never altered.

The docking of *U564* provided more drama for the weary crew, mixed with humour soon to become legendary within the U-boat service. Just before entering Brest's inner harbour with its assemblage of bandsmen, honour guard, flotilla officers and Brest's mayor among others, Suhren's keen eyes spotted his friend Horst Uphoff among the dockyard crush. As usual acting with more spontaneity than careful thought Suhren bellowed across by megaphone 'Well Hein (Uphoff's nickname) are the Nazis still at the helm?' When his question was met with murmers of assent Suhren promptly shouted for both engines full astern, much to the amusement of his waiting crowd. As Suhren's U-boat moored against the hull of a derelict barge the usual array of welcoming faces were present. The flotilla staff, Brest's mayor and his wife and several army officers, recently returned from Russia for a period of recuperation in the backwater of Brittany, all lined the jetty's side. Unfortunately, in their enthusiasm to get closer to the U-boat several army officers walked from the jetty onto the barge's makeshift roof, collapsing it and causing several serious injuries. As Suhren remarked:

'Even in port *U564* did pretty well for excitement!'

Among the decorations awarded to Suhren's crew after their successful voyage was a German Cross in Gold for the boat's Chief Engineer, Oblt. (Ing) Ulrich Gabler. This patrol marked the end of Suhren's operational career. He left command of *U564* and the ranks of 1st U-Flotilla for a staff position.[62] His final debriefing by Dönitz as commander of *U564* ended with a gentle but firm rebuke. Suhren was regaling his Commander-in-Chief with the story of his Navigation Officer lightening the atmosphere of the submerged U-boat after undergoing retaliatory depth-charging by remarking 'It's as dark as a bear's arse in here.' Dönitz failed to see the humourous aspect of this. Suhren had already earned his commander's displeasure years before as a young *Leutnant* aboard *U48* by swearing during gunnery drill. Now Dönitz reminded him:

'You are now a prominent figure, with all your decorations, whom people listen to. Think carefully before you open your mouth, and choose your language more carefully.'[63]

In Kiel *U441* began her first patrol as part of 1st U-Flotilla. Slipping from the harbour at 0700hrs Kptlt. Klaus Hartmann started the gruelling journey to his new base of Brest. However, due to a crewman becoming dangerously ill aboard the cramped U-boat, Hartmann aborted his mission, arriving in Trondheim on 27 September in order to transfer his sick man to hospital.

19 September: *U117* slipped from Kiel for its first operational patrol at 0700hrs. She did not sail to join her sister-ship *U116* at the Atlantic front but for transport duties between Norway and Germany. Meanwhile, on 22 September *U116* left Lorient to act as U-tanker in the North Atlantic. From 29 September she refuelled six boats: *U221*, *U258*, *U356*, *U618*, *U43* and *U106*. Having completed his mission, new commander Oblt.z.S. Wilhelm Grimme set course for Lorient, radioing a message to that effect to Kerneval and was never heard of again. The fate of Type XB *U116* remains unknown.

---

[62] Initially Suhren held the post of instructor at the 22nd U-Flotilla (2nd U-boat Training Division – 2ULD), later he was to become commander of all U-boats stationed in Norway, *FdU Nord*.

[63] *Nasses Eichenlaub*, Reinhard Suhren.

1 October: On a day of considerable U-boat shuffling and movement Winter recorded the following welcome additions to the fighting strength of 1st U-Flotilla: *U301, U353, U354, U441, U602* and *U663*. On that same date that the first of the new boats, *U301*, and a finally repaired *U563*, departed Kiel at 0700hrs, further north *U441* sailed from Trondheim at 1220hrs. *U117* began the return journey for Kiel from Bergen at 1430hrs, arriving at 2100hrs the following day. *U117* continued to shuttle between Norway and several of the Baltic ports before departing for a minelaying mission from Königsberg on 12 October. Three days later while the boat was en route to Reykjavik to sow her minefield, Winter recorded the passing of the large U-boat's operational control from 1st U-Flotilla to Bergen's 11th U-Flotilla.

15 October: Kptlt. Hermann Kottmann left Brest as new commander of *U203* at 1700hrs. Son of a Wehrmacht officer, Kottmann, ex-officer aboard the *Graf Spee* at the time of her scuttling and subsequently Watch Officer aboard *U203* between November 1941 and August 1942, had been recalled from Germany to command his old boat. He had been preparing to commission a new U-boat after leaving Mützelberg's command. The following day the latest *Ritterkreuz* winner of 1st U-Flotilla ended his patrol in Brest. Krech brought *U558* into dock at 2000hrs, claiming 32,500 tons sunk.

October continued to see U-boats commissioned or transferred to Brest's 1st U-Flotilla. On the 19th *U440* arrived, bearing the scars of light damage after entanglement with escort ships of convoy SC99. In Kiel *U413*, commanded by Kptlt. Gustav Poel, began its first patrol. Sailing initially for Marviken, the U-boat left for Brest on 28 October.

U202 and *U201* returned within a day of each other, the former docking at 1300hrs on 25 October, the latter at 1400hrs the next day. Both commanders claimed success from their patrols. Kptlt. Poser listed his accomplishment as two ships of a combined tonnage amounting to 12,800 tons (in fact he had only sunk the 1,815-ton SS *Achilles*, his second 'victory' the badly damaged 7,191-ton SS *John Carter Rose*, hit by two torpedoes and finally sunk by gunfire from *U201*). *U202* was then immobilized for nearly three months during a total refit.

Schnee's successor Rosenberg had accounted for three ships totalling 15,696 tons (including the aforementioned *John Carter Rose*) during a voyage that took the boat as far south as Venezuela, though he over-claimed his total at 22,100 BRT. During Rosenberg's subsequent debriefing by Dönitz the young commander was compelled to report that his boat had spent several hours in pursuit of hydrophone noise that transpired to be a herd of whales. This confession persuaded BdU to assign trained crewmen to several U-boats in order to familiarize inexperienced commanders and hydrophone operators with underwater sounds both natural and man-made, and hopefully increase the flagging rate of convoy interception among his men.

27 October: Three boats of the 1st U-Flotilla sailed during the day. In Kiel at 0700hrs Kptlt. Kurt Nölke began his inaugural voyage as commander of *U263*. Meanwhile at 1800hrs in Brest two veteran U-boats put to sea. *U564* began her first patrol under the command of Oblt.z.S. Hans Fiedler, Reinhard Suhren having transferred from his illustrious command. *U653* began its fifth war patrol with Kptlt. Gerhard Feiler, still smarting from his previous failed August patrol, cut short by aircraft attack. Three days later they were joined at sea by the final 1st U-Flotilla sailing of the month. Kptlt. Walther Schug's aging *U86*, sole Type VIIB of the Flotilla, began its fifth patrol.

28 October: *'U599 Vermisst zwei Stern.'*

Nearly two months after Kptlt. Wolfgang Breithaupt had taken his newly commissioned boat *U599* to sea from Kiel he still had achieved no successes to record. After slipping from Kiel on 27 August the U-boat had participated in two group operations, *Lohs* and *Wotan*, both in the North Atlantic. Weather had hindered the former group's attack on convoy SC100 during mid-September, while a combination of the natural elements and strong air defence frustrated the latter group when shadowing convoy SC104. After days of dogged pursuit, U-boats finally broke through and SC104 suffered before the *Wotan* pack dispersed. Eight ships were sunk in total, but none by Breithaupt.

On 16 October the scattered *Wotan* group were directed in rapidly deteriorating weather to intercept the newly detected convoy ON137, sighted in the grey drizzle by *U704*. For three days the other U-boats struggled to make contact, but never succeeded, the sole shadowing boat, *U704*, herself losing touch with the merchant ships and never regaining it. Fuming that even the weather had turned against his U-boats, BdU cancelled the operation on 19 October.

Breithaupt, low on morale and fuel, headed for the boat's new home port of Brest. Travelling surfaced on 24 October north-east of the Azores *U599* was sighted and attacked by Pilot Officer B.P. Liddington's Liberator while the 224 RAF Squadron heavy bomber flew distant cover for convoy KX2. In a single devastating salvo the charging aircraft cleanly straddled *U599* with depth charges. There were no survivors.

1 November: Winter recorded the following transfers to and from the 1st U-Flotilla:

U116 to the 12th U-Flotilla (Bordeaux), although unbeknown to Winter the U-boat was already destroyed;

U263 from Kiel's 5th U-Flotilla to 1st U-Flotilla (in transit to Brest);

U413 from Danzig's 8th U-Flotilla to 1st U-Flotilla (in transit from Marviken);

U439 from Kiel's 5th U-Flotilla to 1st U-Flotilla (preparing for departure from Kiel).

5 November: Oblt.z.S. Hans-Joachim Bertelsmann took new Type VIIC *U603* from Kiel to Kristiansand. The freshly worked-up U-boat would then proceed to its combat flotilla home at Brest. She passed into Winter's flotilla ranks on 9 December after uneventful weeks of duty in the North Atlantic.

6 November: Kptlt. Hermann Kottmann returned *U203* to Lorient following its first patrol after the death of Mützelberg. The one-time Watch Officer under Mützelberg had begun his commander's career successfully. Gliding into the Keroman submarine bunkers at 1015hrs the U-boat displayed 13,131 BRT of pennants from a conning tower bedecked with flowers and adorned with a new emblem. Consisting of a red turtle, the painting had been added to *U203*'s conning tower sides, the front already crowned by the twin-shield crest of the city of Essen, sponsoring town of the U-boat.[64] The colourful U-boat and crew were honoured with a new nickname amongst flotilla-mates, 'Kottmann's Circus'. Salutes were exchanged with the customary honour guard before the engine noise died away and celebrations began. Bearded and clad in grimy fatigues stinking of mildew, the U-boat crew relished their welcome from fellow sailors and the nurses at Lorient's military hospital.

The boat's patrol had begun with disappointment after *U203* pursued an escorted tanker to no avail, as part of *Streitaxt* pack near the Canary Islands. During Kottmann's unsuccessful attack destroyer retaliation brought depthcharge damage to the boat's diesels, necessitating difficult onboard repairs. However, the distant sighting of thirty-seven-merchant ship convoy SL125 passing their patrol line soon rewarded the eight-strong U-boat group. A single straggling Danish tanker had given the path of SL125 away to a solitary stalking member from the *Streitaxt* pack who followed the unwitting Dane to its parent convoy. During the ensuing four-day action, much of it hampered by bad weather, Kottmann attacked and sank the 5,178-ton British MV *Hopecastle* (incorrectly logged by Kottmann as 5,300-ton freighter SS *Nagpore*) with torpedo and deck cannon and later the 7,131-ton British SS *Corinaldo* in the same manner. In total the pack claimed twelve of the convoy's ships destroyed, totalling 85,656 tons, before overwhelming Allied air strength arrived to shelter the convoy. In his official naval history *The War at Sea* Captain Roskill recounts that the loss of life among this Allied convoy was 'severe' – 426-men killed. Dönitz ordered the attacks discontinued on 1 November and *U203* set course for Lorient, fuel bunkers decidedly low.

Two other 1st U-Flotilla boats had less triumph at sea. Both *U602* and

---

[64] During the cruise crewmen had caught and killed a large turtle, augmenting their rations with turtle soup.

U563 had experienced no successes as part of *Puma* group's difficult attacks on Halifax convoy HX212. Both boats slunk into port on 6 November, the former tying up in Lorient at 1015hrs, the latter, commanded by her new captain Kptlt. Götz von Hartmann, at 1500hrs that afternoon in Brest. The following day two more frustrated *Pumas* docked at Brest, *U301* at 0900hrs and *U441* three hours later, both maiden patrols, both complete failures. The latter's experience was typical and Kptlt. Klaus Hartmann had nothing to show for his patrol. Participation in the *Panther* and *Puma* groups and failed attacks on HX212 and one of her escort ships, HMCS *St Laurent*, were the sum total of the month-long voyage. Despite continued attempts to engage ships from HX212, von Hartmann was consistently driven under and out of range by combined air and surface escort attacks. A depressing notation ended entries against 6 November's date in the Flotilla War Diary: '*U116 Vermisst ein Stern.*'

11 November: On Armistice Day 1942 an interesting guest from Bordeaux-based 12th U-Flotilla tied her mooring lines in Brest. Wide-beamed Type XIV *Milchkuh U463* arrived at the mouth of the huge U-boat bunker during early afternoon. Her commander, KK Leo Wolfbauer, had effectively completed his second refuelling mission, operating in the ruthless North Atlantic.

12 November: Transferred from Kiel's 5th U-Flotilla to 1st U-Flotilla, *U439* began its initial operational voyage under the command of Kptlt. Wolfgang Sporn. Slipping from Kiel at 0800hrs, the U-boat nosed towards the sea and action in the North Atlantic.

Another Flotilla addition, Kptlt. Hans Hunger's *U336* accompanied Sporn on his outward voyage, both boats trailing in the wake of their minesweeping escort. Hunger was forced to abort to Kiel with mechanical difficulties after enjoying only a single night of his patrol, the next evening at 2200hrs returning to his home port for fifteen days of repair to the boat's engines. After the work had been completed *U336* shipped out once more. This time she was accompanied by a second new boat, *U628*, commanded by Kptlt. Heinrich Hassenschar, the two boats sailing at 0800hrs for the Atlantic and ultimately Brest.

17 November: The sinking of three Flotilla boats was confirmed, their numbers and case notes recorded by Winter in his War Diary: *U353* (FdUG 13260A5), *U597* (FdUG 13261A5) and *U582* (FdU 13262A5).

Kptlt. Werner Schulte and his entire forty-five-man crew of *U582* were killed as part of the *Luchs* patrol line operating west of Ireland. Before joining the group Schulte had torpedoed and sunk the Norwegian 2,993-ton freighter MV *Vibran*, the boat's sixth kill. On 3 October *U260* sighted convoy HX209, transmitting homing signals to the remaining fifteen *Luchs* U-boats. In appalling weather with high winds screeching across a vicious sea, no concentrated attack could be made by the pitching and struggling German submarines. Lookouts fought against the elements in vain attempts to locate their target. Despite oil-skin protective gear and thick leather gauntlets, water poured through shivering men's clothing, coursing along chilled bodies and slopping into sodden sea boots. There was no protection from nature's punishment. Thick webbing safety harnesses were used, but even they occasionally failed. Further to the U-boats' miseries solar storm interference reduced the effectiveness of radios to nil impeding yet further any progress at concentrating the boats by BdU direction.

On 5 October the convoy target received air cover from US Navy Catalinas based in Iceland, operating at the limits of their range. Lieutenant G.F. Swanson located *U582* while she struggled towards the convoy and dived to the attack with a salvo of depth charges, bracketing the boat as she attempted to evade. *U582* sank rapidly, her entire crew taken to the bottom with their ship in a matter of minutes.

Kptlt. Eberhard Bopst and forty-eight others died aboard *U597* during the U-boat's second patrol. After nearly a month at sea, initially as part of the *Panther* pack and then as *Leopard*, *U597* had yet to score. Bopst was directed toward the lumbering convoy ONS136 on 11th October, making heavy going in terrible weather conditions. That evening Bopst sighted a convoy straggler and attempted to attack with torpedoes but the steel fish missed due to increasingly high seas as the U-boat was thrown about uncontrollably.

Subsequently *U597* tried again to contact the enemy convoy, running at maximum allowable speed the following day in a mountainous sea. Lookouts struggling to locate the merchant ships also failed to locate attacking Liberator of 120 Squadron at about 1200hrs. The approaching aircraft had homed swiftly on what they initially described as the 'wake of an unidentified craft', the slender grey hull gradually becoming discernible. Approaching directly in a long diving attack Squadron Leader T.M. Bulloch selected eight shallow-set Torpex depth charges, but released only six. The steel drums were dropped perfectly, framing the U-boat in a close-set pattern. As they erupted the British Squadron Leader reported that the U-boat target had been blown to pieces, a large fragment of debris barely missing his aircraft's rear turret. No survivors were expected or seen in what was 120 Squadron's first U-boat kill.

The final loss recorded that day was that of another new U-boat, embarked upon its maiden operational voyage. *U353* had left Kiel on 22 September, transferring from 5th to 1st U-Flotilla. Her commander Oblt.z.S. Wolfgang Römer (named 'The Little Man' by his crew due to his slight stature, and previously the commander of Type II training U-boat *U56*) had slipped the moorings at 0700hrs and begun his journey through the 'Rose Garden' to the Atlantic battleground.[65] The passage became at once terrifying to novice sailors and uncomfortable to all. During 5 October Römer was compelled to travel submerged for the entire day due to the severity of surface conditions, howling winds and driving breakers churning the green sea into a furious tempest. Römer's boat also formed part of the *Leopard* group that *U597* had belonged to and began to approach the newly detected SC104 on 14 October.

Over the ensuing two days air and sea escorts drove away repeated attempts by the Germans to engage the forty-eight-ship convoy. As the ten columns of ships made their way at only 7 knots *U353* made yet another attempt to close. Thankfully winds had dropped and the sea assumed a long rolling swell instead of its customary fury. Now, however, different complications presented themselves – overcast and misty conditions reduced visibility to a mere mile.

At around noon Römer, concerned at the close conditions, ordered his boat submerged to 20 metres for a hydrophone sweep. Unfortunately he refused to decrease the U-boat's speed and she glided through the water with motors at 120 rpm, optimal performance from her hydrophones coming between 60 and 90 rpm. Above her the destroyer HMS *Fame* (flagship of British Escort Group B6), zigzagging two miles ahead of the convoy's fourth column, obtained a firm ASDIC bearing at 50°, 2,000 yards distant. Her captain, Commander Heathcote, wasted no time and immediately ordered speed increased to 15 knots and an attack plotted using an initial pattern of ten depth charges set for 50 and 140 feet.

Twenty-six-year-old Römer remained blissfully unaware of the approaching danger. He lingered in his small private 'cabin' lying in his bunk and ignoring requests by his hydrophone operator to reduce speed. Like many captains he had little faith in hydrophones. Instead he elected to rise to periscope depth and attempt to observe the convoy prior to surfacing for a run on diesels. While the U-boat approached the required depth there was a sudden cry from the hydrophone operator as he heard *Fame*'s propellers, seconds later audible to the entire crew as she roared above. Numerous small splashes followed and seconds later the deathly clicking of depth charge fuses before all hell broke loose aboard *U353*. In ten shattering explosions the U-boat was pummelled out of commission. Lighting failed, electric motors ceased to function and stern hydroplanes refused to answer their controls. Water began to spurt from the stern torpedo tube and through the forward-mounted search receiver, quickly flooding the bilges and presenting the potential problem of flooded batteries. Römer bellowed for his boat to go deeper in an attempt to evade the British attacks, but the boat's Chief Engineer reported all instruments damaged and no control over the U-boat possible. Römer was left with little choice and as *U353* plunged to unknown depths he ordered all tanks blown and the U-boat surfaced. The chilling noise

---

[65] The 'Rose Garden' was an area of sea between Iceland and the Faeroe Islands where Allied aircraft regularly jettisoned unwanted bomb loads knowing that German U-boats were frequently present. It was often shallow and considered an extremely high-risk area for German submarines by 1943.

of her hull creaking audibly beneath the strain of withstanding tons of crushing water pressure added impetus to efforts at arresting their descent. The Chief blew number five tank aft, followed by number one tank forward and the U-boat shuddered to a halt before beginning to ascend. All hands were assembled in the control room and prepared to abandon ship.

Aboard *Fame* Heathcote had ordered preparations made for a Hedgehog attack when *U353* abruptly broke surface at a steeply inclined angle, breaching like a whale before slamming down onto the Atlantic swell. Heathcote instantly ordered speed increased to 18 knots and prepared to ram. All weapons that could be brought to bear began to fire, as did distant cannons aboard the passing convoy, venting the merchantmen's fury on Römer's boat. On board *U353* there was a brief moment of almost absurd comedy as Römer became wedged fast in the conning tower hatch, having to be pushed through by straining crewmen from behind. As he was extricated and threw himself over the side, *Fame* struck the U-boat a glancing blow passing over her and dropping five shallow-set (50 feet) depth charges.

German submariners tumbled from their ship before Römer realized that both he and his Chief Engineer were floating in the sea, and their boat was not sinking, with nobody aboard to scuttle her. At roughly the same time a British boarding party made their way from the now-stationary *Fame* to *U353*. They climbed hesitantly aboard, led by P.M. Jones, but managed only five minutes before the U-boat went under, retrieving nothing of lasting value. Six Germans were killed in the action, the remainder, including Römer, plucked from the sea by *Fame* and Norwegian-crewed corvette HMS *Acanthus*. Following damage suffered during the ramming of *U353*, Heathcote was obliged to limp home to England alone.

21 November: Kptlt. Gustav Poel eased *U413* into port at 1200hrs. Brest's U-boat officers had turned out to greet and congratulate the newly transferred arrival from Kiel. While still in the early days of the boat's voyage Poel received news of the Allied 'Operation Torch' landings, which had begun on 8 November as Allied troops stormed ashore in Morocco and Algeria, outflanking the Afrika Korps in a vice that finally squeezed Rommel out of North Africa. Instructions received from BdU aboard *U413* ordered the U-boat to proceed at full speed for the area west of Gibraltar, hoping belatedly to intercept invasion shipping. On the morning of 14 November, while en route, Poel encountered convoy MKF 1 west of Lisbon. The northbound convoy comprised empty British troopships accompanied by newly created escort carriers HMS *Biter* and *Dasher*. Perfectly plotting and executing a submerged attack, Poel torpedoed and hit 20,107-ton troopship MV *Warwick Castle*. The crippled giant sank in thirty minutes after the torpedo pentrated her below the waterline on the port side of number 3 hold, blowing hatch covers over the crow's nest lookouts. Hit at 0850hrs, she was ordered abandoned at 0905, five minutes after Poel had struck her with a second torpedo

161

in almost exactly the same spot. Within 15 minutes she had been evacuated, sixty of her 295 crew and fifty-four of 133 service personnel aboard going with her to the bottom, killed either by the initial attacks or drowning in a heavy sea beneath brief but savage rain squalls.

U413 then joined the *Westwall* group stationed off Gibraltar attempting to interfere with 'Torch' invasion shipping. Massive anti-submarine air and sea patrols, however, frustrated the U-boats in their mission. Of seventeen boats deployed, two were sunk and five disabled, *U413* among the latter.

On 19 November Poel was approaching convoy KRS 3 on the surface when he was located and attacked by a 608 Squadron Hudson. Despite succeeding in crash-diving away from the enemy bomber, Flying Officer A.F. Wilcox dropped four depth charges slightly ahead of the disturbed water where *U413*'s twin-ruddered stern had moments before disappeared. The detonation destroyed Poel's periscopes, forcing him to abort his mission and proceed to Brest. A full month of repairs was required to make the damaged submarine seaworthy, but Poel's efforts in sinking the British troopship received commendation from Dönitz.

29 November: The U-boat base at La Pallice played host to *U263* returning from its first patrol and claiming 20,000 tons sunk. Thirteen days after leaving Kiel Kptlt. Kurt Nölke had received notification while at sea of the Allied landings on North Africa. Proceeding at high speed to his new operational area off Gibraltar, *U263* joined the *Westwall* group, swinging into action on 19 November.

After sighting convoy KRS 3, heading for Gibraltar's naval anchorage, twenty-eight-year-old Nölke attacked immediately. During well-executed submerged daylight attacks he torpedoed and sank the heavily laden 7,244-ton Norwegian freighter MV *Prinz Harald* and 5,123-ton British SS *Grangepark*. A third attack was foiled when the single torpedo launched exploded against the net defence of SS *Ocean Pilgrim*.

However, after daring to press home his effective assault, Nölke was not to escape the convoy's escorts. Pouncing onto *U263*'s ASDIC trace, British ships subjected Nölke and his men to 119 depth charges during hours of tenacious hunting. Aboard the U-boat there was severe damage from the repeated hammer blows and, after finally slipping free from the grasp of angry escorts, Nölke aborted his mission and set course for France.

Their ordeal was not yet over. On 24 November en route for Brest *U263* was sighted and attacked by a 233 Squadron Hudson. Sergeant E.H. Smith further devastated the boat with four depth charges, causing critical damage and rendering her unable to dive. Nölke contacted BdU and was instructed that he had the option of putting in to El Ferrol, Spain, and being interned if he deemed his boat unsailable as far as the sanctuary of France's Atlantic coast. While this option was discussed aboard the crippled boat another air attack by a 59 Squadron Flying Fortress, and later still a third attack from a

405 Squadron Hudson made continuing to France appear virtually suicidal. The U-boat was a floating wreck, though still capable of movement. Her perilous condition was not improved by having an unexploded depth charge wedged fast in her deck casing.

At this critical moment Junkers Ju88 bombers belonging to KG 40 arrived to provide air cover, the black crosses painted beneath the fast bombers' wings acting as a rejuvenating tonic to Nölke's exhausted crew. Further comfort was provided by 10th U-Flotilla's *U511*, aborting a patrol after her commander Kptlt. Freidrich Steinhoff began to suffer a mysterious illness upon reaching the combat zone. The two retreating U-boats travelled in company with flak weapons manned and crew adorned with life jackets in the event of complications. Nölke, having made his decision to return to France, limped into La Pallice on 29 November, the offending depth charge carefully removed and detonated elsewhere by Kriegsmarine explosives experts. His boat would require almost total rebuilding before becoming operational again and during the next thirteen months briefly became one of Dönitz's experimental flak boats before reconversion to standard configuration before her next sailing.

1 December: At 1500hrs 'The Lion' inspected the men and equipment of the 1st U-Flotilla. Visiting Brest to tour the headquarters of both 1st and 9th U-Flotillas, Dönitz held informal and familiar talks with all his available officers. Ideas were exchanged and a 'first hand feel' given to the BdU, now stationed in far away Paris on the *Avenue Maréchal Maunoury*.

Winter also recorded in the War Diary the transfer of more valuable U-boats to his command: *U336, U603, U628* from Kiel's 5th U-Flotilla; *U435* and *U456* from Bergen's 11th U-Flotilla (the former not passing into 1st U-Flotilla until February after transit from Norway).

Also noted on that day is the return of *U566* at 1200hrs, accurately claiming 4 252-tons of enemy shipping. Oblt.z.S. Gerhard Remus had sunk a single freighter, the British SS *Glenlea* from convoy ON143, while part of the *Natter* pack south-west of Ireland. After taking the ship's captain prisoner, the U-boat resumed her patrol before receiving the 8 November transmission of instructions regarding redirection of U-boats to Gibraltar. Joining the *Westwall* group Remus was patrolling the prescribed zone when Sergeant E.H. Smith's 233 Squadron Hudson surprised the boat and damaged her with depth charges. For the second consecutive patrol Remus was forced to abort and return to base, this time trailing a thick stream of leaking oil. *U566* would not be operational for another two months, requiring extensive structural repair work.

3 December: *U301*, commanded by Kptlt. Willy-Roderich Körner, left Brest at 1700hrs. The U-boat was passing from Winter's command to the Mediterranean and La Spezia's 29th U-Flotilla. She eased through the heavily defended Straits of Gibraltar on the night of 9/10 December, docking at her new flotilla base mid-morning four days later. The following month the boat was gone, sunk by a single torpedo from the British submarine HMS *Sahib* on 21 January 1943. The 'mousetrap' of the Mediterranean had claimed another boat.

5 December: After her gruelling working-up period *U225* transferred from 5th to 1st U-Flotilla with her sailing from Kiel bound for the North Atlantic. The following day 'visiting' U-boat *U463* left Brest at 1600hrs for its third operational refuelling patrol. The Type XIV would return from this and the next patrol before being sunk north-west of Cape Ortegal in the effective British effort to hunt down the U-tankers.

Also on 6 December in Lorient Kptlt. Kottmann took *U203* out to the battlefield again. Destined for a month-long North Atlantic patrol the crew were rested and ready. Lorient boasted many attractions for fatigued Kriegsmarine men after concluding a patrol. Aside from the obvious traditional sailor's pastimes of women and drinking, German Naval Command had requisitioned facilities for their seamen, similar to those in and around Brest. The resort area of Carnac boasted accommodation for relaxing U-boat crews where they were able to enjoy sweeping beaches and even an imitation Bavarian tavern. Of course the local Breton fare was also open to the Kriegsmarine, and generally it has been remarked that relations with the local population was cordial if not better.

7 December: The 1st Flotilla's elderly Type VIIB submarine *U84* returned flying a solitary 8,000-ton victory pennant, docking at 1230hrs. Kptlt. Uphoff's patrol had succeeded in claiming a single Allied ship. The 7,459-ton British SS *Empire Sunrise* from SC107 was torpedoed and sunk, after already being damaged by *U402* and straggling badly. Further attacks by *U84* were driven off by air support, although other *Veilchen* group boats managed to claim fourteen more ships during the running battle, losing two of their own number in the process.

30 December: *U564* arrived at Brest after unsuccessful patrolling against convoy ON143 and the 'Torch' landings. *U584* departed for the North Atlantic, Kptlt. Joachim Deecke ordered to join the *Falke* group 500 miles west of Ireland. Last of the New Year departures was Kptlt. Hans Kapf for his first operational patrol in command of *U632*. He too had been ordered to join the *Falke* group.

8.

CRESCENDO

1 JANUARY 1943 to 31 MARCH 1943

1 January 1943: Amid floating ice and freezing conditions, new Bremer-Vulkan boat *U268* transferred from 8th U-Training Flotilla to its combat unit 1st U-Flotilla. Sailing initially for Bergen her commander, OblzS Ernst Heydemann, ordered the boat fuelled and final maintenance undergone before departing for action in the convoy war.

3 January: Oblt.z.S. Günther Rosenberg took *U201* from Brest at 1450hrs. The veteran boat's ninth war patrol, second under command of Rosenberg, was spent in the North Atlantic. Proceeding to the patrol area west of Ireland *U201* had orders to join the *Falke* group hunting westbound ONS convoy traffic.

7 January: As *U86* put into Brest empty-handed after operations with the *Westwall* group, her companion boat *U203* also docked, claiming 11,000 tons of 'ocean liner' sunk in action as part of the *Spitz* group. Kptlt. Kottmann had been involved in the ferocious attack on convoy ONS154 during two nights beginning on 27 December. The ten-strong *Spitz* pack (including flotilla mates *U225* and *U440*), accompanied by another 11-boats in the *Ungestüm* group (with 1st U-Flotilla boats *U336* and *U628*) descended on the forty-five merchantmen led by Canadian Escort Group C1. The escorts comprised destroyer HMCS *St Laurent*, five corvettes, *Battleford, Chilliwack, Napanee, Shediac* and *Orillia*, and the Free French-crewed fighter catapult ship HMS *Fidelity*. Trailing behind the convoy was rescue ship *Toward*, battle-hardened veteran of Atlantic war. Unfortunately for the convoy there were many short-comings among the escort. Although the five corvettes were equipped with effective Type 271 centimetric radar, the majority of the operators were new and inexperienced at handling the equipment. The Escort group had had no opportunity to exercise together as a unit and achieve any form of real cohesion. Pitted against multiple, and often experienced, U-boats, the small warships were soon overwhelmed.

ONS154 had been routed towards the Azores in order to skirt the North Atlantic area savaged by winter storms, although the merchant ships

165

continued to be battered by roaring westerly gales. On the evening of 27 December the gathered 'Wolf Pack' which had shadowed the merchant train struck with calculated ferocity. Oblt.z.S. Wolfgang Leimkühler on his first patrol in command of new Type VIIC *U225* opened the scoring for 1st U-Flotilla boats. He sighted and stalked the British tanker SS *Scottish Heather* while she refuelled the corvette *Chilliwak*. Due to the small warships' limited range a British oiler had been included in the convoy for refuelling purposes. As *Chilliwak* was finishing her fuelling a single torpedo struck and badly damaged the 7,100-ton tanker, forcing her to break away from the convoy and return to Scotland's Clyde shipyards. This put an end to attempts at re-fuelling the small pitching and rolling corvettes. Before the Germans could begin their attack proper brief respite was granted to ONS154 with a curtain of dense fog swiftly lowering over flattening seas. Most U-boats were either voluntarily disengaging to reload or lost contact in diminishing visibility. It was however only a temporary reprieve. Late on the afternoon of 28 December the fog dissipated and a warm sky glowed above calm Atlantic waters. The Allied merchant ships could not have wished for worse luck.

That evening Leimkühler, having regained contact through his sharp-eyed bridge watch, returned and again attacked. Already preceded by other U-boats of both packs, *U225* launched two separate torpedo attacks. The first double torpedo salvo lanced from the U-boat's bow tubes and scored killing blows on the 5,273-ton British steamer SS *Melmore Head*, third ship in column eleven of the lumbering convoy. The freighter exploded in a welter of flames and sank rapidly. A single stern torpedo hit and damaged the British SS *Ville de Rouen*, the 5,083-ton cargo-carrier later given the coup-de-grace by *U662*. In his second attack Leimkühler launched four individual shots into the packed convoy ranks. One hit and damaged Belgian tanker MV *President Francqui*, the 4,919-ton ship in ballast later finished off by *U336*, another brand new flotilla boat scoring her only victim during the convoy action, while two others smashed into the convoy Commodore's ship SS *Empire Shackleton*. Aboard the crippled 7,068-ton steamer Admiral Egerton (Convoy Commodore) ordered the vessel abandoned as she began to settle by the head with a rapidly flooding, and thankfully empty, number one hold. She too was to be finished off by another U-boat later, *U435* putting her under with combined torpedoes and gunfire, miraculously without her cargo of 1,000 tons of ammunition for the Royal Canadian Navy being detonated.

Kptlt. Hans Geissler's *U440* attempted to add its weight to the battle, but despite firing torpedoes into the fray, made no sinkings. The last of the newly operational Flotilla boats involved, Kptlt. Heinrich Hasenschar's *U628*, blooded itself by finishing off the damaged British 5,029-ton steamer SS *Lynton Grange* on the evening of 29 December. *Spitz* boat *U406*, using newly developed 'FAT' acoustic torpedoes, had previously hit the ship, causing her crew to abandon the stumbling hulk. Following the despatch of the *Lynton*

166

Grange Hasenschar attempted a torpedo run against an escorting corvette, but, despite claiming a hit, all his torpedoes missed.[67]

For his part in the action *U203*'s commander mistakenly claimed success. Kptlt. Kottmann's torpedo shot missed its intended target, the torpedo 'porpoising' and skimming ineffectually between densely packed merchant ships. After disengaging and making an eventual return to Brest the veteran U-boat was consigned to the yards for nearly three months of complete over-haul and refit.

By 31 December the U-boats engaged against ONS154 were low on fuel and Dönitz cancelled further attacks. British escort reinforcements were also arriving to bolster the struggling convoy. Dönitz calculated the battle as a victory for the Kriegsmarine – fourteen ships sunk for a total of 69,378 tons and at no loss to themselves. It was a satisfying end to 1942, but in a month of otherwise meagre results for the U-boat arm. German joy was not lessened by British despair over the scale of the disaster. The Canadian Escort Group was criticised for lacking aggressiveness in its response to the U-boat attack and the entire Canadian escort force was sent back into training to be replaced by seasoned British units.

8 January: Three more of the flotilla's victors from the ONS154 convoy battle returned to Brest at 1300hrs and heroes' welcomes: *U225* (mistakenly) claiming the astronomical total of nine steamers for 52,919 tons; *U628* claiming a corvette and single *Dampfer*; *U336* claiming *Keine Versunken*, although having finished off the damaged tanker MV *President Francqui*.

Convoys destined for the support of 'Operation Torch' remained high on U-boat attack schedules into the beginning of 1943. Most devastating to Allied hopes in North Africa was the loss of seven out of nine oil tankers in convoy TM1 on 8 January. Ten U-boats of the *Delphin* pack, exhorted by radio messages from Dönitz to 'Help your comrades in Tunis', accounted for 100,000 tons of oil desperately needed by vehicles of the Anglo-American North African forces. Despite the humiliation suffered in high Admiralty circles, further oil and supply convoys received valuable assistance when on 9 January ULTRA code-breakers mastered the latest set of German Enigma settings. Intelligence regarding U-boat dispositions, unable to be supplied before TM1 met its fate, allowed re-routing of future oil and supply convoys, the U-boats contacting destroyer 'hunter-killer' groups in their place.

[67] The 'FAT' (*Federapparat Torpedo*) ran a wandering course with regular 180° turns, and was found to be extremely useful against convoys. This steering device could be fitted to both standard G7a and G7e torpedoes, and meant that the torpedo could be fired towards an enemy formation from oblique angles and left to run in random search of a target. From the end of 1942 onwards it was manufactured at the rate of roughly 100 per month, and equipped U-boats in the Atlantic, providing a greater choice of weaponry and thus wider scope for variations in attack technique.

10 January: *U435* returned to the ranks of 1st U-Flotilla after seven months under the command of Bergen's 11th U-Flotilla, and her commander sporting his new Knight's Cross awarded while in Norway. Entering port in Brest at 1200hrs Kptlt. Siegfried Strelow's boat displayed three victory pennants gained during her transfer voyage while part of the *Ungestüm* group's attack on ONS154, and amounting to a claimed destroyer and 14,000 tons of *Dampfer* (steamer). Strelow had attacked and missed the destroyer HMCS *St Laurent* in the early morning of 29 December, sinking the damaged SS *Empire Shackleton* instead. *U435* also accounted for the Norwegian 5,701-ton SS *Norse King*, already damaged by *U591* later that day. Strelow's 'destroyer' came on the evening of 30 December when he torpedoed the high-sided fighter catapult ship HMS *Fidelity*. Despite the ship streaming AND nets, Strelow fired two torpedoes at the French-manned ship, both of which penetrated the anti-torpedo nets and exploded in dull roars of flame and steam. The ship rapidly went under, after which Strelow reported that '300 to 400' survivors were drifting in overcrowded life rafts. Given the worsening winter conditions he doubted their chances of survival. He was correct. All 337 men from her crew perished, as did thirty-seven survivors of other sinkings rescued by *Fidelity*, including the Convoy Commodore Admiral Egerton.

In January the weather deteriorated rapidly in the Atlantic. Storms reduced U-boat operations to nothing. Whatever naval units were still operating needed all of their energies in preserving their existence against the elements, rather than any possible threat from enemy forces. Hideous weather made U-boat operations useless, even remaining alive atop a teetering conning tower became a challenge, let alone observing the chaotically tumbling horizon for enemy targets. As Dönitz recorded in his post-war memoirs:

> 'The last months of 1942 had been exceptionally stormy in the North Atlantic. But in January 1943 the elements seemed to rage in uncontrolled fury. Storm followed storm and very considerably enhanced the difficulties of U-boat operations.'[68]

On the Allies' side, although no German interceptions were made in the first half of January, eight merchant ships foundered, four ran aground and upwards of forty suffered severe weather damage. To top matters off, nearly a third of all escort vessels were removed from duty with storm damage. For once the misery at sea was nature's work not man's.

U-boats still sailed, although the majority of their time was spent lying up at sea in anticipation of clearer weather. Attempts at reconnaissance were virtually abandoned and lengthy periods were spent submerged to allow drained men to conserve their energy. Oblt.z.S. Ernst Heydemann's new boat *U268* began its first operational sortie at 1000hrs on 10 January. *U202* left

---

[68] *Ten Years and Twenty Days*, Karl Dönitz p. 316.

Brest on 12 January, newcomer to 1st U-Flotilla *U456* leaving Bergen two days later.

14 January: Kptlt. Götz von Hartmann's *U563* returned to Brest at 1200hrs, thankful to be leaving the atrocious Atlantic conditions behind. A single victory was all there was to show for over a month at sea, von Hartmann claiming a steamer of '6,000 tons' sunk. This sole success had come on 18 December, nine days into the patrol while the boat had been bound for *Westwall* operations west of Spain. The British steamer SS *Bretwalda*, part of military convoy MKS 3-Y from Gibraltar, was torpedoed and sunk by von Hartmann before destroyers drove him off. Distressingly, several newly developed Pi2 magnetic pistols used by von Hartmann had failed to detonate against other targets within the convoy; memories of Norway's disastrous torpedo crisis continued to haunt the U-boat service. Von Hartmann, who had taken command of the boat from Bargsten while she lay in Blohm & Voss's expansive repair yards, reported that his diesels still had 'quirks', the last thing needed on a combat U-boat.

22 January: Another U-boat returned to Brest claiming a single 6,000-ton steamer sunk. At 1200hrs Kptlt. Klaus Hartmann brought *U441* into her concrete berth after over a month at sea. One fortnight after his 13 December Brest departure, Hartmann had sighted the straggling Dutch freighter SS *Soekaboemi*, damaged by *U356* during the bitter action against convoy ONS154. *U441* closed the ship and sent her under with torpedoes, the first success for the boat and the only one for her five-week patrol.

28 January: Kptlt. Wolfgang Sporn took *U439* from Brest for 'special duties'. Within five days he had returned, his mission cancelled. He was transferred to staff duties and his boat received new commander Oblt.z.S. Helmut von Tippelskirch. Kptlt. Feiler accompanied Sporn's boat from Brest at 1500hrs, his *U653* ordered to the inhospitable North Atlantic.

30 January: While the Atlantic rocked with turbulent natural forces, in Berlin there was turbulence of a very different nature. In the increasingly remote world from which Hitler controlled his military machine, he remained nervous to the point of paranoia regarding the use of his surface battle fleets. The sinking of the *Bismarck*, more than any other event, influenced his train of thought towards the Kriegsmarine mothballing its surface fleet, and concentrating on U-boat assaults. Reliance on submarine naval warfare was something that he belatedly became convinced of in December 1942 when the cruiser *Admiral Hipper* was damaged as part of a disastrous surface attack on an Arctic convoy that escaped unscathed. Hitler was furious, accusing his Admirals of cowardice and demanding that the surface fleet be scrapped.

The showdown that occurred between *Grossadmiral* Raeder and Hitler on

6 January 1943 resulted in Hitler (encouraged by a gleeful Göring eager to improve his and his Luftwaffe's somewhat lacklustre standing in Hitler's eyes at the expense of Raeder) demanding the scrapping of the German surface ships, their steel to be used for tank production and the mounting of their heavy cannon in shore batteries. Raeder, after vain attempts at pointing out the fallacy of this move, handed in his resignation, putting forward Vizeadmiral Dönitz's and Vizeadmiral Carls' names as possible successors. Thus Dönitz became the head of the Kriegsmarine on 30 January 1943, promoted to Grossadmiral. Despite his personal emphasis on U-boats as their Commander in Chief and initial agreement with Hitler's plans, it was ironically he who eventually changed Hitler's mind regarding the planned scrapping of the capital ships. Hitler revoked his decision, but the large surface ships were never used to their full potential again.[69] Now the Atlantic ports were left to the smaller vessels of the Kriegsmarine. Winter's entry into the Flotilla War Diary recorded:

'BdU Dönitz becomes *Oberbefelshaber der Kriegsmarine* and Grossadmiral.'

Accompanying his exalted status as Chief of the Kriegsmarine Dönitz was forced once again to move his headquarters. The new location lay near the heart of German military and political power. While U-boat headquarters were set up in a building in Charlottenburg, named Koralle, staff officers occupied the nearby *Hotel am Steinplatz*. The new headquarters complex was operational by 31 March. With Dönitz's elevation to C-in-C Kriegsmarine he named his deputy Admiral Hans-Georg von Friedeburg as *Führer der Unterseeboote* (Commander of U-boats – FdU).

February found the strength of 1st U-Flotilla that had been recuperating in Brest putting to sea in fresh assaults against British convoy traffic. *U628*, *U225*, *U566*, *U603*, *U84*, *U435*, *U665*, *U439*, *U86*, *U306*, *U440* and *U441* all slipped from their French berths and hammered into the Atlantic, crews refreshed by their periods ashore.

On the Allied political front a new revitalized effort was decreed to defeat Dönitz's U-boats. During January 1943 Prime Minister Churchill and President Roosevelt convened the SYMBOL conference at Casablanca to decide the conduct of the war during 1943. After two weeks of hard bargaining several key principles were agreed on, but one remained absolutely at the highest priority:

'The defeat of the U-boat must remain a first charge on the resources of the united nations.'[70]

[69] The unsuccessful candidate Admiral Carls, a distinguished career man, was killed in action two weeks before the end of the war.
[70] *The Second World War*, W. Churchill, Vol. IV, p. 554 – 'The conduct of the war in 1943.'

11 February: Returns were disappointing for *U584*. Tying up once again in Brest at 1300hrs, Kptlt. Joachim Deecke and his exhausted men had spent the better part of six weeks battling the elements as part of two separate wolf packs. Off the west coast of Ireland, expected Allied shipping had never appeared, the only conflict for Deecke and his men being with the depressing conditions aboard their boat.

14 February: The same group – *Falke* – that Deecke had belonged to west of Ireland, yielded meagre results for Kptlt. Hans Karpf's *U632*. Claiming one steamer of unknown tonnage, Karpf had actually sunk two ships during this his maiden patrol and transfer journey from Kiel. While lying in wait for ON convoys Karpf had torpedoed and sunk a straggler from convoy UGS 3, the 6,773-ton Panamanian tanker SS *C J Barkdull* on 10 January. This was one of only four ships sunk by U-boats in the first half of January 1943.

U632 then received its first experience of air attack after being located while surfaced by an RAF B17 of 206 Squadron. Pilot L.G. Clark attacked the submarine with an intended seven-depth-charge salvo. Three of the lethal canisters hung up inside the bomber, but the remaining four were close enough to cause minor damage to Karpf's boat. Clark mistakenly claimed a kill, while the crash-dived U-boat crept away to safety.

Moved east after reported sightings of convoy HX224 west-north-west of Rockall, *U632* chanced upon his second kill, a British convoy straggler MV *Cordelia*. Swiftly attacking the heavily laden tanker Karpf hit her with two torpedoes, the ship exploding in a dazzling display of destruction. The U-boat crew fished one survivor from the water. Once aboard *U632* the dazed British Chief Engineer volunteered the information – why is not clear – to Karpf that the slow moving convoy SC118 was only a matter of two days behind HX224.

The young German instantly appreciated the value of this information and transmitted it to BdU, where it was found to tally with recent *B-Dienst* radio intercepts giving proposed Admiralty sailing instructions for an undisclosed convoy. Dönitz immediately concentrated his boats in the area and formed the *Pfeil* pack to lay in wait. Karpf however could not participate in the operation, his fuel critically low. *U632* set course for Brest, taking on board only sufficient fuel for the journey from Type XIV *Milchkuh U460* on 10 February in the central North Atlantic.

17 February: *U413*, slipping into Brest at 1200hrs, flew two pennants totalling 10,000 BRT from her conning tower. Kptlt. Poel's first score had been while part of the *Jaguar* group north-east of Newfoundland. On 22 January Poel attacked and sank a straggler from convoy SC117, the 3,556-ton Greek SS *Mount Mycale*. Full-scale coordinated group attacks against the convoy were, however, continually frustrated by radio communications problems between the boats and BdU.

The U-boat's second kill came about as a result of the intelligence gathered from Karpf's British prisoner. After finally receiving coherent orders from U-boat command to concentrate in the central North Atlantic, *U413* joined the thirteen-strong *Pfeil* group lying in wait for convoy SC118. On 4 February contact was made by *Pfeil* boat *U187*, helped in his search for the Allied ships by the accidental triggering of a brilliant white snowflake flare from the Norwegian freighter SS *Vannik*, and the pack closed for the kill.

The sixty-three-ship convoy, laden with supplies primarily for Russia and plodding at six knots through a leaden swell, presented a huge target for the approaching Germans. The convoy's real strength lay in her protection – British Escort Group B2, comprising four British destroyers (Senior Officer Commander F.B. Proudfoot's HMS *Vanessa*, HMS *Vimy*, *Witch* and *Beverley*), American coast guard cutter *George M. Bibb*, four corvettes (British HMS *Campanula* and free-French *Abelia*, *Lobelia* and *Mignonette*) and the ubiquitous rescue ship *Toward*. Shadowing U-boats clung tenaciously to the convoy as the group concentrated, despite atrocious weather. Blinding snow, hail and ferocious winds taunted the U-boats, but still they persevered in their hunt.

The battle began with British destroyers fixing the position of the Type IX *U187* using their HF/DF, homing on the U-boat's sighting report. The 10th U-Flotilla boat was the first casualty as scattered *Pfeil* boats made contact and began their assault. BdU directives exhorted the commanders to new heights in order to smash the Allied supply train. At one point Dönitz branded in the minds of his men that they were directly helping the flagging war in Russia by sinking potential supply ships, transmitting:

'At 'em! Operate ruthlessly to relieve the Eastern Front!'

His men were only too aware of the collapse of Germany's Sixth Army at Stalingrad on 2 February.

On the evening of the 5th at the northern end of the patrol line *U413* found the straggling American SS *West Portal* and sank the 5,376-ton ship with all hands. It was Poel's sole success from the battle, which raged until 9 February west of Ireland and expanded with both Allied and German reinforcements. During the five days of fierce combat eleven ships for approximately 60,000 tons (claims from the U-boat skippers amounting to fourteen ships of 109,000 tons) were sunk for the loss of three U-boats, and severe damage to three more from aircraft racing out to cover the convoy on 8 February. It was a disappointing result for BdU, and a rate of attrition that the U-boats could not maintain. Dönitz later noted:

'It was perhaps the hardest convoy battle of the whole war.'

26 February: *U456* docked at her new home port Brest at 1600hrs after transfer from Bergen's 11th U-Flotilla. Kptlt. Max-Martin Teichert and his crew had taken part in *Landsknecht* pack attacks on convoy HX224 during early February, sinking two ships (SS *Jeremiah van Rensselear* and the tanker

MV *Inverilen* for a combined 16,633 tons) and damaging escort sloop HMS *Londonderry*.

On 4 February Teichert received orders to proceed at speed to the interception of convoy SC118 but failed to participate in the attacks. Following the end of that battle and refuelling from *U460*, Teichert set course for Brest, chancing upon and sinking British 700-ton SS *Kyleclare*. As *U456* entered the military harbour and prepared to dock she flew three pennants for 21,000 tons, an over-claim of 3,667 tons.

1 March: Winter noted the following transfers to 1st U-Flotilla:

'New boats *U305*, *U306*, *U415* from Danzig's 8th U-Flotilla, veteran *U209* from Bergen's 11th U-Flotilla.'

2 March: Kptlt. Hunger slipped from Brest for *U336*'s second operational patrol. His destination was the fiercely escalating Atlantic battleground. Five days later the 1st U-boat Flotilla War Diary recorded the presumed loss of one of its oldest and most successful Type VIIC U-boats: '*U201 Vermisst ein Stern*.' The official BdU communiqué sent to Brest had been placed inside Winter's War Diary. It continued:

'Boat left Brest on 3/7 outbound. Last reported 17/2 from (grid area) Bruno Caesar 3136 under escort attack. Fate of the crew unknown.
    For Relatives: Boat was in the North Atlantic on convoy operation and is still in that area.
    Summary: For 1st U-Flotilla. Until the final possible day elapses BdU War Diary won't admit loss.'

U201 had been at sea since 3 January, operating in the North Atlantic. Oblt.z.S. Rosenberg joined the *Falke* patrol group and as soon as he had reached his patrol quadrant proceeded to lie in wait for westbound ONS convoys.

After weeks of chafing inactivity twenty-one U-boats formed a new patrol line south of Cape Farewell named *Haudegan*. By 15 February fuel was running low for the Type VIICs and orders were received from BdU to proceed to a refuelling area and rendezvous with a *Milchkuh* supply vessel. En route, *U69* sighted the elusive convoy ONS165, issuing a brief homing transmission for other *Haudegan* boats. *U201* quickly arrived and the two U-boats approached their target on 17 February in gale-force winds, tempestuous currents and mountainous seas.

Unfortunately for the two attacking U-boats, British Escort Group B-6, commanded by experienced U-boat hunter Commander S. Heathcote, provided the convoy's escort. Aboard two of the British destroyers, HMS *Viscount* and Heathcote's HMS *Fame*, 'Huff-Duff' and radar operators had got position fixes on both *U69*'s beacon and the two small surfaced submarines. Both destroyers ran straight down the bearings indicated, dropping depth charges as they neared their prey. Confusion remains as to who actually sank who, the previously most accepted scenario being that HMS *Viscount* destroyed *U69* with depth charges while HMS *Fame* blew *U201* to the surface and then finished the crippled boat by ramming her and sprinkling the area with more shallow-set charges. Recently, however, this theory has been reversed. In Axel Niestlé's comprehensive study *German U-Boat Losses During World War Two*, he states:

> 'Original postwar assessment changed by FDS/NHB in April 1997. The attack by the destroyer *Fame* on 17 February 1943 . . . formerly credited with the destruction of *U201*, actually accounted for the sinking of *U69*.'[71]

If so then *U201* was indeed sunk by HMS *Viscount* during the confused mêlée. Both U-boats left no survivors. The 'Grey Wolf' that had achieved fame during 1941 and 1942, particularly under the command of Adalbert Schnee, was no more.

9 March: Kptlt. Hasenschar returned to Brest after success in the Atlantic. As part of *Ritter* group, his *U628* sighted convoy ON166 on 22 February, homed to the target by contact boat *U604*, Hasenschar attacking next morning. The sixty-three-ship convoy, escorted by predominantly American Escort Group A3, became aware from careless German radio chatter of the growing number of U-boats closing on them again. They had already undergone repeated attacks (one of which Wolfgang Leimkühler's *U225* had participated in), losing several ships and claiming one U-boat destroyed during their Atlantic crossing.

For the second of ON166's ordeals under fire there were in fact elements of three separate 'Wolf Packs' bearing down on the Allied ships, *Ritter*, *Knappen* and *Taifun*. The combined total of U-boats engaged reached nineteen before the battle had finished. Hasenschar's early morning torpedo attack hit and damaged two tankers, MV *Winkler* and MV *Glittre* (both were subsequently finished off by *U223* and *U603* respectively). *U628* was located by hunting escorts and pounded with depth charges from USCGC *Spencer* but managed to escape, electric motors purring as the U-boat dropped deeper into the Atlantic, dipping below the depth charge attack.

On 24 February *U628* shared the credit for sinking the 4,391-ton Norwegian MV *Ingria* with *U600*, and the following day sank the British Liberty Ship 7,264-ton SS *Manchester Merchant* with two torpedoes. This, the final ship of the convoy to be sunk, took thirty-seven men with her to the bottom. Dönitz concluded that the battle was a success, counting '23 ships

---

[71] *German U-Boat Losses During World War Two*, Axel Niestlé. p. 224.

sunk for 132,171 tons for the loss of one U-boat'. In fact, fourteen ships had been sunk for a combined total of 78,700 tons and four U-boats had been destroyed during the build-up to the attack and the six-day running fight. It marked severe losses for both sides and was one of the largest convoy actions of the war.

10 March: *'U268 Vermisst ein Stern.'* The official report from BdU continued:

'Boat left Bergen 10 January. Last reported 18 February requesting bearings for Lorient. Fate of the crew unknown.

For relatives: Boat was successful during operations in the North Atlantic, and one large tanker had been sunk. Presumed lost due to air attack.'

During the U-boat's first operational sailing Oblt.z.S. Ernst Heydemann had indeed sunk a large ship from convoy HX222. During the afternoon of 17 January 26-year-old Heydemann, operating as part of the *Habicht* group, sighted the convoy and requested permission to fire. Authorized to launch his first combat attack, he singled out the largest ship in sight and fired torpedoes at the 14,547-ton Panamanian factory ship SS *Vestfold*. Loaded with Allied military equipment the huge vessel erupted into flames and sank, taking with her three 143-ton Landing Craft Tanks – LCT *2239*, LCT *2267* and LCT *2344* – raising *U268*'s score to an aggregate four ships for 14,976 tons. No other boats participated in attacking the convoy, judged by BdU too near to Iceland-based aircraft for U-boats to operate effectively.

This single sinking was to be the boat's last. During early February *U268* joined the *Haudegen* group shadowing small convoy SG 19, but to no effect. Days later Heydemann, low on fuel, set course for Lorient and the U-boat's first taste of conquered France.

On the night of 19 February, while travelling surfaced, bridge lookouts were stunned by the sudden appearance of a blinding shaft of white light arcing from the darkness and pinning the U-boat squarely within its broad beam. Moments later four shallow-set depth charges straddled the boat and water stinking of cordite erupted around her. The hull was shattered and *U268* disintegrated and sank with all forty-five crew still aboard. Flying Officer G.D.Lundeon of 172 Squadron in his Wellington VII (MP505 'B') had successfully used the newly developed Leigh Light for the first time[72].

---

[72] Squadron Leader Humphrey de Vere had developed the large aircraft-mounted searchlight in response to problems of attacking U-boats at night. Once the U-boat was detected by on-board radar the 24-inch radar-controlled light was switched on at a range of about 1,000 yards, allowing the pilot and gunners to home on the target visually, while also blinding return fire. It was simple in concept and extremely effective in use.

14 March: '*U582 Vermisst zwei Stern.* No new information.'

Meanwhile further U-boats put to sea from Brest: *U632*, *U563*, *U584* and *U413* all began operational patrols during March as the weather gradually moderated in the Atlantic.

23 March: '*U665 Vermisst ein Stern.*' The depressing regularity of BdU loss notification continued with the presumed demise of another U-boat on her maiden war patrol.

> 'Boat left Kiel 20 February. Last reported 21 March stopped 36 hours before meeting with escort. Fate of crew unknown. Little hope of survival.
>
> For relatives: Boat experienced success in North Atlantic operations and had sunk by torpedo an enemy steamer. Believed lost during their return journey.'

Oblt.z.S. Hans-Jürgen Haupt had sailed his new command from Kiel on 20 February for North Atlantic operations. Joining ten other boats, *U665* formed part of the *Ostmark* group, strung in a line south of Greenland and lying in wait for convoy SC121 sighted by *U405* on 6 March. Accompanied by seventeen other U-boats from *Wildfang*, *Burggraf* and *Neptun* groups, *Ostmark* attacked over the night of 9/10 March. Although twelve ships were sunk Haupt had no success in the fray.

On 14 March *Ostmark* U-boats were joined by three *Burggraf* boats and formed a new pack named *Stürmer*. Proceeding into the central Atlantic in search of convoy SC122 contact was made on 16th and the large pack moved to attack. *U653* had been the contact boat, spotting a convoy's fragile-looking mastheads in the distance and radioing a sighting report:

'*Beta, Beta. BD 1491 Geleitzug Kurs 70*' (convoy course 70).

In fact it was a different and faster convoy to that originally sought. To compound the impending battle fast Halifax convoy HX229 was rapidly over-hauling SC122, its forty merchant ships escorted by a scratch team of four destroyers and two corvettes, loosely named British Escort Group B4. The slower moving SC122 convoy of fifty merchant vessels and British escort Group B-5 were heading directly for the *Stürmer* line, unaware of its presence after an intelligence blackout of Enigma intercepts between 10 and 19 March.

B-Dienst decrypts on the other hand provided valuable information of the two convoys' routing, allowing Dönitz the unprecedented chance of grouping three packs – *Stürmer*, *Dränger* and *Raubgraf* – into a single assaulting force, numbering in total some thirty-eight U-boats against a drawn-out group of ninety lumbering merchant ships.

In high seas with howling gale-force winds the first torpedoes were unleashed on 16 March. This initial attack was launched by 1st U-Flotilla's *U603* as Kptlt. Hans-Joachim Bertelsmann torpedoed and sank the

176

Norwegian freighter MV *Elin K*, after firing three FAT torpedoes and one electric. Kptlt. Siegfried Strelow's *U435* fired four FAT torpedoes at Liberty ship targets, hitting and damaging SS *William Eustis* (later finished off by *U91*). Strelow claimed hits on three other ships and a tanker during the ensuing mêlée but these claims remain unconfirmed. From the total of attacks made by U-boat during the initial clash, ten ships for 72,000 tons were definitely sunk, by seven of the attacking U-boats.

Meanwhile there was confusion in Berlin as *Stürmer* boats subsequently clashed with SC122 100 miles to the north. BdU believed the initial target to have been this convoy and now concluded that the new attacks were against HX229, when in actuality the reverse was true and BdU's initial surmise correct. Dönitz and his staff proceeded to treat the entire operation as one large convoy action and immediately ordered all boats to attack, slipping the leash and allowing his wolves to run wild.

U665 chanced upon the straggling British Liberty ship SS *Fort Cedar Lake*, previously damaged by *U338*. Sinking it with a single torpedo Haupt had made his only kill. Despite small returns for 1st U-Flotilla's U-boats, by the operation's end twenty-one Allied ships had been sunk for the loss of a single boat. Taken as a single action, it remains the biggest convoy battle of the Second World War. Significantly, newly introduced VLR Liberator bombers finally drove off the U-boat attackers, the freshly deployed aircraft marking a turning point in Allied fortunes.

U665 began the trek to La Pallice on 20 March, three days after reporting to BdU the decision to return and being directed by Dönitz to the southern port. Men aboard slowly allowed the tension of battle to drain from them, although vigilance remained vital while the U-boat was surfaced. Any lowering of attention could be fatal, as it proved for Haupt and his men.

British Coastal Command's 19 Group began the first of a series of antisubmarine air offensives over Biscay on the same day that *U665* started to return on 20 March. Lasting for eight days 'Operation Enclose' involved 115 aircraft, many armed with centimetric radar (impervious to Metox detection) and Leigh Lights, covering a box between 7° and 10.5° west.

Two days later in heavy rain that had reduced visibility to roughly 500 yards, she was located near Bishop Rock and sunk by a single depth charge attack from Sergeant J.A. Marsden's 10th OTU (Operational Training Unit) Whitley bomber. The aircraft's rear gunner asserted that the shallow-set depth charges had cleanly straddled the area slightly ahead of the swirl left by *U665*'s stern, still visible as the U-boat attempted to crash dive to safety. No trace was ever found of the forty-six men aboard.

25 March: The entry for this date continued to reflect what can be seen in hindsight to have been the beginning of the U-boats' final decline: '*U225 Vermisst ein Stern*'

'The boat left Brest on 2 February. Last reported 7 February from (grid reference) Bruno Emil 24 with weather report. Fate of the crew uncertain.

For relatives: Boat is possibly missing in action against North Atlantic convoys.'

Oblt.z.S. Wolfgang Leimkühler and his forty-five-men-crew went down with their U-boat after being depth-charged by Flying Officer R.T.F. Turner's 120 Squadron Liberator bomber. One day after joining *Ritter* group west of Ireland *U225* had been surprised while travelling on the surface and sunk in seconds of shattering Torpex detonation.

26 March: Claiming 6,000 BRT of enemy shipping *U202* arrived alongside *U603*, the latter flying pennants for one tanker of 6,000 BRT and one steamer of 5,000 BRT.

After two months and fourteen days Kptlt. Poser brought *U202* into Brest at 1100hrs. The U-boat had left the Breton harbour during January to operate against shipping bound for the Mediterranean. In predictably terrible weather Poser's boat had joined the fifteen others of *Delphin* pack and patrolled the waters stretching from the Canary Islands to Gibraltar.

It was a largely unsuccessful voyage, one small coastal convoy sighted – Gib. No.2 – but attempted attacks were abandoned due to strong air support. During the first half of February the drudgery aboard *U202* was relieved by news of Poser's promotion to Kptlt. In the words of the boat's War Diary a 'terrific feast' was held aboard the cramped and damp submarine, while a nearby U-boat 'fired a deck gun salvo' in honour of the occasion.

After refuelling from *U118* south-west of Madeira between 12 and 14 February, the *Delphin* group swept westwards in search of contacts. On 23 February Poser's alert bridge watch spotted the mastheads of convoy UC 1 and the chase began. With roaring diesels the boat pounded through high seas to close the unsuspecting Allied ships. Crashing headlong into chaotic breakers the U-boats pursued their targets 'at the speed of a cyclist.'[73] Finally contact was established within firing range. *U202* launched attacks against three of the convoy's tankers, sinking the 7,989-ton American SS *Esso Baton Rouge* and damaging SS *Empire Norseman* (later sunk by *U558*) and MV *British Fortitude*. Escort USS *Lonsdale* located Poser's boat and subjected it to three hours of depth-charges, causing minor damage, before abandoning the uncertain contact. Relief replaced terror aboard *U202*'s dripping interior and the boat turned heel and crept away to safety.

On 1 March *U202* and four other U-boats were again refuelled, this time from tanker *U460*, before forming a new patrol line named *Tümmler*. As part of this group Poser participated in abortive attacks against the heavily

---

[73] *Ten Years and Twenty Days*, Karl Dönitz, p. 318.

defended American convoy UGS 6, claiming to have torpedoed two ships, although Allied records dispute this. Poser also reported after the assault that, as escort vessels had launched their own counter-attack, *U202* narrowly missed being rammed by fellow *Tümmler* boat *U569*. Following this disputed failure *U202* received fuel from aborting Type IX *U109* and proceeded home to Brest.

In the early morning approach to Brest's entrance channel Poser rendezvoused with his *Sperrbrecher* escort, following in the large ship's wake. As if in final reminder that the war was now being taken by the Allies into what were once considered safe harbours for U-boats, two mines exploded between *U202* and her *Sperrbrecher* escort. This time the lethal traps had been neutralized, but future Allied plans to choke the entrances to harbours with mines would plague all Kriegsmarine shipping for the remainder of the war.

U603 entered Brest U-boat bunker also at 1100hrs. Claiming one tanker of 6,000 BRT and a single steamer of 5,000 BRT from the massive battle against SC122 and HX229, Oblt.z.S. Bertelsmann had in fact sunk three Norwegian ships: tanker MV *Glittre* (already damaged by *U628*), 5,214-ton MV *Elin* and shared in sinking 5,964-ton MV *Stigstad*.

28 March: '*U116 Vermisst zwei Stern*' – the loss was confirmed due to the boat being long overdue. The following day Kptlt. Krech reported in person to Winter the claimed 9,000-ton ship sunk in the course of continuing operations against Gibraltar convoys. After two months and twenty days at sea the rusted U-boat returned to Brest, her wooden deck grating green with accumulated sea moss. While sailing for his designated patrol area, Krech had received orders to rendezvous with 2nd U-Flotilla's *U109* in order to transfer one of his Warrant Officers to assist the U-boat during its home voyage. Her commander, Knight's Cross bearer and 'Ace' Heinrich 'Ajax' Bleichrodt, had finally succumbed to nervous exhaustion and broken down during his boat's patrol. Despite orders from Dönitz to continue the voyage under command of the ship's First Officer, the U-boat was heading for Saint Nazaire, Krech's Warrant Officer was put aboard to assist in watch-keeping and administrative duties.

As part of the *Rochen* group *U558* had scoured the seas between southern Biscay and the Azores in search of American convoys to Gibraltar. On 23 February Krech scored his only victory. During the late evening he torpedoed and sank the straggling tanker SS *Empire Norsemen*. The 9,811-ton ship had been hit earlier that day by Poser's *U202*, while part of convoy UC1, and had fallen out of line to be left alone in hostile waters south of the Azores. Whatever their actual achievements had been thus far in the war, U-boats had a profound effect on the psyche of merchant mariners and straggling from a convoy came to be viewed as certain death. In this case the crew attempting frantically to repair damage to their struggling ship were correct.

The following month, while part of newly raised *Tümmler* group, Krech launched an attack against three destroyers escorts of convoy UGS 6 but missed with a full bow salvo of four torpedoes. The convoy was pursued for eight days but lost only four ships to U-boat attack.

1 April: *U653* lay in the cavernous U-boat bunker at La Pallice, having docked the previous evening. Kptlt. Feiler claimed three steamers sunk totalling 15,000 BRT during two months on patrol. In fact he had only sunk the American 7,176-ton SS *Thomas Hooker* after the crew had abandoned ship following severe storm damage in the central Atlantic as part of convoy ON169. His other recorded 'victories' were probably the damaging by torpedo of MV *Madoera* and near miss on SS *Delilan*, both ships from ON166.

During the voyage *U653*, a boat that had already experienced one man lost overboard during its career, suffered further tragedy at the hands of an inhospitable sea. Crewmember Heinz Theen remembers:

'The operational region was east of Newfoundland. On the fourth day we crossed Biscay without 'problems' or interference from the British, making a good fast passage.

I was with my Third Watch from 0400hrs to 0800hrs in increasingly heavy weather. The conning tower was often submerged, but the boat always climbed free. My watch and I had at first harnessed ourselves during the second hour as the swell strengthened. At the beginning of the watch – at 0400hrs – we stood completely dry on the bridge, no spray coming there. By the end of the watch, when the swell had grown to strength 6 to 7, and the Third Watch was totally drenched, we shouted down that the First Watch would get 'somewhat wet' during watch changeover. These times were 'shit weather.'

'The First Watch appeared dressed as 'seals' [slang for 'heavy rain gear'] at the changeover. I saw the new watch harnessed correctly with the *Karabinerhaker des Gurtes* connected to its mounting [within the bridge panelling]. Then I handed over the watch to IWO Oblt.z.S. Werner Laudon, after making sure that he too was harnessed. I wished the IWO a good watch, and he said to me '*Obersteurmann* (Navigator), I will try my best for four hours so that the IIWO has better weather when we change over. You weren't very successful during your watch! Enjoy yourself over breakfast where at least you can stay dry!' They were the last words that I exchanged with IWO Laudon. I still didn't know at the time that I would never see him or his watch again.

'On 13 February, at precisely 0800hrs over breakfast, I heard noise coming when water entered the control room from the bridge, before the bridge completely flooded. Noise from the bilge pump and both diesels (at 1200hrs we were supposed to patrol with only one diesel) could be heard. Suddenly, at 0810hrs, I heard no diesel noise at all. I went to the control room where I asked *Maatrose* Tragessor why the diesel wasn't working. Tragessor explained to me that the air intake for the diesel's air supply was saturated with water. Nearly a minute later the diesel sprang back to life.

'Jokingly I said 'The First Watch must think itself already ready for the changeover in three and three quarter hours. The cruise can not always be beautiful!'

'I had been in the control room for five minutes by then, until I noticed that the sound of water, distantly heard previously from above the control room, was now missing. The bridge hatch was closed. *Zentrale-Maat* and the helmsmen told me the First Watch had apparently closed the conning tower hatch about seven minutes ago. I climbed up to open the conning tower hatch and was startled to find nobody on the bridge; I could see no one from the First Watch. The bridge was empty! *U653* had spent seven minutes sailing blind. Despite well-fastened harnesses, four seamen had been snatched by the cruel sea in an instant to their death. By 1200hrs we had searched and found nothing.'

After communicating the disaster with BdU Feiler was informed that replacements could be transferred to *U653* for its entire missing watch party. Operations against the shipping traversing waters between the United Kingdom and America continued to be both hazardous and difficult due to that implacable enemy, nature. Rain, snow, gale-force winds and torturous seas conspired to make all sailors' lives miserable during the first months of 1943. On 9 March *Bootsmaat* Walter Mayer also paid the ultimate price and was lost overboard from the continuously pitching *U653*. Even sturdy Kriegsmarine safety harnesses were not infallible.

9.

THE FIGHT AGAINST ALLIED
AIR POWER

1 APRIL 1943 to 31 DECEMBER 1943

April 1943 found Dönitz in the unprecedented position of having eighty-seven attack boats available to be sent into the North Atlantic maelstrom. From Brest 1st U-Flotilla hurled *U203*, *U628*, *U732*, *U456*, *U566*, *U439*, *U418* and *U202* against a strengthening enemy as the Battle of the Atlantic reached its crescendo. Two of these boats were new to combat, *U732* and *U418* transferring from Danzig's 8th U-Flotilla, the latter sailing under command of the youngest skipper in Atlantic U-boats, 22-year-old Oblt.z.S. Gerhard Lange.

March's results from U-boat operations had provided much encouragement to Dönitz. The combination of well-handled *B-Dienst* intercepts on Allied shipping routes and the – unbeknown to the Germans – temporary loss of Enigma intelligence to Allied code breakers had helped to provide numerous sinkings for Atlantic U-boats. The 'Black Gap' was still available for exploitation by U-boats, although VLR B24 Liberators were beginning to appear and escort carriers had proved difficult to operate in foul Atlantic conditions. Conversely, communication and teamwork with KG40 *Kondors* had reached a new high, submarines finally benefiting from priceless aerial reconnaissance.

In effect, though, the majority of these conditions found during March were only temporary. The optimistic projections of BdU for a final decisive onslaught against the convoys and severing of Great Britain's supply route were not to bear fruit. In fact they were unlikely to even if events had continued along their previous course. Despite considerable pessimism in the British Admiralty, and thoughts of abandoning convoying completely as 'unworkable', author and ex-US Navy submarine skipper Clay Blair states an often ignored fact in his excellent book *Hitler's U-boat War – The Hunted*:

> 'Although obviously a terrible spike indeed, the U-boat successes on the North Atlantic run in March (1943) did not come close to cutting this vital lifeline to the British Isles. The sinking figures also bear repeating. Sixteen convoys composed of about nine hundred merchant ships, plus

escorts, sailed east and west over this route in March. The scores upon scores of U-boats were able to mount decisive attacks on only four of the eight eastbound convoys: Halifax 228 and 229, and Slow Convoys 121 and 122. These attacks resulted in the sinking of thirty-nine out of about 450 merchant ships in the eight eastbound convoys. The loss of 8.5 percent of all the laden merchant ships sailing east that month hardly constitutes a 'crisis of crises."

Germany's all-out April assault aimed at closing down both UK bound and North Africa bound convoys fizzled and died. On 6 April British Coastal Command opened its own offensive against the Biscay U-boats, code-named Enclose II, swiftly to be followed by other more powerful anti-U-boat operations. The spectre of Allied aircraft began to haunt U-boats day and night. Soon the Bay of Biscay would earn the grim nickname '*Tal des Todes*' (the Valley of Death).

12 April: New Flotilla boat *U305* docked in Brest at 1036hrs, two victory pennants representing hard-won sinkings in the North Atlantic. Kptlt. Rudolf Bahr had commissioned his U-boat on 17 September 1942 at Lübeck's Flenderwerft. Finally, on 27 February 1943 Bahr had slipped from Kiel for the boat's inaugural journey, transferring operational command from 8th to 1st U-Flotilla. *U305* sailed to join *Stürmer* group operating against eastbound convoy SC122 off Ireland's north-western quarter. The eighteen *Stürmer* boats made contact on the night of 16/17 March after a sighting by *U338* and the hunt began. Bahr launched his attack during the following evening, torpedoing and damaging the 8,789-ton SS *Port Auckland* and sinking the 4,256-ton SS *Zouave*. As the British steamer *Zouave* took its cargo of iron filings to the deep Bahr reloaded tubes and placed himself in a favourable position from which to deliver the coup-de-grace to his first victim, the damaged British refrigerator ship. A little after midnight SS *Port Auckland* suffered a second torpedo hit, buckled and sank. As the action developed into the sprawling battle between nearly forty U-boats and convoys SC122 and HX229 *U305* received the unwanted attention of angry escort ships, pummelled by savage depth-charging and forced to run silent and endure the fury from above.

Following the conclusion of the running fight, *U305* proceeded with other U-boats from the battle to bolster newly arriving U-boats in a fresh group named *Seewolf*. Combined with the *Seeteufel* pack, a massive patrol line was established in the hunt for eastbound SC123. On 27 March, in disgusting and difficult conditions, lookouts on *U305* sighted the convoy and Bahr ordered homing signals sent for the remaining pack boats. In all, twenty-two U-boats were ordered to close on Bahr's signals, four making contact with escort destroyers within a matter of hours. It was at the moment of engagement that nature unleashed the full fury of a bitter storm. Winds rose to hurricane force and U-boats were forced either to submerge or cling grimly to the wildly bucking surface and try to trail the sea-battered convoy. As the decision was being made aboard each U-boat whether to submerge and lose their elusive quarry, aircraft from Iceland arrived and decided the issue, driving the U-boats under.

Any attempts to attack the scattered convoy were futile. Surfaced U-boats were harried by aircraft and hammered by the sea. Tons of water shipped through conning tower hatches and more than once U-boats were completely submerged, bridge watches clinging desperately to the conning tower as they struggled to break surface and breathe again. Contact was lost on 30 March and never regained. In total one ship had been sunk. It was a bitter disappointment.

As Bahr entered Brest with his hard-won pennants fluttering, *U440* also returned from patrol to La Pallice. Winter's entry beside the U-boat's number was brief and concise: 'No Tonnage'. Similarly disappointing results were logged by *U564* on 15 April. The latter boat returned to La Pallice minus one crewman, Midshipman (*Fähnrich*) Heinrich Feuerhake lost overboard in heavy seas on 28 March.

16 April: Veteran U-boat *U86* docked in Brest at 1130hrs. Kptlt. Schug claimed two steamers for 13,000 BRT sunk during this, his boat's sixth patrol. He had actually, and probably unknowingly, drastically inflated his achievements. As part of the *Neuland* pack in action against HX228, Schug torpedoed and badly damaged with FAT torpedoes the 5,464-ton British steamer SS *Jamaica Producer* during the night of 10/11 March. The ship was later towed to harbour for repair.

Following an unsuccessful role in the huge SC122/HX229 battle, *U86* later was part of the doomed attempt at attacking convoy HX230 while with the *Seewolf* pack. Failure on both counts added nothing to the U-boat's spirits and dejectedly the boat returned to Brest, refuelling north of the Azores from *U463* while en route.

18 April: Kptlt. Götz von Hartmann ended his last cruise aboard *U563* at 1130hrs inside the safe concrete enclosure at Brest. The patrol claimed four steamers sunk for a total of 31,000 BRT. Von Hartmann had begun his tally after pursuing convoy HX231 southeast of Greenland. Operating as part of *Löwenherz* group, *U563* seriously damaged the American tanker MV *Sunoil*, already straggling due to engine trouble, on 5 April (the tanker was later sunk by three torpedoes from *U530*). The U-boats' operations were severely hampered not only by tenacious convoy escorts but also aircraft from Iceland and Northern Ireland, constantly attacking U-boats and driving them under where their effectiveness was virtually nil, lacking the necessary speed to manoeuvre to an attack position. Without the speed of diesels available to close a target, U-boats were powerless to press attacks while forced to dive away from the surface. On 7 April weary lookouts atop *U563*'s tower spotted an RAF 86 Squadron Liberator dropping from the skies on an attack path. Von Hartmann ordered an emergency crash dive to save his boat from depth charges he knew would follow. Unfortunately for two crewmen the dive had come too quickly; Petty Officer (*Oberbootsmaat*) Christian Wieland and Seaman Second Class (*Matrosengefreiter*) Rudolf Schädlich were both lost overboard, probably killed in the water by the ensuing blasts.

Despite this disaster, *U563* continued operating, forming part of new group *Lerche* south-east of Cape Farewell. The boat scored three more torpedo hits, this time against convoy HX232. In the early morning darkness von Hartmann sank the 7,117-ton British MV *Pacific Grove* and the Dutch 2,666-ton SS *Ulysses*. In the same attack he hit and damaged MV *Fresno City*, the British ship sunk by *U706* later that day. These were the last successes for *U563*, the worn and tatty U-boat proceeding home after taking on fuel from *U462* north of the Azores.

22 April: '*U632 Vermisst ein Stern.*'

> 'Boat left Brest on 15 March. Last reported 6 April, Grid reference AK38 after convoy.
>
> For relatives: Boat had success in the North Atlantic operating against convoys, and had sunk one destroyer.'

Flight Lieutenant C.W. Burcher's 86 Squadron Liberator killed Kptlt. Hans Karpf and his forty-seven man crew during an attempt to attack convoy HX231. Operating as part of the *Löwenherz* group, Karpf sank the 7,065-ton Dutch freighter SS *Blitar* during the early morning of 6 April. Later that same day Burcher sighted the surfaced U-boat 18 miles from the convoy's position. Approaching along the submarine's track, he dropped to 50 feet in order to release four depth charges above the boat. With mounting annoyance, the pilot registered that only one of his depth charges had released, falling wide of the target. While gunners peppered the U-boat with fire they saw men scrambling down inside the conning tower and the sleek grey hull began to submerge.

Flight Lieutenant Burcher roared around for a second attack, this time achieving a perfect four-depth-charge 'straddle' across the U-boat's still visible stern. There was no doubt about the result of their attack. In massive geysers of dirty water the U-boat was destroyed, depth charges splintering the hull and sending the entire crew to their deaths. Gunners reported sighting 'oil and a black object', believed to be a body, floating in the area of detonation.

28 April: After leaving Brest on 24 April at 1800hrs *U566* was back in the concrete shelter following damage inflicted by enemy aircraft, the second time that this U-boat had returned to Brest with serious battle damage. On the night of 26 April, while proceeding surfaced through Biscay, the Leigh Light

of a 172 Squadron Wellington bomber had surprised *U566*. Pilot Sergeant A. Coumbis, from Rhodesia, framed the boat with his blinding searchlight and managed to inflict serious damage with six depth charges. Kptlt. Hornkohl's U-boat returned fire at the attacker and miraculously succeeded in driving the Wellington away. The problems aboard *U566* were critical, however, and she was unable to dive. Water threatened to swamp the vessel while surfaced, any increase in external pressure would be undoubtedly fatal. Making the perilous return journey, vulnerably surfaced *U566* received cover from both Junkers 88 aircraft and *Vorpostenboote* from Brest's *7. Vorpostenflottille* as she neared the Brittany coast.

Staggering into harbour at 0930hrs, *U566* was examined by flotilla engineers and then consigned to the yards for serious rebuilding that would take the better part of two and a half months. Her crew disembarked and celebrated survival against the heavy odds stacked against them.

Dönitz was aghast at the huge increase in casualties caused by enemy aircraft. Accordingly, on 1 May BdU issued an order that would have disastrous consequences for many U-boats. All U-boats traversing the Bay of Biscay were now ordered to travel submerged at night and surfaced during the day in groups of three or more. The night now afforded no shelter from air attack; at least by day the impending threat could be visually detected. As part of standing order (*Ständiger Kriegsbefehl*) 483, once under aircraft attack the boats were to remain surfaced and 'shoot it out' with the aircraft. Additional flak weapons were added to crowded conning towers and the U-boats began to implement this new policy. U-boat deck guns, all but useless by this stage, had been ordered removed to compensate for the steady increase in weight brought about by additional anti-aircraft weapons. Coincidentally, the 131-aircraft British Biscay anti-submarine air offensive 'Operation Derange' hit its stride at the beginning of June. Losses among the U-boats were casting a pall of depression over men of the 1st and other Flotillas. Germany's glory days for submariners appeared to be not much more than a distant memory.

5 May: *U415* arrived at 2130hrs in Brest after her first operational patrol from Bergen. The U-boat had logged sinking two steamers for 15,000 BRT, but like so many others suffered severe damage from air attack during the return transit across Biscay. Kptlt. Kurt Neide had joined the *Seeteufel* group to attack a feeder convoy from Iceland that was attempting to join ONS1. All attempts at interception were thwarted by strong air and surface escorts and eventually the attack called off. Similarly the next interception planned against HX230 was foiled by both atrocious weather and the ferocity of air cover provided by long-range bombers. Tempers were high and spirits low aboard *U415*.

Neide next took his boat to the west and joined *Meise* 'Wolf Pack' northeast of Newfoundland. The group was lying in wait for convoy HX234, sighted finally on 21 April. As *U415* thundered into action a second convoy was discovered, ONS 3 westbound for the United States and well placed for interception. Five boats split from the main pack to deal with this development, *U415* included. In the early morning of 21 April Neide attacked and sank two British steamers, the 4,917-ton SS *Ashantian* and 5,486-ton SS *Wanstead*. These were two of only three ships sunk, as contact was lost in blinding fog and impenetrable snowstorms. Ironically, it was only the dire weather that provided the Germans with cover from aircraft.

After *U415* began the slog to Brest on 25 April she refuelled from *U487* before heading south-east. While the U-boat proceeded surfaced a little after midnight on 1 May she was located and attacked by Flight Sergeant P.W. Phillips' 172 Squadron Wellington. The Leigh Light slung below the British bomber framed *U415* as she gamely returned fire with all flak weapons. Six depth charges damaged the boat, which in turn hit and damaged Phillips' aircraft. Neither side were incapacitated and the skirmish ended as rapidly as it had begun.

During the morning of 2 May *U415* was attacked again, this time by a 461 Squadron Sunderland, but to little effect. That afternoon Neide's frustration boiled over as his boat was the object of a third attack. Flight Sergeant N. Earnshaw brought his 612 Squadron Whitley straight at the damaged boat, firing machine guns and dropping depth charges. After returning fire, Neide, contrary to Dönitz's instructions, ordered the boat submerged. Two depth charges rocked *U415* as a parting gesture and more damage was inflicted. It was a painfully weary crew who stepped ashore at Brest three days later.

9 May: Another new arrival, *U306*, docked in Brest that evening at 2000hrs. Her commander also claimed two steamers sunk, for an estimated 20,000 BRT. Skipper Kptlt. Claus von Trotha had undertaken a virtually identical patrol to *U415*, the U-boat's two victories coming from an attack on HX234 while part of the *Meise* group. During 22 April *U306* sank the British 10,218-ton MV *Amerika* and the 7,176-ton American Liberty ship SS *Robert Gray*. Unlike *U415*, however, von Trotha's boat escaped the attention of the RAF during its return to base.

14 May: *U732* completed its first Atlantic patrol, tying up in harbour with two victory pennants showing 13,000 BRT strung from her periscope. Oblt.z.S. Claus-Peter Carlsen was mistaken, however. His new boat had sunk nothing during its five-week patrol, unconfirmed – and probably premature – detonations heard underwater aboard the escaping U-boat hastily taken as proof positive of a merchantman kill.

15 May: '*U203 Vermisst ein Stern.*'

The last of 1st U-Flotilla's 'Ace' U-boats was finally reported missing. Her ultimate communication with BdU had been a weather report on 25 April. Kptlt. Hermann Kottmann had left port on 3 April to join the *Lerche* group south of Iceland, the U-boat sailing from Brest with the customary commissioning pennant flowing from the commander's flagstaff. After no success in action, *U203* formed part of *Meise* group and, like *U415*, split from the main pack to attack convoy ONS 3 on 21 April. Kottmann again achieved no triumph and after the operation was called off due to inclement weather *U203* began the return march to Brest empty-handed.

Six hundred miles south of Cape Farewell on 25 April, Easter Sunday, Kottmann sighted the escort carrier HMS *Biter* of Escort Group 5, providing cover for convoy ON54. No doubt anxious to sink such a significant ship, particularly after dreary disappointment elsewhere, the U-boat was ordered to battle stations and prepared to attack. Beginning his approach at high surface speed, Kottmann was 'Dfed' by destroyer HMS *Hesperus*. The latter immediately communicating the impending threat to HMS *Biter* a Swordfish biplane of the carrier's 811 Naval Air Squadron which was already aloft was directed to the contact, surprising the U-boat and managing to drop two shallow-set depth charges on the crash-diving *U203* at approximately 1830hrs. Fortunately for the U-boat crew this aircraft had only been able to carry the two depth charges during its take-off, lack of wind preventing any extra weight aboard. While Kottmann submerged, the Fleet Air Arm pilot called for assistance from another escort destroyer, HMS *Pathfinder*, and marked the area of submergence with flares.

Swiftly obtaining good ASDIC results, Commander E.A. Gibbs launched five depth-charge attacks from *Pathfinder*, dropping nearly forty separate charges, while HMS *Biter* flew a second of its nine Swordfish to join the hunt. The escort carrier itself then closed on *U203*, dropping two depth charges, one of which failed to detonate. Beneath *Pathfinder*'s accurate hammering the U-boat reeled in agony. At some stage during the rapid dive a diesel exhaust valve had not seated properly and water had begun to enter the pressure hull. Under the accurate depth-charging this trickle became a flood and Kottmann had no choice but to surface before his boat became unstable with tons of water sloshing throughout her bilges.

When *U203* dramatically broke surface near *Pathfinder* the German crew came under concentrated and accurate fire while they tumbled from the conning tower. Eleven men were lost with the slowly sinking U-boat, including the ship's Chief Engineer, Oblt (Ing) Friedrich Albatant, who had remained below inside the hull to ensure that the boat sank (he received a posthumous Iron Cross First Class for this act of heroism). Kottmann and thirty-seven shivering men were rescued, and the 1st U-Flotilla's last 'Ace' U-boat, responsible for sinking 96,724 tons of enemy shipping during its brief career, was gone.

19 May: *U628* returned from its third patrol claiming four steamers sunk for 22,000 BRT and a '*Korvette*'. Kptlt. Hasenschar had in actuality sent a confirmed single 5,212-ton ship to the bottom. The U-boat shared the credit for another of 7,134 tons and had damaged yet another for 5,081 tons. The corvette escort from convoy ONS 5 claimed as sunk was logged by

Hasenschar as being hit and destroyed during the morning of 5 May, but has never been confirmed by Allied records.

While Hasenschar brought his boat back from the Atlantic battleground he sighted convoy HX237 and, realizing the opportunity before him, proceeded to shadow. The convoy was already under attack by the *Drossel* pack but as Hasenschar debated joining the battle the U-boats' operation was abandoned in the face of saturating air and surface escorts.

During the whole of May eight 1st U-Flotilla U-boats put to sea for Atlantic patrols: 5 May, *U603*, 8 May, *U558* and *U336*, 12 May, *U305*, 20 May, *U435*, 26 May, *U440*, 27 May, *U669* and 29 May *U563*. Two of them were sunk within five days of leaving harbour.

On 31 May *U563*, commanded by her new skipper Oblt.z.S. Gustav Borchardt, was surprised by Wing Commander W.E. Oulten's Halifax bomber while surfaced. The 58 Squadron bomber attacked with machine guns and nine depth charges, causing severe damage to the U-boat. Borchardt refused to give in, however, and, remaining true to his orders, returned fire while radioing distress calls. A second 58 Squadron Halifax arrived and proceeded to attack with nine depth charges. This time the aim was bad and all nine explosives fell wide of their target.

While the two bombers circled, yet more Allied aircraft arrived. Flight Lieutenant M.S. Mainprize and Flying Officer W.M. French both brought their Sunderland flying boats into the fray. Mainprize of 10 RAAF Squadron bracketed the U-boat with depth charges, followed by French's 228 RAF Squadron aircraft. This time *U563* was doomed and circling Allied airmen could clearly see '30 or 40 Germans' in the water. The rear gunner of Oulton's bomber later said:

> 'The U-boat was obliterated in the plumes of the explosion. As the plumes died away I saw the bow and stern again, then the remainder of the U-boat, wallowing in the depth-charge pool.'

Despite a search by Junkers 88 aircraft the following day no survivors from the fifty-three-man crew were found.

The same day that *U563* met her end *U440*, commanded by new captain Oblt.z.S. Werner Schwaff, was also attacked on the surface by an Allied aircraft taking part in the 'Derange' Biscay offensive. Initially Flight Lieutenant D.M.Gall, flying Sunderland 'R' of 201 Squadron, was unsure as to the identity of the submarine:

> 'We all expected him to dive and when he did not I asked my navigator to check whether we were near one of the "free lanes" for our own submarines.'

It then appeared to Gall that the submarine began to flash a message to his flying boat, and he again queried his navigator to verify the rather bizarre code sequence that was evidently being signalled. At that moment:

'It was my Scottish rear gunner who eventually put my mind to rest by calling on the intercom, "He's no' flashin' Skipper, he's firin"'!'

With Pilot Officer Martin, a passenger aboard, manning the Sunderland's forward turret Gall began his attack. The conning tower started to take hits from the heavy machine guns and bodies could be seen dropping from the *Wintergarten* (the lower *Flakvierlinge*-equipped extension aft of the conning tower's existing *Turm 0* flak platform) from which German flak still roared.

Despite heavy return fire Flight Lieutenant Gall straddled the racing boat with depth charges, initially dropped wide but striking a bull's eye as the U-boat, altering course to evade, turned into them, and, her bows rising vertically in agony, she sank stern first. There were no survivors, 1st U-Flotilla had lost another forty-six men. During five operational patrols the U-boat had sunk nothing.

U-boat Command had already taken what they considered the next step in their fight against aircraft. However, their experiments at converting seven U-boats into flak boats, designed to lure enemy aircraft into battle so as to destroy them, ultimately failed. Dönitz and his staff still hadn't realized that although Metox was proved to be all but useless at that point, it was not the reason that enemy aircraft could so efficiently locate U-boats. Clutching at the straws of improved radar detection equipment, Dönitz based the idea of the so-called '*Unterseebootflugzeugfalle*' (submarine aircraft-trap) on the crew's ability to 'see' the enemy approach. *U441* of Brest's 1st U-Flotilla was the first such flak boat, designated 'U-Flak 1'. A Type VIIC boat, as well as the usual anti-aircraft stations of the rear kiosk and '*Wintergarten*' she had her conning tower extended forward, providing a third weapon position. In the stern-facing *Wintergarten* was a single-barrelled 3.7cm weapon, itself positioned beneath the four barrels of a shielded 2cm quad *Flakvierling*. The forward extension carried another fearsome *Vierling*, rounding out the lethal increase in firepower. The heavily armed U-boat, sacrificing some fuel storage capacity for the increased weaponry, was intended to either sail independently as a 'trap' or to escort other U-boats heading for the Atlantic.

Feelings among her crew about their new role were a mixture of trepidation and resignation. Within earshot of the men destined to attempt the first '*Flakfalle*' operation other U-boat crews had named them the '*Himmelfahrt kommando*' – suicide squad. Spirits sagged accordingly.

Her initial anti-aircraft sortie from Brest began at 1000hrs on 22 May 1943, under command of new captain Kptlt. Götz von Hartmann, late of *U563*, the previous commander, Klaus Hartmann, incapacitated in hospital wrestling with a severe case of pneumonia. With sixty-seven men aboard, including a doctor, two engineers to test newly installed radar detection equipment, and an additional team of specialist gunners, the U-boat's four days at sea resulted in the shooting down of Flying Officer H.J. Debden's Sunderland 'L' from RAF 228 Squadron two days later. While cruising surfaced in map grid reference BF4948 *U441* finally attracted the attention of the British aircraft, which immediately began an attack run with depth charges. Despite one of the U-boat's *Vierling* weapons not being fired (poor welding at the weapon's base had weakened under exposure to sea water, making the weapon unstable and therefore preventing its firing) the sudden flak barrage evidently surprised the British attackers and the huge flying boat received fatal cannon hits. All crewmen aboard the Sunderland were killed as it slammed into the sea only 300 yards from *U441* at 2050hrs. Although successful at destroying the British attacker, there were injured among the U-boat crew and their ship received moderate damage to her bow from the British depth charges released immediately before the Sunderland crashed. The fact that the U-boat itself did not emerge unscathed from the skirmish appears to have escaped the notice of Dönitz and other members of BdU Staff. They were delighted with the 'potential' of the aircraft trap and ordered work to be hurried up on the remaining seven U-boats designated for conversion. In the meantime the Atlantic war had come to a head.

24 May: As *U584* tied up in Brest at 2200hrs claiming two steamers sunk for 12000 BRT (in fact a single American ship SS *West Madaket* for 5,565 tons) the Battle of the Atlantic reached its inevitable conclusion. Orders issued from BdU directed all remaining boats still at sea to proceed to the waters west of the Azores, well clear of the North Atlantic killing ground. The previous day Dönitz and his staff had estimated that so far in May thirty-one U-boats had been lost; in fact the total was even worse, standing at thirty-three. This tremendous rate could not be maintained and Dönitz withdrew from the battle. He stressed to his commanders that the decision to withdraw was a 'temporary measure' and that they must do their utmost to maintain morale among their men.

To disguise the withdrawal, Dönitz assigned thirteen Type VII U-boats, including 1st U-Flotilla's *U202*, to broadcast fake radio messages from the North Atlantic in order to maintain the illusion of strength in the area. British Enigma intercepts alerted the Admiralty who promptly sank three of them.

On 24 May Dönitz recorded the following words in his diary:

> 'Wolf Pack operations against convoys in the North Atlantic, the main theatre of operations and at the same time the theatre in which air cover was strongest, were no longer possible. They could only be resumed if we succeeded in radically increasing the fighting power of the U-boats. That was the logical conclusion to which I came and I accordingly withdrew the boats from the North Atlantic.We had lost the Battle of the Atlantic.'

29 May: In Brest the sombre mood of defeat hung in the air. Winter made little note of BdU's decision – indeed only hindsight marks it as the true moment of irrecoverable collapse – continuing to relate the day-to-day routines of Flotilla procedure. Unfortunately they were often bleak entries to be included.

> 'U456 Vermisst ein Stern.'
> 'Last reported 12 May from (Grid Reference) Bruno Dora 6569, asking for help from U89.'

On 12 May veteran of arctic operations Kptlt. Max-Martin Teichert was operating as part of the *Drossel* group during his second patrol from Brest. Intercepting convoy HX237 on 11 May Teichert torpedoed and sank the 7,138-ton British freighter SS *Fort Concord*. This was to be the end of U456's brief winning streak. The following day, as Teichert pounded through the sea surfaced, his boat was surprised and attacked by Flight Lieutenant J. Wright's Liberator bomber. The 86 Squadron aircraft immediately dropped a *Fido* homing torpedo, which sought its target and exploded against the U-boat's hull. Damaged but not sunk, U456 radioed nearby U89 for assistance, the last message received from the struggling boat. Keeping the circling aircraft at bay by using all available flak weapons, Teichert managed to survive until nightfall and attempted to run home. Fate, however, was not going to let him go that easily.

Early the following day Sunderland 'G' of 423 RCAF Squadron located the limping boat and began to attack her. Two depth charges were dropped from 50 feet, rocking the boat with their explosions, but not finishing the German's miseries. Gunfire flew between the U-boat and flying boat and soon Teichert had reports from lookouts of approaching destroyers. HMS *Opportune* was rapidly nearing the crippled boat. Further chaos was added by the arrival of Swordfish aircraft that dropped smoke float markers beside the hunted boat. In a desperate effort to evade, U456 submerged and was never seen again. It is believed that previous damage from the homing torpedo had caused structural weakness which resulted in a catastrophic hull failure as Teichert attempted to escape by going deep. If there was any hope for the doomed Germans it was taken away by a short sharp depth-charge barrage launched from *Opportune*.

Later U448 chanced upon the bodies of two of Teichert's crew, recovering them and giving the dead men a proper military burial at sea. Max-Martin Teichert's final epitaph was the awarding of a posthumous Knight's Cross on 19 December 1943.

'U209 Vermisst ein Stern.' Last contact with Kptlt. Heinrich Brodda had been made on 6 May by U954, another of the *Star* group to which U209 belonged. In thick fog patches the U-boat group attempted to close on convoy ONS 5. On 7 May Squadron Leader B.H. Moffitt sighted the U-boat and dived his Catalina to wave-top level to attack with machine guns and depth charges. The RCAF aircraft released four shallow-set depth charges, which appeared to straddle the target, obliterating any sight of the crash-diving

U-boat. There was no more contact with *U209*, Brodda and his forty-five-man crew presumed sunk by the Catalina attack.

1 June: The days of gloom received some relief on this day as Werner Winter celebrated his promotion to Korvettenkapitän. However, the respite was short lived. The following day the 1st U-Flotilla War Diary received new BdU loss notification: '*U439 Vermisst ein Stern.*' Oblt.z.S. Helmut von Tippelskirch was mere hours out from Brest on 27 April when he received orders to join *Drossel* group north-west of Cape Finisterre. During 3 May two convoys were reported bound from the British Isles to Gibraltar, 275 miles due east. The first convoy consisted of fifteen coastal craft (MGBs, MTBs) escorted by auxiliary trawlers HMS *Bream* and HMS *Coverley*, the second composed of twenty-eight LCTs accompanied by trawlers HMS *Huddersfield Town* and Norwegian *Molde*. Both convoys were on similar courses but separated by approximately ten miles.

Aboard *U439* the decision was taken by her skipper to intercept the first convoy of coasters and the boat leapt forward with engine throttles wide open. At approximately 2300hrs on 3 May *U439* had located his target convoy and begun to shadow. Fellow *Drossel* boat *U659* of Brest's 9th U-Flotilla was also approaching the convoy after failing to locate the second of the two British convoys. Sea conditions were difficult and neither boat was aware of the other's presence.

Aboard *U439* preparations were being made for a surface attack when the horizon lit up following a third unknown U-boat's successful torpedoing of British MGB *657*, which exploded into angry flames. Von Tippelskirch's Watch Officer, described by crewmen as being 'by nature lazy and easygoing', was preparing for the attack, torpedo-firing being his responsibility while surfaced. Apparently the flames and subsequent British star shells distracted him and he paused to gaze at the blazing spectacle, as did the crewman assigned the port sector of the bridge watch. At that moment von Tippelskirch ordered a slight alteration of course to port, his boat making nearly full speed in its attack run. With a grinding crash *U439* lurched viciously as she collided with *U659*, also launching an attack and also distracted by far off fireworks.

Kptlt. Hans Stock had no time to order his crew to evacuate *U659*. While he had apparently survived the impact atop the boat's conning tower, below him the entire control room was crushed, a massive hole in the hull allowing tons of water to swamp the boat's mangled interior. Water and oil poured inside flooding her quickly. In the words of a survivor from *U439*:

> 'A few minutes later a big wave swallowed her and sent her to the bottom.'

As soon as the impact had occurred von Tippelskirch ordered *U439* thrown into full astern. While the U-boat struggled backwards, both diesel exhausts became blocked and the pressure hull filled with choking blinding fumes.

Water flooded into the bow torpedo room and the watertight hatch closed. However, the boat's Chief Engineer, Kaptlt. (Ing) Adolf Rau, was unable to re-establish trim in the bow-down submarine, her forward tanks ruptured and unable to blow. Ordering aft tanks flooded, some balance was restored, but the U-boat was left so low in the water that there was no choice but to abandon ship before she was swamped.

Atop *U439*'s conning tower von Tippelskirch signalled the floundering *U659* to pick up his crew, not realizing that his opposite number was sinking as well, and more rapidly. Initially a reply was received, believed to be saying that the 9th U-Flotilla boat would gladly pick up survivors. A rapid second response flashed that they too were sinking, immediately after which the U-boat disappeared. Hans Stock and his First Lieutenant had descended into the interior of *U659* to speed up their boat's evacuation, and were trapped and drowned in the deluge.

U439 was also rapidly going down. As the conning tower sank lower into the sea a wave rode over the hull from astern and the U-boat submerged for the final time. Her First Lieutenant, perhaps realizing that his tragic lapse of concentration had been the main cause of this disaster, refused a life belt and was last seen clutching the conning tower as it went beneath the surface.

At 0300hrs British MTB *670* of the coastal convoy's starboard column slowed to investigate oil patches found floating in the convoy's path. The small British craft subsequently rescued nine men from *U439* and three from *U659*. Von Tippelskirch was not among the survivors. Two hours after the sinking, HMS *Coverley* struck 'a submerged object' in the vicinity, perhaps the remains of *U439*, which was believed to have been suspended in mid-water due to air trapped behind hatches sealed during evacuation. If so, this final impact probably sent the wreck to the depths.

10 June: *U84*, *U306* and *U732* all left from Brest bound for operations in the Central Atlantic region, west of the Azores. Two days later a fourth Flotilla boat sailed for the same destination, *U415* putting to sea at 0700hrs. Later that evening a new U-boat arrived in Brest after weeks of patrol. At 2030hrs on 12 June Oblt.z.S. Werner Techand brought *U731* into its new base, after departing from Kiel on 29 April. The boat had achieved no result for its patrol, and had been used since the withdrawal order of 24 May to broadcast dummy radio signals from the North Atlantic area. The same day that *U731* arrived, Winter recorded further dismal fortunes for 1st U-Flotilla: '*U418 Vermisst ein Stern.*'

Oblt.z.S. Gerhard Lange had taken his new command, *U418*, from Kiel on 24 April to join the raging battle in the North Atlantic. After thirty-nine days at sea the newly operational U-boat had nothing to show for its patrol except frayed nerves, rubbed raw by the constant attentions of enemy aircraft. Time and again this U-boat and others of the *Donau* groups had been hampered and harassed by incessant and strong aircraft cover for Allied convoys. Finally, low on fuel and after spending time as one of Dönitz's radio decoys, Lange ordered course set for Brest. At 1100hrs *U418* was approaching the final leg of its home journey when lookouts spotted the small speck of an approaching British Beaufighter.

Aboard the British fighter-bomber Flying Officer Bateman and his navigator Flight Sergeant C.W.G. Easterbrook had not actually seen the surfaced U-boat. Inside the cramped aircraft was a third man – passenger, observer and Royal Navy specialist in U-boat warfare, Lieutenant Commander F.J. Brookes. Brookes saw *U418* some ten miles distant after scrutinizing the grey Biscay expanse through binoculars. Bateman immediately began an attack run.

Aboard the 236 Squadron aircraft was a new weapon in the anti-submarine arsenal. Solid-head 25lb rockets fitted on under-wing rails had just been introduced to the RAF anti-submarine squadrons and Bateman was fresh from three days of training with them. As the Beaufighter streaked toward *U418* lookouts raised the alarm and Oblt.z.S. Lange began a crash dive. Approximately 800 yards from the U-boat, when the conning tower and stern were still above water level, Bateman fired his first two rockets, followed seconds later by two more. Streaking away from the aircraft, trailing bluish smoke behind them, the four rockets smashed into the hull waterline, ripping enormous holes in the submarine and passing through the other side.

There was no chance for Lange and his men. Whoever survived the scything projectiles was dragged 200 metres to the seabed as *U418* catastrophically flooded in seconds. A green patch of disturbed water was all that marked the grave of forty-eight Kriegsmarine submariners.

13 June: *U413* returned to Brest. Her skipper, Kptlt. Gustav Poel, claimed two ships sunk, totalling 10,000 tons. However, after taking part in four group operations – *Meise, Star, Fink* and *Donau 2* – Poel had in fact sunk nothing. Two unexplained detonations following an attack at 1420hrs on 25 April were what Poel assumed were sinkings. The U-boat, like so many sister-ships, had been frustrated by intense surface and air escort activity and fog during several attempted assaults against North Atlantic shipping. Also like other boats, following BdU's order to withdraw, *U415* spent considerable time roving the North Atlantic as part of the futile radio deception plan.

14 June: '*U564 Vermisst zwei Stern*'.

> 'The boat departed Bordeaux 9 June. During 14 June it was attacked and sunk by enemy aircraft in (Grid Reference) Bruno Fritz 7549.
> Twenty-eight soldiers dead. Eighteen, plus the commander, rescued.'

Kptlt. Feiler's veteran *U564* was one of five U-boats conforming to the new BdU directive and proceeding in company across Biscay. The surfaced boats were under orders to stand and fight if attacked by aircraft, their most likely antagonist. Streaming in line astern Feiler's boat was accompanied by large Type IXs *U159*, *U185* and two Type VIICs *U415* and *U634*.

During late afternoon on 13 June a pair of Sunderlands belonging to 228 RAF Squadron were patrolling separately the southern expanses of Biscay. At 2000hrs Flying Officer L.B. Lee, pilot of Sunderland 'U' DV967, sighted the remarkable train of German submarines and without hesitation dived to attack the procession. Spotted by alert bridge lookouts, flak beginning to hurl towards the onrushing aircraft when it was at a distance of 600 metres. Singling out *U564*, that was slightly separated from the rest, Lee was able to straddle the U-boat with depth charges before the intense anti-aircraft fire ripped his aircraft to shreds and it crashed headlong into the waves. There were no survivors from the Sunderland's eleven-man crew.

Unfortunately for Feiler though, Lee's attack had borne fruit. The U-boat was heavily damaged by the close depth-charge attack. Among the on-board problems was one that ruled out continuing the war patrol – *U564* was unable to dive. After being appraised of the situation, BdU ordered Kptlt. August Maus, captain on Type IXC-40 *U185* from Lorient's 10th U-Flotilla, to escort *U564* south to the Spanish coast where Feiler could attempt repairs. The commander of Bordeaux's 8th Destroyer Flotilla prepared to send *Z24* and *Z32* out from Le Verdon to rendezvous with the two U-boats and relieve Maus of escort duties, while KG 40 for their part were also assembling Junkers 88 air cover for the crippled U-boat. The three remaining German submarines continued toward the open Atlantic, while *U185* and *U564* headed south into the night.

By unhappy coincidence the next day marked the opening of a new RAF anti-submarine air campaign centring on an area of the Bay of Biscay not far from Spain's north-west coast. Code-named 'Musketry' this new Allied offensive utilized all Coastal Command's 15 and 19 Groups' fighting strength, withdrawing their potent anti-submarine aircraft from convoy escort duties. A second sector further west, code-named 'Seaslug', was to remain the domain of 15 Group VLR Liberators and other long-range aircraft. Ten squadrons of B24 Liberator bombers (five British and five American) formed a heavy backbone to this second onslaught. Air Marshal Sir John Slessor, AOC-in-C of Coastal Command, was determined to capitalize on the new German policy of remaining surfaced and firing back at aircraft, using Dönitz's misguided strategy against his own boats.

Slessor's orders were that the Musketry area was to be constantly 'swept' by seven aircraft at a time, flying parallel tracks three times a day. Aircraft encountering U-boats were instructed to radio a three-digit code number signifying a confirmed sighting. Once contact had been made, the decision as to whether to attack or wait for support was left in the pilot's hands. Leigh Light aircraft would continue to patrol the area at night, but by now it was well known that Dönitz had ordered his U-boats to submerge during darkness and surface by day when they had some chance of detecting an approaching threat. Although the likelihood of U-boat interception appeared slim Leigh Light aircraft could at least provide nuisance value and keep U-boats pinned underwater where their batteries would be slowly drained.

At first light on 14 June the two slow-moving U-boats were approaching neutral Spain. They spotted a distant Allied flying boat, but remained unseen themselves. Aboard both U-boats maximum attention was given to the sky with all flak weapons armed and ready for action. By 0940hrs the first anti-aircraft rounds were fired, unfortunately successfully aimed at two Focke Wulf FW200 *Kondors* that had belatedly arrived as part of their air escort. The angry crews of both graceful aircraft communicated their feelings to the U-boats and sheered off.

Later that afternoon the two U-boats, still constrained to a maximum 10 knots by Feiler's damage, were finally detected by their enemies. Australian Sergeant A.J. Benson, pilot of Whitley 'C', 10th Operational Training Unit, sighted them 90 miles north-west of Ferrol at 1439hrs. The large bomber began circling as both *U564* and *U185* opened fire whenever Benson drifted into range. The coded sighting report was transmitted and two hours later Squadron Leader J.G. Stronach's unwieldy Hampden of 415 Squadron also arrived and began to circle. Benson then opened his attack.

While his gunners sprayed both U-boats Benson roared toward *U564*, straddling her with six depth charges, enveloping Feiler's boat in a spume of detonation. It was the end for *U564*, her hull fatally ruptured by powerful Torpex, the boat's spine crumpled by the blast beneath her keel. Feiler's crew frantically tried to halt the rapidly flooding tide within their pressure hull, but to no avail. Their British attacker had not escaped retribution, however. Accurate flak, particularly from *U185*, wrecked the aircraft's hydraulics and starboard engine. Limping away, Benson was forced to put down into the sea 80 miles south-west of the Scillies.[74]

Maus, aboard *U185*, briefly and unsuccessfully attempted to attach a towline to the ailing *U564*, but the latter gradually swamped and went to the bottom. Only Feiler and seventeen men were rescued, the remainder either killed in the initial blasts or trapped inside vainly battling to save their ship as *U564* made her final dive.

Stronach's still shadowing Hampden was preparing its own attack when KG40's Ju88 escort arrived on the scene, pouncing on the obsolete British bomber and shooting it down for the loss of her entire crew. Feiler and his surviving men were later transferred aboard newly arrived *Z24* (*Z32* having turned back with turbine problems) during the evening for return to Bordeaux.

---

[74] After three days and nights in a rubber dinghy French fishing trawler *Jazz Band* rescued Benson and his four crew. They were subsequently landed at Morgat on the Crozon Peninsular and handed over to the German troops stationed there. The five men became POWs in two separate Stalag Luft camps.

23 June: '*U202 Vermisst ein Stern*' – presumed lost.

'Last report on 1 June from (grid reference) Anton Jot 6335, giving weather conditions.'

Kptlt. Günther Poser had left Brest at 1745hr on 29 April, bound for the climactic battles in the North Atlantic. *U202* joined the small *Lech* group (completed by *U91* and *U664*) positioned south of Greenland. On 15 May the three U-boats were combined with four other wolf packs – *Iller, Inn, Isar* and *Nahe* – in order to form the ultimately unsuccessful *Donau* 1 and 2 groups. During 18 May the mass of U-boats was directed south-east to intercept Allied convoy SC130. That same day Poser encountered *U91* in mid-ocean and her skipper, Oblt.z.S. Heinz Hungerhausen, exchanged megaphone greetings with Poser. Apparently, as the two U-boats proceeded towards their mutual target, Poser had an interesting and opportunistic idea. *U91* was equipped with GEMA radar and Poser desired to test the capabilities of his onboard Metox radar detector. Hungerhausen agreed to activate the equipment so that Poser could determine the efficiency of his Metox set. What he neglected to do, however, was to notify his Metox operator below of the impending test. While both U-boats ploughed through the sea Hungerhausen switched on his radar, causing a shriek of alarm from *U202*'s Metox operator that they were being detected by 'enemy radar force 6!' As ratings raced for the bow compartment *U202* crash-dived to evade their 'enemy', leaving a bewildered *U91* behind them.

Poser was described later by a crewmember as either incredibly cool under pressure or rather indolent. In a later British appraisal of prisoner interrogation from *U202* it was recorded that Poser:

'Hardly ever rose from his bunk where he spent a good deal of his time – he was either imperturbable or lazy, it is not quite clear which.'

If indeed Poser was cool under fire then even his calm was to be tested severely during the coming battle – the *Donau* operation was a disaster, no ships sunk for the loss of three U-boats. After Dönitz's order to withdraw, *U202* spent days as a radio decoy before heading for Brest on 27 May. The stop in Brest was planned to be brief, *U202* needed to take on fuel and then proceed to Kiel where the tired boat was due for a complete refit. Four days into the return voyage, a little before 1000hrs, lookouts sighted distant ships, and, after a careful approach, Poser determined that they were warships of the Royal Navy Support Group 2, not the hoped-for congregation of merchantmen. Poser then made a fatal mistake – he dived.

Aboard the lead sloop HMS *Starling* Group Senior Officer, Captain F.J. Walker, received reports of a firm ASDIC contact. Previously the Royal Navy Group had homed on HF/DF direction finding from a long signal sent by *U202* to base, bemoaning his lack of fuel. The five strong group – Royal Navy sloops HMS *Starling, Wild Goose, Cygnet, Woodpecker* and *Kite* – was en route to participate in the Musketry anti-submarine drive, Support Group 2 originally having been earmarked for convoy escort between Gibraltar and Great Britain, but assigned to the operation by C-in-C Western Approaches after suggestions from Air Marshal Slessor. As Slessor had put it to his naval counterpart, now would be a 'good moment to employ a surface hunting group' in co-operation with Coastal Command. After sailing from Liverpool on 16 June, the sloops were approaching their Musketry station at 45° 30'N by 12° 00'W. Conditions were good; a force two north-easterly wind brushed an otherwise calm sea. Visibility stretched as far as eight miles. It was perfect for an anti-submarine mission. Altering course, *Starling* approached the U-boat contact and prepared to depth charge.

During the 30 minutes that ensued HMS *Starling* made five depth-charge attacks, three individually and two as a barrage with HMS *Wild Goose* and *Kite*. At 1138hrs British hydrophone operators reported hearing the U-boat blow tanks. Gun crews were cleared for surface action and everybody waited in silence for the grey steel to break surface. Aboard *U202*, Poser was attempting to deceive the circling sloops. He had released nineteen *Bold* canisters and then gone deep, zigzagging at between one and a half and three knots in his attempt to creep away. The deception did not work; almost immediately the experienced Captain Walker had seen through the ruse.

Between 1436hrs and 1844hrs HMS *Woodpecker* and *Wild Goose* continued the depth-charging, a total of 252 depth-charges having been released since the attack began. With continued, though sporadic, ASDIC contact, the British knew that all they had to do was wait and Poser would be forced to surface in order to recharge his batteries. More German *Bold* released did little to fool the British during the evening. For the U-boat crew the agony of propellers humming above and depth charges thundering against their steel tomb continued.

Finally at 2402hrs *U202* surfaced 1,800 yards from HMS *Starling*. The sloop immediately opened fire with 4-inch main cannon and Oerlikon anti-aircraft weapons at the U-boat which lay wallowing at a standstill. *Starling* began an attack run, and as German crewmen tumbled from the conning tower *Starling* scraped down the U-boat's port side, straddling *U202* with depth charges from her port thrower set to explode at 50 and 140 feet. Twenty-seven rounds of 4-inch ammunition, fuses on 'safe', were fired point-blank at the U-boat, ripping enormous holes in the hull and conning tower without exploding.

The U-boat shuddered in agony before settling deeper by the stern, still refusing to go under. Scramble nets were thrown out and HMS *Starling* rescued two officers, including Poser, and fifteen ratings, while *Wild Goose* picked up a further two officers and ten ratings, the majority of German survivors wounded to some degree (later one of the Germans died of his severe wounds and was buried at sea with full military honours).

The action had lasted for 14 hours and completely reaffirmed British faith in ASDIC. Furthermore, Captain Walker and the other commanders had managed to see through the use of diversionary *Bold*, a total of seventy-six of the bubble making decoys having been deployed by *U202*.

1 July: *U628* departed Brest at 0730hrs for her fourth war patrol. Four days later, on 5 July, *U566* also sailed from Brest at 0700hrs. Kptlt. Hans Hornkohl was attempting his third patrol as commander, this time his destination the old hunting grounds of America's east coast in a renewed attempt by Dönitz at seizing the advantage for his U-boats. The renewal of operations against America was, however, destined to fail. Past German glories of '*Paukenschlag*' were determined by American anti-submarine commanders to never be repeated.

8 July: After an initially 'successful' anti-aircraft sortie by *U441* in May, the boat slipped from Brest at 0800hrs. By the mission's conclusion there was no longer to be any disguising the unsuitability of a U-boat as an anti-aircraft platform. During her previous patrol as an 'aircraft trap' *U441* had claimed victory with the shooting down of a heavy Sunderland flying boat. This time, however, she attracted the attention of three nimble and powerful 248 Squadron Beaufighters and suffered badly from furious cannon fire.

At 1405hrs Flight Lieutenant C.R.B. Schofield and his observer, Sergeant J.A. Mallinson, sighted *U441* two miles to port and immediately banked the lead aircraft towards their foe with the two other Beaufighters trailing line astern. Aboard *U441*, sailing through grid-reference BF4894 west of La Pallice, lookouts had also sighted the RAF fighters and guns were fully manned. Kptlt. Götz von Hartmann was present among the eighteen or so people in the U-boat's extended conning tower. The weather was clear, blighted by occasional showers and a moderate breeze. Due to the gentle Atlantic wind the sea state was a softly rolling swell, rocking the U-boat as gunners attempted to line up their sights against the onrushing Beaufighters. Therein lay the inherent problem with a U-boat as gun platform – it would not keep still.

U441's stern *Vierling* began to fire at Schofield's fighter and he remembers tracer shells 'the size of golf balls' flashing by the cockpit as the slower-firing but potentially more devastating German 3.7 cm cannon began to join in. Schofield pressed the trigger of his own weapons and devastating cannon fire lanced toward the crowded *Wintergarten*. Peeling away in evasive action, the first Beaufighter was followed by both others scoring direct hits amidst German gunners. Men were seen scrambling for cover, one lying prone on the scarred deck and yet another in the sea. A small explosion was followed by fire towards the aft of the conning tower, probably caused by stored ammunition exploding. Ten men were killed (three non-commissioned officers and seven seamen) and thirteen wounded aboard *U441*, including her commander, Kptlt. Götz von Hartmann, and all three Watch Officers. While men raced to help those still living the ship's onboard *Marinestabsarzt* (medical officer, equivalent to Kapitänleutnant) Paul Pfaffinger, the only uninjured officer aboard the battered U-boat and in Dönitz's estimation ' a keen and amateur yachtsman', ordered her dived away from the Beaufighters and took her back to Brest. Von Hartmann's War Diary entry related the events as Pfaffinger took command of the U-boat:

> 'While I fell into my bunk, the IWO as replacement commander lacked the necessary overall view of the situation [and had also been wounded in the attack – author's note], the IIWO was incapacitated by severe wounds, so *Stabsarzt* Dr. Pfaffinger replaced me on the bridge.'[75]

The blackened and twisted U-boat limped into her home port at 2330hrs on 13 July. This time the nurses present were not there to throw flowers, but to carry badly wounded men from their painful odyssey. The boat was destined for three months in the shipyard for reconversion to a more conventional state. There was no longer any mistake about the worth of a U-boat aircraft trap. In fact all U-boats received increased anti-aircraft artillery during 1943, reducing the gap in on-board ordnance between standard configuration and the special flak ships. The idea of 'slugging it out' was abandoned, as were the short-range aircraft traps. Dönitz later wrote:

> 'So far as the U-boat Command was concerned . . . this action showed that a submarine was a poor weapon with which to fight aircraft, and all further modification work on U-boats as aircraft traps was abandoned.'[76]

Despite these words, Brest's 9th U-Flotilla's *U621* continued its conversion to 'flak boat'. Its career as such would last for one brief mission in late August 1943, before reconversion to its original state. Similarly *U256* and *U953* briefly sailed as 'flak boats'. Dönitz was still fully aware of the implications of Allied air power over the Bay of Biscay. In the BdU War Diary on 11 July he remarked:

> 'If we cannot succeed in driving the English forces off from Biscay further losses will be inevitable. The danger is particularly serious for damaged U-boats returning.'

24 July: *'U435 Vermisst ein Stern'* – presumed lost.

Kptlt. Strelow and his forty-seven-man crew were yet more victims of overwhelming Allied air power. Ordered at the end of May to patrol the blue waters south-west of the Azores, *U435* began searching for Gibraltar-bound

---

[75] Paul Pfaffinger was awarded the German Cross by Dönitz on 28 August 1943 for this action, the only U-boat medical officer so honoured.

[76] *Ten Years and Twenty Days*, Karl Dönitz, p. 412.

American convoys. The sea remained depressingly empty for the hunting U-boat, and, as part of the *Trutz* patrol line, Strelow worked his way towards the east in search of contact.

Reformed into *Geier 1, 2* and *3* patrol lines, sixteen U-boats began to approach Gibraltar. *U435* was part of *Geier 2* and on 8 July Strelow received instructions from BdU that he may return to base if needed, rather than stay within a highly dangerous sector swarming with enemy aircraft. Strelow did not act soon enough.

In the Allied camp Air Marshal Slessor had asked that RAF squadrons based in Casablanca and Gibraltar widen their U-boat searches further north in support of the Musketry and Seaslug offensives. Accordingly, the relevant squadrons obliged. On 9 July a Leigh Light-equipped Wellington of Gibraltar's 179 Squadron sighted and attacked *U435*, Flying Officer E.J. Fisher cleanly straddled the diving U-boat with four depth charges; and neither she nor her crew ever surfaced again.

While July dissolved into overwhelming disaster for Winter's Flotilla, August promised no reprieve. Meagre results had been achieved by what few U-boats had been in operation. In Norway *U956* nominally joined 1st U-Flotilla for the last six months of 1943. Because the Russian convoys had been suspended for most of that time the U-boat spent miserably cold patrols cruising the frozen waters near Bear Island in search of non-existent targets. Hitler's insistence still held portions of the Kriegsmarine pinned to defence of the Arctic Circle. *U956*'s most dangerous encounters were with icebergs and polar bears.

The familiar paper slips of two more official BdU communiqués were entered into the 1st U-Flotilla War Diary on 10 August.

> '*U558 Vermisst ein Stern, U628 Vermisst ein Stern*' – presumed lost.

Kptlt. Günther Krech's *U558*, veteran of the heady days of February 1941 when boat and crew joined the 1st U-Flotilla alongside men such as Wohlfarth, Schnee and Mützelberg, was no more. Krech had sailed from Brest for his tenth war patrol at 0730hrs on 8 May. He had battled through the same aircraft-induced inferno as all boats at sea during the ensuing weeks, scoring no successes for himself. Freed from pack activity in early July, Krech sailed to the coast of Portugal in search of the Gibraltar traffic.

On either side of the U-boat's conning tower was painted the boat's emblem of a parson pointing to his eye, above the legend '*Holzauge sei Wach*' (Wooden eye, be alert). Based upon an old German folktale of a minister with a false eye always on the search for his unfaithful wife's lovers, it was an exhortation to the crew's vigilance to provide them with targets and protect them from others. This vigilance was to save the boat from an encounter on 15 July off Cape Roca when a single Wellington bomber of 179 Squadron sighted and attacked the submarine. Krech elected to remain surfaced and his gunners, forewarned by sharp lookouts, put up such a barrage of flying lead

202

that their attacker missed the boat, depth charges splashing harmlessly wide.

Two days later their fortune deserted them as Wing Commander A.E. Clouston from Gibraltar's 224 Squadron sighted *U558* in mid-afternoon through a rainsquall. New Zealander Clouston dove to attack the boat despite heavy and prolonged flak. The B24 bomber was hit several times until it hurtled above the U-boat releasing twenty-four small anti-submarine bombs. As the damaged Liberator roared away her rear gunner strafed the boat, which disappeared in a welter of spray. *U558*'s bow emerged from the blinding wall of water as Krech wildly manoeuvred his boat. They were hit, but not out of the fight, the port diesel bunker leaking but his boat still able to dive. The minute that Clouston's aircraft had passed Krech ordered the bridge cleared and the boat to dive. Thus began the so-called 'Battle of Seconds'. By the reckoning of submariners it would take 20 seconds to clear the bridge and be ready to submerge. During those precious moments the U-boat had no anti-aircraft defence, gunners racing for the conning tower hatch. If timed incorrectly against the actions of an attacking aircraft it provided a vital, and potentially fatal, opening in which to attack a helpless, surfaced submarine. It was a race many U-boat crews lost. Krech, however, was an experienced skipper and had judged that Clouston was out of bombs. He was unfortunately mistaken.

The ungainly looking bomber wheeled quickly around for another pass over *U558*. This time Clouston attempted to drop another stick of twenty-four bombs, but twelve remained obstinately hung inside the bomber's belly. A dozen were dropped, falling wide but knocking men still in the conning tower off their feet. Krech managed to submerge in time but his boat had suffered further debilitating damage. Clouston circled above and then departed as Krech struggled onwards towards Brittany, forced to resurface his tattered U-boat.

Lieutenant C.F. Gallimeier of 19 Squadron, USAF, was next to find the shambling U-boat on 20 July. As *U558* approached the edge of the Allied Musketry zone, the American Liberator attacked Krech from port. This time the vigilance of bridge watch had faltered and Gallimeier's 'F' B24 took the boat completely by surprise. In panic the ship's diesels were suddenly shut off, a mistake that would cost them dearly. While gunners ran to their posts Gallimeier dropped seven depth charges along the boat's port flank from stern to bow. Flak, only beginning now that the bomber had dropped its load, stitched upwards into the aircraft's port inner engine and waist gunner, wounding the American in both legs. More geysers of water hammered the boat as the depth charges exploded, but still they continued, afloat and mobile. Unrelenting German return fire struck the now circling B24, but with all eyes on Gallimeier the Germans did not at first notice another aircraft arrive.

Flight Lieutenant G.A. Sawtell's 58 Squadron Halifax opened fire on *U558* with cannons, the U-boat now heeling badly as she ran in ever-constricting circles. The Halifax's turret gunners scored several hits and observed

Kriegsmarine men falling from the conning tower now running with blood. Then, abruptly, the guns fell silent aboard *U558*. Unbeknown to Allied aircrews seawater was slowly flooding Krech's U-boat. Once the batteries had become submerged noxious chlorine gas began to fill the hull, forcing men to leave the interior and escape outside, aslo preventing access to ammunition stored internally. *U558* was now helpless.

Seeing an opportunity to attack, Sawtell raced over Krech's boat and dropped eight shallow-set depth charges while the Germans were abandoning ship. The accurate explosions killed most still alive in the water and served only to speed an already sinking boat on its way. Machine-gun fire was reported by survivors to have peppered the water among floating men before both bombers departed. Six survivors were seen by the airmen to enter a dinghy they had launched, surrounded by '30 to 40' bodies, more dead than alive.

Krech, wounded in the spine and thigh, was one of those aboard the dinghy, alongside his Chief Engineer Oblt. (Ing) Siegfried Steckel and four ratings. Most survivors still in the sea, clutching the dinghy's outboard grab straps, died over the following days from exhaustion, their wounds, drinking seawater in an attempt at quenching thirst or the after-effect of inhaling chlorine gas. On 24 July Squadron Leader T.M. Bulloch sighted the dinghy and dropped emergency packs to its wretched occupants. The following day Canadian destroyer HMCS *Athabaskan*, en route to Plymouth after playing a part in the Bay of Biscay anti-submarine drive 'Operation Percussion', rescued Krech, his Chief and two surviving ratings.

Kptlt. Heinrich Hasenschar's *U628* was yet another victim of the suffocating Allied air cordon around Biscay. On 2 July, one day after leaving Brest in company with *U648*, Hasenschar made his final contact with base from grid reference Bruno Fritz 7382. The two U-boats then proceeded along separate paths towards their patrol areas. Squadron Leader P.J. Cundy, pilot of Liberator 'J' of 224 Squadron, chanced upon a surfaced *U628*, destined for the central Atlantic.

Cundy and his crew were taking part in a 'Derange' operational patrol, carrying newly developed 35lb anti-submarine bombs, hollow-charge weapons dropped in sticks of eighteen, and four depth charges. At 1402hrs the Liberator first caught sight of *U628*. In the words of Peter Cundy:

> 'The U-boat captain was not asleep and saw us coming. He opened fire with all armament, including a 37mm cannon, while the aircraft was still a mile away and, as range closed, he scored hits on us.
>
> 'My gunners were not idle. They returned a hot fire and one of the U-boat crew was seen to fall overboard. We had stopped a few bullets; there was a hole in a tank and the petrol was flowing over the engine exhaust. I thought there might be a fire at any moment, but we carried on and dropped our depth charges, one of which hit the U-boat abaft of the conning tower and bounced off into the sea.'

Cundy circled for a second attack as *U628* began to sink lower in the water. The next attack comprised the remaining three depth charges and clearly straddled the boat, shrouding it in a cascade of churning water. As the blast subsided Cundy and his crew saw that their target was gone, a dark brown patch of oil with several bodies and struggling survivors the only traces to be seen. None of the Germans who escaped the U-boat were ever seen again, another forty-nine-crewmen killed in Biscay.[77]

11 August: Kptlt. Claus von Trotha brought *U306* into Lorient harbour at 1730hrs. Sailing slowly past the moored hulks in front of the gigantic Keroman bunkers, von Trotha watched as his Watch Officer handled the docking of the U-boat. Heavily gauntleted crewmen threw thick woven rope fenders alongside the U-boat's hull and retractable bollards were raised to accommodate mooring lines.

As well as the commander's jackstaff with its long commissioning ribbon, *U306* flew four pennants totalling 27,000 BRT of torpedoed steamers. Two months at sea had taken its toll on the weary crew but they at least had some results to show for their labours; four confirmed and one probable. During early July the boat had patrolled the seas between the Cape Verde islands and the West African mainland. Sighting a coastal convoy on 16 July Von Trotha logged several submerged attacks and the destruction of four steamers.

Although celebrations at the traditional homecoming banquet that evening in Lorient continued with vigour, there was only one victory confirmed for Von Trotha. In his stalking pursuit of the small convoy between grid references EK79 and EK49, from five separate torpedo launches only the 5,882-ton British freighter MV *Kaipara* was reported hit, badly damaged by the first torpedo.

Further reinforcements were en route for the mauled Flotilla. New boats *U238*, *U422* and *U963* had all departed Kiel between 12 and 17 August. They followed recent BdU orders and all made a refuelling stop in Norway before attempting their journey into the Atlantic. This was a reflexive decision take by Dönitz following the loss of nine out of ten supply U-boats. The slow and unwieldy *Milchkuh* submarines were high on the Allied hit list, falling easily to aircraft of the 'Derange', 'Musketry' and 'Seaslug' operations, although more by coincidence than the often-mentioned ULTRA-based assault against the tankers.[78] The operational strength of 1st U-Flotilla by 18 August was twenty-four boats, including the three new additions in transit.

19 August: Spirits within the 1st U-Flotilla, indeed the entire *Unterseebootwaffe*, sagged after months of increasing losses. During July alone

---

[77] Cundy's Liberator made the return flight to St. Eval. After landing, the aircraft was found to be so badly damaged that it was written off.

[78] See *Hitler's U-Boat War – The Hunted*, Clay Blair, p. 356.

thirty-seven U-boats had been destroyed, twelve of them in Biscay. Desperately trying to minimize the horrendous level of casualties suffered by his U-boats traversing the 'Valley of Death', Dönitz issued fresh instructions to his men:

> 'All boats are ordered until further notice to proceed (on the return passage in the Biscay area) on the 'Pinang' route, i.e. hard under the Spanish coast.'

During August Dönitz and the staff at BdU had altered many of the fundamental operational directives previously issued to U-boat commanders. From 2 August U-boats were no longer to travel through Biscay in groups. Nor were they ordered to remain surfaced and 'fight it out' with the enemy. They were to creep solo both in and out of their home ports, hugging the shelter of neutral Spain while returning.

From 13 August the use of Metox aboard U-boats was forbidden. Tests proved that the radar detector did indeed radiate a weak signal, thought to be the method by which Allied aircraft could find U-boats with such uncanny accuracy. Of course this was a fallacy. Yes, Metox did radiate, but German refusal to accept that Allied engineers had managed to make a workable centimetric radar, let alone one small enough to fit inside an aircraft, was the root of the problem. The new German radar detector *Wellenanzeiger* FuMb 9 *Zypern* (nicknamed *Wanze G1*, or 'bed bug') had been rushed into production, and was to be used instead of Metox. There were several improvements with the new design. Instead of laborious manual frequency search the *Wanze* had an automatic search capability. It also had a permanently fixed aerial, the *Runddipol* (round dipole). Unfortunately, despite German beliefs, and almost irrelevantly, this too emitted weak signals. Use of the G1 was thus immediately discontinued, replaced by improved non-radiating G2 as of 5 November 1943. A third detection set, *Borkum*, was also issued in the interim period while boats were changing from *Wanze* G1 to G2.

After a continued spate of undetected air attacks, a further weakness was discovered in the equipment. It was belatedly found that *Wanze* did not cover the frequency range of centimetric radar. A further detector, FuMb7 *'Naxos'*, was required to augment the *Wanze*. By November 1943 1st U-Flotilla boats began to be so equipped.

Despite a slump in spirits among the men of Germany's frontline U-boats, there never appeared a hint of reluctance to sail against the enemy. Years after the war Erich Topp provided an insight into the absolute willingness of U-boats to put to sea against increasingly heavy odds:

> 'Much of the credit goes to Dönitz, he was magnetic and charismatic, and he played a vital role in maintaining morale at a high level. In addition, when we left our home port in Germany or in France we . . . were reducing our lives to a few maxims, the most important one to be a band

206

of brothers. There was a great loyalty to the service and to Dönitz. Also, the navy felt the strain of the mutiny of 1918; it could not allow any hesitancy or doubt in this war; it couldn't allow even a hint that might recall the actions of 1918.'

23 August: Two U-boats put to sea from Brest: 1st U-Flotilla's *U305* and 3rd U-Flotilla's *U645*. They faced the nightmare 'Valley of Death' before combat in the North Atlantic, Dönitz having decided to attempt a renewal of operations against Atlantic convoys. Kptlt. Rudolf Bahr's *U305* was one of fifteen U-boats sent during the final week of August to form the 'Wolf Pack' *Leuthen* south-south-west of Iceland.

The first half of August had seen U-boats licking their wounds in French ports after devastating losses from the 'Musketry' and 'Seaslug' offensives. Dönitz was now determined to take the fight beyond Biscay once again, helped by his new radar detectors, *Bold* noisemakers, *Aphrodite* radar decoys (balloons trailing silver foil, difficult to launch and unpopular although often effective) and new improved T5 *Zaunkönig* homing torpedoes; escort killers. These torpedoes had been demanded by Dönitz to be ready for use by 1 August, and some eighty were. The *Zaunkönig* (Wren) torpedo was seen as a potential saviour for Germany's struggling U-boats. Able to be fired towards the enemy from any position, it was tuned to seek the exact pitch of sound generated by escort ships' propellers. The weapon, however, had one crucial drawback not yet recognized, which was to result in frequent over-claiming from eager U-boat commanders. With a maximum range of 5.7 kilometres and a short arming range, U-boats were compelled to dive deep immediately after firing the weapon for fear of becoming the torpedo's target. Submerged, the German crew would be subjected to the cacophony of noise that accompanied convoy battle. Detonation of the torpedo, or indeed any torpedo, was often heard, and although the results were unverifiable commanders regularly claimed the attack as a certain kill. This particular fault would not become immediately apparent to U-boat command and early results were accordingly overstated, leading to an exaggerated view of the weapon's effectiveness.

26 August: '*U84 Vermisst ein Stern*' – presumed lost.

Kptlt. Horst Uphoff had last communicated with BdU to report the torpedoing of a '6,000-ton steamer', left burning by the U-boat on 16 July, and another possible '7,000-ton steamer' from five nights later. One month and six days into his Caribbean patrol Uphoff reported his status from grid reference DC 8596 following a BdU request for information and was ordered to begin his homeward trek.

Uphoff was given instructions to take on fuel for the journey from *U117*, unknown to BdU already sunk on 7 August. *U84* next received orders to rendezvous with *U740* south-west of the Azores. This also failed due to the latter boat undergoing severe air attack and having to abort the meeting.

U84's next rendezvous was to be even less fortuitous. The facts surrounding subsequent events are still unclear. Some sources quote the U-boat being attacked by Avenger aircraft belonging to USS *Core* on 24 August; others make no mention of this, saying that the U-boat went missing with no definite cause. The most accepted version of events is that an Avenger from USS *Core* attacked Uphoff's boat. Catching the surfaced U-boat by surprise, the American commenced a shallow dive as *U84* began to submerge, releasing a single Fido homing torpedo. Nothing was ever heard of Uphoff or his forty-five men again.[79]

28 August: *U731* slipped from Brest for its second operational patrol. Oblt.z.S. Werner Techand took his ship to sea, destined for the hunting grounds south-south-west of Iceland of the *Leuthen* pack, probably the most well equipped U-boat group to put to sea, and carrying Dönitz's hopes for a renewal of North Atlantic success.

31 August: *U732* docked in Brest claiming two steamers probably sunk during two and a half months at sea, primarily operating within the confines of the Caribbean. Oblt.z.S. Claus-Peter Carlsen claimed one ship sunk, one torpedoed and likely destroyed, as well as two other hits of unknown effect during three seperate attacks launched against New York to Cuba convoy NG 376 west of Great Inagua Island on the night of 1 /2 August. In total Carlsen had launched four torpedoes and 'observed hits on two ships with flashes and fountains, detonations were heard'.[80] After suffering fierce retribution from gunboat escort USS *Brisk*, Carlsen was able to slink away to safety. Oddly, there were no ships listed as missing from NG 376's convoy manifest when it arrived at Guantanamo, Cuba.

1 September: On the fourth anniversary of war *U566* returned to Brest from its tenth voyage. Kptlt. Hornkohl had received the special mission of planting twelve TMB mines in the approaches to Chesapeake Bay, near Norfolk. The difficult task was carried out on the night of 30 July, Hornkohl retreating at the completion of his mission to submerge in deep clear water after signalling the coded message 'AFKP', signifying success.

The following day a US Navy aircraft discovered a surfaced *U566*, sparking a badly handled and ineffective search by aircraft and blimp. On 5 August Hornkohl sighted a New York to Guantanamo convoy and closed for an attack. An escort vessel turned toward the U-boat and Hornkohl launched his escort-killer torpedo directly towards it. In a shattering explosion the 2,265-ton gunboat USS *Plymouth* (*PG-57*) was fatally holed and sank rapidly.

---

[79] Axel Niestle records that the attack by USS *Core*'s aircraft was on a 'nonsub target'. If this is indeed correct then *U84* is still missing from unknown causes.

[80] Personal correspondence with Claus-Peter Carlsen, 10 February 2001.

Ironically the US Navy gunboat was originally German, built by Krupp in 1931, the luxury steel-hulled yacht owned by W.K. Vanderbilt before hostilities and her donation to the US Navy.

This incident sparked another chaotic American search by aircraft and blimp. The net result was *U566*'s shooting down of a US Navy Avenger from squadron VB-128, the pilot, Lieutenant F.C. Cross, being drowned after his aircraft crashed into the sea. A second Avenger also never returned to its airfield after dropping bombs wide of the U-boat. It was probably hit by flak and lost some time en route for home. Hornkohl's escape from the American coast towards France continued to be punctuated by several more aircraft skirmishes, all dealt with successfully by *U566*'s experienced flak gunners. The U-boat was forced to deploy its newly developed *Aphrodite* radar decoys in the first week of August after attracting the unwanted attentions of three US Navy destroyers from Norfolk. Whether the balloon counter-measures were successful or not is unknown, but the destroyers failed to find *U566*. Hornkohl's claim upon arrival in Brest was one destroyer sunk and one aircraft confirmed. The carefully laid mines yielded nothing for the Germans.

2 September: Brest's U-boat contingent cheered more departing U-boats, *U584* sailing to join the *Leuthen* pack in the North Atlantic; *U603* following a week later to become part of *Rossbach*; *U336* following later still on 14 September, also for *Rossbach*.

8th September: A strange visitor made an appearance in Brest's military harbour. Japanese blockade-runner *I8* arrived from Lorient with Torpedoboot escort, having docked in France after a two-month voyage from Japan. Aboard the massive vessel were supplies of wolfram, quinine, rubber and other commodities difficult for the German war machine to obtain. Traversing the oceans between Japan and occupied Europe had remained the domain of converted cargo ships until 1943, which saw a determined and successful Allied onslaught against them. Submarines were not entirely suited to the enterprise, but at least the Japanese *I8* could carry enough to make this hazardous venture profitable. Winter and his 1st U-Flotilla officers played host to the Japanese crew, both in Brest and at the *Château de Trévarez* deep within Brittany's rolling countryside before *I8* began her return journey to the Far East.[81]

U415 returned during the evening, tying up in Brest at 2100hrs. Kptlt.

---

[81] For the return to their home country they embarked torpedoes, aircraft engines, AA guns and ten German advisors. Captain Shinji Uchino brought his submarine into Japanese waters in early 1944, docking at Kure on 21 December. The Imperial Japanese Navy sent five submarines to German-occupied Europe of which only three (*I30*, *I29* and *I8*) successfully arrived and stayed in Lorient, and were sunk during their return voyages.

Niede's second patrol, lasting nearly two months, had begun in company of four other boats on 12 June. After the devastating Sunderland attack that had incapacitated *U564*, and led ultimately to her sinking, Niede had continued west towards the azure waters of the Caribbean. Once refuelled west of the Azores from *U535*, *U415* operated initially north of Guiana for several fruitless days. Joining five other Caribbean boats, Niede then proceeded to hunt for targets in the outflow of the Orinoco River, sailing from Trinidad to the mouth of the Amazon.

During his patrol Niede attempted two attacks on heavily defended convoys near Trinidad. Aircraft and surface ship attack, hammering the boat away from the vulnerable merchant ships, frustrated both approaches. *U415* had no success. Heat inside the boat added its own debilitating burden to a patrol fraught with depth-charging and alarm dives. Finally, in early August, Niede began the home journey, his Type VIIC critically low on fuel. Ordered to rendezvous with *U117*, Niede wasted precious diesel patiently waiting before the realization that the ex-minelayer supply boat had been sunk. BdU arranged another rendezvous with stand-in tanker *U525*. Five days, and more fuel, later this U-boat too was deemed already sunk. Finally a successful refuelling was undertaken from another provisional tanker *U847* on 27 August. It was a crew suffering from nervous and physical exhaustion who disembarked inside Brest's floodlit U-boat bunker.

11 September: Two similarly unsuccessful Flotilla boats arrived in Best at 2200hrs. *U653* had also experienced depth-charge attacks and heat-induced misery in the Caribbean. Added to the woeful spate of heavy air attacks was the extra burden for *U653* of tropical fever contracted by skipper Kptlt. Feiler and a good many of his crew. Starting home for France on 4 August with a raging temperature, Feiler spent two weeks searching for the same refuelling U-boats that *U415* had sought, finally also refuelling from *U847* on 11 September. As the crew took their first steps on French soil, suffering the wobbly gait of men too long at sea, Feiler had reached his limit of endurance. After treatment for his condition he was reassigned by Dönitz from combat U-boats to other duties.

The other returning U-boat *U86* had begun its patrol by sailing through the 'Musketry' and 'Seaslug' offensive areas, bound for West Africa. Surviving this initial hurdle Kptlt. Walter Schug took his Type VIIB, one of the Flotilla's oldest boats, south of Liberia for futile and barren patrolling. Schug was ordered to rendezvous with another West African boat *U445* on 11 August, the latter's on-board physician reported to BdU as 'desperately ill'. Schug, also with a doctor onboard, Kaptlt (*Marinestabsarzt der Reserve*) Joachim Abel, made speed to the meeting until informed that the 25-year-old Lieutenant (*Marineassistenzarzt*) Heinz-Konrad Fuhrmann had died. Like his Flotillamates, Schug had difficulty obtaining fuel for his return, the British onslaught against U-Tankers having achieved devastating success.

15 September: Despite the decision to refrain from 'U-boat aircraft trap' operations, the sinister silhouette of a 'Flak boat' bristling with weaponry entered Brest harbour at 1830hrs. *U271* had begun conversion to its new anti-aircraft role during late July. Kptlt. Curt Barleben participated during *U271*'s transfer to Winter's flotilla from Danzig's 8th U-Flotilla in Dönitz's decoy radio operation during June, arriving in France on 16 July. Docked in Lorient,the boat had undergone intense work on its conversion before sailing north to Brest on 14 September. Two weeks of drills in the *Rade de Brest* followed by provisioning and preparation would take until the beginning of September. Then the top-heavy boat would put to sea for its second operational patrol, Winter recording in the War Diary for 27 September that the boat's preparation was complete. FdU West Rösing, no stranger to 1st U Flotilla, also arrived to brief the commander for his forthcoming mission.[82]

23 September: In the Arctic the underemployed Narvik U-boats continued to patrol. At 1130hrs Oblt.z.S. Hans-Dieter Mohs began *U956*'s second combat voyage. This time attached to *Monsun* group operating between Bear Island and Spitzbergen the boat sailed aimlessly until 4 November in search of non-existent convoys. It was to be the last operation as part of 1st U Flotilla, control of the boat passing to Bergen's 11th U-Flotilla during December.

2 October: *U271* and *U413* slipped from Brest at 1600hrs. Diesels throbbed as the two boats surged through the narrow entrance channel to Brest in the cleared path left by their *Sperrbrecher* and *Vorpostenboote* escort. Both boats were destined for the further declining fortunes of Germany's Atlantic front, Dönitz's renewed convoy offensive already in shreds.

Hundreds of miles to the north new Flotilla boat *U424* began the journey from Germany to refuel in Norway before also heading for the Atlantic and her first war patrol under command of Oblt.z.S. Günther Lüders.

7 October: Kptlt. Claus von Trotha left Brest at 1700hrs. His boat *U306* was embarking on its third war patrol in an ambitiously planned assault on the MK – KM convoy lanes between the British Isles and the Mediterranean. Only days out of Brest the boat was forced to return with mechanical difficulties, resailing on 14 October at 1330hrs. Named *Schill* group, there were ten U-boats in total, *U228, U262, U306, U333, U358, U466, U707* and the fearsome but flawed flak boats *U211, U441,* and *U953*.

---

[82] The post of FdU West (*Führer der U-Boot West*) had come into being during July 1942, originally stationed in Paris but moving to Angers at the beginning of 1943, occupying the beautiful *Château de Pignerolles*. Hans Rösing, veteran of the 'Weddigen' Flotilla, held this post as administrative chief for France; responsible for recording arrivals and departures from Atlantic bases, resupply of the U-boat flotillas stationed in France and control of construction programmes within his region.

Alongside Flotilla-mate *U441*, 9th U-Flotilla's *U211* and 3rd U-Flotilla's *U953* were assigned to the group in an attempt to counter the heavy Allied air support which had necessitated the curtailing of operations against this convoy route in June 1942.

U441 did not set sail from Brest until 17 October, under new command. The boat's original commander Kptlt. Klaus Hartmann had – confusingly – replaced wounded Kptlt. Götz von Hartmann.[83] Battle damage repaired and losses made good by the surprisingly overwhelming number of volunteers from Brest's U-boat men, *U441* slipped away to sea at 1600hrs.

Below Winter's notation of Brest departures came yet further grim news: '*U669 Vermisst ein Stern.*'

Oblt.z.S. Kurt Köhl had left Saint Nazaire at 0800hrs on 29 August. The boat's second only patrol, the first spent on June's radio-decoy attempt after leaving Kiel for France, *U669* had been ordered to undertake a special operation. The 30-year-old commander had been assigned 'Operation *Kiebitz*', an ambitious attempt at rescuing German U-boat POWs from Canada.

POW Camp 30 was located in Bowmanville, Ontario. Housed in the utilitarian wooden barrack huts were several veteran U-boat skippers such as Hans Ey (*U433*), Horst Elfe (*U93*) and the 'Tonnage King' himself Otto Kretschmer, grouped together within the camp under the self-styled name 'Lorient Espionage Unit'. Along with various key officers also resident behind the wire, these men were planning to tunnel out of the camp and rendezvous with *U669* at Pointe de Maissonette, Chaleurs Bay.

The audacious plan had been hatched by the prisoners and communicated to Dönitz using a simple code hidden within their mail to Germany. Instructions and maps were likewise mailed back using the same basic code system or hidden within gift parcels. Unbeknown to BdU and the Kriegsmarine prisoners, Allied camp authorities had intercepted their coded mail and were fully appraised of the scheme. They saw not only the chance to foil the attempted escape but perhaps net an operational U-boat into the bargain.

On the night of 7th September as Köhl brought *U669* towards Cape Ortegal and the planned pick-up point the Leigh Light of Pilot Officer E.M. O'Donnell's Wellington bomber from 407 Squadron, RCAF, located him. In the face of intense flak from his startled U-boat quarry, O'Donnell succeeded in straddling *U669* with five depth-charges, pulverizing the steel pressure hull and sending all fifty-three men aboard to their graves.[84] The 'Lorient

---

[83] The two von Hartmann's earned themselves nicknames to alleviate the confusion of their identities. Klaus von Hartmann was 'Brown' and Götz von Hartmann was 'Blue'. The term 'Brown' was often meant as a reference to Nazi party members, although in this case it most definitely was not – it referred instead to their eye colour.
[84] After realising that *U669* had been lost, Dönitz assigned the mission to 2nd U-Flotilla's *U536*. Allied authorities attempted to capture the boat but failed, sinking her instead. The skipper and sixteen men became POWs in Canada.

Espionage Unit' remained captive, their tunnel intercepted before the planned breakout.

8 October: Kptlt. Horst Hepp arrived at his new base of Brest during midday. Alongside *U238*'s commissioning ribbon and battle ensign streamed pennants accounting for five steamers totalling 24,000 BRT sunk and three more damaged. Hepp and his crew rejuvenated Brest's Flotilla base with their score, the highest seen for months. Momentarily the accumulated clouds of depression parted for Winter and his Staff.

U238 had departed on this her first mission from Kiel during 12 August. Travelling first to Norway for minor rust treatment and refuelling, Hepp finally slipped from Trondheim on 5 September for the front line. He was one of the nineteen boats that would eventually comprise the well-equipped *Leuthen* group of Dönitz's renewed Atlantic battle. Early on 20 September contact was made with convoy ON 202 and four *Leuthen* boats began to close the merchant ships, *U238* among them.

Twenty-five year old Hepp tried to approach the sixty-eight-ship convoy stealthily but was quickly detected and driven away by escort corvette HMS *Polyanthus*. Hepp was not to be put off, however, and after hours spent carefully shadowing the corvette on its return course he found the convoy, slipped through the escort screen and at 0932hrs on 20 September launched two torpedoes at the crowded shipping. Beneath a blue sky, bright though lacking warmth, his first torpedo struck Liberty ship SS *Theodore Dwight Weld*, while the second struck another American SS *Frederick Douglass*. The *Weld* died rapidly as the torpedo impacted the ship's port side at Number 3 hold adjacent to the fuel oil tanks. Within seconds the engine room exploded breaking the ship in two. Her stern sank immediately, while the bow section drifted away to be swamped later that day. No boats were lowered, such was the speed of her sinking, and twenty merchant crew, including the master, and thirteen navy men were lost. One further badly injured crewman died later aboard the British rescue ship *Rathlin*.

The second ship hit by Hepp dropped out of line with heavy damage. The torpedo had holed the Liberty Ship on its port side between Number 4 and 5 holds, exploding in the sand ballast, and water flooded her quickly, submerging the engines as she settled deeper into the sea. As her panicked engine room crew vacated the lower decks crucial watertight doors leading to the holed drive shaft tunnel were left open, hastening her demise. Her black master, Adrian Richardson, was abandoned by his Second Officer and Chief Engineer (both white) along with a sizeable number of her crew shortly after the torpedo impact. The entire complement of thirty-nine crew, twenty-nine Naval Armed Guard and a young black female stowaway successfully abandoned ship aboard four lifeboats, later saved by the *Rathlin*. Lifeless and drifting, the lumbering ship could not make way, and was later finished off by *U645*. She could have been saved if her crew had not made such a hasty departure. The destruction of SS *Frederick Douglass* was unfortunate in more ways than one. American Naval historian Samuel Morison wrote:

> 'The vessel had a Negro master, several Negro officers and a crew that was about half Negro and half white. Consequently, she was considered an experiment in race relations. These unfortunate events . . . would have called for no particular comment but for the racial composition of *Douglass*'s crew, and the feeling of some of *Weld*'s survivors that the *Douglass*'s lifeboats might have made an effort to rescue them. In this writer's opinion, the personnel of the torpedoed vessels reacted as individuals; some well and courageously and others in a despicable and cowardly manner; Captain Richardson behaved according to the best traditions of the sea.'[85]

None of this American drama was apparent to the men aboard *U238* and, elated at his first combat successes, Hepp cautiously retreated in the face of angry and numerous surface escorts, supported by VLR aircraft. Diving deep into the Atlantic the victorious U-boat slipped away, the sound of exploding bulkheads and thrashing propellers still reverberating through her steel hull.

U238 lost contact with ON 202 the following day and stumbled blindly through thick fog in an attempt to relocate its targets. After the blanketing fog thinned on 21 September Allied aircraft began to throw their weight against the *Leuthen* boats. The increased flak armaments carried by all Atlantic U-boats successfully warded off many attempted attacks, but could not sway the tide of battle completely. During 22 September Hepp again made contact with ON202 and prepared for a second assault.

At 0414hrs the following morning he slipped through the escort screen and fired a full salvo of two TIII torpedoes, two FATs and a single TIII from the stern tube.[86] Multiple explosions were seen and Hepp logged the destruction of four ships sunk and one damaged. In fact he had sunk the Norwegians MV *Oregon*, SS *Skjelbred* and British steamer SS *Fort Jemseg*. Two other ships were hit and heavily damaged though remaining afloat. In total 23,048 tons had been sunk by *U238*, a further 7,176 tons shared with *U645*. Hepp had achieved the highest score in the Atlantic for months.

22 October: Kptlt. Rudolf Bahr's *U305* returned triumphant from the battle against ON202/ONS18 as part of the *Leuthen* pack. Although claiming two destroyers sunk using the new *Zaunkönig* torpedoes, Bahr had only sunk one, the Canadian HMCS *St. Croix*. Hit first and disabled by Bahr's initial attack at 2151hrs on 20 September, *U305* returned an hour later to finish off the

---

[85] *History of United States Naval Operations in World War II – Vol X The Atlantic Battle Won*, Samual Eliot Morison, pp. 140–142.
[86] The TIII '*Falke*' (Falcon) torpedo was a modified G7e electric torpedo with acoustic guidance system, the first of its kind for the Kriegsmarine.

listing Canadian. During this second attack another torpedo from *U305* had sped towards HMS *Itchen*, exploding in the ship's wake, but thought by Bahr to have hit.

Two U-boats were reported missing: '*U643 Vermisst ein Stern, U336 Vermisst ein Stern.*'

Kptlt. Hans Harald Speidel had taken *U643* on its inaugural combat patrol from Bergen on 14 September for transfer to Brest via the North Atlantic. Hans Speidel remembered:

> 'After several training courses I was appointed as commanding officer of *U643*. I had a good forty-nine-strong crew, including twenty veterans and a naval doctor who was sent aboard as it was anticipated there could be injuries from aircraft attacks.'

One hour before *U643* was to leave Bergen the ship's doctor unexpectedly began his service aboard Speidel's boat. The navigator suddenly became ill and after examination by the doctor he was pronounced unfit to go to sea and interned in Bergen's military hospital.

It was to be a patrol that lasted only twenty-five days. Conforming to expectations the U-boat was attacked while surfaced by Liberator bombers of 86 and 120 Squadrons, and battered to a standstill by depth charges. *U643* lay bow-down and listing to starboard as her crew abandoned ship amid continual machine-gun fire from circling bombers. German sailors launched dinghies from her bow until there erupted a huge explosion from the forward torpedo room (*Bugtorpedoraum*) killing several of the fleeing crew still atop her splintered deck casing.

Allied destroyers of Support Group 3 that had raced to the scene dropped nets to rescue survivors, many of whom were too weary to climb aboard, falling back into the sea and drowning. In total twenty-three men were saved, including the commander, Chief Engineer Oblt (Ing) Karl-August Kennepohl, and the ship's medical officer. Aboard HMS *Orwell*, one of the British rescuers, Sub-Lieutenant Ian Wedderburn, remembered the German medical officer in particular:

> 'The doctor was more disposed to talk especially when he was with the surgeon of HMS *Orwell*, helping to attend to the German wounded ratings; he wanted to know where we would be landing the survivors, and if it would be the Clyde because he had an aunt living in Argyll.'[87]

U336 was already a veteran of three patrols as part of 1st U-Flotilla. Her commander, Kptlt. Hans Hunger, had also left Brest on 14 September bound for the same battleground as *U643*. Also, like *U643*, Hunger's boat was a victim of Allied aircraft.

On 5 October Flight Sergeant G.C. Allsop sighted the surfaced U-boat

[87] *Autumn of the U-Boats*, Geoffrey Jones. p. 88.

from the cockpit of his 269 Squadron Halifax. Without hesitation he brought his bomber into a shallow dive to attack *U336* with eight solid-shot rockets. As the missiles flew towards their target trailing thick smoke, the German submarine attempted to evade, spewing light flak towards Allsop's aircraft. Most of the projectiles were seen to impact the U-boat, which immediately ceased firing, as *U336* slewed to a halt and began to sink by the bow. During the boat's death throes a final spurt of flak beat out a futile tattoo towards the circling bomber, perhaps triggered by the dying hand of one of the U-boat's gunners. In moments the guns were silenced, all fifty crewmen dead with their U-boat as she submerged a final time.

29 October: '*U566 Vermisst zwei Stern.*' Kptlt. Hans Hornkohl en route to the Mediterranean from Brest was sighted and attacked in the darkness of early morning on 24 October. Sergeant D.M. Cornish was flying his 179 Squadron Leigh-Light Wellington bomber west of Oporto when the U-boat was detected by on-board radar. Diving to attack, the Wellington suffered moderate damage to its tail plane from German flak, but succeeded in dropping six depth charges close enough to *U566* to disable the submarine. Cornish was forced to break off the attack and proceed back to his home airfield, low on fuel.

Aboard *U566* Hornkhol learned that his boat was not only unable to dive but not capable of manoeuvring at all. Faced with few viable options, the decision was made to scuttle her. In an orderly evacuation her entire crew took to their dinghies and watched their boat disappear beneath the waves. Some time later the Spanish trawler *Fina* rescued the crew and landed them in Vigo, Spain, from where they were eventually repatriated to France and back to the war.

1 November: Winter recorded further transfers to and from his flotilla as BdU attempted to bolster the Atlantic U-boat force: *U307* to Trondheim's 13th U-Flotilla; *U471* from 5th U-Flotilla; *U426* and *U629* from 11th U-Flotilla; *U741* from 8th U-Flotilla; *U625* from 13th U-Flotilla.

2 November: Unsuccessful *Leuthen* and *Rossler* boat *U731* arrived in Brest at 1700hrs. Oblt.z.S. Werner Techand had accomplished nothing during this, the boat's second patrol. Techand and five 'Lords' (ratings) showed wounds sustained during a prolonged series of attacks from Pilot Officer H.M. Smith's Hudson bomber on 4 October. The 269 Squadron aircraft made three separate attack runs over the U-boat before *U731* was able to dive to safety. This marked the end of Techand's operation as he ordered the mission aborted for France.

While underway for Brest lookouts sighted SC143 during the night 8 /9 October, issuing a contact report which brought other *Rossler* boats in to attack. *U731*, however, took no part in the ensuing brief battle that resulted in the disastrous loss of three U-boats for two merchant ships sunk.

3 November: *U271* limped into Brest at 1330hrs, the U-boat's foray as a flak ship ending in near disaster. After departing Brest during early October Kptlt. Curt Barleben had set course for the seas west of the Azores to provide anti-aircraft protection for refuelling U-boats. Travelling in company with another Flak U-boat, 9th U-Flotilla's *U256*, Barleben arrived at his predesignated station during 12 October, their charge being *U488*, one of the few remaining *Milchkuh* U-boats. The Type XIV boat was vital for the long-distance operations of Germany's Type VII U-boats; more so now that most of her fellow supply submarines had been sunk.

However, before the arrival of the two flak boats *U488* had been forced northward by patrolling American aircraft of the carrier USS *Card*. *U271* and *U256* spent hours searching for the tanker in order to offer their protective umbrella until, on 21 October, the inevitable happened and Avenger aircraft from USS *Card*, only 35 miles away, located *U271* and began to attack her. In subsequent strafing and depth-charge attacks one of the U-boat's flak weapons was disabled and a crewman killed. Barleben seized a brief opportunity to escape by diving away, fearful of further aircraft arriving from the newly operational Terceira airfield on the Azores. His U-boat was battered and scarred after the short combat. Further action as a flak ship was deemed impossible and *U271* aborted its mission, heading once again for Brest. After arrival in the concrete pens *U271* was transferred to dry dock and scheduled for reconversion to its original state.

8 November: *U441* sailed into Brest harbour in a similar condition at 0400hrs, hidden from prying eyes by the cloak of early morning darkness. Her third sailing as a flak boat had again ended with severe damage to the submarine. As part of the *Schill* extended patrol line Kptlt. Klaus Hartmann had been preparing for the imminent action against combined convoys MKS28/SL138 when his boat was pounced upon by unidentified Allied aircraft. During the ensuing fire fight *U441* again took a pounding and was forced to break away from the action. Damage aboard was found to be too serious for the crew to remedy so the mission was aborted and *U441* taken home. Meanwhile the *Schill* operation spiralled downwards into another disaster at the hands of enemy escorts.

Three days after *U441*'s return BdU ordered the reconversion of all 'aircraft-traps' to their original state, without exception. In Günther Hessler's study commissioned by the British Admiralty after the war he states:

> 'Operational conditions had changed since this type of boat was conceived; she could no longer be used in the Bay of Biscay, owing to the strength of enemy air opposition, nor could she be employed further afield, or against convoys, since she carried insufficient fuel and torpedoes. In fact, compared with the operational U-boat, which in addition to her normal fuel and torpedo-carrying capacity possessed an

AA armament nearly as powerful as that of the flak-U-boat, the latter was no longer worthy of its title.'[88]

11 November: As two U-boats slipped from Brest at 1400hrs for operations west of Portugal, *U86* and *U238* putting to sea with a comparatively muted send-off, Winter recorded in the Flotilla War Diary the presumed loss of one more U-boat: '*U584 Vermisst ein Stern.*'

Kptlt. Joachim Deecke and his crew had been host to a small team of *B-Dienst* specialists aboard their boat concerned with monitoring Allied convoy radio signals during the forthcoming patrol in the North Atlantic. At 1630hrs on 2 September *U584* had sailed from Brest to join the *Leuthen* group. During the dangerous transit of the Bay of Biscay Deecke was attacked several times at night by Allied aircraft, arriving undetected by newly installed *Wanze* radar-detection equipment.

Following orders from BdU, when *Leuthen* boats attempted to engage convoy ON202 and ONS18, most U-boats targeted the escorts with their newly developed TV *Zaunkönig* acoustic 'escort-killer' torpedoes. On 21 September at 0610hrs Deecke attacked HMCS *Chambly* with a single *Zaunkönig*. After a run of seven minutes and fifty seconds, Deecke and his crew, submerged and retreating at speed, heard their torpedo detonate, wrongly assuming a hit. Their corvette target had, however, evaded the torpedo, which exploded harmlessly in the ship's wake. Although the *Zaunkönig* was an effective and thoroughly tested weapon it suffered from an extremely sensitive Pi4 firing pistol. As the weapon often criss-crossed turbulent wake seeking its acoustic signature target, they frequently detonated prematurely. As stated earlier, U-boats departing the scene submerged became prey to the illusion of high successes against Allied convoy escorts.

Following the abandonment of *Leuthen* operations, *U584* joined the newly created *Rossbach* group, formed to intercept ON 203. This and subsequent searches for ONS19, SC143, HX259 were all failures: no contact and so no sinkings.

Low on fuel Deecke, along with several other U-boats, attempted to rendezvous with *U488* for replenishment. During 10 October a man was lost overboard, swept away to die in the Atlantic wastes. Between 11 October and 31 October *U584* made attempt after attempt to meet with the tanker, each time frustrated by either worsening weather conditions or enemy aircraft. Finally, during the last day of October *U584* met 9th U-Flotilla boat *U91* also homebound to Brest. The two submarines began the difficult task of fuel transfer, heavy unwieldy pipes strung between the surfaced boats as harnessed crewmen fed precious oil into *U584*'s empty bunkers.

Unfortunately for the two boats, at their most vulnerable, an Avenger aircraft from USS *Card* arrived on the scene and began to circle while calling for reinforcement. After sporadic flak was fired towards the American aircraft,

---

[88] *The U-Boat War In The Atlantic*, Günther Hessler, Volume III, p. 35.

Kptlt. Heinz Hungerhausen aboard *U91* ordered the refuelling pipe cast off and his U-boat dived. A brief signal was later sent to BdU warning U-boat command that the refuelling had been aborted and that Hungerhausen's last glimpse of *U584* was as she also prepared to dive before the aircraft pounced.

While Lieutenant W.S. Fowler circled above the scene, support from two other avengers arrived and he began his own attack. *U584* was in the process of submerging when Fowler dropped a 'Fido' homing torpedo slightly ahead of the U-boat's swirl. A single explosion followed by oil and debris rising to the surface marked the end of the U-boat, its crew and the *B-Dienst* team, fifty-three men in all.

16 November: *'U732 Vermisst ein Stern.'*

Oblt.z.S. Claus-Peter Carlsen had taken *U732* from Brest at 1600hrs on 17 October. Bound for Toulon, *U732* was scheduled to transfer flotillas after her passage through the Gibraltar bottleneck into the Mediterranean. The boat's third patrol was to be her last, with no credited sinkings so far.

During the night of 30 October the U-boat's bridge watch heard aircraft attacking what they presumed was another submarine nearby. The alarm was raised and *U732* slipped beneath the surface for two hours. The following morning another cautionary dive to 300 feet was made, the U-boat proceeding at slow speed as she crept towards Gibraltar.

Later that day the chilling sound of distant depth charges was heard before a strong hydrophone trace heralded the arrival of the anti-submarine trawler HMT *Imperialist*. At 1300hrs near Cape Spartel Lieutenant Commander B.H.C. Rodgers' trawler dropped a pattern of ten depth charges on its freshly acquired ASDIC trace that was *U732*. To the German crew's dismay their U-boat was blasted to the surface by charges exploding beneath their keel. As the U-boat broke surface she came under prolonged and accurate cannon fire from *Imperialist*, charging toward them. Hits were taken by *U732* before Carlsen managed to get his battered boat crash-dived. A further ten depth charges followed the U-boat down, then a final parting shot of eight as *U732* tumbled deeper. Out of control, the U-boat struck the sandy seabed at approximately 100 fathoms (585 feet). Aboard *Imperialist* the U-boat was presumed sunk by their attack and Rodgers broke off the assault to continue anti-submarine patrolling, crewmen painting the silhouette of a U-boat on their ship's bridge (later Rodgers received the DFC for the 'sinking' of *U732*).

Nearly 600 feet below him the U-boat was in sad shape. After assessing the various damage reports, it was found that W/T equipment was inoperable, as were the compass and both periscopes. Several diving tanks appeared to have been punctured and, perhaps most crucially, the pressure hull had begun to leak, cracked by the depth-charging. Carlsen ordered total silence aboard the U-boat as necessary personnel undertook essential repairs, and *U732* drifted with the tide to the audible scraping of sand beneath her keel. Eight hours passed before the boat was made ready for an emergency attempt at surfacing.

Sand had entered the hydroplane shafts, causing them to become jammed in the 'hard rise' position.

As breathing air aboard the damaged boat became thicker and heavier with carbon dioxide and the creeping paralysis of oxygen starvation crept over the crew, Carlsen prepared to order his boat surfaced, using the last 400lbs of compressed air available to blow tanks. As the U-boat neared the surface the captain ordered the cap of the stern torpedo tube opened, and as a last vague attempt, the torpedo was fired. However, it missed its target completely. Worse was to follow as, with the loss of weight and compensating blast of water too slow to maintain trim, the U-boat began to rise.

U732 crashed headlong to the surface in an otherwise empty sea. Carlsen immediately ordered diesels fired as the crew sucked greedily on fresh sea air flooding the humid interior. The U-boat had an extreme list to starboard and made heavy way through the water. With destroyers circling nearby, Carlsen commanded cumbersome *Aphrodite* radar decoy balloons released. It was to no avail.

As the crippled boat ploughed slowly west she was bracketed squarely in the piercing searchlight of the British destroyer HMS *Douglas*. Astern of *U732*, aboard the pursuing Royal Navy ship, Lieutenant Commander K.H.J. Phibbs ordered his guns to open fire and hits were scored almost immediately killing several of the Kriegsmarine crew. Bowing to the inevitable, Carlsen directed the boat abandoned and scuttled. He was remembered by survivors to be checking the life-jackets of crewmen ascending to the conning tower and 'coolly handing out reserve life-jackets which were stacked near the bridge' to those escaping crewmen who had forgotten theirs. Finally, as the German survivors were swimming away, and the Chief Engineer Günter Feist had ensured that scuttling would take place, HMS *Douglas* fired a brief round with machine guns at *U732*, then passed over the sinking boat, dropping ten depth charges to ensure its doom. Oblt.z.S. Claus-Peter Carlsen and eighteen men were rescued, thirty-one died with their ship.

20 November: Further unusual visitors were recorded by Winter. *UIT21* (ex-*Guiseppe Finzi*) and *UIT22* (ex-*Alpino Bagnolini*) arrived from Bordeaux's 12th U-Flotilla. The high-towered ex-Italian U-boats from the Atlantic BETASOM command had been seized by the Kriegsmarine following Italy's capitulation and commissioned into their ranks during October 1943 as transport boats. Both were engaged upon familiarization trials for their respective crews. (*UIT21* never became operational, decommissioned in Bordeaux on 15 April 1944 and blown up on 20 August, while *UIT22* departed for the Far East in January 1944, but was destroyed by aircraft south of Cape Town on 11 March 1944).

21 November: *U415* and *U653* both slipped from Brest headed for operations west of the British Isles as part of the *Coronel* group, lying submerged in wait for westbound convoys.

Flotilla-mate *U413* returned at midday following one month and nineteen days of unsuccessful hunting. Kptlt. Gustav Poel had participated in *Schlieffen* group operations south-west of Iceland. This U-boat group, harried by aircraft from Icelandic airfields, failed to dent target convoy ONS 20, a single straggling ship being sunk, while several U-boats were sunk or damaged due to Dönitz's instructions to stay surfaced and 'fight it out' in force at the time. Although newly fitted double 2cm anti-aircraft weapons proved highly trustworthy regarding their rate of fire and reliability in action, the small-calibre shell seemed to lack the necessary force to disable oncoming aircraft. There was one further disadvantage to the increased level of flak weaponry aboard Type VII U-boats. In even a moderate swell the submarines rolled badly, now top-heavy with cannons and armour plating. Swaying as much as 30° – 60° on some occasions – from the vertical was routinely reported, making life physically more demanding on U-boat crews, often young and inexperienced.

To compound German miseries, aboard Poel's boat was an experimental radar (*Grenzwellenekapfänger*) as well as direction finding equipment (*Presskohle*) accompanied by a small operating team on board. Another U-boat belonging to the group, *U631*, also carried the equipment for this evaluation patrol. Stationed at opposite ends of the patrol line, the task of both boats was to track enemy convoy movements, reporting course changes. The mission was deemed a failure. Several reports were incorrect, one particular report by Poel tracking a convoy on a north-westerly course, in direct conflict with *U91*'s hydrophone report of the convoy taking a south-westerly course. BdU opted to follow *U413*'s directions, which were unfortunately inaccurate, the *Schlieffen* pack haring off for hours in the wrong direction.

Unrewarding participation in *Siegfried*, *Körner* and *Tirpitz* packs followed before *U413* ended its dismal fourth complete combat patrol.

24th November: *'U306 Vermisst ein Stern.'*

Kptlt. Claus von Trotha's participation in *Schill* operations against MKS 28/SL138 was brief and unsuccessful, his final communication with BdU received on 25 October from Grid reference BE 85. Six days later after being located by two escorts' ASDICs – destroyer HMS *Whitehall* and corvette HMS *Geranium* – the U-boat was attacked with fearsome Hedgehog barrages. Minutes after the charges had detonated, the British ships retrieved splintered internal woodwork from the disturbed grey water. Claus von Trotha and his fifty-man crew were killed during the U-boat's third war patrol.

Late November and early December found several U-boats arriving in harbour, only two departing for patrol, *U305* on 8 December at 1700hrs and *U731* slipping from the concrete pens at 1600hrs on 19 December. As weather deteriorated at sea with the grip of winter tightening, meagre results were replaced with no gains at all for 1st U-Flotilla in combat. New boat *U426* arrived at 1130hrs on 29 November, one ship torpedoed and sunk – the British SS *Essex Lance* (6,625 tons) straggler from ONS 20 – during seven weeks at sea. Oblt.z.S. Christian Reich, ex-Watch Officer aboard *UA* and

U202, ended his first combat command mission with one wounded crewman hospitalized at Brest, injured in an aircraft attack during the *Schill* deployment, and a second crewman killed. Another newcomer, Oblt.z.S. Henning Schümann's *U392*, sailed for Brest, slipping from the bomb-damaged city of Kiel on 2 December after seven months of working up in the Baltic.

Oblt.z.S. Karl Boddenburg's *U963* finally arrived in Brest on 3 December at 1000hrs, no victories to the boat's credit. Boddenburg's first attempt at transferring from Trondheim's frozen waters in early September had resulted in debilitating damage from pack ice and a premature return to Trondheim. Sailing again during early October *U963* participated in *Siegfried*, *Körner* and *Eisenhart* operations before sailing empty-handed to Brest.

The final new arrival, *U424*, entered the Brest military harbour at 1000hrs on 15 December. Next to the entry regarding Oblt.z.S. Günter Lüders' newly operational U-boat Winter recorded the familiar *'Keine Tonnen'* entry. German fortunes continued to fade to nothing.

U238 restored a measure of pride to the flotilla upon its return on 12 December. Kptlt. Horst Hepp (incorrectly) claimed the sinking of a single Corvette during the *Schill* action against MKS30/SL139. At 2315hrs on 19 November Hepp had fired a solitary *Zaunkönig* torpedo at the convoy escorts but to no effect, the Germans misled by the distant sound of detonation. Hepp also landed two captured RAF men, their aircraft ditched on 27 November after being shot down in flames nearby. Unwittingly, the two men were indirectly responsible for the loss of two of *U238*'s crew and five men injured three days later.

After Hepp had interrogated the two British prisoners he sent a lengthy, and pointless, report to BdU of his findings. Nearby Allied ships used their accurate 'Huff Duff' equipment to pinpoint the U-boat, which had been ordered to rendezvous with *U764* in order to hand over the prisoners. Zeroing in on the rendezvous, Avenger and Wildcat aircraft from USS *Bogue* attacked both U-boats while surfaced, through heavy flak. Lieutenant J.E. Ogle's Avenger managed to hit *U238* badly, killing the two men and wounding five, including the commander. Diving away from the hostile aircraft, Hepp aborted his patrol and returned to Brest.

3 December: While combat raged in the Atlantic and Biscay KK Werner Winter closed the book on Kptlt. Hans Karpf and his crew of forty-seven; *'U632 Vermisst zwei Stern.'*

> 'No new information, except boat is believed to have sunk an 8 000BRT "Nordana" type steamer on 6 April [in fact the Dutch 7,065-ton SS *Blitar*].
>
> 'Supplementary message for 1st U-Flotilla: In case no definite news arrives before 10 December, letters are to be sent after Christmas.'

Christmas came and went for the 1st U-Flotilla, the last in its brief existence.

10.

ATTRITION

1 JANUARY 1944 to 30 JUNE 1944

New Year's Day 1944 found 1st U-Flotilla at an on-paper strength of twenty U-boats:

U238 – Kptlt Horst Hepp, dry-docked in Brest undergoing damage repair.

U263 – Kptlt Kurt Nölke, nearing completion of re-conversion to normal configuration from that of a 'flak boat' following over a year in La Pallice dry dock repairing severe damage sustained in November 1942.

U271 – Kptlt Curt Barleben, reconversion from 'flak boat' completed and the boat preparing for patrol in eight days.

U276 – Kptlt Rolf Borchers, still in Kiel preparing for baptismal patrol.

U305 – Kptlt Rudolf Bahr, at sea as part of *Borkum* pack north-east of the Azores.

U311 – Kptlt Joachim Zander, operating west of Ireland as part of three-boat *Rügen 5* pack.

U392 – Oblt.z.S. Henning Schümann also operating west of Ireland, Schümann's boat as part of four-boat *Rügen 4*.

U413 – Kptlt Gustav Poel, moored in Brest undergoing routine between-mission maintenance.

U415 – Kptlt Kurt Neide, returning from operations north-west of Cape Ortegal as part of *Borkum* pack.

U424 – Oblt.z.S. Günter Lüders, undergoing routine maintenance in Brest.

U426 – Oblt.z.S. Christian Reich, preparing for the boat's second patrol after repairing damage inflicted by air attack during November.

U441 – Kptlt. Klaus Hartmann, nearly completed the removal of extra flak weapons from the boat's brief but spectacular 'flak boat' career.

U471 – Kptlt. Friedrich Kloevekorn, operating as part of *Rügen 3* west of Ireland.

U603 – Oblt.z.S. Rudolf Batz, the U-boat undergoing a complete refit at Brest.

U625 – Kptlt. Hans Benker, patrolling as part of *Rügen 6* west of Ireland, the young commander only one day from tragedy.

U629 – Oblt.z.S. Hans-Helmuth Bugs, returning to Brest from Cape Farewell with passengers aboard.

U653 – Oblt.z.S. Hans-Albrecht Kandler, operating as part of *Rügen 6*.

U731 – Oblt.z.S. Graf von Keller, proceeding from Brest to the sea west of Ireland to join *Rügen* boats.

U741 – Oblt.z.S. Gerhard Palmgren, freed from operations as part of *Sylt* pack west of Ireland and reforming with *Rügen* boats for fresh patrolling.

U963 – Oblt.z.S. Karl Boddenberg, preparing for the boat's second patrol after maintenance inside Lorient's Keroman bunker.

5 January: At 1700hrs Oblt.z.S. Hans-Helmuth Bugs brought *U629* around mid-channel Mengham buoy and into Brest's natural harbour enclave. Sailing past the concrete boundary of the military inner harbour, Bugs' crew lined up on their forecasing to take the salute of their small reception committee. *U629* had been in action since December 1942 as a member of Bergen's 11th U-Flotilla, transferring to Winter's Flotilla from the Arctic wastes during November 1943. After sailing from Narvik on 21 November Bugs and his men had spent all of the final month of 1943 in the Atlantic and were claiming their first ever combat victory.

Early December was spent as part of *Coronel* group lying west of the North Channel, before *U629* was transferred to *Amrum* once the expected ONS 24 convoy had evaded reconnaissance patrols. The extended line of U-boats spent weeks weathering winter storms and once again achieved nothing. However, during the interminable gales and violent tempests Bugs completed a mission of mercy to at least justify his boat's presence in the Atlantic.

On 16 December, another *Coronel* boat, 9th U-Flotilla's *U284*, on its first combat patrol, suffered critical damage in raging seas. While the U-boat began to flood, her engines seized completely, putting her at the mercy of the elements. Her commander, Oblt.z.S. Günther Scholz, issued a distress call, which was answered by the arrival of *U629* on 21 December, when the entire crew of *U284* was transferred to *U629* and the dying U-boat scuttled. Bugs, with his ship crowded to its absolute maximum, ordered a course laid for his new base at Brest.

While passing north-east of the Azores Bugs observed what he reported to be a 'small convoy'. Stalking into position for a brief hit-and-run attack, *U629* fired a single *Zaunkönig* torpedo towards a lumbering escort ship at 0234hrs on 29 December. Aboard the submerged and retreating U-boat a detonation

224

was heard, followed by the unmistakable noise of a sinking ship – bulkheads creaking and exploding under strain. Claiming a '*Zerstörer*' sunk Bugs continued for port. There are no Allied records of a ship lost from this attack.

One day short of Brest the overcrowded submarine was sighted by Flying Officer H. Czyzun's Leigh-Light-carrying Wellington of 304 Polish Squadron and immediately attacked. Amid sparse return flak the Wellington dropped six depth charges and sprayed nearly 1,500 rounds of machine-gun fire over *U629*, causing light damage but extreme anxiety among the nearly 100 men aboard. Bugs radioed for help and BdU despatched two outbound U-boats, Brest's *U426* (1st U-Flotilla) and Lorient's *U539* (10th U-Flotilla), to assist. A pair of Benodet's *24. Minensuchflottille* minesweepers was also sent from the Breton coast to aid Bugs in whatever way they could. It transpired that the assistance was unnecessary, *U629* and its swollen crew landing safely the following day in Brest. *U426*, one of her would-be rescuers, was not to be so fortunate.

6 January 1944: Two more U-boats returned to Brest with varying tales of victory or misfortune. *U625* arrived from Trondheim, transferred from the 13th U-Flotilla. Oblt.z.S. Kurt Sureth docked the U-boat at 1000hrs, after being in command for four days. The ex-First Watch Officer had been thrust into his captaincy by the death of the boat's commander Kptlt. Hans Benker. After leaving the boat's home in Norway on 15 November, *U625* had taken part in several abortive attempts at pack operations, hampered by bad weather and persistent Allied aircraft.

On 2 November at 2138hrs, beneath an overcast night sky, Benker's U-boat was surprised on the surface by a British B24 Liberator bomber. Firing back with all available weapons, *U625* managed to drive away their assailant. The reprieve was only temporary as a second Liberator of 224 Squadron renewed the assault. With gunfire peppering the conning tower and the four-engine bomber preparing a depth-charge attack, Benker chose to submerge and his bridge was cleared in moments in preparation to dive. But with several gun crews having to make their way through the constricted conning tower hatch, time worked against him. There was also a further complication. In their haste to get below the two-pronged *Naxos* antennae was left in place on the U-boat's bridge. One of the most fundamental problems with early German submarine radar detectors, apart from their unreliability, was that the antennae had to be removed prior to diving. The wire cable connecting antennae to receiver snaked from the conning tower rim, through the hatch and down into the pressure hull.

As Benker attempted to dive, water flooded through the conning tower hatch, held open by the *Naxos* cable. The submarine was being operated by an experienced and veteran crew who had the nose dipping beneath water only seconds after the captain's cry of 'Alarm!' Frantically shouting for the dive to be cancelled, Benker and a second crewman, *Maschinengefreiter*

Woepe, were left atop the conning tower in knee-deep water attempting to remove the problem antennae as *U625* dived. Amid the confusion of orders and counter-orders the boat submerged, leaving both men outside. Whether they freed the cable or not is unclear, in any event firm pressure on the conning tower hatch would have cut the wire and enabled a safe dive. Crewmember Bruno Bragel remembered:

'First that order reached the *Zentralle*. Blowing tanks and closing valves. The first bridge crew came down, presumably realizing the Kommandant was not with them, but that the dive manoeuvre was already far advanced and that the conning tower hatch at the top had closed while the Kommandant and a man from the bridge crew (*Mechanikergefreiter* Woepe) tried to work on retrieving the aerial.

'By then the boat had already reached 11 meters before rising. Immediately after the tower hatch was free the Second Watch Officer sprang onto the bridge. The bridge was empty. He heard cries from the Kommandant and bridge man from the right aft. He went immediately on both diesels full ahead and turned hard to starboard. The First Watch Officer was called to the bridge and took command. On the return heading calls for help were heard and we headed towards them, slowing down. The intention to switch to E-motors had to be abandoned as the aircraft was approaching again – type Lancaster (sic). Both diesels were again ordered full ahead in the direction of the faint shouting.

'The plane hit about 200 metres before dropping a sonar buoy. It then went out of sight at about 270°. We slowed and switched briefly to E-motors in order to hear better. Weak cries were heard to port and we turned towards them. Engine noise (from aircraft) was getting louder so the diesels were restarted. At the presumed scene of the accident two inflated one-man rafts and four life vests were dropped.

'On the port and stern beams men were on lookout. The aircraft came over again and again, but didn't seem to find us. Because of this we had to start the diesels again, to retain manoeuvrability for the next approach.

'2201 hrs: The bridge man was seen forward and to port and was caught by one man. In spite of sharp lookouts from the bridge, port and stern, we didn't see the commander. Visibility was clear. It was possible to see any objects on the water up to 500 meters.

'*Maschinengefreiter* Woepe's statement confirmed my assumption that the commander had drowned. Woepe stated that he went overboard with the commander and they had been close together in the water both calling for help.'

Meanwhile, on the same day that Oblt.z.S. Kurt Sureth brought *U625* home, *U415* arrived in Brest at 1200hrs claiming two enemy destroyers sunk. Kptlt. Neide had departed for his third patrol on 21 November. After endless waiting as part of the *Coronel* pack west of Great Britain, during which time sporadic Luftwaffe reconnaissance failed to find any targets for the boats, *U415* was attached to the *Borkrum* group, 400 miles north-west of Cape Ortegal. Originally planned to operate against combined convoys MKS 33/SL142 the group was directed to find and attack the escort carrier USS *Card*, sighted by FW200 *Kondor* and BV222 aircraft belonging to KG40, on 22 December. The aircraft had been flying air reconnaissance for three German blockade-runners returning from the Far East – *Osorno, Alsterufer* and *Regensburg* – each carrying vital supplies from Japan destined for Bordeaux and distribution to Germany's Wehrmacht. The presence of the escort carrier and its destroyer screen was seen as a definite threat to the large German merchantmen and *Borkum* boats were assigned the task of intercepting the Allied 'hunter-killer' group. While the U-boats attempted to attack the carrier Task Force, *Zerstörer* and *Torpedoboote* sailed from Bordeaux in order to escort the blockade-runners to safety.

Several of *Borkum*'s boats made contact with their target during the night of 23/24 December. While some were driven off by destroyers' depth charges, Neide managed to creep into a suitable firing position from which to attack both the escort carrier and her vigilant destroyer screen. At 0143 a spread of three FAT torpedoes were loosed toward USS *Card* and one of her escorts, USS *Decateur*. The torpedoes missed both ships, but after eight minutes a detonation was heard, leading Neide to believe that he had hit the destroyer *Decateur*.

U415 spent the daylight hours stalking around the Task Force's perimeter, Neide's torpedomen labouring to reload in preparation for nightfall. During the day he had sighted convoy OS62/KMS36 and decided to launch his second attack against the escorts of this merchant train. *U415* made its second attack at 2057hrs that evening, firing another FAT spread toward the destroyer screen. This time the audible roar heard within the boat was definitely that of an enemy ship sinking, the British destroyer-leader HMS *Hurricane* hit and sunk in a holocaust of flame by a single torpedo on Christmas Eve.

During *U415*'s home leg to Brest she was sighted and attacked by the ever-present RAF, Flight Lieutenant I.J.M. Christie's 58 Squadron Halifax narrowly missing the U-boat with six depth charges. After briefly returning fire, Neide dived his boat to safety and proceeded for several hours zig-zagging submerged.

All of the German blockade-runners safely landed in Bordeaux, although the bold foray, code-named 'Operation Trave', to escort blockade-runner *Alsterufer* through Biscay, mounted by destroyers of the *8.Zerstörerflottille Z27, Z23, Z24, Z32, Z37, ZH1* as well as all the boats of *4.Torpedobootflottille*, ended in tragedy for the Germans. The German force encountered strong British cruisers HMS *Glasgow* and HMS *Enterprise* while attempting to rendezvous with their merchantman. During the ensuing disastrous battle the

Kriegsmarine lost the destroyer *Z27*, as well as *T25* at 1540hrs and *T26* twenty minutes later. Between the three ships there were 395 men killed.[89]

7 January: On this day BdU dissolved his last patrol lines still operating west of the British Isles. U-boats in the six small *Rügen 1* to *Rügen 6* lines were ordered to operate singly within their present patrol area. This marked the final abandonment of advanced patrol lines as a standard location and attack formation for German submarines. Henceforth the 'Wolf Pack' attack would only be put into effect when air reconnaissance was available and functioning effectively. From that day onward solo U-boats would be confronted with the increased power of Allied escort forces while operating single-handed.

January's sailings from Brest amounted to only five boats: on the 8th, *U271* at 1700hrs; 17th, *U441* at 1600hrs; 25th, *U413* at 1600hrs, 28th, *U238* at 1700hrs; 29th, *U424* at 1700hrs. The last of these, Lüders' *U424*, lasted fourteen days before the luckless U-boat was destroyed with her fifty-man crew by depth charges from Royal Navy sloops HMS *Wildgoose* and *Woodpecker*. Lüders had been attempting to open his score by attacking convoy ON223 as part of the *Igel 2* group. An unforgiving enemy ended the U-boat's brief career.

9 January: '*U86 Vermisst ein Stern.*'

The sole remaining Type VIIB belonging to 1st U-Flotilla had left Brest on Armistice Day 1943, at 1400hrs. Kptlt. Walter Schug began his eighth war patrol with operations as part of the *Schill* group west of Portugal. Constantly harried by aircraft, no success was recorded by any of the U-boats attempting to intercept combined convoy MKS30/SL139. On 22 November the remaining *Schill* boats were reformed into the aptly named *Weddigen* pack. Situated west of Spain, this group lay in wait for the following convoy MKS31/SL140, but again they waited in vain. During the night 22/23 November the Allied convoy slipped past the U-boat patrol line without detection.

Kptlt. Schug made his last contact with friendly forces on 28 November from Grid Reference Cäser Fritz 6247, as BdU cancelled the *Weddigen* operation. After this final communication the U-boat vanished. Originally she was thought to have been sunk the following day by three Avenger aircraft from the escort carrier USS *Bogue*. It has since been determined that this attack was most probably against *U764* which escaped without damage. After repeatedly failing to report his position to BdU, Schug and his crew were

---

[89] Korvettenkapitän Wilrich von Gartzen's *T25* sank at 1540 hours with eighty-five men killed; Kapitänleutnant Joachim Quedenfeldt's *T26* followed at 1600 hrs with ninety dead. *U505* rescued thirty-three men from the former, including her commander while an Irish cargo ship picked up ninety survivorts from *T26*, again including her commander. Aboard *Z27*, among the 220 dead were her commander *Korvettenkapitän* Günther Schultz and the commander of 8th *Zerstörerflotille*, Kapitän zur See Hans Erdmenger.

declared *Vermisst ein Stern,* the rating later raised to two stars and backdated to 14 December 1943. Since the re-evaluation of its cause of sinking no discernible reason has been found for her demise.

20 January: New addition to the Flotilla, *U392*, commanded by Oblt.z.S. Hermann Schümann, arrived in Brest claiming a single destroyer and possibly a freighter sunk during their transit from the training waters of Kiel. While operating west of Ireland as part of the *Rügen 4* group, Schümann sighted what he considered to be 'three or four freighters' with only a light escort. He launched a bow salvo of three FAT torpedoes against eight escorts for the fifty-four-ship convoy HX271 near Rockall on 26th December. His first torpedo 'porpoised' and prematurely detonated, his second he claimed to see hit an escort 'directly beneath her bridge', while the third was heard to detonate after a run of three minutes and one second. Despite his conviction of success there were no casualties reported by the Allies.

Six days after Schümann's docking another fresh boat arrived from Kiel. *U311*, commanded by Kptlt. Joachim Zander, tied up at 1000hrs after an unsuccessful two months at sea.[90] Likewise, new U-boat *U741* docked beneath the concrete shelter at Brest, her commander Oblt.z.S. Gerhard Palmgren also having no triumph to report.

20 January: As if to erect a final epitaph over Dönitz's anti-aircraft U-boat experiment, Kptlt. Kurt Nölke and his fifty-man crew were killed aboard *U263* as the boat attempted a trial dive near La Pallice. At the completion of her repairs Nölke's U-boat had been hastily reconverted to her normal configuration following the cancellation of flak boat operations. While undergoing a test cruise offshore from La Pallice Nölke reported that his trial dives had been unsatisfactory and the U-boat had suffered damage as the result of going deep. While still in the process of making a further transmission to headquarters the signal abruptly stopped in mid-sentence. It is believed that structural damage as a result of the deep diving trial had weakened her hull and *U263* flooded, plummetting to 35 metres. Trapped inside the stricken U-boat by the speed of their sinking, all of her crew perished.

21 January: '*U426 Vermisst ein Stern.*'

Oblt.z.S. Christian Reich's second patrol had begun on 3 January at 1600hrs. The following day he was ordered to run at full speed to the assistance of Oblt.z.S. Hans-Helmuth Bugs' *U629*, under air attack with over 100

---

[90] During its period of work-up in the Baltic *U311* had participated in trials of camouflage plating to be attached to a U-boat's conning tower in order to reduce energy reflection by enemy radar waves. Although the camouflaging effect was confirmed, the trials were deemed unsuccessful and the quarter wave plate was found not to be resistant to seawater corrosion.

men aboard. After hours of pushing his boat to the limit of its surface speed, diesels pounding with exertion, Reich was informed that his mercy mission was unnecessary as Bugs had managed to slip away from the persistent Liberator. Speed was reduced and a more cautionary sailing procedure adopted, but no amount of vigilance was able to prevent *U426* from location by enemy aircraft.

On 8 January Flying Officer J.P. Roberts of 10 Squadron, RAAF, sighted the lone wolf U-boat west-south-west of Brest and began his attack. German lookouts had also seen the approaching Sunderland, its ungainly appearance belying the effectiveness of the huge flying boat. Reich swiftly weighed his options and elected to remain surfaced and fight it out. Ammunition was hastily hauled on deck and gunners manned their heavy weapons as the Sunderland approached at a height of 50 feet.

Roberts' first attack was foiled by his depth charges remaining lodged within their racks, refusing to release. The Australian gunners, however, took a grim harvest of the U-boat's bridge crew and gunners, splintering the U-boat's deck casing with prolonged and accurate fire. Roberts prepared for his second bomb run, this time releasing six shallow-set depth-charges directly over the turning U-boat. *U426* disappeared in a geyser of water as the depth-charges detonated.

After the spray had subsided the U-boat could be seen sinking by the stern, with the crew abandoning ship. Strafing the dying U-boat once more, she was finally seen to go totally under. None of her crew of fifty were ever rescued.

The first three weeks of February witnessed only a single 1st U-Flotilla boat putting to sea. On the 5th *U603* sailed at 1700hrs for the North Atlantic. The cheering crowds were now a distant memory of the glory days for Germany's U-boats. Comrades from the Flotilla still gathered to bid farewell to departing U-boats, but there was now a strained tension about each new sailing. The tables had turned and the odds were no longer good for success, or even survival. French well-wishers were scarce. There was no disguising the fading fortunes of the Third Reich, and citizens of the occupied country who may once have been happy to entertain and consort with the conquerors were keen to keep their distance from the decaying Nazi empire. *U603*'s fifth war patrol was the first under new commander Kptlt. Hans-Joachim Bertelsmann, and, reflecting the sinking fortunes of 1st U-Flotilla, it would be their last. After no reported success Bertelsmann was located and sunk by USS *Bronstein* 580 miles north of the Azores. Her crew of fifty-one vanished without trace.

7 February: '*U305 Vermisst ein Stern.*' Kptlt. Rudolf Bahr and his crew had taken part in the *Borkum* group operation in support of Germany's three blockade runners before falling to the depth charges of destroyer HMS *Wanderer* and frigate HMS *Glenarm* on 17 January 1944. There were no survivors.

18 February: Oblt.z.S. Alexander Graf von Keller returned to Lorient from his first patrol as *U731*'s commander. Like many other commanders from recent operations he claimed two unsubstantiated victories, one destroyer and one steamer. This assumption came as a result of a torpedo attack launched against convoy KMS41/OS67 and its escorts in grid reference BE2964. Firing a spread of three torpedoes at 0011hrs, von Keller assumed that two hits were made against a single steamer in the convoy, and that a further explosion heard after two minutes and thirty seconds was scored against an escort's propeller noise. There was no damage recorded by the Allies. Following the attack, *U731* managed to shake off pursuit by deploying several *Aphrodite* radar decoys. The balloons laden with aluminium foil strips raced away on a stiff breeze, dancing across the ocean and distracting searching Allied radar operators with false echoes, allowing Von Keller's boat the opportunity to escape.

During *U731*'s weeks at sea as part of the *Stürmer* group panic had seized the staff at BdU. On 29 January aerial reconnaissance reported a suspected invasion force approaching the French Biscay Coast. All thirteen *Stürmer* boats were ordered to break off operations in the Atlantic and head at top speed for the threatened area. Within hours the false alarm had been rescinded as a bewildered Spanish fishing fleet became the focus of intense Luftwaffe and Kriegsmarine scrutiny. Invasion fever was epidemic within the Wehrmacht.

A second *Stürmer* boat, *U984*, put into Brest on 24 February. Like Von Keller, her commander Oblt.z.S. Heinz Siedler claimed a single destroyer sunk. Again, it was a probable premature detonation that had been heard, the explosion after twelve minutes and thirty seconds wrongly assumed to have been a hit on its destroyer target. Before docking at Brest *U984* weathered multiple aircraft attacks on its approach to Brest. The sky had become crowded with enemies and ruled by the Allies.

28 February: Newly operational *U276* sailed from Kiel to Bergen. She became part of the *Mitte* group, formed to repel a possible invasion of Norway by the Allies. The order had gone out from Berlin to create this anti-invasion group on 16 February and effectively tied twenty-one U-boats to the inactive coast of Norway when Atlantic operations were stumbling to a near fiasco state.[91] The following day *U392*, *U625* and *U741* slipped from Brest bound for the battleground of the Atlantic.

Coupled with the numerous sailings from German and French ports were several U-boats returning from patrol. Ex-flak boat *U441* joined the ranks of U-boats claiming the destruction of an enemy destroyer. While submerged, the U-boat commander and crew had heard the detonation of their Gnat

---

[91] Fregattenkapitän Schutze, *FdU Ost*, commanded the impotently static group, spread between Narvik and Stavanger.

torpedo after two minutes and twenty-five seconds, erroneously assuming a fatal hit. *U413* returned to port at 1615hrs on 27 March, claiming an enormous tally of four destroyers and a single steamer sunk. Kptlt Gustav Poel had been carrying out a lone wolf patrol south-west of Ireland when he encountered convoy KMS41/OS67 on 11 February. In two separate early morning attacks with Gnat torpedoes Poel heard two detonations after eleven minutes, twenty-five seconds, and twelve minutes, twenty-four seconds. He logged in his War Diary:

> '12 February. 0424hrs. Visibility 1 600 to 8 000 metres. Fired TV torpedo from tube V at southerly destroyer. Torpedo launched on surface; heavy explosion after 11 minutes 25 seconds.
>
> '0435hrs. Destroyer not seen. Obscured by diesel exhaust and bad visibility. Radio intercept of convoy R/T indicates hit obtained. One destroyer briefly and excitedly reports condition, then nothing more. Another destroyer goes to her aid and later reports incident to a third; sinking of the destroyer may therefore be taken as certain.'[92]

Again, like so many others, he mistakenly, though understandably by the account of the action in his ship's diary, claimed the target sunk. Submarine-hunting destroyers rushed to the area and began sweeping the sea for any trace of the phantom U-boat. Their R/T procedure was lax and intercepted messages allowed Poel to evade his pursuers.

Nine days later *U413* achieved its sole indisputable success. In an effort by German Naval Command to tie down enemy forces, several U-boats were ordered to operate near to the British coastline. However, air and surface anti-submarine patrolling were so heavy that the U-boats thus deployed were forced underwater for most of their time. With a maximum submerged speed of only 7 knots, enemy surface ships were relatively safe from effective attack. While patrolling North Cornwall *U413* was spotted by a fishing boat that immediately notified authorities of its presence. A small force of destroyers arrived to hunt the U-boat that had the temerity to close upon British shores, HMS *Warwick* falling to a single torpedo from *U413*, blown in two west of Trevose Head.

During 21 March Poel stumbled on to a small convoy, launching two attacks a little after 2300hrs. While retreating submerged one Gnat detonation was heard after two minutes, thirty-five seconds, and a single explosion from a three torpedo FAT spread reverberated through the U-boat's steel hull thirteen minutes after firing, none of which have ever been confirmed. Further jubilation ensued aboard *U413* with notification by radio that Gustav Poel had received the Knight's Cross for the reported sinking of four enemy destroyers.

The end of Poel's operational career followed their return to Brest.

[92] *The U-Boat War in the Atlantic*, Günther Hessler, Vol III, p. 57.

Transferring during April to a staff post as a unit leader at Mürwik's Naval School, Poel was replaced by Oblt.z.S. Dietrich Saches, former commander of training boat *U28* until she was lost in an accident at Neustadt.[93]

March and April were notable for the transfer of six new boats to 1st U-Flotilla: *U394*, *U821* and *U987* in March, *U292*, *U736* and *U740* in April. However, by far the most numerous entries in 1st U-Flotilla War Diary from March 1944 are notices of loss – confirmation of previous notation and the loss of new U-boats.

7 March: *'U271 Vermisst ein Stern.'*

Kptlt Curt Barleben's U-boat was engaged in its third war patrol when a US Navy Liberator sighted and attacked the surfaced submarine west of Galway Bay, Ireland. The ex-flak boat was part of the six-strong group *Hinein* attempting to intercept convoy KMS 40. On 27 January VB 103 Squadron's Lieutenant G.A. Enloe sighted the U-boat running 'surfaced and at high speed' and attacked with a perfect six-depth-charge pattern. The front and beam turret guns aboard the aircraft opened fire as Enloe approached. The Liberator passed over the boat's port beam at an altitude of only 50 feet, dropping his charges about 50 feet apart. Explosions straddled *U271* abaft of her conning tower, four to port and two to starboard. As all momentum was lost aboard the crippled U-boat the stern lifted and then began to settle. Winds gusting up to 40 knots prevented the Liberator crew from watching the boat go under, *U271* becoming obscured in heavy seas. Passing over the estimated position of the attack the Americans sighted a light green patch of water – no debris, oil slick or survivors.

15 March: *'U238 Vermisst ein Stern.'*

U238 had slipped from Brest at 1700hrs on 27 January. The sky had been iron grey and those on the U-boat's bridge shivered beneath the piercing bite of Atlantic winds. The boat was headed for waters west of Ireland to become part of *Igel 2* group – twelve U-boats in search of convoy ON 223.

During 6 February Kptlt. Horst Hepp received orders to concentrate north of the Azores following a Luftwaffe sighting of huge combined convoy MKS 38/SL147. No doubt Hepp dreamed of repeating his earlier North Atlantic success of late 1943. The boat's final communication with BdU was recorded during 9 February from grid reference Bruno Emil 2282, before *U238* was sighted and attacked by convoy escorts of Johnny Walker's devastatingly effective Support Group 2. During the morning of 9th February two British sloops, HMS *Kite* and *Magpie*, ten miles ahead of the convoy body, sighted Hepp's boat, which immediately dived. *Kite*'s captain Lieutenant Commander W.F.R. Seagrave, feared that the submerged U-boat may attempt to attack his ship with a *Zaunkönig* escort-killer torpedo and so

---

[93] Poel later went on to a post within BdU (Org.) from January 1945 to the war's end.

ordered a single depth charge dropped as a precaution. His hunch was validated as a single TV torpedo streaking towards his ship was detonated by the ensuing shock wave, only twenty yards short of its target.

The hunt began in earnest as U-boat and ASDIC operators vied to obtain the upper hand. Captain Walker aboard HMS *Starling* joined the search for *U238* shortly after noon. A second *Zaunkönig* was foiled by another depth charge from HMS *Kite*, this time exploding so close that the sloop suffered minor damage. Depth-charge patterns were periodically dropped on ASDIC contacts, but with no apparent result. HMS *Magpie* then added a hedgehog barrage to the disturbed water, followed by another depth charge pattern from *Starling*. This time there was a visible result. The hedgehog attack caused a second submerged explosion, compounded by *Starling*'s charges. Debris floated to the surface from the destroyed U-boat that had taken eight separate hedgehog attacks and 238 depth charges. None of the fifty German crew survived.

21 March: '*U625 Vermisst ein Stern.*'

> 'Last reported: Several emergency battle reports. The boat sinking as a result of heavy battle damage. Presumed definitely sunk.'

Oblt.z.S. Siegfried Straub had taken U625 from Brest on the leap year's 29 February for its first patrol since the death of her previous commander Hans Benker. Eight days from Brest BdU received a report that one of *U625*'s diesels, as well as her *Wanze* and *Naxos* equipment had ceased to function. Emergency repair directions were radioed from BdU and the boat continued along its course. Operating as part of the loosely deployed *Preussen* group west of the British Isles, Straub's boats was surprised, on 10 March while surfaced, by a Canadian 422 Squadron Sunderland flying boat.

Flight Lieutenant S.W. Butler's aircraft proceeded to attack with six depth charges as the U-boat began to return fire. Initially flak was fired at the Sunderland while it was out of range, so Straub gambled on the aircraft staying shy and ordered his men below in an attempt to dive. The 'Battle for Seconds' had begun. U625 had only just dipped below the surface when Butler's charges exploded around her, throwing the U-boat into turmoil. Multiple damage was reported and Straub ordered tanks blown and the boat surfaced.

Again the flak weapons were manned and tracer arced towards the circling Sunderland. Straub apparently had no directional control, U625 observed by the Canadians to be circling slowly to starboard. Keeping out of anti-aircraft fire range Butler radioed for reinforcement as he tracked the crippled German.

Straub recognized his hopeless predicament and decided that his ship could not be saved, giving the order to prepare to abandon her. He radioed a distress signal to U-boat control and prepared scuttling charges. Two other *Preussen* boats were directed to rescue the crew, *U256* and *U741*, and the entire fifty-four-man crew abandoned ship in rubber rafts and dinghies. As *U625* sank behind them the Germans huddled together to await rescue. Butler also radioed a directional report for the German crew to be captured before departing the scene. No trace of Straub or his men was ever found.

28 April: '*U392 Vermisst zwei Stern*' – confirmed loss.

As part of the futile continuation of U-boat transfer to the Mediterranean *U392*, commanded by Oblt.z.S. Henning Schümann, left Brest on 29 February alongside *U629* and *U276*. Schümann took his boat south in preparation for penetrating the tightly patrolled Strait of Gibraltar.

During the early morning of 16 March a Catalina aircraft of US Navy VP 63 Squadron located the surfaced U-boat with newly developed MAD (Magnetic Anomaly Detector) equipment, south-west of Portugal's Punta de Tarifa. Lieutenant R.C. Spears dropped flares and sonobuoys on the U-boat before radioing for reinforcement. After his first pass, Spears turned to make an attack with twenty-four Mark IV contact pistol retrorockets. Firing the weapons in salvoes of eight, three direct hits were observed, the U-boat staggering beneath hammer-blow impact. Two other Catalinas arrived to undertake similar attacks and *U392* suffered further severe damage from the impact of two more rockets.

Unable to finish the task, all three Catalinas continued to circle while British frigate HMS *Affleck* and destroyer HMS *Vanoc* arrived to hurl depth charges on the now submerged U-boat. Hedgehogs fired from both ships added to the maelstrom of explosive power aimed at Schümann's boat. *U392*, already weakened by the rocket attacks, did not survive the ordeal, nor did her fifty-two-man crew.

30 April: '*U653 Vermisst ein Stern.*'

Veteran U-boat *U653* finally ended her career in the sea west of the British Isles. Attached to the *Preussen* group, Oblt.z.S. Hans-Albrecht Kandler was located on radar by a Swordfish aircraft from carrier HMS *Vindex*. Kandler immediately crash-dived away from the biplane, which marked the spot with flares. Unfortunately for *U653*, Johnny Walker's Support Group 2 escorted HMS *Vindex*, the escort carrier on her first sailing. HMS *Starling* and HMS *Wild Goose* closed to track the U-boat, quickly located on ASDIC by the latter. Walker, aboard *Starling*, prepared to attack with a pattern of depth charges designed to drive the boat deeper before *Wild Goose* attacked with a second pattern.

In what must have been a lucky strike, the first set of depth charges ruptured *U653*'s hull and the U-boat immediately sank into oblivion. Commander D.E.G. Wemyss aboard *Wild Goose* was apparently rather vexed at the poaching of what was believed to be 'his' U-boat. Walker, understanding the unwritten etiquette that he had unwittingly violated, radioed to Wemyss:

'Very much regret my unwarrantable intrusion into your game.'

Again, like so many other U-boats, there were no survivors from the fifty-one men aboard *U653*.

3 May: Oblt.z.S. Gerhard Palmgren docked *U741* at 0800hrs. The initial week of their patrol had been spent searching for survivors of *U256*'s sinking on 10 March. Although life rafts were seen as the U-boat sank, no trace of her crew was found. During the search Pilot Officer E.M. O'Donnell's 407 Squadron, RCAF, Wellington located *U741* and attempted to attack with depth charges. Gunners manning the U-boat's heavy AA weapons extracted a measure of vengeance and hit the bomber, which crashed into the sea streaming smoke, leaving no survivors.

13 May: In the face of heavy and prolonged losses an order was issued to the effect that no Type VIIC U-boat should be at sea for more than eight weeks at a time. Also the intention was stated not to allow any boats to sail for the Atlantic without a *schnorkel* and the new FuMO 61 *Hohentweil* radar.[94] However, practical realities – Allied disruption of production and transporting machinery components through France to the bases – meant that this plan was not able to be fully implemented.

The *schnorkel* apparatus, when fitted, allowed submarines to remain underwater while using their main diesel engines, venting exhaust and supplying fresh air, thereby increasing underwater speed and the ability to remain submerged on long voyages, and also allowing the submerged charging of batteries. It was originally a Dutch design, incorporated in their four *Onterzeeboote O21* to *O24*. With the occupation of Holland in 1940 the Germans retrieved several examples of the design within Dutch shipyards but did not appreciate the importance of their find until three years later. After redevelopment it was rushed into production by the Germans in the hope of reducing the danger to U-boats that were still forced to surface at night in order to recharge batteries, while British aircraft could scour the seas as if it were bright daylight with their effective radar. Although an imperfect and often unpopular device, it was seen as a last hope for older mainstay submarine designs such as the Type VIIC.

17 May: '*U311 Vermisst ein Stern.*'

> 'Last reported 2 April outbound from (grid reference) Anton Lucie 91
> . . . one destroyer and one steamer sunk.'

Kptlt. Joachim Zander had slipped from Brest on 7 March bound for the North Atlantic. En route Zander's boat was attacked by an RAF Flying Fortress, the U-boat gunners shooting the 206 Squadron aircraft down with

---

[94] This radar was introduced into the U-boat fleet during March 1944. It was particularly effective in locating enemy aircraft at between 15 and 20 kilometre range.

concentrated anti-aircraft fire. Heading for the Preussen pack area west of the British Isles, *U311* encountered the heavily guarded tanker convoy CU 17, sailing from the Caribbean, on 17 March. Zander radioed his contact and immediately fired a TV *Zaunkönig* at an escort destroyer. Although the torpedo missed, a detonation heard within the submerged U-boat was enough to convince the crew of success. They then paid dearly for their attempt. Four hours of nerve-shredding ASDIC and depth charges followed before Zander skilfully managed to slip away.

The following day *U311* prepared a new attack, but was located by escort destroyer USS *Daniel T. Griffin*'s sonar. Despite the American desperately attempting to home on the U-boat's signal, Zander managed to penetrate the destroyer screen and fire two FAT torpedoes into the dense convoy. An enormous explosion marked the impact against the American 10,342-ton tanker SS *Seakay*. Crippled and listing, the tanker was later finished off by escorts. Zander had made what was only the fourth merchant shipping kill for five barren months, eluding his pursuers and breaking away to safety.

Following orders to dissolve the *Preussen* group, Zander continued hunting around Ireland's west coast. He met his nemesis on 22 April after being sighted by Canadian Support Group 9, three frigates and one corvette. In severe and accurate depth charge attacks HMCS *Swansea* and *Matane* destroyed *U311*, along with Kptlt. Zander and fifty crew.

The beginning of June 1944 found Dönitz and his Staff Officers, particularly BdU, conferring at length over the very ability to wage U-boat warfare against an overwhelmingly superior enemy. Meanwhile all of the French based flotilla commanders had met with FdU West *Fregattenkapitän* Hans Rösing in La Baule to discuss the threatened Allied invasion amongst other pressing concerns. On 1 June the BdU War Diary reflected the acute state of depression regarding the state of Germany's U-boat war:

> 'For the officers and men of the U-boats, the task of tying down enemy forces is a particularly heavy responsibility. . . . Now, chances for attack are comparatively remote, while those of not returning from operations are very high. In the past few months an average of only 70% of all boats has returned from operations.
>
> 'It is imperative to continue the U-boat war, because once it has come to a standstill we shall be unable to resume. . . . The U-boat arm has shown that it can survive the darkest hours. Equipped with new weapons it must face the battle ahead with that same unshaken confidence that it has even today, however serious may be the losses.'

The same day five new U-boats were transferred to the operational command of 1st U-Flotilla: *U243*, *U396* and the new Type VIIC-41 *U1007*, all based in Norway as part of the *Mitte* group; *U637* (in the Baltic) and *U292* (already destroyed en route from Norway to the North Atlantic). Subtracted from the Flotilla strength, *U987* was placed under command of Bergen's 11th

U-Flotilla. She too was in Norway, moored at Stavanger as part of the *Mitte* group.

During the last two weeks of May five U-boats set sail for the English Channel. The small group, designated *Dragoner*, was tasked with testing the suitability of *schnorkel* use under combat situations. From 1st U-Flotilla Kptlt. Klaus Hartmann took *U441* from Brest on 20 May as the second *Dragoner* boat to put to sea. Planned to operate against Allied cruisers and destroyers north of the Ouessant Islands, the five boats, working in conjunction with shore-based radar, experienced little apart from a continual harassment by aircraft and surface hunters. The best that could be said from the experimental cruise was that all five boats returned to port intact, no mean feat by June 1944.

6 June: The death knell of the German Navy stationed in Western France was sounded on the 6 June 1944, with the Allied 'Operation Overlord' landings in Normandy, now famously known as D-Day. Heralding this turning-point for the Second World War, in Brest at 0138hrs that morning, was the sound of a mine explosion echoing around the cliffs of the *Goulet de Brest*. *M4031 'Pesce Spada'* a twenty-year-old ex-Italian fishing boat of the *Industria Pesca & Sottoprodotti* fleet, attached to *40.Minensuchflottille* since 1942, was no more.

At 0315hrs Brest's two U-boat flotillas were placed on *Alarmstreife II* – invasion alert. News of the Allied parachute landings had arrived at BdU ten minutes earlier, and both *Mitte* and *Landwirt* groups were placed on immediate readiness.

One of the most contentious events related to activities of 1st U-boat Flotilla at the time of the D-Day landings is the so-called 'ramming order'. The source of this controversy is a brief passage in Herbert Werner's classic book of his Second World War experiences *Iron Coffins*. Written as a factual account of his U-boat career during the Second World War he relates an episode in May 1944 when FdU West (*Führer der U-Boote West* or Senior Officer Western U-boats) Kapt. Hans Rösing was present at the compound of the 1st U-Flotilla. Apparently he had been sent by BdU to brief the flotilla commanders about plans to intercept the expected Allied invasion shipping. There were fifteen U-boat skippers seated at the long conference table as well as Rösing and Flotilla Chief Winter. According to Werner's account Rösing began the meeting with a small preamble regarding the necessity of preparation for an invasion that nobody could predict would happen when or where. He finished his short speech with:

> 'This is where you gentlemen step in. Headquarters' directive is short and precise: Attack and sink invasion fleet with the final objective of destroying enemy ships by ramming.'[95]

---

[95] *Iron Coffins*, Herbert Werner, p. 213.

Needless to say an order of this magnitude provoked silent outrage among the assembled skippers, who requested clarification from Rösing and received the same bland words again. The very nature of U-boat warfare runs completely against an idea such as this. To sacrifice one of the dwindling number of functional U-boats in vain attempts at ramming enemy shipping would be wasteful to the point of tragic stupidity.

However, there has been much dispute as to whether this order was ever actually given. The 1st U-Flotilla War Diary does not mention it. Horst Bredow, former U-boat crewman and founder and operator of Altenbruch's 'U-boot Archiv', indignantly states that Dönitz never gave such an order to be passed on to his men, although Bredow was not present in Brest at this or any other time. On the other hand Heinz Marbach, captain of U953 and present at the conference has backed Werner's account, confirming this astonishing event in Harald Busch's book U-Boats at War.

There is a possibility that both Werner and Bredow are correct. In a personal account of the U-boat war Kptlt. Peter Erich Cremer, captain of U333 from La Pallice's 3rd U-Flotilla, recalls an Order of the Day given by Dönitz to his U-boat men regarding anti-invasion measures:

'Every enemy vessel which serves the landing, even if it ferries only half a hundred sailors or a tank, is a target demanding the full commitment of the boat. It is to be attacked even if one's own boat is put at risk. When it is a matter of getting at the enemy landing fleet, no thought must be given to the danger of shallow water or possible mine barriers or any other consideration. Every man and every weapon of the enemy destroyed before the landing reduces the enemy's chance of success. But the U-boat which inflicts losses on the enemy at the landing has fulfilled its highest task and justified its existence, even though it stays there.'[96]

While Dönitz had not directly insisted that his commanders ram their submarines into enemy vessels Kriegsmarine officers greeted the order with scorn. They had spent the previous four years of war attempting to keep themselves and their crews alive while sailing against their enemies. The idea that they were now expected to sacrifice themselves in a bid to halt massive invasion shipping was absurd. The order apparently given by Rösing, quoted as a direct command from BdU, was probably delivered as an interpretation of Dönitz's Order of the Day phrased in his own words. KK Rösing has been described in post-war studies of the subject as an 'unimaginative man' and Werner for his part tends to depict him with barely disguised contempt as a somewhat superfluous officer, more interested in his tennis rackets and hairstyle than any specific purpose within U-boat command hierarchy.[97] Possibly

---

[96] *U333 The Story of a U-boat Ace*, Peter Cremer.
[97] On the other hand Reinhard Suhren refers to Rösing as an excellent commander (of *U48*) and more than capable of dealing with the task of effective leadership.

Rösing, or even Winter, added the final embellishment of 'ramming' to Dönitz's already astounding Order of the Day. Whatever the truth, no U-boats attempted such an insane act and the issue continues to be a source of much debate.

The vanguard of German U-boats put on immediate alert in Brest following the 6 June landings sailed that evening for Normandy, as part of the formidable thirty-six-boat *Landwirt* group. They had spent the entire day in chafing inactivity awaiting their orders from BdU to depart. Most of these boats were still held in reserve, ordered to lie at 200 metres depth outside their home ports. By adopting this course of action these U-boats avoided the possibility of becoming trapped by a second Allied invasion landing, something that Hitler firmly believed in much to the detriment of the forces immediately available to his commanders in Normandy. However, among these thirty-six submarines, Brest's U-boats, the closest to the invasion front (known as the *Holzbein* group), were ordered to head straight for the Cherbourg Peninsula and engage the enemy fleet. Of the fifteen boats available in Brest only eight were equipped with the *schnorkel* allowing them to proceed to the battle submerged. The remaining seven boats of the Brest group, which did not possess the *schnorkel* (accompanied by a *schnorkel*-equipped *U441*), were ordered to 'proceed on surface at top speed to English Coast'. In the words of Herbert Werner:

> 'The message was even more insane than our present standing order from Headquarters. It required me and seven of my friends . . . to remain on the surface and race unprotected toward the southern English coast at a time when the sky was black with thousands of aircraft and the sea swarmed with hundreds of destroyers and corvettes.'[98]

Of the fifteen U-boats that put to sea from Brest only five reached anywhere near the Allied fleet.

In the bright moonlit night of their departure the extended column of eight surfaced Type VIIC U-boats, six from 1st U-Flotilla, shone like beacons to British bombers. The sea had a gentle one-metre swell, and excellent visibility stretched in all directions. Leading the procession was the *schnorkel*-equipped *U441* – Kptlt. Klaus Hartmann as Senior Officer for the group – followed by *U413*, *U373* (3rd U-Flotilla), *U740*, *U629*, *U821*, *U415* and *U256* (9th U-Flotilla). Radar detection equipment aboard the U-boats emitted the shrill chorus of multiple threats. All around the line of German submarines were British aircraft, waiting for the moment to strike. Trailing the column, gunners clutching anti-aircraft weapons and scouring the threatening skies for enemies, *U256* and *U415* were the first to go. Shortly after 0130hrs two

---

[98] *Iron Coffins*, Herbert Werner, p. 218.

Liberator bombers of the RAF's 53 Squadron, which darted into view from the bow quarters, negating effective use of the U-boats' anti-aircraft weapons until they had passed astern, attacked the U-boat procession. The two rearmost boats were rocked by accurate depth-charge drops, but after putting up heavy return flak, two aircraft were observed to crash into the sea. *U256* was credited with definitely downing one of the attacking Liberators, while the other was thought to have fallen to a combination of U-boats' flak. Following injury inflicted by Flight Lieutenant J.W. Carmichael's 53 Squadron Liberator, *U256* was forced to return to port, dropping out of line with extremely heavy damage.

During the fierce exchange of gunfire a Wellington bomber of 179 Squadron also barrelled into view, turret machine guns blazing, to partake in the fray. Flight Lieutenant W.J. Hill's bomber evaded the heavy anti-aircraft fire after straddling Oblt.z.S. Herbert Werner's *U415* with depth charges, hurling the boat upwards and jamming her rudder to starboard. The bombing run had been so accurate that the starboard saddle tank of *U415* suffered a massive dent where a lethal drum had struck the boat and rebounded before sinking to its pre-set detonation depth. As the Wellington roared overhead, a Liberator bomber attacked from starboard with cannons thundering. Hits were scored on the bridge and men injured by fragments of flying metal, including Werner, his head lacerated by shell fragments. *U415* had begun to settle by the stern and Werner ordered all available ammunition brought to the bridge and rubber dinghies prepared in the event that evacuation became necessary. The Liberator swooped for a second attack, this time from port. However, the Allied aircraft had misjudged the return fire and 2cm cannon rounds ripped through the steel airframe, causing the aircraft to spiral away and smash into the sea barely 800 metres from the boat. *U415* was, however, reduced to ruins. The *Wanze* had been destroyed and the boat barely controllable. Werner followed *U256*, the two injured boats limping separately back to Brest, hounded by aircraft and prowling destroyers.

Period Admiralty reports credited 224 Squadron's Canadian Flying Officer Kenneth Owen Moore with achieving a unique feat of arms during the early hours of 7 June – two U-boats sunk during the course of a single patrol. According to reports, while flying his Liberator bomber near Ouessant Island, his crew made radar contact with a surfaced U-boat 12 miles ahead of their position. Approaching the target, the Navigator, Flying Officer Alec Gibb, opened fire with the bomber's nose turret as Moore released six depth charges to straddle the boat. Blown completely out of the water, she sank instantly. Oblt. Hans-Helmut Bugs and the entire fifty-two-man crew of *U629* went down with her. Ten minutes later, another radar contact appeared and the Liberator made a second successful attack, this time sinking Oblt. Detlef 'Teddy' von Lehsten's *U373*, the commander and forty-six men later being rescued by French fishermen and returned to Brest, leaving four men behind.[99] However, after recent analysis of this confusing tangle of U-boat versus aircraft combat, historians have concluded that *U629* was in fact sunk by Flight Lieutenant J.W. Carmichael, the pilot responsible for knocking *U256* out of the fray. In his comprehensive book *Hitler's U-Boat War* American author Clay Blair attributes the sinking to Carmichael, as does Axel Niestlé in the authoritative *German U-boat Losses During World War Two*. Carmichael reported attacking a U-boat at 0513hrs, dropping his depth charges just forward of the conning tower. After the explosions all flak stopped apart from several wide shots believed fired by the hand of a dead flak gunner. The U-boat was considered likely to have been sunk and now has been named as *U629*. However, even if this was the case, Moore was later responsible for sinking 1st U-Flotilla's *U441* on the night of 8 June, thus earning the accolade accorded to him. The ex-flak boat that had weathered many violent air attacks during its career was sent to the bottom with all hands by Liberator depth charges.

During 7 June another of the non-*schnorkel* group was forced to abort from its mission. *U963* was knocked out of the fight with damage caused by a 53 Squadron Liberator to the north-west of Ouessant. Aboard *U413* there was no triumph either. Oblt.z.S. Dietrich Sachse's boat clashed in the morning darkness of 8 June with Flying Officer J. Spurgeon's 502 Squadron Liberator. Despite having its port engine disabled during the brief combat the RAF bomber managed to inflict enough damage on *U413* to force its return to base. Only two of the eight U-boats that left Brest without *schnorkels* survived until 9 June. The following day *U740*, commanded by Kptlt. Günther Stark, disappeared west-south-west of the Scilly Isles. There is some confusion as to whether the U-boat was sunk by Flight Lieutenant A.K. Sherwood's 120 Squadron Liberator, or from an unknown cause. Whichever is correct, the boat and fifty-one crew were never heard from again. *U821* outlived her by one day.

Of the eleven Norwegian-based *Mitte* group that sailed on 8 June to patrol for possible invasion forces bound for Norway only one was a 1st U-Flotilla boat. Kptlt. Hans Märtens took *U243* from Flekkefjord during the early morning and proceeded to the North Atlantic. Three days later the U-boat sighted what was perceived to be an enemy aircraft, which the flak crew promptly shot down. The joy at this easy victory was short-lived for the

[99] For this spectacular and deadly mission Moore received the Distinguished Service Order and an American Silver Star. Among his crew there were awarded two Distinguished Flying Crosses and one Distinguished Flying Medal. Von Lehsten suvived the war, after having another boat sunk beneath him in March 1945 when the Type XXI *U3508* was bombed and sunk. His last command, another Type XXI boat, *U3044*, he scuttled on 5 May 1945 as part of the German 'Operation Regenbogen' – the disabling of captured submarines contrary to the surrender terms.

Kriegsmarine crew. Approaching the aircraft's soaking occupants in their rubber dinghy Märtens was shocked to find that they were German – the aircraft had been a Junkers 88. The U-boat and their irate passengers returned dejectedly to Bergen on 12 June.

It was not only the U-boats of Western France who had suicidally challenged the Allied invasion. The last three surviving *Zerstörer* of *8.Zerstörerflottille*, *ZH1*, *Z24*, *Z32*, departed Brest in company with the sole survivor of *5.Torpedobootflottille*, *T24*, on the evening of 8 June. By early morning the following day shattered debris and bodies were washed ashore along northern Brittany, *Z32* and *ZH1* pounded to oblivion by Allied destroyers, the remaining two ships damaged and fleeing south.[100]

On 15 June *U743* sailed from Kiel to reinforce the Atlantic U-boats of 1st U-Flotilla. Oblt.z.S. Helmut Kandizor, ex-First Watch Officer and subsequent temporary commander of *U333*, lasted fifteen days at sea before his boat was attacked by an 86 Squadron Liberator bomber west of Norway and forced to abort to Bergen with damage. During the repair work *U743* received a *schnorkel* in what would amount to a vain bid at prolonging the boat's operational life.

17 June: 'U731 Vermisst ein Stern.'

Another of 1st U-Flotilla's boats ordered to transfer to the Mediterranean, *U731* was intercepted on 15 May by two MAD-equipped Catalinas of US Navy VP 63 Squadron. Hit by retrorockets and damaged, Oblt.z.S. Alexander Graf von Keller's U-boat *U731* struggled underwater to escape her tormentors but was easily located by ASDIC aboard the sloop HMS *Kilmarnock* and the anti-submarine trawler HMS *Blackfly*, summoned by the Catalinas. Sloop captain Lieutenant Commander K.B. Brown ordered a combination of depth charges and hedgehogs fired, destroying the U-boat and crew within minutes.

19 June: *U741*, equipped with a new *schnorkel*, slipped from Brest on a special mission in company with three other boats, *U309* (9th U-Flotilla), *U390* (7th U-Flotilla) and *U212* (3rd U-Flotilla). Oblt.z.S. Gerhard Palmgren had been ordered to transport anti-tank and machine-gun ammunition to the garrison of Cherbourg, now isolated and cut off by advancing American troops. However, en route to Normandy, on 23 June *U741* was recalled when it was discovered that the entrance to Cherbourg harbour had been blocked by the beleaguered garrison. Palmgren returned to Brest. His cargo would soon be needed in the home port of 1st U-Flotilla.

---

[100] Both *Z24* and *T24* were sunk by Allied aircraft near Le Verdon on 24 August at the climax of 'Operation Kinetic'.

11.

DEFEAT AND EVACUATION

1 JULY 1944 to 31 AUGUST 1944

5 July: '*U422 Vermisst zwei Stern*, confirmed loss.'

Sent from Kiel to Bergen for refuelling during late August 1943, Oblt.z.S. Wolfgang Poeschel, aboard *U422*, left Germany and Danzig's 8th U-Flotilla. Transferring to Brest's 1st U-Flotilla via the North Atlantic, Poeschel was ordered to join the *Leuthen* group in action south-south-west of Iceland. *U422* slipped from Bergen on 8 September, her diesels echoing off steep fjord walls as the U-boat trailed its escort towards open water. It was a patrol dogged by air attack.

In thick fog twenty-three-year-old Poeschel joined other *Leuthen* boats stalking combined convoy ON 202/ONS18 north of the Azores. As the fog dissipated over the following two days Allied aircraft began to shadow the gathering wolf pack. Early on 23 September a Liberator bomber from 10 Squadron, RCAF, attacked *U422*, Squadron Leader J.F. Green dropping two depth charges, badly wounding two crewmen and lightly injuring a third. As Poeschel crash-dived to safety in a drifting fog patch the Canadian bomber lost contact before being able to make a second attack. After communicating his plight with BdU, *U422* was ordered to rendezvous with *Milchkuh U460* in order to transfer casualties into the care of the supply U-boat's doctor *Marinestabsarzt* Dr. Konrad Bürker.

On 4 October *U422* was approaching the rendezvous area along with several other boats intent on replenishment. Allied intelligence reports based on intercepted Enigma transmissions had triggered the routing of escort carrier USS *Card* to the area. At 1140hrs Lieutenant (jg) R.L. Stearns was flying at 4,000 feet on the last leg of a regular dawn anti-submarine patrol when he sighted the group of objects about 15 miles ahead. As he grew nearer, gradually losing altitude, he realized it was four submarines moving together. Stearns had chanced upon the stunning spectacle of four surfaced U-boats, *U460*, *U422*, *U455* and *U264*, the latter having just finished refuelling. He made a contact report while circling the formation. As they began to spread out and put up a thick flak barrage the Avenger pilot decided not to await a fighter escort and immediately began his attack, dropping a single bomb

244

and being forced to circle in frustration while awaiting reinforcement, his sole remaining weapon a 'Fido' torpedo.

Eventually Lieutenant (jg) D. E. Weigle arrived as back-up Avenger and the U-boats formed a close circle and began to dive. Two Wildcat fighters were next on the scene and picked the boat putting up the most intense anti-aircraft barrage as their target for strafing. After three runs this boat submerged leaving two subs, *U460* and *U422*, one for each Avenger. The two remaining U-boats then formed into column, still undergoing Wildcat strafing. Stearns attempted to manoeuvre into an advantageous position to attack *U460* with his 'Fido' but was not quick enough, as the refuelling submarine submerged. He held his 'Fido' and prepared to attack the last surfaced U-boat. Under intense Wildcat strafing attacks *U422* began to submerge, seen to turn sharply to port while part of her stern was still above the surface. Stearns lowered his wheels to slow his aircraft and started his run up the U-boat's track. He followed the boat in its turn and dropped his homing torpedo. The weapon hit 50 feet in front of the point of submergence, ran ahead for about 20-25 seconds, then turned sharply to port and exploded. A brown slick formed followed by large amounts of debris. Beneath the oil-streaked water Poelsen and his forty-eight-man crew died. The supply U-boat *U460* also sank during the incident, thought to have exceeded its depth and been crushed by natural water pressure in its attempt to escape.

On 5 July 1944 Allied High Command issued orders for the opening of 'Operation Dredger', a concerted drive against U-boats and their escorts. Battle-hardened and experienced 'Hunter-Killer' groups of British warships began roaming Biscay and the Western Approaches. Their commanders had taken early lessons to heart and the resultant increase in U-boat sinkings was the reward. By this stage of the war the Bay of Biscay region was a virtual no-go area for any U-boat, except underwater or by extreme stealth under cover of darkness. The ships of the *Vorpostenflottillen* were among those tasked to accompany German submarines in and out of their home ports, providing anti-aircraft cover and the always welcome addition of extra eyes straining into the distance for the first signs of danger.

Pitched battles were fought between the Allied Task Forces and small Kriegsmarine escort ships, often within sight of the French coast. The Ouessant Island chain, known to be a rendezvous point between U-boats and their escorts, was a particular focus for Allied attention. On 6 July a gun battle between the British and German ships erupted, lasting from 0145 hrs to 0215 hrs, with the tenacious smaller German vessels finally driving off their assailants. The primary targets for the Allies, a pair of U boats from 3rd and 9th U-Flotillas, had already left the scene. However, despite keeping control of the battlefield, the Germans had suffered the most. Two escort ships, *V729* and *V728*, were seriously damaged, requiring work in the Brest repair yards, while *V715* drifted listlessly under a pall of black smoke at the south-east corner of Fromveur Channel. There, at approximately 0600 hrs, after the crew were evacuated in the face of sheets of flame she finally sank, a carpet of glowing debris marking her departure. 'Operation Dredger' had begun in devastating style, the constant whittling away of Brest's *Vorpostenboote* depriving arriving and departing U-boats of valuable surface support.

11 July: Two small lines were entered in the Diary against this date, but they reflected the continuing run of bad luck experienced by men of the 1st Flotilla. Under orders from FdU West two U-boats were sent out from Brest to patrol within an 80-mile radius of the vital harbour in an attempt to tackle any British destroyers, now virtually blockading the French ports. Both *U415* (Oblt.z.S. Herbert Werner) and *U963* (Oblt.z.S. Karl Boddenburg) departed from Brest on 11 July at 2200hrs. By now Kriegsmarine men were well aware of the constant threat of air attack during both day and night and they gingerly made way towards the open sea, submerging immediately once past Pointe Saint Mathieu. Their small escort ship took the first opportunity to discharge its responsibility for the submarines and race back to the apparent safety of Brest harbour. Much to the surprise of both captains there then followed two days of fruitless patrol as the U-boats swept an empty sea. The Royal Navy was, for once, conspicuous by its absence. However, the German submarines became paralysed by unrelenting Allied air assault hounding them as they surfaced for precious gasps of clean air and a chance to recharge flattened batteries. The boats finally returned to the shelter of their pens having achieved nothing but a decline in crew morale.

14 July: Bastille Day. KK Winter's diary entry for this date was yet more bad news: within the sanctuary of Brest military harbour itself two men killed and one of the dwindling number of seaworthy boats destroyed. *U415* had struck a mine, possibly one laid by the RAF as far back as 28 May, part of their 'Jellyfish No. 5' field, near the mole that fringed the western perimeter of the harbour. It is believed that the mine responsible for the sinking had become stuck to the anti-torpedo nets strung across the mouth of the U-boat bunkers. Thought to have been observed falling into the military basin by sentries atop the bunker's roof, exhaustive sweeping was carried out. If the mine had indeed become lodged in the heavy nets it would explain why no trace of it was found before *U415*'s fateful transfer. The luckless U-boat had been without its commander at the time, Oblt.z.S. Werner having succumbed to nervous exhaustion and overslept. Instructed to transfer berths by the 1st U-Flotilla's Chief Engineering officer, impatient and unwilling to wait any longer for Werner's expected appearance an hour earlier at 0900hrs, *U415* was manoeu-vring to an alternative berth under the orders of the ship's First Officer, OblLt.z.S. Karl-Heinz Meinert Neumann, with her noisy diesel engines instead of the standard practice of running on electric until clear of the inner harbour. These thumping underwater vibrations activated the mine's acoustic trigger and it exploded directly beneath the U-boats keel, breaking her back, throwing two men violently through the air and severely injuring many more inside the ship's steel hull. Officers from inside the Naval Academy headquarters ran to join the growing throng of startled onlookers. Others raced to the scene in small boats, among them a distraught Werner. The shattered boat eventually slipped beneath the oily surface after the remains of her equally shattered crew had been evacuated. Both men who had been catapulted clear by the blast, *Matrose* Wolfgang Brandt and *Matrosenobergefreiter* Heinz Wegat, were killed, their bodies later recovered by harbour patrol craft.

The 1st U-boat flotilla was not the only Kriegsmarine unit at Brest to suffer during this day of French celebration. A mine also sank one of the submarines' familiar *Vorpostenboot* escorts. *V713 'Leipzig'* went under in minutes beneath the guns of the Italian-manned Toulbroch battery, leaving nothing but debris and struggling crewmen drifting in the swell of the *Goulet* entrance to mark her passing.

The final entry on this page of the War Diary was an official despatch from BdU dated 16 July, couched in the same dispassionate words as always and perhaps becoming all too familiar to Winter.

> '*U243* (Märtens) will be declared *Vermisst ein Stern* on 3 July 1944. Vessel left Bergen 15th June. Last report: weather, from Anton Max 41 on 27 June. British broadcasts reported 38 men in captivity. Date of loss uncertain. For family members: boat lost in Atlantic. Reason for loss unknown. Part of the crew in prison.'

Kptlt. Hans Märtens had received a message on 2 July diverting his ship from its patrol area in the Western Approaches to Brest to 'await further developments'. Six days later *U243* was sighted and attacked by first one and then a second Sunderland of 10 Squadron, RAAF, straddling the surfaced boat with depth charges. A USN Liberator of VP-105 arrived and added further depth charges to the fray. The crew abandoned ship, the pilot of the first Sunderland, Flying Officer W.B.Tilley, credited with the sinking and awarded a DFC. According to German survivors, while struggling in the water the U-boat men were subsequently strafed by patrolling American aircraft. Seven hours after the sinking the Royal Canadian Navy destroyer HMCS *Restigouche*, part of an 'Operation Dredger' hunting group, arrived having been vectored to the wreck site by the circling aircraft and plucked thirty-nine men from the water. However one of the rescued men, Kptlt. Märtens, later died of severe head wounds sustained during the attack. This raised the number killed from his ship to twelve. By lingering in the vicinity of a hostile coastline in daylight Canadian Captain David Groos risked much in order to save the weakened German crew, never hesitating in his mission of mercy, respectfully remembered by those Germans who survived for his gallant act.

Between 16 July and 19 July the only activity in Brest noted by Winter involved *U963* (Oblt.z.S. Karl Boddenburg) as she slipped in and out of Brest on further futile patrolling in the approaches to Brittany's coast, tying up again within the concrete shelter at 0900hrs on the morning of the 19th. The only contact with the enemy had been further crash dives due to aircraft and the distant thunder of depth charges in the Channel – Operation Dredger achieving results. Winter then attached two more of BdU's official communiqués, both dated 18 July 1944:

'— Secret — *U821* (Knackfuß) will be declared *Vermisst ein Stern* on 10th June 1944. Vessel left Brest 6th June. Sunk by aircraft on 10 June before Quessant (sic). One man rescued. Probably rest of crew remained. For family members. Not reported yet. Vessel lost in action against invasion aircraft. No hope for rescue.'

Within view of Ouessant Island four Mosquitoes of 248 Squadron initially sighted *U821*, commanded by Oblt.z.S. Ulrich Knackfuss, on 10 June 1944. Part of the ill-fated *Landwirt* attacking force bound for the beachheads of Normandy, Knackfuss' boat was travelling dangerously exposed on the surface. Having left port on the evening of the Allied landings the U-boat had come under air attack shortly after separating from her escorts at 0100hrs on 7 June. *U821* alternated between harrowing periods on the surface recharging batteries and submerged cruising to the accompaniment of distant depth charges.

Around 1400hrs on 8 June destroyer screw noises were heard and Knackfuss prepared to attack. Firing a single T5 from tube 2 the young commander was astonished by the 'wonder' *Zaunkönig* missing its target. Within half an hour Knackfuss prepared another attack but the distance was deemed too great. By that time the U-boat's huge batteries were low on charge, holding only 3,400 ampere-hours. Knackfuss laid his boat on the sandy seabed and proceeded to wait for further targets to stray before his torpedo tubes. Toward 1600hrs multiple propellers of a British sweep group were heard by hydrophone passing to starboard, fading away to leave eight hours of ominous silence. In the face of an absence of activity Knackfuss decided to surface into what was a cool clear night.

Within 15 minutes of throwing open the hatch FuMo contact revealed an approaching aircraft at 15,000 metres. Minutes later the blinding spear of a Leigh Light framed startled U-boat flak gunners who immediately opened fire. Three bombs arced towards them, landing to starboard, badly wounding five of the bridge crew and injuring three others. Knackfuss bellowed for his wounded to be taken below and ordered the tanks flooded and *U821* crash-dived to the bottom. *Bootsmaat* (Petty Officer Third Class) Dietrich remembered:

'Noises indicating leaks came from 2nd port and 4th starboard ballast tanks (fuel) and there was presumably also loss of fuel towards noon. Repeated aerial bombs were dropped over boat, presumably in oil slick. CO intended to go to reception depth at programme time, send message of intention to return, and start home because U-boat badly down by

248

stern. Because of leakage of fuel from ballast tanks (fuel) 2 and 4 it was necessary to blow ballast tank 1. Maintenance of depth very difficult. When boat steering at reception depth stern broke out of water.'[101]

After sighting no enemy presence with a speedy periscope search, *U821* surfaced to immediately receive another air attack. Suffering further glancing blows, the U-boat plummeted below and endured several ensuing depth-charge attacks. Knackfuss found himself caught in a difficult predicament. Above him lurked an implacable enemy, while within the submerged U-boat battery power was fading rapidly with never enough time surfaced and under diesel power to charge properly. Without electric current the screws could not turn and *U821* would either sink or be forced to confront her tormentors on the surface. Finally, as the desolate coastline of Ouessant hove into periscope view, his small element of choice was removed – the electric cells were exhausted. *U821* surfaced beneath the flimsy protection of a friendly coast.

Two fighter aircraft, which Knackfuss believed to be friendly, were immediately seen heading west from Ouessant lighthouse. Ten minutes later four Mosquitoes of 248 Squadron appeared against a clear sky. At a range of one and a half miles the British pilots saw the sleek grey hull approximately three miles to the north-west of Ouessant. Without hesitation the 'wooden wonder' fighter-bombers hurtled downwards cannons blazing as the submarine came within range. Mounting twenty-four individual attacks within ten minutes, the Mosquitoes unloaded 5,000 rounds into the U-boat and the surrounding sea. German gunners managed to hit and damage the Mosquito flown by Flying Officer S.C. Nunn in the starboard radiator, until the aircraft following scythed down the Kriegsmarine submariners. In a spray of blood their shattered bodies were pitched over the side by the devastating cannon fire. Many wounded Germans slipped from the bloodied deck and drowned.

After their sixth firing pass over the boat the RAF crews counted at least twenty Germans, dead and alive, in the vessel's oily wake. Suddenly there was an explosion from the U-boat's conning tower, probably storage bottles for *Aphrodite* gas detonating after being struck by aircraft cannon fire. She slowed considerably as the Mosquitoes expended the last of their ammunition and could only circle above in frustration. But for the Germans there was to be no reprieve. Arriving from the northern horizon was a white-painted Liberator bomber of 206 Squadron. Flight Lieutenant A.D.S. Dundas brought his bomber, serial number EV943 'K', around instantly for a pass above the wallowing boat. Releasing five depth charges as his gunners sprayed the hull, he made several near-misses. Attempting to attack again with a spread of six, he was foiled by the depth charges refusing to release. A third attempt yielded the same results until finally, on his fourth pass, they dropped free and clearly straddled the U-boat's hull. Enormous jets of spray obscured

---

[101] Report GKDOS 120/44, from 1st U-Flotilla to BdU Ops.

U821 and when they cleared she was seen to have bodies lying in the *Turm 0* and *Wintergarten* as well as huge holes along her saddle tanks. In a swirling mass of bubbles and debris *U821* slid stern first beneath the sea, leaving three men on the surface visible to the circling aircraft in their life jackets. A small trawler of the Brest *Hafenschutzflottille* had meanwhile headed out towards the scene to pick up survivors, observed by Wehrmacht troops stationed on Ouessant Island. But the trawler crew themselves came under attack by six Mosquitoes of the same squadron that had originally disabled Knackfuss' boat. In the ensuing gun battle, which also involved the watching troops on nearby Ouessant, one Mosquito was downed by anti-aircraft fire while the German trawler was sunk.

In fact there were six wounded U-boat men afloat in the swirling water behind *U821*. After inflating a small one-man rubber dinghy, several badly wounded men were pushed aboard by their comrades in the water and the pitiful group attempted the exhausting journey to Ouessant. In the fierce currents that have marked the area as hazardous to shipping throughout the ages the lightly wounded men clinging to the dinghy's exterior faded away one by one until only Dietrich remained. Realizing that his wounded comrades that were still aboard the small inflatable dinghy were also dead from their injuries, he pushed their bodies over the side and dragged himself aboard. From the two combined German sinkings the barely conscious *Bootsmaat* Dietrich was the only survivor, plucked from the sea by a Brest-based *Vorpostenboot* originally sent to escort the boat safely into harbour. Four floating bodies from the U-boat crew were also recovered. BdU's War Diary documented that:

> 'Because of enemy action (air) a further search was suspended. According to statements further survivors were not anticipated.'

The second communiqué within 1st U-Flotilla's War Diary read:

> '— Secret — *U767* (Dankleff) will be declared *Vermisst ein Stern* as of 3 July 1944. Vessel left Narvik on 22nd May. Last report, weather, 6 June from Anton Luci L2. Report of chase stations Atlantic – one man captured. Date of loss not confirmed. For family members: vessel operated in North Atlantic. Reason for loss unknown. Because of reports beyond our control from the enemy, the loss of the most part of the crew is to be presumed.'

In fact the Allied reports were correct. *U767* had been on her inaugural combat patrol when Royal Navy ships of 14 Escort Group detected her on 18 June. Two destroyers, HMS *Havelock* and HMS *Fame*, made combined depth-charge and hedgehog attacks on their target within the Gulf of Saint Malo. Despite fire from distant German coastal batteries of KK Walter Hubbert's MAA (*Marine-Artillerie-Abteilung*) 608, the attacks were successful. The sole German survivor broke the surface with escape gear, having been blown free of the flooding submarine by air escaping from her stern. HMS *Fame* rescued the dazed German and the ships of the Escort Group moved out of artillery range, covered by smoke from HMS *Hotspur*. Oblt.z.S. Walther Dankleff had been on his first patrol as commander of *U767*. Their sole success recorded as the sinking of British frigate HMS *Mourne* on 15 June.

No more activity within Brest was recorded until 22 July when 3rd U-Flotilla *U953* (Oblt.z.S. Karl-Heinz Marbach) returned. During his twenty- eight day patrol Marbach claimed three merchantmen hit (including a confirmed sinking of 20,000 BRT) and one destroyer. In fact the sole sinking was British merchantman SS *Glendinning* for 1,927 tons, torpedoed south of Worthing. On the day of his return from patrol Marbach was sent to Berlin in order to receive the Knight's Cross from Dönitz.

20 July: Shock waves ran through the Wehrmacht on hearing the news of the attempt on Hitler's life. All available officers and warrant officers of the 1st U-Flotilla gathered in their mess hall within the Naval Academy to meet their commander KK Werner Winter. Herbert Werner, still recovering from the shock of losing his boat *U415*, remembered Winter entering the room with his staff:

> '(His) face was stony as he demanded attention. '*Meine Herren*, I have the duty to inform you of the contents of a teletype I have received from Admiral U-boats. This morning an attempt has been made on the Führer's life. However, he escaped injury. The would-be assassin, an Army officer, has been captured. I can assure you that the Navy had no part in the plot. Gentlemen, there will be no change whatsoever. The war will go on until final victory.'
>
> 'The disclosure shocked the crowd. Our reaction ranged from disbelief to deep concern. The assembly dispersed in confusion and anger. The news soon echoed throughout the compound: the crews were told immediately before they could be surprised by propaganda on the British radio station "Calais".'[102]

The following day Werner had more personal business to attend to as *U415* was wire-dragged across the muddy bottom of the military harbour by two tugboats and placed in dry dock. There, lying forlornly on her starboard side, the full extent of her damage was laid bare: her stern hull had been split wide open revealing bent and cracked ribs, the diving tanks were ruptured, propeller shafts bent and rudders and hydroplanes utterly destroyed. She was stripped of all valuable equipment and abandoned within the U-boat bunker dry dock, her berth no longer needed for servicing functional U-boats.

25 July: '*U292 Vermisst ein Stern*' – presumed lost.

Oblt.z.S. Werner Schmidt slipped from Bergen on 24 May 1944 bound for

---

[102] *Iron Coffins* Herbert Werner, p. 236.

the North Atlantic on his first patrol as commander of newly 'worked-up' *U292*. The Type VIIC-41 boat lasted three days into its patrol before Flight Lieutenant V.E. Camacho's 59 Squadron Liberator surprised the inexperienced bridge watch. Patrolling north-east of the Shetland Islands, Camacho made a single pass with six depth charges, taking hits from the hastily manned flak weapons within *U292*'s *Wintergarten*. Despite the bomber's port engine suffering damage the bomb run was near perfect, *U292* straddled by charges and blown into oblivion. She briefly wallowed in the swell before slipping beneath the surface with her fifty-one-man crew.

1 August: The day dawned in Brittany with the 'U-boat meadows' at *Château de Trévarez* reduced to ruins following a successful raid by five Mosquitoes of 613 Squadron. No longer would the grand red brick building and its sumptuous grounds play host to German or Japanese submariners.

Coupled with this blow to morale came a more devastating operational development. The British began 'Operation Kinetic', an Admiralty plan to achieve during August the complete elimination of all remaining Kriegsmarine vessels in Western France. Concentrating on the coastline stretching between Bordeaux and Brest, the operation continued the well-established Allied theme of air and naval cooperation. It was promoted as a move to force a decision along the Atlantic Coast and was firmly backed by Prime Minister Winston Churchill amongst others. In command of the operation was Vice-Admiral F.H.G. Dalrymple-Hamilton, lent to Western Approaches Command from the British Home Fleet, aboard the cruiser HMS *Diadem*. With all eyes on the desperate ground combat in central France, the feeling among the Allied High Command was that it was almost a 'tidying-up' operation.

'Operation Kinetic' had two goals: the elimination of the Kriegsmarine in the west and the assisting of the American ground forces' liberation of France's Atlantic coast. For this proposed knockout blow the now familiar Royal Navy 'Escort Groups' and 'Task Forces' were used to blockade French Atlantic ports with aggressive patrolling, while RAF Coastal Command aircraft were in turn tasked with increasing still further their level of anti-shipping attacks. For their part RAF Bomber Command committed fifteen Lancasters of the famous 617 Squadron (guided to their target by two of the squadron's Mosquito pathfinders) to bombard Brest's U-boat pens using 12,000 lb tallboy bombs.[103] The combined weight of the air and sea forces

---

[103] This squadron had been responsible for the 'bouncing-bomb' raids on 16 May 1943 that breached the Mohne and Eder dams in Germany's Ruhr valley. They actually succeeded in penetrating the Brest U-Boat pens with their massive bombs on 5 August 1944, but no vessels within the concrete shelters were seriously damaged. One of the attacking Lancasters was shot down into Douarnenez Bay near St. Anne de Palud. A subsequent raid on 12 August saw no Lancasters lost despite heavy flak, but similar mediocre results, more hits on the bunker and two tankers sunk.

involved was unleashed on 1 August, and the next thirty days would witness a combat ferocity that Brittany had not yet seen during this war.

2 August: *U413* sailed from Brest, bound for the English Channel. It lasted eighteen days in action. Oblt.z.S. Dieter Sachse attacked convoy ETC 72 near the Isle of Wight on the evening of 19 August. Although claiming two ships sunk with TV torpedoes, he in fact destroyed one, British steamer SS *Saint Enogat*, adding 2,360 tons to the boat's existing score of 30,139 tons since October 1942. It was the U-boat's swan song.

The following morning a three-destroyer Royal Navy 'hunter-killer' group tracked *U413* down and attacked with depth charges. Between them HMS *Wensleydale*, *Vidette* and *Forester* battered the U-boat into an irretrievable state and she began to flood, crashing to the sandy bottom only 30 metres below. Several men were trapped in the forward torpedo compartment, their senior ranking man the boat's Chief Engineer Oblt. (Ing.) Karl Hütterer. With remarkable calm the men waited for the creeping water to rise above waist level and then opened the torpedo-loading hatch inset into the compartment ceiling above them. In a rush of bubbles and escaping air Hütterer was blown clear and rose to the surface above, the only survivor.

Meanwhile the ground war in Brittany began in earnest. France's Resistance members received their call to rise against the Germans with a coded message over the BBC, while the US 6th Armoured Division, led by Major-General R.W.Grow, smashed through the outskirts of Dinan.

Also on the second day of August Artillery General Wilhelm Fahrmbacher was promoted to command of the German XXV Corps holding Brittany. Theoretically comprising 343rd, 353rd, 265th, 275th Infantry Divisions, and with General Bernhard Ramcke's *2.Fallschirmjäger* Division also attached, his forces stretched from north of Brest to Saint Nazaire. In fact many of his units had been shattered in Normandy and were either no longer within his sphere of command or were mere shadows of their former selves. His mission brief held three aims: preserve the submarine bases; deny the Allies use of any Atlantic ports as supply heads; and tie down the maximum number of allied units. Fahrmbacher's first actions were to bring him into direct conflict with the overall commander of the region's Kriegsmarine forces, KA Kähler, when he ordered the immediate evacuation of numerous coastal garrisons, and their troops moved to the nearest *Festung* city. Informed of this action by General Rausch of the 343rd Infantry Division, as he pulled his men away from the vulnerable coastline above Le Conquet and between Saint Nic and Concarneau, Kähler was furious. As *Seekommandant Bretagne* he should at least have been informed of these hasty withdrawals and at best would have vetoed the movement of troops away from such sensitive areas. In many regions German soldiers abandoned easily defended positions often without informing nearby Kriegsmarine units manning vital posts such as radars, lighthouses, searchlight batteries and minor ports. Radars were constantly picking up signs of Allied activity around Brittany's coast. Without these 'eyes and ears' there would be no hope of countering any possible amphibious attacks, still anticipated at any moment. The huge guns of the coastal and inland batteries would also be blind without accurate radar-based target plotting.

On 3 August Winter noted the deployment of some of his men in the positions around Brest:

> 'At 1030hrs a company under the command of Oblt. List deploys in positions formerly held by the army.'

4 August: American troops pierced the scanty German lines in Normandy. At the hillside town of Avranches the anticipated breakthrough occurred, American troops flooding through the gap and racing for Brittany and the rear of the Wehrmacht's Normandy front. At OKM Dönitz recognized the threat developing to his Biscay bases and began steps to evacuate his U-boats while there was still time.

Emphasis was placed on equipping U-boats in Brest and Lorient with *schnorkels*, while those boats unable to be so fitted were prepared for transfer to the southern ports of Bordeaux and La Pallice. Complications arose as American troops and French *Maquis* pressed towards Brest and large numbers of demoralized and undisciplined German troops, retreating hastily before the enemy, took shelter in Brest's U-boat pens, the only place safe from Allied bombs. Huge disruption was caused to work in progress and the atmosphere became tense and often ugly as Kriegsmarine sailors attempted to carry out their duties, often fending off panicked soldiers at gunpoint.

Benodet, home of the *2.Minensuchflottille*, was deserted by the German Army, leaving naval troops stationed there bewildered and demoralized by their sudden lack of armed support. The confused naval troops appealed to Brest for instructions and received nothing more than a curt 'Stay put and await orders' in reply. Morlaix, Saint Brieuc, Lézardrieux were all vacated prematurely, as was the massive and strategically important artillery battery at Paimpol.[104] *Vizeadmiral* Krancke, *Marinegruppenkommando-West* in Paris, upon learning of this last event, promptly ordered the 203mm cannons to be reoccupied, only to be told that Army engineers had destroyed them. Krancke was not well disposed towards the army at the best of times, now he positively

---

[104] Kriegsmarine men left behind during the Wehrmacht evacuation of Saint Brieuc were rescued by ex-*Vorpostenboot* sailor Oblt.z.S. Brusgatis and his select group of men who sailed three small lobster-fishing snail boats into the harbour on the night of 5/6 August. They then sailed their vessels to Brest, dodging FFI gunfire and Allied destroyers before arriving four days later. Brusgatis, whose yacht sported a large red sail, admitted that he attempted to make his men look more like Breton fishermen 'using old coats and hats', and always whistled 'La Marseillaise' when approached by the enemy. In the words of a fellow officer, he was 'a bit mad'.

railed against them, Fahrmbacher in particular. In hindsight, Fahrmbacher's actions can be seen as entirely reasonable, shortening his lines in order to defend fortresses that offered greater chance of holding.

On the American side events were also causing frustrations to the commander of the US Third Army. With only 100 miles to Brest, the 6th Armoured Division had been ordered to halt by his immediate superior US VIII Corps Commander, General Troy Middleton, enabling troops to mop up resistance in Dinan's centre, by-passed during the advance. When General Patton found Grow's troops stationary he became enraged and overruled General Middleton's command by ordering Grow:

> 'Don't take any notice of this order, or any other order telling you to halt, unless it comes from me. Get going and keep going till you get to Brest.'

But the few hours respite that the Germans had received were to prove vital. Shortly afterwards the Americans reached Huelgoat with minimal interference. However, here the thrusting American troops encountered veteran German paratroopers of Major Becker's 2nd Battalion (7th Regiment), not so easily discouraged at the sight of advancing armour. In the dense forest surrounding the town the lightning Allied advance slowed as they fought grimly against stubborn Germans, losing thirty Sherman tanks in close-quarter combat. The vicious and protracted battle amongst the trees, which ended with an orderly German withdrawal, was an augury of things to come.

The following day as *l'île de Batz* was evacuated by the Germans, Kriegsmarine men of Oblt. Heinz Jungjohann's anti-aircraft unit, Crozon's detachment from Brest's III Naval Flak Brigade, also fought a pitched battle, but this time with the French Resistance on the rounded hill of *Menez-Hom*. German morale was sinking to a new low in most areas with confusing orders and counter-orders flying in all directions. The 104 garrison troops recently taken off *l'île de Batz* were ordered by Naval Command to reoccupy the island. This order itself was in turn countermanded when OKW discovered that the installations on the island were already destroyed. Days later FFI troops captured the bewildered men near Brest, with no orders and no idea in which direction they were supposed to be heading.

Gradually, however, a structure was imposed on the chaos. General Fahrmbacher, now out of favour with his superiors, was ordered to leave his headquarters at Lorient and proceed to Brest aboard one of the remaining *Vorpostenboot* in order to coordinate troop movements with *Vizeadmiral* Kahler. This instruction was rescinded before it could be executed, however; the route was too dangerous and Brest had more than its fair share of commanders on the spot already. Kahler meanwhile had finally agreed to the withdrawal of many of General Rausch's troops. It was too late to reoccupy most of the abandoned and destroyed German installations, and, after discussions with Rausch, he saw no choice but to concur with the General's plans for strengthening what areas were still defensible. Strongpoints were consolidated against the advancing French and American soldiers, and relative calm descended on the Germen defenders. The massively thick city walls of Brest, with parts dating back to Gallo-Roman times, were reinforced and prepared for the American avalanche. A call for surrender from General Middleton was predictably refused by *Oberst* Hans von der Mosel, *Festungkommandant Brest*. By nightfall on 7 August the Germans were clearly able to see the impending American attack forming. KK Hans Dr Luck, commander of the Kriegsmarine Flak Group 805, reported a huge concentration of American tanks between Kersaint and Plabennec.

At sea the ships of the remaining small-vessel German flotillas were disappearing quickly. With the blockading British ships squeezing the perimeters of Brittany's Kriegsmarine ports, the Germans' ability to move was becoming severely hampered.

8 August: FdU West was forced to evacuate Angers, arriving at La Rochelle with a mobile radio truck. Rösing had decided to use the (so far) unthreatened port as the location of his new headquarters. Meanwhile in Brest British Stirling and Halifax bombers clogged the harbour approaches with mines while American Marauder bombers attacked any ships visible within the anchorage. Among the casualties left burning and beyond salvation following the attack was the 9,323 ton U-boat depot ship *Spichern*. The ship was so heavily damaged that the day following the raid she was towed out of harbour and scuttled in the entrance channel as a block ship.

9 August: 1st U-Flotilla noted the loss of another U-boat: '*U736 Vermisst ein Stern.*'

'Operation Kinetic' claimed the first of its thirteen U-boat kills. Oblt.z.S. Reinhard Reff had taken *U736* from Lorient on 5 August after his boat had undergone two months of repairs to aircraft-inflicted damage. Easing from the harbour as evening grew darker the U-boat dived as soon as it was clear of the coastline. Attempting to operate the boat's *schnorkel* the device malfunctioned and diesel gases spewed into the pressure hull as the engines greedily sucked in what air was within it. Many crew suffered ruptured eardrums and minor carbon monoxide poisoning before the diesels were shut off and electric motors activated. To compound problems, *U736* was detected only hours into its patrol. The British frigate HMS *Loch Killin* fixed the U-boat by radar and then ASDIC, dropping an unerringly accurate depth-charge pattern around Reff's desperately twisting boat.

Aboard *U736* chaos exploded at the same moment as the multiple charges and it became immediately apparent that the U-boat could remain submerged no longer. Ordering all tanks blown, Reff and his men were propelled rapidly upwards before their ascent ended in an abrupt impact with something above the U-boat's hull. Opening the conning tower Reff gazed aghast into the equally astonished faces of British sailors. *U736* had surfaced beneath *Loch Killin*'s stern. On board the Royal Navy frigate Lieutenant Commander S. Darling bellowed for small arms to be broken out as Oblt.z.S. Reff and several of his crew returned fire towards Royal Navy machine gunners, some only metres away. There was no real contest and bullets stitched across the battered conning tower before Reff and seven men stepped from the tower onto the frigate's quarterdeck with arms raised in surrender. Both ships remained locked together for several minutes, allowing eleven more German sailors to board the victor's decks before the weight of *U736* finally dragged the U-boat away into the depths. Twenty-eight men, most probably killed during the brief gun battle, were either still aboard as she began her final dive or drifting lifeless in the summer swell.

10 August: 6th U-Flotilla's *U270* left Lorient, under command of Oblt.z.S. Heinrich Schreiber, who had never previously had command of an operational U-Boat. The boat was being used to evacuate important members of 1st U-Flotilla from Brest, and had sailed with only a scratch crew to enable greater passenger capacity. After arrival in the besieged port and embarkation of the specified personnel she had eighty-one-men crammed inside her, slipping precariously past blockading British ships and heading south.

On 12 August near the destination port of La Pallice, *U270* was attacked by Flying Officer D.A. Little's 461 Squadron, RAAF, Sunderland flying boat engaged on 'Kinetic' sweeps. Depth charges were successfully dropped from the aircraft's wings and damage was such that the boat was rendered unable to dive. Schreiber continued southward, but after an hour it became obvious that *U270* was becoming increasingly unstable. In the face of dwindling survival odds, the order was finally given to abandon ship. As the men assembled on deck a Leigh-Light-equipped 179 Squadron Wellington flew towards them with its massive searchlight trained on the boat. The startled men leapt from the U-boat's casing but no attack was made. *U270* sank in the early hours of 13 August, seventy-one survivors, including *U270*'s commander, later picked up by a British destroyer.

Dönitz, realizing the inevitability of Brittany falling, had ordered the Breton ports' arsenals to concentrate all their efforts toward equipping U-boats with the *schnorkel* device. While Allied ships south of Penmarc'h bombarded German forces at Concarneau with impunity, *Sperrbrecher 157*, commanded by KK Notholt, was loaded in Brest with *schnorkel* parts bound for the still unthreatened ports of La Pallice and Bordeaux. Only a small escort was to be provided for this clandestine sailing. Two armed trawlers of *7.Vorpostenflottille* – *V719* and *V720* – were assigned to accompany the *6.Sperrbrecherflottille* ship. Although the mission was ultimately a success, Anglo-Canadian 12 Escort Group – five 1 500-ton destroyers, HMS *Albrighton*, HMCS *Assiniboine*, *Skeena*, *Qu'appelle*, and *Restigouche* – intercepted the small convoy. Within minutes *V720* was aflame and sinking, only

257

seventy-five men suriving long enough to surrender to members of the French resistance in La Palue.

11 August: An American 300-bomber raid pulverized Brest and its environs. Twenty-five high-altitude bombers attacked Camaret's Grand Gouin artillery emplacements and those at Toulbroch, Kerbonne and Portzig. There was little to be destroyed within Brest's city walls itself. Mountains of rubble lay everywhere and roads were often difficult to define, let alone be usable amid such profound devastation. Previous attacks had focused primarily on the U-boat bunkers, any visible ships at anchor in the harbour or any of the surrounding gun emplacements. Thunderbolt fighter-bombers added their weight to the developing land battle with low-level sweeps over enemy installations. Winter's War Diary makes mention of the escalating damage day after day:

> 'Towards evening, air raid on the marine school area. Structural damage in *Haus Loof, Haus Prien.*
>
> 'Bombs [that fell] on the west bunker caused no major damage. Many hits in the area around the marine school. This raid caused one death. Otherwise no injuries to personnel.
>
> In the morning, another air raid on the marine school. Direct hit in the west wing and in the ceremonial hall. Other bombs lie on the sports ground and in the ravine close to the western part of the marine school, and in the harbour area.'

Now with the Germans declaring their intention to fight for the ports of Brittany, a fate reminiscent of Italy's Monte Cassino and Caen in Normandy was to befall the cities which housed these once vital harbours. Within Brest more outlying garrisons retreated into the German perimeter – Benodet was finally completely abandoned, retreating Germans harassed on their way to Brest by French Resistance and FFI members. Meanwhile repeated appeals for air support from the Luftwaffe went unheeded; Guipavas and Lanveoc aerodromes had long since been abandoned and the nearest squadron, KG100, was grounded by lack of fuel.

All U-boats still found in Brest harbour were made ready to transfer out:

> '*U766* [6th U-Flotilla in Brest since the end of July] departs for redeployment in the south. Intermittent fighting in progress on the perimeter of the fortress. Mines dropped on the marine school area in the night of the 7th/8th are cleared. On the night of the 9th the military harbour is mined again.'

12 August: In the still darkness of morning Oblt.z.S. Herbert Werner, late of *U415*, sailed his new command, 3rd U-Flotilla's *U953*, complete with forty technicians and as many crew from his last boat as could fit aboard, out of the trap that Brest had become. His last minute reprieve from death or capture in Brest had been granted two days previously by Winter. The boat's commander, Kaptlt. Heinz Marbach, had been prevented by the rapid American advance on Brest from returning to the port from Berlin where he had received his award of the Knight's Cross, his command passing to the boatless Werner.[105] Carrying several civillian passengers, Werner also received permission to also embark all able-bodied men from *U415*, scouring the front-line trenches in search of them. They were all happy to sail, death at sea being at least something accepted by sailors, which death on land in trench warfare was not.

Exiting the narrow entrance channel to Brest was not easy, the bottleneck swarming with prowling MTBs intent on preventing any such escape attempts. Werner submerged while still in the Goulet, creeping gingerly by reefs and wrecks littering the seabed until in the open sea where a course could be laid for La Pallice.[106]

The dawning of 12 August was to reveal two important changes to the Breton battlefront. The spearhead unit of the American advance, 6th Armoured Division, after receiving a bloody nose at the hands of Brest's heavy flak guns turned tank killers, was transferred south to attack Lorient, leaving only an Armoured Combat Command – CCA – and the 2nd, 8th and 29th Infantry Divisions to conquer Brest. The war of movement in Brittany was over; from now on it was to be archaic and brutal siege warfare. Relative calm descended on the city as the American infantry reinforcements moved to their concentration areas. German paratroopers stopped an initial attack by the already positioned CCA, halted near Guipavas. Only weeks earlier the city would have been wide open to a lightning American attack, but on the German side the energetic *Fallschirmjäger* General Bernhard Ramcke had replaced *Oberst* Hans von der Mosel as *Festungkommandant,* the latter becoming his deputy. His presence served to stiffen German resolve and raise the morale of his soldiers.

Ramcke had earlier reported to his commander-in-chief, Göring, 'Brest is in chaos', but now he directed his considerable energy into imposing order upon his command. The second phase of the ground battle was ready to begin, Brest was coming under increasing fire, dominated by American artillery stationed on high ground in the newly conquered Presqu'Ile de Daoulas. The Naval Academy, U-boat base and its labyrinthine tunnel network became the control centre of the city's defenders.

---

[105] Marbach was later transferred to command the Type XXI *U3014*, but the boat never saw action.

[106] After transferring his passengers to shore at La Pallice and possible transport to Germany. Werner took *U953* to Norway, departing the Biscay Coast on 7 September – contrary to popular belief not the last U-boat to leave France – and arriving in Bergen on 11 October after a voyage completely submerged.

13 August: The 1st U-boat Flotilla witnessed the departure of its last seaworthy boat as Kptlt. Karl Boddenberg and his crew prepared to sail *U963* from Brest for the final time.

In the course of the *U963*'s outfitting the previous day two men were killed as a result of sporadic Allied bombing by Lancasters of RAF Bomber Command's 1 Group. *Bootsmaat* Albrecht Sekula died instantly, killed by the blast of a dockside explosion, while crewmate *Maschinenobergefreiter* Helmut Laskosky died later of his wounds in a tunnel behind the U-boat bunkers, now functioning as a field hospital. Easing out of the Goulet de Brest on her electric engines, the U-boat slipped past patrolling Allied ships, using the early darkness as a cloak, and headed for La Rochelle. A final tragedy took place on 21 August as the boat was nearing her southern sanctuary. During a crash dive at 0017hrs in response to approaching enemy forces *Bootsmaat* Hans Reiler was lost overboard. His body was never found.

The defunct flotilla's final commander, KK Werner Winter one of the few surviving 'Aces' of the early years, became commanding officer of the German Naval troops defending Brest. Brittany had all but slipped from the German grasp. The rest of 1st U-Flotilla's War Diary records the ebbs and flows of the savage battle for Brest.

Winter recorded after the departure of *U963*:

> 'The remaining soldiers of the U-Flotilla proceed south. East and west bunkers (of the Naval Academy) to function as fighting unit command centres. Enemy shelling from the north-east on the city. Numerous hits on the support base of the 9th U-Flotilla. No losses.'

On 14 August the weapons store at Brest Arsenal began supplying any remaining German garrisons in Audierne Bay by clandestine night missions. The intrepid Oblt.z.S. Brusgatis and his miniature fleet of lobster boats were employed for this task, silently ferrying arms and ammunition to Concarneau and Lezongar on the night of the 21 August.[107] The following night Audierne Bay was to become the scene of the final stand for Brest's *Vorpostenboote*.

Far to the north, also on 21 August, 1st U-Flotilla's Oblt.z.S. Helmut Kandizor left Bergen with *U743*, following repair work. A final signal was received that day from Kandizor and then no more was ever heard from him.

---

107 Earlier that month Kriegsmarine men left behind during the Wehrmacht evacuation of Saint Brieuc were rescued by Oberleutnant zur See Brusgatis and his small group of men who sailed three small lobster-fishing sial boats into the harbour on the night of 5/6 August. Brusgatis made his final appearance in the story of Brittany's liberation on 28th August. Still leading his colourful lobster fleet he sailed into the small anchorage of Lesven to embark 300 troops waiting for evacuation. Hoisting sail, he and his men set course for Lorient, where their unique 'warships' were finally retired amidst the blasted ruins of *Festung* Lorient.

Under orders from BdU not to provide passage reports or any transmissions except by special request, *U743* vanished.

Immediately following the end of the war, *U743*'s sinking was attributed to frigate HMS *Helmsdale* and corvette HMS *Porchester Castle*. It is now thought to be an incorrect assumption. The two British ships did indeed sink a U-boat, probably *U484*, but Kandizor's submarine was nowhere in the vicinity of the attack, 150 miles west of Malin Head. Kandizor's sailing orders at that time were to head for grid square AL63, whereas the British attacks on a U-boat took place in square AM 5170, some way to the west, and an area that *U743* would not venture into without specific orders.

On 5 September BdU ordered a passage report from Kandizor upon passing grid square AL63. There was no acknowledgement. The following day a reminder was sent, also remaining unanswered. Finally on 6 October, after the disbanding of her parent unit, *U743* was posted as missing with effect from 10 September.

Brand new flotilla addition *U925* also mysteriously vanished while on its baptismal combat sortie. *Oberleutnant der Reserve* Helmuth Knoke, after nearly a year as Watch Officer aboard 12th U-Flotilla's *Milchkuh U462*, began his first patrol as commander from Kristiansand on 24 August. A final passage transmission was received two weeks later as *U925* neared the Faeroes, before repeated communication requests from BdU were met with silence. Knoke and his fifty-man crew were most probably the victims of extensive Allied minefields, either dying trapped within their sinking ship or as they struggled to survive the intense cold of the Norwegian Sea.

25 August: '*U741 Vermisst ein Stern* with effect from 10 August 1944'.

> 'According to English radio broadcasts *Maschinenmaat* Leuser is in captivity.'

Following his aborted mission to resupply German troops in Cherbourg Oblt.z.S. Gerhard Palmgren had sailed from Brest on 5 July for the English Channel. His transit to the combat zone had been arduous in the extreme. Caught on the surface by 'Operation Kinetic' destroyers mere hours from Brest he had crash-dived and escaped, but only after suffering damage to the U-boat's forward periscope from shellfire. On 12 July, while hugging the south coast of England, *U741* had become entangled in the sweeping gear of an Allied minesweeper, ripping the U-boat's radio antennae free and snaring the port propeller. Palmgren waited for the seas to empty and surfaced to cut free the wire cables. But his worries were far from over and later, while running at *schnorkel* depth, *U741* had her *schnorkel* and periscope all but destroyed after she was rammed by an unidentified Allied ship.

Repairs were no longer possible at sea and Palmgren opted to sail for Le Havre, where his father FK Karl Pamgren had recently taken command of the *38.Minensuchflottille*. On 15 July *U741* arrived in the port. The crew of *U741* found Le Havre devastated by Allied air attacks and barely functional. During the night of 24 June 234 Lancaster bombers had smashed the harbour in an attempt to eradicate the *Schnellboote* menace. During that and subsequent raids they very nearly succeeded: four *Torpedoboote* (light destroyers) and thirteen *Schnellboote* littered the harbour floor. Gingerly easing through the clogged harbour, Palmgren docked his tattered U-boat and began the laborious repair work. After tying up and going ashore he received a tardy radio signal from FdU West Rösing advising not to attempt landing at Le Havre due to the considerable damage to the port. However, he was in time personally to congratulate his father on the award of Oak Leaves to his Knight's Cross four days earlier.

Two weeks later Palmgren prepared once again to sail. In order to mislead observant Allied agents he emerged from Le Havre harbour with a severe artificial list during the day, returning painfully slowly to dock. That night with less fanfare he covertly sailed again, this time destined for the Isle of Wight.

During the afternoon of 15 August he sighted and attacked Allied convoy FTM 69. Staying submerged, he fired two torpedoes, one of which hit *LST 404*, causing considerable damage but not sinking her. Only able to submerge in the shallow coastal waters to approximately 70 metres, *U741* was quickly located by corvette HMS *Orchis*, which tenaciously hammered the U-boat with two depth-charge attacks and two with the ship's Hedgehog. Aboard *U741* there was no hope. The pressure hull collapsed and flooded the bow-down submarine. Eleven men, mainly diesel-room crew, were trapped in the U-boat's stern compartment as the water steadily rose. In a final desperate bid for survival, Leo Leuwer and another engine room stoker opened the torpedo-loading hatch and were blown free of the U-boat by escaping air. Only Leuwer survived, his companion died as he floated in the swell, while no others of the forty-six-man crew ever emerged from their iron tomb.

Brest had been completely cut off and under siege since 6 August. German paratroops positioned near Le Menez-Hom and the hills south of Chateaulin fought their way into the city to assist the flagging men of the 266th Division. This infantry unit had been virtually reduced to Lt Col. Fürst's 899th Regiment, augmented with Ukrainians grouped into the *639 Batallion Russe*. A single Engineer Company, various Luftwaffe personnel and a company each of Naval Infantry and U-boat men whose boats were either lost or non-serviceable rounded out the defending troops. Despite the welcome addition of Ramcke's tough *Fallschirmjäger*, the Germans could not hold off inevitable defeat, but they could make the Americans pay a dear price and under Ramcke's driving leadership the defending Germans had established no less than seventy-five strongpoints within the city by the time the American sledgehammer swung. Kriegsmarine sailors found themselves in the front line of an infantry war.

On 16 August Marine Artillery Oblt. List, of 1st U-Flotilla staff, led a mixed Kriegsmarine and Army platoon-sized shock group into action against French Maquis before the perimeter of *Festung* Brest. In fierce house-to-house combat, fought with small arms and grenades while artillery fire hurtled over-head, the French 'Terrorists' broke and ran, leaving twenty-three to become prisoners, as well as a small cache of arms. One German was killed in the vicious engagement, and, despite their inexperience at ground fighting, Kriegsmarine troops aquitted themselves well. List himself received the Iron Cross First Class from Winter for his command of the small action, as did several of his men.

During the battle for Brest Allied Intelligence benefited unexpectedly from the capture of Kriegsmarine Enigma settings for the month of September. Hard on the heels of American and British combat troops was a small U.S. Navy Forward Intelligence Unit (Task Unit 125.8) attached to 30 Assault Unit, Royal Marines. One of the Task Force, Lieutenant (jg) Angus MacLean Thuermer, remembered the event:

> 'It had been found by a scouting party out between VIII Corps troops and the German fortress forces. It had come bouncing down the night before dropped by parachute from a German light plane that had been trying to put the package inside the Brest Citadel.
>
> It was funny stuff, on flimsy mimeograph paper in two colours. '*M-Schlüssel* settings for September' was at the top of the page. It didn't take Lt. Commander George Kidd and Lt. Irwin Kitchen more than about 12 minutes to look at those sheets, grab their bedrolls, gas a jeep, and take off for Omaha beach.'[108]

The first concentrated and direct American assault on '*Festung Brest*' was launched on 21 August 1944. It was a ferocious combat that swung in all directions, attack, counter-attack and defence merged into one as the defenders were pushed deeper into the city by American troops forced to fight for every street and every building. Overhead flew the aircraft of the RAF and USAAF, supporting American tanks and infantry with rocket and napalm fire. The end was never really in doubt, the Germans could not take the number of casualties that were inflicted on them, but still the battle dragged on night and day.

The Kriegsmarine began to evacuate their last functioning vessels. Seven ships of the 7. *Vorpostenflottille* attempted to break out of the pocket and head south to the ports not yet threatened with capture. It failed and all seven ships were sunk. The British warship HMS *Warspite* shelled the city on 25 August adding extra flames to the inferno that the once proud port had become. In the process of her voyage to Brest she had engaged the massive 35.2cm guns of the inland German battery at Lochrist, near Le Conquet, known as the 'Graf Spee' emplacement, in an inconclusive artillery duel. Nearby farm-houses and suburbs were shaken to their foundations by the thundering guns and shattering explosions of *Warspite*'s massive shells.

---

[108] *What To Do If Your Moustache Falls Off*, Angus MacLean Thuermer, p. 244.

The following night at 2230hrs Oblt.z.S. Gerhard Matschulat took his 9th U-Flotilla *U247* from Brest, carrying several men from Winter's flotilla. They lasted six days at sea, depth-charged and sunk south-south-west of Land's End on 1 September.

28 August: KK Winter attached the text of one of his final radio reports from Brest:

> 'Situation report: Frontline battles concentrated to the north. Heavy air last days. Today calmer. Artillery fire over entire fortifications. Garrison of Quessant (sic) is to be withdrawn. Fu.M.O. now only at St. Mathieu. Because of fighter-bombers U-escorting service only possible with small vessels. Following the filling up of *U256* Diesel there is only the fortress reserves.'

With the end of 'Operation Kinetic' came extinction of the Kriegsmarine in Western France. Pressure exerted by the force of Allied naval and airborne power destroyed the remains of the German surface flotillas. By the end of the operation the British calculated that they had annihilated at least ninety-three enemy vessels. This staggering list was broken down as: thirteen U-boats, seventeen large surface vessels (a total of 82,000 tons), two Destroyers (with a third scuttled in Bordeaux) and sixty-two small battle craft (*Vorpostenboote, Minensuchboote* etc.). It was also widely acknowledged that the massacre of the *Sperrbrecher* and *Minensuchboote* resulted in many ships being destroyed by minefields now left unswept. Twilight had long since descended on the German occupation.

By 28 August 1944 the Allied watch on Brittany's coast was being held by a reshuffled and downsized Force 26 (HMS *Bellona*, HMS *Tartar* and HMS *Ashanti*), Force 27 (HMS *Mauritius* and HMCS *Iroquois*), Force 28 (HMS *Ursa* and Polish destroyer *Piouru*), the AA Ship *Conqueror*, thirteen MTBs, two Destroyer Escort Groups and the always present RAF aircraft. As an example of the importance placed upon the semi-regular troops of the FFI and French Resistance, on 28 August HMS *Bellona* transferred nine tons of foodstuffs, forty machine guns, 20,000 rounds of ammunition and 12,000 cigarettes to a French trawler south of the Gironde for use by the local Maquis. In return, and in true French style, the grateful British crewmen received a large consignment of edible-crabs.

12.

THE FLOTILLA DISSOLVED

1 SEPTEMBER 1944 to

21 SEPTEMBER 1944

1 September: At Penmarc'h French-speaking Canadian signals troops were landed from HMCS *Iroquois* to ascertain the situation on the ground. Their reports on German movements and strength, based on information from the local Resistance, were invaluable to the Allies. Fierce fighting continued in the blasted battleground of Brest. With heavy use of napalm and phosphorus bombs and shells, the Americans forced the German defenders back. The massive Fort Montbarry, built in 1776 and stubbornly defended by *Fallschirmjäger*, only fell after prolonged attack by flame-throwing 'Crocodile' tanks, artillery and infantry.[109] Meanwhile the last U-boat of 9th U-boat Flotilla, *U256*, left the bunker on 3 September under the command of Flotilla Commander KK Heinrich Lehmann-Willenbrock who carried the final letters home of many trapped naval men. The U-boat was barely serviceable following damage sustained during the Liberator attack on 7 June, but she succeeded in slipping through the Allied cordon and headed for Bergen, completing the perilous journey aided by a makeshift *schnorkel*.

The 1st U-boat Flotilla, premier unit of the Kriegsmarine *Unterseebootwaffe*, officially ceased to exist on 3 September 1944. KK Werner Winter signed his final entry as *Chef der 1.Unterseebootflottille* before handing the War Diary to Lehmann-Willenbrock for transfer to OKM headquarters. His concluding hurried pencil entry voiced familiar patriotic phrases expressing his and his men's belief in *'Volk und Führer'* and trust in Germany's ultimate victory. The words may have seemed empty to Winter as he wrote them from the command bunker behind the imposing Naval Academy, home to the flotilla since 1941, now standing battered by bombing and unusable. The Flotilla was no more, her boats transferred first south and ultimately – those that would survive – to Norway and eventual surrender. Most personnel who could have been evacuated had been, the remainder joined their comrades in the front line trenches and foxholes or sheltering inside the tunnels behind

---

[109] These British tanks belonged to 141 RAC (The Buffs), 79th Armoured Division, and operated in support of the American troops.

the U-boat pens. The combat efficiency of these ex-sailors varied enormously and often, despite undoubted courage, they lacked the basic knowledge needed to stay alive in the inferno of infantry warfare. *Leutnant* Tollkien, company commander of 12th Company, 2nd *Fallschirmjäger* Regiment, remembered the arrival of U-boat men in his position facing the advancing Americans:

> 'The mission assigned to the 12th Company, 2nd Regiment, was to occupy Hill 103 that constituted the central point, particularly warm, as we were to find out later. It was here in fact that the Americans made their first breach in the fortified perimeter around Brest. The company received reinforcements . . . the entire crew of a U-boat [unidentified]. Real drama then followed. Those guys were really brave. They expressed their desire to fight. We told them to calm down, but in vain. They fought and died with their words 'They will not pass!' It was terrible.'

At the moment of dissolution the strength of 1st U-Flotilla was a mere six U-boats. Only one of the six had ever operated in Brest – *U963* which had departed for La Pallice on 13 August. Three others, *U396*, *U773* and *U1199*, had spent only brief months on Flotilla strength, stationed in Norway for the duration of their service. The fifth and sixth flotilla members were *U722*, transferred administratively to the Flotilla during August 1944 while non-operational in Kiel, and *U743* in transit from Bergen and sunk at some time during the journey. Before the war had ended three of the other remaining boats had also been sunk.[110] There could be little doubt that Germany's time was fast running out. The 'Weddigen' Flotilla had weathered five years of war with Great Britain, to the exact day. The Third Reich would only outlive it by eight months.

Meanwhile the battle for Brest ran its course. Outlying Breton islands surrendered one after another, Ouessant succumbing in the most dramatic and confused manner. German troops had evacuated the island on 29 August, but twenty-five soldiers returned four days later to carry out demolition work and also hunt for several deserters who were now fighting for the FFI![111] After two days of cat-and-mouse skirmishing across the scrub-covered island the remaining twenty surviving Wehrmacht men surrendered on 5 September.

---

[110] *U743* was sunk sometime during transfer, as stated, *U396*, *U722* and *U1199* were sunk in action during 1945; *U963* was scuttled by her crew near Portugal at the German surrender, while *U773* surrendered at Trondheim.

[111] Two Austrian soldiers had decided to desert, arranging their escape from the German Army with a leading local figure on Ouessant, Noél Pennec. On the third agreed day M. Pennec was a little surprised to find twelve would-be deserters instead. During the ensuing days thirty English sailors landed from the sloop HMS *Rochester* and augmented the FFI men of the island.

On 15 September Winter radioed OKM in Berlin:

> 'U-boat base and 9th U-Flotilla have been forced to capitulate after several days of brave fighting. . . . Heil our Führer!'

The shell of Brest city eventually surrendered on 18 September 1944, the garrison's last commander, *Oberst* Erich Pietzowka (commander of 5th Batallion, 2nd Fallschirmjäger Regiment), surrendering to Colonel Chester J. Hirschfelder of the 2nd US Infantry Division all German forces remaining east of the Penfeld, while recently promoted *Generalmajor* Hans von der Mosel surrendered those to the west. Also taken into captivity on this day was *Admiral* Otto Kahler at the head of his Kriegsmarine troops, one of whom was KK Werner Winter.

Fighting along the Crozon Peninsular witnessed the same dogged defence and hand-to-hand combat that Brest had seen. The south-eastern base of the peninsula had succumbed to the American onslaught, surrendered by General Rauch of the 343rd Division. Crozon itself was finally conquered by brave and obstinate attacks from the tiring American troops; Camaret followed and then Pointe de Pen Hir with its enormous artillery emplacements. The final act of this drama came two days later on the Presqu'Ile de Que'lern, near Roscanvel, when Ramcke saw that the useless death of his men no longer had any military purpose and so surrendered Finistère to the US Army. He had fulfilled his promise to Hitler to hold out until the end of September at least.

Following the end of resistance from the concrete bunker and its serpentine tunnel complex, Intelligence officers of Task Unit 125.8 searched the deserted U-boat pens for anything of value. Lieutenant (jg) Angus MacLean Thuermer, U.S.N.R (and former Associated Press foreign correspondent in Berlin) recalls entering Brest bunker:

> 'We went directly to the German Navy's U-boat 'pens', as we called them. The Germans used the English word 'box'. My first impression on entering the U-Boat pens was of their immensity; they were cavernous and dark inside. A [crippled] U-Boat [*U415*] in the Number 1 pen seemed so small. Additionally, in this first pen there was a hole through the roof. The iron rods that are woven into concrete were hanging down.
>
> 'No U-boat men surrendered to us. The 29th Infantry Division took the place. We came in on their heels. . . . Officers of the F.I.U. combed through the Brest pens and the flotilla headquarters office built into the massive structures, but found precious little of intelligence value.'[112]

The officers found no trace of the daily records concerning operations of 1st U-Flotilla. Inside a room they considered likely to have been the commander's

---

[112] Angus Maclean Thuermer.

office Lieutenant Thuermer found what appeared to be a 'one-stringed oriental guitar'. Perhaps this was a memento of the visit to Brest by the blockade-running 2,231-ton Japanese submarine *I8* during September 1943.

The human cost of this 'battle of prestige' for the Germans was 10,000 dead (and the destruction of three of their combat divisions – 266th, 343rd, 2nd *Fallschirmjäger* – with all three commanding officers prisoner) and 38,000 men taken prisoner. The American Army suffered 9,831 casualties. It has never been established exactly how many French civilians died, both those caught in the crossfire and those in the Resistance. One conservative estimate for this death toll is 965 and 740 injured. Luckily the Germans had evacuated most of the citizens of Brest to the surrounding countryside at the beginning of August. But their city was destroyed. In the ashes lay the last silent remains of Germany's 1st U-Flotilla, the shattered Naval Academy headquarters now still and empty, the sailors either captured by the American Army or en route to other units in southern France or Norway. The camouflaged building complex was pitted and scarred from multiple explosions. Winter's headquarters bunker to the rear of the main building, still adorned with huge red crosses to mark its field hospital status, remained in service until American medical personnel were able to evacuate the wounded.

Below this towering edifice the enormous concrete U-boat bunker, holed by Lancaster carried Tallboy bombs and surrounded by the detritus of recent battle, held only the corpse of *U415* as mute memorial to the 128 U-boats and their crews who at some stage during the previous five years had made up the strength of 1st U-Flotilla. The official record, the flotilla's War Diary, found its way back to BdU and filing as part of the sombre record of a worldwide conflict already lost by Germany.

Within seven months the Third Reich was finished. Hitler was dead, shot in the head by his own hand, his ashes scattered over the torn ground outside the Reich Chancellory after SS officers had doused his corpse with petrol and set it alight. *Grossadmiral* Dönitz was named in Hitler's will as his successor, establishing a hasty government in the North German town of Flensburg with himself as Reich President. His was the task of capitulating to the Allies.

The Third Reich passed into history, as did all of its fighting formations. Where once the world had trembled to the crash of tank tracks, aerial bombing and U-boat attack, an exhausted peace descended over Europe as the flames of destruction gradually subsided. To the victors went the spoils: prisoners, advanced German weaponry, documentary records and tracts of land, all siezed and held by various Allied nations. Within the hard-won rewards lay virtually the entire paper history of the Kriegsmarine, captured and taken to England by the men of 30 Assault Unit, Royal Marines. Because of Donitz's desire to preserve Germany's naval history and the successful completion of the small British unit's mission, the story of the 1st U-Flotilla remains with us today.

Appendix One

U-BOAT TYPES OF THE

1st U-FLOTILLA.

TYPE II U-BOAT

Dimensions: 44 metres × 4.1 metres × 3.9 metres (draught)

Displacement: 250-tonnes (364-tonnes dived)

Complement: 3 officers, 22 crew.

Rated Diving Depth: 330 feet.

Armament: 3 × 53.3cm (21") torpedo tubes at bow below the designed waterline.

5 × torpedoes or 12 TMA (18 TMB) mines.

1 × 2cm/30 AA cannon (1200 rounds) on a detachable deck mounting.

Propulsion: 2 × MWM RS 127 S 6-cylinder 4-stroke 350 horsepower super-charged diesels, in compartment two. 2 × SSW PG VV 332/36 double commutator- type 205 horsepower electric motors in compartment one. 1 × 62-cell AFA 36 MAK 580 battery in battery boxes without rubber shock absorbers (7160 amp hours) or 1 × 62-cell AFA 44 ML 570 battery (8380amp hours) for *U8, U11, U57, U58, U137* to *U152*.

Speed: 12.7 knots surfaced/7.4 submerged.

The small single-hull (i.e. the outer skin of the submarine is the pressure hull with supporting frames inside) Type II A-D U-boats were laid down as coastal submersibles, based on a combination of the 1933 redesign of 1918 Type UF submarines, the First World War UBII Class and aspects of the Finnish/German *Vessikko* model. Models A and B possessed a single periscope, while C and D incorporated a second attack periscope housed within the tiny conning tower. Capable of a radius of action of 3,450 miles at 12.7-knots surfaced speed, their underwater endurance was 35 miles at 4 knots. Comprising three watertight compartments within the single hull, diving tanks were located in the bottom of compartment two while trim tanks lay in compartments one and three. The fuel oil bunker in turn was immediately aft of the trim tanks. A major advance in German design work meant that U-boats had welded pressure hulls instead of weaker rivets. This pressure hull had a maximum rated diving depth of 150 metres, well over contemporary standards. Two 3-bladed propellers of 85cm diameter pushed the single-ruddered U-boat. For vertical manoeuvring they were equipped with two hydroplanes forward and two aft. The main obvious physical difference between the various marks was found in the arrangement of flooding slots along the hull sides.

In all, fifty such submarines were constructed. They were not ideal for operational use, unstable in moderate to heavy seas and capable of only low surface speed and limited endurance. Living and working conditions aboard were primitive in the extreme for the crew, the internal space having no real subdivision. As Erich Topp remembered:

> 'They were fast to dive – the same as a Type VII. But there was not much room, I had not even a special part for the commanding officer, I was sleeping in the bow room where all the torpedoes were, and I had no privileges on board.'

Moreover, in order to conform to the rulebook of submarine warfare, U-boats were initially compelled to surface and fire a warning shot over the bow of any merchant shipping intercepted. The idea of firing a burst of 2cm cannon fire in order to intimidate a large cargo vessel must have appeared faintly ridiculous to many commanders and crew.

Plate 1 shows Oblt.z.S Wolfgang Lüth's Type IIB *U9* – the 'Weddigen boat', carrying a conning tower decoration of Otto Weddigen's First World War Knight's Cross.

TYPE VII U-BOAT
Dimensions: 67.1 metres × 6.2 metres × 4.8 metres (draught).
Displacement: 769-tonnes (865-tonnes dived)
Complement: 4 officers, 40-56 crew.
Armament: 4 × 53.3cm (21") torpedo tubes at bow below the designed waterline.
1 × 53.3cm torpedo tube at stern above the designed waterline (or below the waterline from *U45* (Type VIIB) onwards).
11 × torpedoes or 22 TMA (33 TMB) mines initially increased to 14 × torpedoes or 26 TMA (39 TMB) mines from *U45* onwards.
1 × TK 8.8cm/45 deck cannon
1 × 2cm AA cannon.

Armaments aboard the Type VIIC U-boats were altered considerably during the course of the war. The German Type VII U-boat kept 'ready use' 8.8cm ammunition in an externally mounted 80cm diameter by 120cm deep watertight container. The lid for this was at deck level just forward and to port of the deck gun.

More anti-aircraft weaponry was added during the war (even to the point of the so-called 'Flak Boats' covered within the text) and from 1943 onwards deck cannon were removed having become largely obsolete. From 1944 the standard above deck weaponry fitted was 1 × 3.7cm AA cannon (1 195 rounds) plus 2 × twin 2cm A cannon (4 380 rounds).

Within the 1st U-Flotilla the main below deck weaponry also varied as follows:
U80 had only two bow tubes (a shortage of available torpedo tubes during construction);

U83, U203, U331, U401 and *U651* possessed no stern tube;

U336, U353, U354, U374, U379, U392, U401, U405, U413, U415, U418, U422, U424, U426, U435, U439, U440, U441, U456, U665, U669, U722, U731, U732, U740, U741, U743, U767 and *U773* possessed no mine fittings.

Propulsion: 2 × *Germaniawerft* F46 6-cylinder 4-stroke 1 400 horsepower supercharged diesels, in diesel room housed within compartment two (or 2 MAN M6 V 40/46 6-cylinder 4-stroke supercharged diesel engines on board *U79, U80, U81, U86*). 2 × BBC GG UB 720/8 double 375 horsepower electric motors in compartment one (there were other variants to this type of motor). 2 × 62-cell AFA 33 MAL 800 battery in battery boxes without rubber shock absorbers (9 160 amps/hour) stored below flooring in compartments three and five. (There were also variations to battery type although the majority of 1st U-Flotilla boats carried the above configuration).

Speed: 17 knots surfaced/7.6 submerged.

The original Type VII boats were developed in 1934, resembling closely a larger version of the single-hull form of a Type II but with the addition of saddle tanks. An ocean-going design, Type VIIs were divided into six watertight compartments. Trim tanks were found in compartments one and six, and main diving tanks and fuel oil bunkers beneath the control room. Further diving tanks were also located in the stern. The regulating tanks were - pressure-tight, while auxiliary tanks located in the outer saddle tanks were not. Very much the U-boat Arm's backbone during the course of the war, Type VII submarines (particularly the Type VIIC of which there were approximately 600 built) underwent many variations to their conning towers in order to accommodate increased flak weaponry, splinter protection, as well as antennae and dipole aerial fittings. From 1943 onwards new Type VIIC U-boats were also fitted with the so-called 'Atlantic stem' a 13cm bow extension. Another additional piece of equipment rushed into emergency production during 1943/1944 was the retractable *schnorkel,* a belated attempt during 1944 to prolong the operational effectiveness of a U-boat virtually obsolete by that stage of the war.

The reasons for the continued German reliance on this outdated design were many, perhaps one of the main factors being its relative ease and cost-effectiveness of production. The Type VIIC had a remarkably strong seamless welded pressure hull capable of diving to 200 metres and often beyond in emergency situations. The improved Type VIIC/41 increased the manufacturers' crush depth to 250 metres.

Indeed when Kptlt. Hans-Joachim Rahmlow's *U570* (3rd U-Flotilla) was captured intact on 27 August 1941 by British anti-submarine trawlers HMS *Northern Chief* and HMS *Kingstone Agate* after being disabled by an RAF Hudson of 269 Squadron, British inspectors were staggered to find the extent of the hull's thickness, its superbly professional welding and the pressure it could withstand. Designers promptly set about developing new depth charges carrying Torpex instead of the weaker TNT (the new improved Torpex was 30% more effective than the previously used Amatol), and capable of exploding on a deep setting of 600 feet rather than shallow settings used up to that point. U-boat captains were thus deprived of the sanctuary of the deep – previously unsuspected by the British and a saviour to their opponents.

Plate 1 shows a mid-war Type VIIC with deck gun removed and conning tower extended aft to provide the *wintergarten* anti-aircraft platform.

TYPE XB U-BOAT
Dimensions: 89.8 metres × 9.2 metres × 4.7 metres (draught).
Displacement: 2177-tonnes dived   **Complement:** 5 officers, 47 crew.
Armament: 2 × 53.3cm (21") torpedo tubes at stern below the designed waterline.
    15 × torpedoes
    Two groups of 12 mineshafts each side of the outer hull (48 SMA mines).
    Six mineshafts in forward outer hull (18 SMA mines)
    1 × Utof 10.5cm/45 deck cannon (200 rounds) – removed from 1943-44.
    1 × 3.7cm AA cannon (2 500 rounds)
    1 × 2cm AA cannon (4 000 rounds) – increased to two cannons 1943-44.
Propulsion: 2 × Germaniawerft F46a 9pu 9-cylinder 4-stroke 2100 horsepower supercharged diesels, in diesel room housed within compartment three. 2 × AEG GU 720/8 double 287 horsepower electric motors in compartment two. 2 × 124-cell AFA 33 MAL 800 accumulator batteries in battery boxes below compartments four and six. (1960 amps/hour).
Speed: 16.4 knots surfaced/7 submerged.

Laid down as ocean-going minelaying submersibles, these U-boats were originally designed in 1938. They had a double hull divided into seven water-tight compartments. Trim tanks were housed in compartments one and two, while diving tanks and fuel were contained in the outer hull, almost square when viewed sectionally. Pressure-tight regulating tanks and further fuel oil bunkers were contained amidships, additional diving tanks located in the bow and stern.

During the course of the war modifications to the submarines' conning tower were the same as for Type VII and Type IX U-boats. A hinged *schnorkel* was fitted from mid-1944 on the starboard after edge of the conning tower casing.

These submarines were the first dedicated mine-laying U-boats built since the First World War and the largest built by Nazi Germany. Designed to carry 66 SMA mines (*Schachtmine* or Shaft Mine) and 15 torpedoes, the 2.15 metres long 1.33 metres diameter mines stored in 12 vertical shafts on each side of the hull. However, the mines were discovered to be defective and an embargo was placed upon their use. Design faults had been found to cause premature explosions, requiring several months of modification to correct, an embargo placed on their use until March 1943.[113] Consequently the four Type XB U-boats constructed served as U-tankers in the *Milchkuhs* (Milk Cow) role, able to carry 240-tons of fuel for attack U-boats to use.

In Plate 1 the sheer size of the U-boat can be gauged, and 12 side-mounted mine shaft entrances seen along the top of her flank.

[113] *U117* was the first U-boat to deploy the redisigned SMA off the Moroccan coast after transfer to Bordeaux's 12th U-Flotilla.

Appendix Two

GERMAN SUBMARINE DEVELOPMENT

1922–1935

As far back as 1922 C-in-C of the Reichsmarine Admiral Behnke had authorized covert construction of a new generation of German submarines. Germany financed design work by thirty of their engineers, ostensibly from the Krupp armaments industry, and controlled by board members of three German shipbuilding yards. Under cover of a Dutch-registered firm, *Ingenieourskaantoor voor Scheepsbouw* (IVS) registered in The Hague, submarine design and construction was begun in Spain and Finland.[114] Former Construction Head at the *Germaniawerft* shipyards, Doctor of Engineering Hans Techel headed the company while KK (ret.) Ulrich Blum held the post of Technical Director.

During 1925 Naval Ministry funds were put into IVS development and an order was also obtained from Turkey for two U-boats. In addition there was the tantalizing prospect of undertaking a portion of Spain's extensive new ship-building programme. KK Wilhelm Canaris, sent by the Reichsmarine as an intermediary in Spanish armament deals – thus ordered the establishment of a dedicated submarine office under the nomenclature 'Au' (*Ausbildung –* Training) in charge of which was KA Arno Spindler. Prototype designs for three different submarine models were completed on paper: one small 250-ton vessel, one medium 500-ton vessel and a 750-ton large model.

Three of the small types (*Vessikos*) and three mediums (*Vetehinens*) were constructed in Finland thanks in large part to retired KK Bartenbach, naval adviser to the Finnish government, former chief of U-boat acceptance commission (UAK) and commander of First World War Flanders U-boat Flotilla. A single large submarine (*E1*) and all initial torpedoes and torpedo tubes were built in Spain, the vessel taking shape in the Echavarrieta shipyard. After several years of this covert arrangement a new and more convenient cover firm was established in 1928, the Berlin-based *Ingenieurbüro für Wirtschaft und Technik GmbH* (*Igewit*) Company. Under this guise the

---

[114] The founders of I.v.S were AG Vulkan-Werft yard in Hamburg and Stettin, and two Krupp-owned yards, Germaniawerft in Kiel and AG Weser in Bremen (another important submarine construction company, Blohm & Voss, was not involved).

fledgling U-boat arm began in earnest. Although shipbuilders in the host countries actually manufactured the products from these Reichsmarine design teams, the knowledge was German and experience in construction of modern designs invaluable for the future of Germany's submarine development.

Spindler also needed a combined team of active-service seamen and engineering officers to take part in the testing of the two German submarines built for the Turkish Navy (500-ton boats *Birinci Inönü* and *Ikinci Inönü*, completed in March 1927). German Naval Command considered that for political reasons, namely the flagrant violation of Versailles Treaty terms, only retired military personnel should be involved, together with a small though highly experienced civilian staff. The connection with the Turkish Navy resulted in two of the retired German officers involved being asked to establish a U-boat training school for Turkish, and of course German, crews.

In Germany Spindler was actively establishing a training programme and, in conjunction with the Naval Arms Superintendent, he managed to start a series of theoretical lectures on U-boats for senior Ensigns. These began in 1927 and were included during the Ensign's torpedo courses at the newly created 'Torpedo and Radio School' in Flensburg-Mürwik. The training equipment used to introduce the principles of underwater warfare comprised film taken during the Great War aboard *U35* and *U139*. On the engineering side, Spindler planned a training programme for future U-boat men to be introduced from 1927 onwards. Trainees were tested on ideas of how to both preserve and develop knowledge and experience gained during the Great War by the Kaiser's U-boat men.

The full training programme was finally initiated during the course for sixty naval Ensigns of the Class of 1925, which was given at the 'Marine Artillery School', Kiel, during the early part of 1929. Hans Schottky, a former lecturer and retired Oblt.z.S. from Flanders Flotilla U-boats *UC69*, *UB59* and *UB117*, replaced Spindler in the U-boat Office during the latter half of 1929. He made great efforts to implement realistic simulator training for Ensigns. His ideas were not, however, adopted by the Naval Ministry, being deemed logistically impractical. Despite this setback for U-boat training development, Schottky and a mixed group of serving officers, retired officers, civilian engineers and sundry officials managed to gain practical experience during the testing of the two now-completed Finnish boats *Vetehinen* and *Vesihiisi* during the summer of 1930 at the small port of Abo.

By 1931, despite certain construction difficulties, the Spanish boat *E1* was also finished. This large submarine had been launched on 22 October the previous year, promptly running aground after hitting the water. *E1* was to be studied by German designers as the possible prototype 'backbone' for Germany's future submarine force (*UA* and the two Type IA boats were the result). Kptlt. A.D. Bräutigam was head of the German testing team. For some years Bräutigam had been in charge of Japan's submarine construction, all of which was similarly based on previous German design work. Also among the assessment team were 54-year-old Kaptlt. (Eng.) Heinrich Papenberg, later head of U-boat construction, as Chief Engineer (*Leitender Ingenieur*, commonly referred to as a U-boat's 'LI') and Hans-Rudolf Rösing from the Finnish design and testing team. *E1* began her trails in Cadiz harbour, Spain, although the end of the Spanish monarchy led to the submarine being sold to Turkey in 1931.

During 1933 *Reichswehrminister* (Defence Minister) von Blomberg ordered the establishment of a fully-fledged submarine school in Kiel-Wik. Kptlt. Slevogt was named as Commanding Officer, with Senior Lecturers Werner Fürbringer, a former U-boat commander, and Hülsmann, and Junior Lecturers Hans-Rudolf Rösing and Kurt Freiwald. On 25 June 1933 the school's first course began.

The inaugural crew comprised eight officers, and 70-80 NCOs and seamen. The training establishment's official title was 'School of Anti-Submarine Warfare' (*Unterseebootsabwehrschule* or UAS), and technically it was incorporated into the Inspectorate of Torpedoes. Theoretical training included lessons in U-boat construction from the point of view of both sailor and engineer, instruction in maintaining stability, weight distribution and trim above and below water, during both peacetime and war conditions, and the use of escape apparatus. Men of the seamen branch received basic training in torpedo firing, and officers and senior ratings in the use of the periscope. Simultaneously, engineering personnel were taught the mechanics and theory of both diesel and electric propulsion units. Hardware used during the intensive courses included an electrically operated steering machine, as well as an electric periscope and gyro compass installation.

Practical training was carried out initially with the aid of primitive though ingenious simulators. These comprised elderly minesweepers (*Minensuchboote*) equipped with a replica submarine control room comprising periscope stub housed within a covered deck compartment. An engine installation made up of half a Type II drive unit complete with submarine steering equipment completed the simulation. Training took place aboard these minesweepers and *CV707* (future design foundation for Type II U-boat) in Finland between May and August 1935. To participate in the Finnish exercises seven officers and six NCOs were sent to Finland thinly disguised as tourists and students.

By November 1934 foreign-based German submarine development had advanced to such a state that component frames of twelve U-boats had been constructed in the Ruhr. Copied directly from tried and tested IVS designs, they were transferred to Kiel in the utmost secrecy where they were stored in *Germaniawerft* and *Deutschewerke* warehouses during January 1935. The diesel and electric engines followed, then torpedo tube armament. On Saturday 16 March 1935 Hitler decreed Germany's rearmament – Army conscription, the establishment of the Luftwaffe and new German battleships

– formally abandoning the Versailles Treaty. On 15 June 1935 *Deutschewerke* shipyards at Kiel launched the small Type IIA coastal submarine *U1*, commanded by 28-year-old Kptlt. Klaus Ewerth. The U-boat school flotilla (*Unterseebootesschulflottille*) later had an attached technical training unit (*Schulverband der Unterseebootschule*) counting six new Type II U-boats, the initial six launched by Germany from 1935 onwards, *U1* to *U6*.[115]

[115] This training school moved to Neustadt in May 1937.

Appendix Three

STRENGTH OF THE 1ST
U-FLOTILLA 1939 TO 1944

Pre-war Years:

Weddigen Flotilla

U7 (Type IIB) nominally within Weddigen Flotilla though officially attached to *Unterseebootesschulflottille*, Neustadt.

U8 (Type IIB) nominally within Weddigen Flotilla though officially attached to *Unterseebootesschulflottille*, Neustadt

U9 (Type IIB) commissioned 21/8/35 into this flotilla

U10 (Type IIB) nominally within Weddigen Flotilla though officially attached to *Unterseebootesschulflottille*, Neustadt

U11 (Type IIB) nominally within Weddigen Flotilla though officially attached to *Unterseebootesschulflottille*, Neustadt

U12 (Type IIB) nominally within Weddigen Flotilla though officially attached to *Unterseebootesschulflottille*, Neustadt

U13 (Type IIB) commissioned 30/11/35 into this flotilla.

U14 (Type IIB) commissioned 18/1/36 into this flotilla. Transferred October 1937.
Participated in operations in Spanish waters between July and September 1937.

U15 (Type IIB) commissioned 7/3/36 into this flotilla.

U16 (Type IIB) commissioned 16/5/36 into this flotilla. Transferred October 1937.

U17 (Type IIB) commissioned 3/12/35 into this flotilla.

U18 (Type IIB) commissioned 4/1/36 into this flotilla. Rammed and sunk on 20/11/36
Raised repaired and transferred to 'Lohs' U-Flotilla.

U19 (Type IB) commissioned 16/1/36 into this flotilla.

U21 (Type IIB) commissioned 3/8/36 into this flotilla.

U23 (Type IIB) commissioned 2/9/36 into this flotilla.

Boats in total	15
Transferred from Flotilla	7

Sunk	1 (6% operational strength)
Remaining boats as at 1/1/39	7

Tenders: *Saar, T23, T156, T158, Donau, Memel, Weichsel* (March 1938 to December 1942).

The strength of 'Weddigen' U-Flotilla on 1st September 1939 to December 1939:

U9 (Type IIB) Aug 35 – Dec 39.
U13 (Type IIB) Nov 35 – Dec 39.
U15 (Type IIB) Mar 36 – Dec 39.
U17 (Type IIB) Dec 35 – Oct 39 transferred to UA-Flotilla.
U19 (Type IIB) Jan 36 – Dec39.
U21 (Type IIB) Aug 36 – Dec39.
U23 (type IIB) Sept 36 – Dec 39.
U24 (Type IIB) Nov – Dec 39.
U61 (Type IIC) Dec 39 – Dec 39.
U62 (Type IIC) Dec 39 – Dec 39.

Boats in total	10
Transferred from Flotilla	1
Sunk	0
Remaining boats as at 1/1/40	9

Tenders: *Donau, Memel, Ammerland* (October 1939 to August 1941), *Weichsel* (March 1938 to December 1942).

The strength of 1st U-Flotilla January 1940 – Dec 1940:

U8 (Type IIB) Apr – Jun transferred to 24th U-Flotilla.
U9 (Type IIB) Jan – Jun transferred to 24th U-Flotilla.
U11 (Type IIB) Jun – Nov transferred to 21st U-Flotilla.
U13 (Type IIB) Jan – 30/5/40 sunk by depth charges.
U15 (type IIB) Jan – 31/1/40 rammed and sunk by German Torpedoboat *Iltis*.
U19 (Type IIB) Jan – Apr transferred to UA-Flotilla.
U20 (Type IIB) Jan – May transferred to UA-Flotilla.
U21 (Type IIB) Jan – June transferred to 21st U-Flotilla.
U22 (Type IIB) Jan – Apr posted missing.
U23 (Type IIB) Jan – June transferred to 21st U-Flotilla.
U24 (Type IIB) Jan – Apr transferred to UA-Flotilla.
U56 (Type IIC) Jan -Nov transferred to 24th U-Flotilla.
U57 (Type IIC) Jan – Sept transferred to 22nd U-Flotilla.

U58 (Type IIC) Jan – Dec transferred to 22nd U-Flotilla.
U59 (Type IIC) Jan -Dec transferred to 22nd U-Flotilla.
U60 (Type IIC) Jan – Nov transferred to 21st U-Flotilla.
U61 (Type IIC) Jan – Nov transferred to 21st U-Flotilla.
U62 (Type IIC) Jan – Nov transferred to 21st U-Flotilla.
U63 (Type IIC) Jan – 25/2/40 sunk after depth charged and scuttled.
U137 (Type IID) Jun – Dec transferred to 22nd U-Flotilla.
U138 (Type ID) Jun – Dec transferred to 22nd U-Flotilla.
U139 (Type IID) Jul-Oct transferred to 21st U-Flotilla.
U140 (Type IID) Aug – Dec transferred to 22nd U-Flotilla.
U141 (Type IID) Aug – Oct transferred to 21st U-Flotilla.
U142 (Type IID) Sept – Oct transferred to 24th U-Flotilla.
U143 (Type IID) Sept – Oct transferred to 24th U-Flotilla.
U144 (Type IID) Oct – Dec transferred to 22nd U-Flotilla.
U145 (Type IID) Oct – Dec transferred to 22nd U-Flotilla.
U146 (Type IID) Oct – Dec transferred to 22nd U-Flotilla.
U147 (Type IID) Dec transferred to 22nd U-Flotilla.
U149 (Type IID) Nov – Dec transferred to 22nd U-Flotilla.
U150 (Type IID) Nov – Dec transferred to 22nd U-Flotilla.

Boats in total	32
Transferred from Flotilla	28
Sunk	3 (9% operational strength)
Missing	1
Remaining boats as at 1/1/41	**0**

Tenders: *Lech* (January 1940 to June 1941), *Ammerland* (October 1939 to August 1941), *Weichsel* (March 1938 to December 1942).

1941:

U79 (Type VIIC) Mar – Sept transferred to 23rd U-Flotilla.
U80 (Type VIIC) Apr transferred to 26th U-Flotilla.
U81 (Type VIIC) Apr – Dec transferred to 29th U-Flotilla.
U83 (Type VIIB) Feb – Dec transferred to 23rd U-Flotilla.
U84 (Type VIIB) Apr – Dec.
U86 (Type VIIB) Sept – Dec.
U201 (Type VIIC) Jan – Dec.
U202 (Type VIIC) Mar – Dec.
U203 (Type VIIC) Feb – Dec.
U204 (Type VIIC) Mar – Dec.
U208 (Type VIIC) Sept – Dec.
U331 (Type VIIC) Mar – Sept transferred to 23rd U-Flotilla.
U371 (Type VIIC) Mar- Oct transferred to 23rd U-Flotilla.

U372 (Type VIIC) Apr – Dec transferred to 29th U-Flotilla.
U374 (Type VIIC) Sept – Dec transferred to 29th U-Flotilla.
U401 (Type VIIC) Apr – Dec.
U556 (Type VIIC) Feb – Dec.
U557 (Type VIIC) Feb – Nov transferred to 29th U-Flotilla.
U558 (Type VIIC) Feb – Dec.
U559 (Type VIIC) Feb – Oct transferred to 23rd U-Flotilla.
U561 (Type VIIC) Mar – Dec.
U562 (Type VIIC) Mar – Nov transferred to 29th U-Flotilla.
U563 (Type VIIC) Mar – Dec.
U564 (Type VIIC) Apr – Dec.
U565 (Type VIIC) Apr – Nov transferred to 29th U-Flotilla.
U566 (Type VIIC) Apr – Dec.
U574 (Type VIIC) Jun – Dec.
U582 (Type VIIC) Dec.
U584 (Type VIIC) Nov – Dec.
U651 (Type VIIC) Feb – Dec.
U653 (Type VIIC) May – Dec.
U754 (Type VIIC) Dec.

Boats in total	32 Plus the temporary experimental additions of *UB1* and *UD1*.
Transferred from Flotilla	12
Sunk	6 (19% operational strength)
Remaining boats as at 1/1/42	**14**

Tenders: *Lech* (January 1940 to June 1941), *Ammerland* (October 1939 to August 1941), *Weichsel* (March 1938 to December 1942).

1942:

U84 (Type VIIB) Jan – Dec.
U86 (Type VIIB) Jan – Dec.
U116 (Type XB) Sept – 11/10/42 unknown loss.
U117 (Type XB) Feb – Oct transferred to 11th U-Flotilla.
U201 (Type VIIC) Jan- Dec.
U202 (Type VIIC) Jan – Dec.
U203 (Type VIIC) Jan – Dec.
U263 (Type VIIC) Nov – Dec.
U301 (Type VIIC) Oct – Dec transferred to 29th U-Flotilla.
U336 (Type VIIC) Dec.
U353 (Type VIIC) Sept – 16/10/42 sunk after depth charged, rammed and boarded.
U354 (Type VIIC) Sept – Oct transferred to 11th U-Flotilla.

U379 (Type VIIC) Jul – 8/8/42 sunk after depth charged and rammed.
U405 (Type VIIC) Mar – Jun transferred to 11th U-Flotilla.
U413 (Type VIIC) Nov – Dec.
U439 (Type VIIC) Nov – Dec.
U440 (Type VIIC) Sept – Dec.
U441 (Type VIIC) Sept – Dec.
U456 (Type VIIC) Dec.
U558 (Type VIIC) Jan – Dec.
U561 (Type VIIC) Jan transferred to 23rd U-Flotilla.
U563 (Type VIIC) Jan – Dec.
U564 (Type VIIC) Jan – Dec.
U566 (Type VIIC) Jan – Dec.
U582 (Type VIIC) Jan – 5/10/42 sunk by Catalina aircraft.
U584 (Type VIIC) Jan – Dec.
U597 (Type VIIC) June 42 – 12/10/42 sunk by Liberator aircraft.
U599 (Type VIIC) Aug – 24/10/42 sunk by Liberator aircraft.
U603 (Type VIIC) Dec.
U628 (Type VIIC) Dec.
U653 (Type VIIC) Jan – Dec.
U656 (Type VIIC) Jan – 1/3/42 sunk by depth charges.
U754 (Type VIIC) Jan – 31/7/42 sunk by Hudson aircraft.

Boats in total	**33**
Transferred from Flotilla	5
Missing	1
Sunk	7 (215 operational strength)
Remaining boats as at 1/1/43	**20**

Tender: *Weichsel* (March 1938 to December 1942).

1943:
U84 (Type VIIB) Jan – 24/8/43 possibly sunk by Avenger aircraft otherwise sunk by unknown reasons.
U86 (Type VIIB) Jan – 29/11/43 possibly sunk by Avenger aircraft otherwise sunk by unknown reasons.
U201 (Type VIIC) Jan – 17/2/43 sunk by depth charges and ramming.
U202 (Type VIIC) Jan – 2/6/43 sunk by depth charges and scuttled.
U203 (Type VIIC) Jan – 25/4/43 sunk by depth charges.
U209 (Type VIIC) Mar – May sunk unknown causes.
U225 (Type VIIC) Jan – 15/2/43 sunk by Liberator.
U238 (Type VIIC) Aug – Dec.
U263 (Type VIIC) Jan – Dec.
U268 (Type VIIC) Jan – 19/2/43 sunk by Wellington aircraft (first successful use of Leigh Light).

U271 (Type VIIC) Jun – Dec.

U305 (Type VIIC) Apr – Dec.

U306 (Type VIIC) Mar – 31/10/43 sunk by depth charges.

U307 (Type VIIC) May – Oct transferred to 13th U-Flotilla.

U311 (Type VIIC) Nov – Dec.

U336 (Type VIIC) Jan – 15/10/43 sunk by Hudson aircraft.

U392 (Type VIIC) Dec.

U413 (Type VIIC) Jan – Dec.

U415 (Type VIIC) Mar – Dec.

U418 (Type VIIC) May – 1/6/43 sunk by Beaufighter rocket attack.

U422 (Type VIIC) Aug – 4/10/43 sunk by Avenger and Wildcat aircraft.

U424 (Type VIIC) Oct – Dec.

U426 (Type VIIC) Nov – Dec.

U435 (Type VIIC) Feb – 9/7/43 sunk by Wellington aircraft.

U439 (Type VIIC) Jan – 4/5/43 sunk after collision.

U440 (Type VIIC) Jan – 31/5/43 sunk by Sunderland aircraft.

U441 (Type VIIC) Jan – Dec.

U456 (Type VIIC) Jan – 13/5/43 lost under attack by exceeding depth following damage.

U471 (Type VIIC) Nov – Dec.

U558 (Type VIIC) Jan – 20/7/43 sunk by Halifax and Liberator aircraft.

U563 (Type VIIC) Jan – 31/5/43 sunk by Halifax and Sunderland aircraft.

U564 (Type VIIC) Jan – 14/6/43 sunk by Whitley aircraft.

U566 (Type VIIC) Jan – 24/10/43 scuttled.

U584 (Type VIIC) Jan- 31/10/43 sunk by Avenger aircraft.

U603 (Type VIIC) Jan – Dec.

U625 (Type VIIC) Nov – Dec.

U628 (Type VIIC) Jan – 3/7/43 sunk by Liberator aircraft.

U629 (Type VIIC) Nov – Dec.

U632 (Type VIIC) Jan – 6/4/43 sunk by Liberator aircraft.

U643 (Type VIIC) Jul – 18/10/43 sunk by Liberator aircraft.

U653 (Type VIIC) Jan – Dec.

U665 (Type VIIC) Feb – 22/3/43 sunk by Whitley aircraft.

U669 (Type VIIC) Jun – 7/9/43 sunk by Wellington aircraft.

U731 (Type VIIC) May – Dec.

U732 (Type VIIC) May – 1/11/43 sunk after scuttled.

U741 (Type VIIC) Nov – Dec.

U963(Type VIIC) Aug – Dec.

Boats in total	47
Transferred from Flotilla	1
Sunk	27 (57% operational strength)
Remaining boats as at 1/1/44	**19**

1944:

U238 (Type VIIC) Jan – 9/2/44 sunk by depth charges.
U243 (Type VIIC) June – 8/7/44 sunk by Sunderland aircraft.
U263 (Type VIIC) Jan – 20/1/44 sunk during diving test.
U271 (Type VIIC) Jan – 28/1/44 sunk by Liberator aircraft.
U276 (Type VIIC) Jan – Jul transferred to 31st U-Flotilla.
U292 (Type VIIC-41) Apr – 2/5/44 sunk by Liberator aircraft.
U305 (Type VIIC) Jan – 17/1/44 sunk by depth charges.
U311 (Type VIIC) Jan – 22/4/44 sunk by depth charges.
U370 (Type VIIC) Jun – Jul transferred to 8th U-Flotilla.
U392 (Type VIIC) Jan – 16/3/44 sunk by depth charges.
U394 (Type VIIC) Mar – May transferred to 11th U-Flotilla.
U396 (Type VIIC) Jun – Sept transferred to 11th U-Flotilla.
U413 (Type VIIC) Jan – 20/8/44 sunk by depth charges.
U415 (Type VIIC) Jan – 14/7/44 sunk by mine.
U424 (Type VIIC) Jan – 11/2/44 sunk by depth charges.
U426 (Type VIIC) Jan – 8/1/44 sunk by Sunderland aircraft.
U441 (Type VIIC) Jan – 18/6/44 probably sunk by Liberator.
U471 (Type VIIC) Jan – Apr transferred to 29th U-Flotilla.
U603 (Type VIIC) Jan – 1/3/44 sunk by depth charges.
U625 (Type VIIC) Jan – 10/3/44 sunk by Sunderland aircraft.
U629 (Type VIIC) Jan – 7/6/44 sunk by Liberator aircraft.
U637 (Type VIIC) Jun – July transferred to 8th U-Flotilla.
U653 (Type VIIC) Jan – 15/3/44 sunk by depth charges.
U722 (Type VIIC) Aug – Oct transferred to 11th U-Flotilla.
U731 (Type VIIC) Jan – 15/5/44 sunk by depth charges.
U736 (Type VIIC) Apr – 6/8/44 sunk by depth charges.
U740 (Type VIIC) Apr – 9/6/44 sunk by Liberator aircraft.
U741 (Type VIIC) Jan – 15/8/44 sunk by depth charges.
U743 (Type VIIC) Jul – Sept missing
U767 (Type VIIC) May- 1/6/44 sunk by depth charges.
U773 (Type VIIC) Aug – Sept transferred to 11th U-flotilla.
U821 (Type VIIC) Mar – 10/6/44 sunk by Mosquito and Liberator aircraft.
U925 (Type VIIC) Aug – 14/9/44 lost to unknown causes
U963 (Type VIIC) Jan – Oct Transferred to 11th U-Flotilla.
U987 (Type VIIC) Mar – May transferred to 11th U-Flotilla.
U1007 (VIIC-41) Jun – Jul transferred to 24th U-Flotilla.
U1199 (Type VIIC) Aug – Oct transferred to 11th U-Flotilla.

Boats in total	37
Transferred from Flotilla	12
Missing	1 (*U743* also later declared missing from 10th September)

Sunk	23 (62% operational strength)
Remaining boats as at 3/9/44	**6**

During the Second World War the 1st U-Flotilla comprised 135 different U-boats (including *UB1* and *UD1* and *U7, U8, U10 – U12* the latter Type IIs only briefly on Flotilla strength).

Of these 65 were sunk (48%), 4 (3%) declared missing and 66 eventually transferred from the flotilla, five after the unit's dissolution.

SOURCES

Unpublished

British Admiralty Anti-U-Boat warfare reports 1940 to 1944.

KTB 1st U-Flotilla.

KTB BdU.

KTB SKL.

KTBs various U-boats.

KTB *Sperrbrecher Sp.19 'Rostock'*.

Hitler's Directive for the occupation of Denmark and Norway, 1 March, 1940 (United States, Office of United States Chief of Counsel for Prosecution of Axis Criminality, *Nazi Conspiracy and Aggression*, 8 vols. and 2 suppl. vol VI, 1003–1005, Doc. No. C-174.)

ULTRA and the campaign against the U-boats in WW2, Commander Jerry C. Russell USN (Studies in Cryptology, NSA, Document SRH-142. Record Group 457, Records of the National Security Agency).

The German declaration of war with the United States, 11 December 1941 (Department of State Bulletin, 13 December 1941.)

Prime Minister Winston Churchill's review of the war to the House of Commons, 30 September 1941 (British Library of Information.)

German Clandestine Submarine Warfare Willard C. Frank Jr. (9th Naval History Symposium Paper)

Gosport Submarine Archives:

    Attacks on U-boats from 1939 to 1945 A1995/217.

    Allied Submarine Successes A1994/098/001.

What To Do If Your Moustache Falls Off – (Fairly True Reports From A CIA Man) Angus MacLean Thuermer (Naval Reserve Lieutenant (j.g.), U.S. Navy Forward Intelligence Unit (Task Unit 125.8) retd.).

Published Books

Bernage, Georges (Editor), *La Bretagne en Guerre 1939 – 1945*, Editions Heimdal, 1994.

Blair, Clay, *Hitler's U-Boat War*, Vols 1 & 2, Cassell 1996.

Bohn, Roland, *Raids Aeriens Sur la Bretagne Durant La Seconde Guerre Mondiale*: Vols 1 & 2, Self Published 1996.

Bohn, Roland & Le Berre, Alain, *Chronique D'Hier*, Vol. 2, Self Published 1994.

Bowyer, Chaz, *Men Of Coastal Command 1939 – 1945*, William Kimber, 1985.

Brown, David, *Warship Losses of World War Two*, Naval Institute Press, 1995.

Buffetaut, Yves, *Les Ports Francais: Les Ports de l'Atlantique 1939 – 1945*, Marines Edition.

Chazette, Alain & Reberac, Fabian, *Kriegsmarine*, Editions Heimdel, 1997.

Churchill, Winston, *The Second World War*, Volumes 1 to 6, Cassell 1948.

Collier, Richard, *The Sands of Dunkirk*, Collins, 1961.

Costello, John & Hughes, Terry, *The Battle Of The Atlantic*, Collins, 1977.

Dönitz, Karl, *Ten Years And Twenty Days*, Lionel Leventhal 1990.

Frank, Wolfgang, *Enemy Submarine*, William Kimber 1954.

Franks, Norman, *Conflict Over The Bay*, William Kimber, 1986.

   Search, Find And Kill, Grub Street, 1995.

Franks, Norman and Zimmermann, Eric, *U-Boats Versus Aircraft*, Grub Street, 1998.

Goss, Chris, *Bloody Biscay*, Crecy Books, 2001.

Gröner, Erich, *Die deutschen Kriegsschiffe 1815 – 1945*, Bernard & Graefe Verlag, 1985.

Hessler, Günther, *The U-boat War in the Atlantic*, HMSO, 1989.

Hildebrand, Hans & Lohmann Werner, *Die Deutsche Kriegsmarine 1939 –1945*, Podzun–Verlag, 1956.

Hocking, Charles, *Disaster at Sea in the Age of Steam* Vols 1 & 2,

Howarth, Stephen & Law, Derek (Editors), *The Battle of the Atlantic; The 50th International Naval Conference*, Naval Institute Press, 1994.

Jacquin, Frederic, *Les Bombardements de Brest 1940 – 1944*, MEB.

Jones, Geoffrey, *Autumn of the U-boats*, William Kimber, 1984.

Korth, Klaus & Lüth, Wolfgang *Boot Greift wieder An*, Erich Klinghammer, 1944.

Lucas, James, *Storming Eagles*, Arms and Armour Press, 1988.

Macintyre, Donald, *Battle of the Atlantic*, Pan, 1961.

Martienssen, Anthony, *Hitler and his Admirals*, E.P. Dutton,1949.

   Führer Conferences on Naval Affairs, HMSO, 1948.

Mordel, Jacques, *Heligoland – Gibraltar Allemand de la Mer du Nord*, Presse de la Cite, 1967.

Morison, Samuel Eliot, *History of the United States Naval Operations in World War II, Vol. X The Atlantic Battle Won*, Little, Brown 1950.

Nesbit, Roy Conyers, *The Strike Wings*, William Kimber 1984.

Niestlé, Axel, *German U-boat Losses During World War Two*, Naval Institute Press, 1998.

Nutting, David, *Attain by Surprise*, David Colver 1997.

Peillard, Leonce, *Histoire Générale de la Guerre Sous-Marine*, Robert Laffont, 1970.

Price, Alfred, *Aircraft Versus Submarine*, Naval Institute Press, 1974.

Rohwer, Jürgen, *Allied Submarine Attacks Of World War Two*, Naval Institute Press, 1997.

   Axis Submarine Successes, Naval Institute Press, 1983.

   The Critical Convoy Battles Of March 1943, Naval Institute Press, 1977.

Ritschel, Herbert, *Kurzfassung Kriegstagesbuecher Deutscher U-Boote 1939-1945, Band 1*, Korntal, 1996.

Robertson, Terence, *The Golden Horseshoe*, Tempus, 2000.

Rössler, Eberhard, *The U-Boat War*, Arms & Armour Press, 1981.

   Vom Original zum Modell: Uboottyp II – Die 'Einbäume', Bernard & Graefe, 1999.

Rust, Eric C., *Naval Officers Under Hitler*, Praeger, 1991.

Sharpe, Peter, *U-Boat Fact File*, Midland, 1998.

Shirer, William, *The Rise And Fall of the Third Reich*, Simon & Schuster, 1960.

Showell, Jak P. Mallmann, *The German Navy In World War Two*, Arms & Armour Press, 1979.

   German Navy Handbook, Sutton, 1999.

   U-Boat Command And The Battle Of The Atlantic, Conway, 1989.

Steen, E.A., *The Norwegian Sea War 1940-1945*.

Stern, Robert C., *Type VII U-Boat*, Arms and Armour, 1991.

Suhren, Reinhard and Fritz Brustat, *Nasses Eichenlaub*, Berlin 1983.

Thomas Publications (1943), *The U-Boat Commander's Handbook* (Translation).

Vause, Jordan, *Wolf*, Airlife, 1997.

Werner, Herbert, *Iron Coffins*, Holt, Rinehart and Winston, 1969.

Whitley, M. J., *Destroyer*, Naval Institute Press, 1983.

Williams, David, *Wartime Disasters At Sea*, Patrick Stephens, 1997.

Wynn, Kenneth, *U-boat Operations of the Second World War; Vols. 1 & 2*, Chatham Publishing, 1997.

Published Scholarly Works/Articles

New Interpretations in Naval History – Selected Papers from the Ninth Naval History Symposium, Edited by William R. Roberts.

INDEX

Poel, Gustav, 155, 11, 171, 195, 221, 223, 232, 233
Poeschel, Wolfgang, 244
Polyanthus, HMS, 213
Porchester Castle, HMS, 261
Porpoise, HMS, 44
Port Auckland, 183
Poser, Günther, 152, 155, 178, 179, 198, 199
Potrero del Llano, 142
President Francqui, 166, 167
Preuss, Joachim, 108
Prien, Günther, 8, 17, 22, 24, 29, 75
Prinz Harald, 162
Prinz Eugen, 79, 80, 87, 117, 126, 137
Pröhl, Willi, 148
Punjabi, HMS, 136

Q

Qu'appelle, HMCS, 257

R

Raeder, Erich, 9, 16, 17, 40, 52, 62, 71, 89, 103, 133, 146, 169, 170
Rathlin, 213
Rau, Adolf, 194
Reeder, Günther, 55
Refast, 128
Reff, Reinhard, 256, 257
Regensburg, 227
Reich, Christian, 221, 223, 229, 230
Reichenbach – Klinke, Kurt, 62
Reiler, Hans, 260
Remus, Gerhard, 146, 152, 163
Renown, HMS, 80
Resercho, 23
Restigouche, HMCS, 247, 257
Reuben James, USS, 108
Riegele, Hermann, 68
Rio Grande, 113, 138
Rio Tercero, 140

Robert Gray, 187
Robin Moor, 91
Rochester, HMS, 78, 113, 266n
Römer, Wolfgang, 159–61
Rona, 64
Rosemonde, 127
Rosenberg, Günther, 146, 152, 155, 165, 173, 174
Rösing, Hans-Rudolf, 4, 74, 77, 78, 211, 237, 238, 240, 256, 262
Rostock, 60, 108
Royal Archer, 21
Royal Oak, HMS, 24

S

S6, 68
S30, 53
Saar, 5, 10, 20
Saches, Dietrich, 233, 242, 253
Sahib, HMS, 164
St. Albans, HMS, 78
St. Apollo, HMS, 78
St. Croix, 214
Saint Dunstan, 62
Saint Enogat, 253
St. Laurent, HMCS, 158, 165, 168
Samphire, HMS, 125
San Felix, 79
San Jacinto, 137
San Tiburcio, 33
Santos, 35
Scania, 104
Schädlich, Rudolf, 185
Schafer, Hans, 99
Scharnhorst 86, 87, 126, 129, 137
Scheer, Werner, 5
Schepke, Joachim, 26, 27, 34, 38, 42, 43, 48, 67, 75, 92, 107
Scheringer, Heinz, 4, 20
Schie, 93
Schirlitz, Ernst, 146
Schlieper, Alfred, 112, 115, 116
Schmidt, Karl, 69
Schmidt, Werner, 251

Schmidt, Werner von, 4, 127, 133, 136, 147, 148
Schmundt, Herbert, 134
Schnee, Adalbert, 9, 72, 75, 94n, 101, 102, 108, 116, 119, 130, 137, 138, 143–6, 148, 152, 155, 174, 202
Schnorkel, development of, 236
Scholz, Günther, 224
Schonder, Heinrich, 59, 60
Schreiber, Heinrich, 257
Schug, Walter, 119, 144, 156, 184, 210, 228
Schulte, Max, 49, 51, 52
Schulte, Werner, 120, 138, 146, 147, 158
Schultze, Heinz Otto, 64, 104
Schümann, Henig, 222, 223, 229, 235
Schuur, Heinz, 31
Schwaff, Werner, 189
Scimitar, HMS, 99
Scotia, 22
Scottish American, 49
Scottish Heather, 166
Scottish Minstrel, 60
Seakay, 237
Seal, HMS, 68, 69
Sealion, HMS, 21
Seeteufel, 69
Seidel, Hans, 153
Sekula, Albert, 260
Shaftesbury, 148
Shediac, HMCS, 165
Shipbuilders:
  Blohm & Voss, 73, 74, 83, 127
  Bremer Vulkan, 73, 74, 165, 169
  Danzigerwerfte, 74
  Deschimag, 58
  Deutschewerke, 2, 61, 63, 76
  Flenderwerft, 183
  Germaniawerfte, 2, 73, 74, 76
  Howaldswerke, 73
  Nordseewerke, 74

297